IN DEFIANCE OF BOUNDARIES

UNIVERSITY PRESS OF FLORIDA

Florida A&M University, Tallahassee
Florida Atlantic University, Boca Raton
Florida Gulf Coast University, Ft. Myers
Florida International University, Miami
Florida State University, Tallahassee
New College of Florida, Sarasota
University of Central Florida, Orlando
University of Florida, Gainesville
University of North Florida, Jacksonville
University of South Florida, Tampa
University of West Florida, Pensacola

IN DEFIANCE
OF BOUNDARIES

Anarchism in Latin American History

Edited by Geoffroy de Laforcade
and Kirwin Shaffer

University Press of Florida

Gainesville · Tallahassee · Tampa · Boca Raton
Pensacola · Orlando · Miami · Jacksonville · Ft. Myers · Sarasota

Publication of this book was made possible in part by a grant from Penn State University–Berks College.

This book may be available in an electronic edition.

22 21 20 19 18 17   6 5 4 3 2 1

First cloth printing, 2015
First paperback printing, 2017

Library of Congress Cataloging-in-Publication Data
In defiance of boundaries : anarchism in Latin American history / edited by Geoffroy de Laforcade and Kirwin Shaffer.
pages cm
Includes bibliographical references and index.
ISBN 978-0-8130-6110-8 (cloth)
ISBN 978 0 8130-6454-3 (pbk.)
1. Anarchism—Latin America—History. 2. Latin America—Politics and government—20th century. I. Laforcade, Geoffroy de, editor. II. Shaffer, Kirwin R., editor.
HX850.5.I5 2015
335'.83098—dc23
2015008841

The University Press of Florida is the scholarly publishing agency for the State University System of Florida, comprising Florida A&M University, Florida Atlantic University, Florida Gulf Coast University, Florida International University, Florida State University, New College of Florida, University of Central Florida, University of Florida, University of North Florida, University of South Florida, and University of West Florida.

University Press of Florida
15 Northwest 15th Street
Gainesville, FL 32611-2079
http://upress.ufl.edu

Contents

Acknowledgments

As noted in the introduction, this project has been brewing for close to a decade, and over those years we have encountered many people who have given wonderful advice and support to see this book to its fruition. First, we must thank our families for the long hours away from them that led to the book that you have in your hands. Second, we wish to thank the editors and staff at University Press of Florida. During the long course of reviews, we worked with a supportive cast of editors, including our original supporter, Amy Gorelick, followed by Sonia Dickey, Meredith Babb, and Erika Stevens. All were consistently positive in their critiques and helped us to weather shifting editors as well as cranky and disappearing reviewers. Third, we wish to thank our respective universities—Norfolk State University and Penn State University–Berks College—for moral and occasional financial support in developing this project. Fourth, we are thankful to the authors of this volume not only for their exceptional chapters that help to illustrate the diversity of anarchism in Latin America but also for their patience. Fifth, we are indebted to many individuals for their insightful (and sometimes frustrating) comments. This book could not have reached this point without frequent readings from Barry Carr, suggestions from Steve Hirsch, the epilogue by José Moya, and comments by David Struthers. To our readers: we trust that this book will help you appreciate Latin American anarchism in new and enriching ways.

Cheers!

Introduction

The Hidden Story Line of Anarchism
in Latin American History

GEOFFROY DE LAFORCADE AND KIRWIN SHAFFER

Many of us were graduate students in the mid-1990s when anarchist history became a growing focus of research on a worldwide scale. This trend grew out of new directions in the history of labor and social history, gender and ethnic studies, the world-historical turn in migration studies and intellectual history, and, most of all, the crisis in socialist and Marxist ideologies that followed the long-anticipated collapse of state-sponsored social engineering. Scholars and activists struggled with outdated teleological paradigms of modernization and class formation, particularly in Latin America, where ominous cracks in the national-popular state, and the dependency theories upon which it rested, were just beginning to birth the social uprisings that would rattle the continent from Chiapas and Oaxaca to La Paz and Buenos Aires. Many on the left welcomed the demise of authoritarian regimes, cautiously embracing the democratic and globalizing claims of grassroots social movements, liberal democracy, and human rights but were weary of the cheerleading and celebrations heralded by right-leaning advocates of an "end of history." In this climate, activists and scholars began to reinvestigate the era of diverse, contending socialisms that culminated in the 1917 Bolshevik Revolution in Russia. In Latin America itself, Marxism had made only timid appearances in the waning nineteenth century, and Communist Parties did not emerge until the 1920s. By this time anarchists had been active throughout the hemisphere for four decades.

Even prior to expressions of modern anarchism, socialist utopianism had existed in Latin America throughout the nineteenth century. In 1828 Robert Owen requested permission to create a collectivist commune in the Mexican state of Texas, and an Icarian settlement inspired by Étienne

Cabet appeared after the territory's annexation by the United States. A Fourierist "phalanstery" or cooperative was created in Aguascalientes in 1850.[1] The Greek immigrant Plotino Rhodakanaty spread the ideas of Charles Fourier and Pierre-Joseph Proudhon among artisans, peasants, and indigenous communities and launched a "School of Reason and Socialism" in Chalco, Mexico, in 1855.[2] That same year, shortly after the fall of the Bogotá Commune, Élisée Reclus, the Belgian geographer who later became an influential spokesperson for anarchist communism, experimented in Colombia's Sierra Nevada de Santa Marta with a rural commune. Located on land confiscated from the *latifundistas*, it was worked by European, Asian, and indigenous artisans and peasants whose empowerment was violently negated by liberal elites. The significance of this experience was not lost on future historians of Colombia who recognized its countercultural challenge to the creole ideologues' definition of national identity.[3]

Italian immigrants who flocked to Brazil during the expansion of the coffee economy in the late nineteenth century also launched utopian experiments of rural communitarian organization such as the Guararema plantation and the Colónia Cecilia in the 1890s. The former was established in the final months of the monarchy by the artisan jeweler Artur Campagnoli with the help of Italian, Spanish, Russian, French, and Brazilian colonists—the latter in Palmeiras, in the southern state of Paraná, where another Italian anarchist, Giovanni Rossi, received a land grant from the departing Portuguese emperor to establish a utopian colony based on universal equality and free love.[4] Both experiments reflected the utopian and experimental aspirations of new immigrants who believed, like the Buenos Aires–based French anarchist Joaquín Alejo Falconnet (alias Pierre Quiroule), that America was a new frontier for "volunteers of anarchy" intent on escaping the chaotic exploitation of Europe and building a new egalitarian society based on cooperative labor.[5] These and other experiments in utopian community-building reflected the importance of equality and freedom by European émigrés who sought to found futuristic micro-societies in the Americas. At the same time, "foreigners" were not the sole voices of libertarian ideals. In Brazil, for example, the experience of the *quilombos* (autonomous societies founded by fugitive African slaves in the seventeenth and eighteenth centuries), struggles for abolition in the nineteenth century, and the idealism of Antônio Conselheiro's rebellious Canudos community in the 1890s fueled the historical imagination of prominent anarchist writers of "native" Afro-Portuguese descent, such as Gabio Luz and Afonso Henriques de Lima Barreto.[6]

Just as these past authors found inspiration in the rebellious struggles of their day, many modern historians looked to "current events" for new frameworks of analysis. A lasting image of the 1999 World Trade Organization protests in Seattle was one of anarchists employing direct action to disrupt the meeting. This challenge to the twin powers of global capitalism and neo-liberal states was broadcast into homes worldwide. The World Social Forum, ongoing transnational protests against the World Bank and the Davos Forum, and similar dramatic events such as the indigenous-led Zapatista insurrection in Mexico epitomized the resurrection of anarchist-inspired themes.[7]

The beginning of the new millennium witnessed a series of new crises in global capitalism. Massive economic chaos in Argentina and the surge in privatization and state deregulation throughout the hemisphere resulted in the pursuit of militant strategies that had once been understood as anarchist forms of direct action: landless peasant movements, factory take-overs by unemployed workers, and "horizontalism" (the reaching out of activists and communities across social sectors in cooperative and barter arrangements, rather than confronting the state head-on or seeking vertical power).[8] Workers, peasants, unemployed, downwardly mobile middle sectors, and landless peasants, disenfranchised economically and politically, fought back not as an imagined Marxian proletariat but as people united in common struggle against contemporary forms of cultural, economic, political, and social oppression. They did not seek change through formal elections or parliamentary reformism but instead articulated profound yearnings of freedom and democratization from below. It is no coincidence that the publication of histories of anarchism in the past twenty years has grown symbiotically with the rise of neo-anarchist social practices during those years.

In recent decades scholars have published new histories of anarchism that expand from Europe and the United States—the traditional center of anarchist studies—to China, Japan, Korea, South Africa, and Egypt. The revitalized historiography of anarchism in Latin America has been well represented in books, articles, conference papers, and Internet forums. Major scholarly conferences have included panels dedicated to anarchist history in the region or have included it as part of larger comparative panels on the movement's diverse expressions and global reach: for example, the European Social Science History Conferences in 2006 (Amsterdam), 2008 (Lisbon), 2010 (Ghent), 2012 (Glasgow), and 2014 (Vienna). Various facets of Latin American anarchism were discussed at Latin American Studies

Association meetings in 2006 (San Juan), 2007 (Montreal), 2009 (Rio de Janeiro), and 2010 (San Diego). The emergence of the North American Anarchist Studies Association in 2008 gave rise to annual conferences blending
activist reflection and scholarship, with papers dedicated to transnational
anarchism in Latin America and the Caribbean in 2009 (Hartford), 2011
(Toronto), 2012 (San Juan), 2013 (New Orleans), 2014 (Surrey, British Columbia), and 2015 (San Francisco). In 2011 a forum in Mexico City brought
together leading writers on Latin American anarchist culture, culminat-
ing in an edited collection in 2012.[9] The continent figured prominently in
the collected volume *Anarchism and Syndicalism in the Colonial and Post-
Colonial World*, a thematic volume on transnational anarchism in Latin
America was published in the journal *E.I.A.L.: Estudios Interdisciplinarios
de América Latina y el Caribe*, and a collection of essays mainly on South
American anarchism was published in French.[10]

The genesis of this book dates back to the middle of the first decade of the
millennium, when it was originally conceived as a multivolume collection
of the best works that had been written, in several languages, since the end
of the Cold War on the history of Latin American anarchism. Originally
the project was conceived as a country-by-country study, but we quickly
realized the futility of that approach, in particular given the broad range of
subjects addressed by Latin American historians of the movement in such
countries as Argentina, Brazil, and Mexico. What appeared more interesting was to convey the different ways historians had approached anarchist
history, and how those histories—while they contributed to local and regional understandings of society and culture, to an extent often underestimated by nationalist scholars—were not "national" per se in their totality
or their scope. After all, anarchists themselves were not "nationalists," so it
seems rather counterintuitive to examine them solely from such an alien
angle. As a result, we chose to focus on authors who skirted the traditional
geographical, chronological, and thematic limits of the historiography and
instead brought fresh directions to the research while unlocking new and
interesting dimensions of the anarchist past.

Earlier studies of anarchism in Latin America tended to be nationally
focused in the sense that they explored anarchist movements within the
territorial and political framework of national boundaries. "International"
events such as the Mexican and Russian Revolutions, the Spanish Civil War,
and the Great War in Europe were regularly chronicled for their impact
on such movements, and "foreign" migrants were generally understood to
have transported their ideas from distant lands. However, when historians

labeled these phenomena "international" and "foreign," they were semantically delineating the "domestic" or national space within which anarchist practice and organization are assumed to be centered. When studying the phenomenon of Latin American anarchism, however, several factors must be kept in mind: preexisting local and regional traditions of radical grassroots rebellion in the provinces in the formative periods of independence, the absence of an inclusive cultural concept of "nation," the preeminence of the state as an authoritarian and centralized construct without such avenues for popular citizenship as universal suffrage or working-class representation, and the role of transatlantic European immigration in the spread of ideas of political dissent and social transformation. As Lucien van der Walt and Steven Hirsch write in their aforementioned volume, "anarchism was not a West European doctrine that diffused outwards, perfectly formed, to a passive 'periphery.' Rather, the movement *emerged simultaneously and transnationally*, created by interlinked activists on three continents."[11] Thus anarchism was local, national, transnational, and transregional before it became aligned as a feature of individual nation-states. Contemporary historians of Latin American anarchism are concerned with the extent to which local, regional, and transnational solidarities embodied oppositional or countercultural practices and meanings and were effective in translating abstract libertarian ideas into concrete actions and lived experiences defending workers and resisting—rather than forging—the modern state.

Anarchism, Nationalism, the Nation-State, and Capitalism

This is not to say that what Latin Americans and other postcolonial activists call the "national question" is entirely irrelevant. Indeed, the same scholars who confined the study of anarchism to national boundaries often denied its incidence on national traditions. David Viñas, José Aricó, and others have observed that historians and activists after World War II tended to view anarchism as an imported doctrine that was a prelude to the history of socialist organizations and nationalist genealogies.[12] The reality is somewhat more complex. The former American colonies of Spain and Portugal were from the 1870s through the 1920s—and in some areas for longer—a terrain of widespread dissemination, diffusion, and adaptation of anarchist ideas, perhaps one of the largest such theaters in the world, Max Nettlau surmised.[13] While as a revolutionary ideology anarchism enunciated clear new beginnings and called for a revolt against the establishment, its effectiveness and credibility depended on the movement's ability to em-bed its practices in real social life. Classical anarchist thinkers anticipated this necessity in their writings on tradition, culture, and the emergence of nationalism.

Élisée Reclus, for example, argued that a critical awareness of past historical development was a prerequisite for the conscious creation of a "future collective history" that would transcend the social conflicts of culturally specific societies.[14] In Latin America, where protracted resistance against the centralization of modern states followed the revolutions for independence in the 1820s, anarchists encountered models of regionalism and federalism that they interpreted as bearing historic potential for the future.[15] Pierre-Joseph Proudhon, who in 1848 coined the expression "permanent revolution" to describe the empowerment of the people from below in the face of growing state oppression in France, developed the principle of federalism that later informed anarchist organizational strategies in Latin America.[16] He saw the diversity and preservation of sovereignty among decentralized polities characterized by cultural pluralism, grassroots governance, an awareness of shared identities, and a capacity for dialogue with the outside as conditions for social liberation.[17]

As Guy Thompson has shown, "conservatives in Mexico and Brazil warned that democratization, federalism and decentralization would encourage Indian caste wars and slave revolts leading to emancipation, which would threaten the post-colonial social edifice."[18] Implicit in Proudhon's critique of French republicanism, in the aftermath of imperial restoration in 1815, liberal revolution in 1830, and the 1848 urban popular uprisings was a rejection of the homogenizing, exclusionary national identity promoted by the state, for which Proudhon substituted a vision of local democracy that would at once protect the people from authoritarianism and empower them with sovereignty. These ideas raised alarm in Latin America and informed elite discourses of "civilization and barbarism" long before the federalist principle was given life by anarchist organizers of the labor movement early in the next century.

For the Russian activist Mikhail Bakunin, the uprisings of 1848 had moved two crucial issues to the forefront: the social question and the national question.[19] He became one of the earliest figures in the nineteenth-century socialist movement to define nationality in response to state-sponsored nationalist revisions of the past: "It is an affinity between people which developed through history, and inspired people with a spontaneous desire for unity which did not necessarily correspond with the rules of affinity enunciated by historians, and should not be imposed from above on the basis of such rules."[20] National movements, he argued, should be supported wherever they arise, provided they are "in the political as well as in the economic interests of the masses" and devoid of "the ambitious intent of founding a powerful State."[21] Instead of a central state, Bakunin argued that a decentralized federation of communes and collectively managed units of labor would give voice to affinities of collective belonging by respecting their autonomy and empowering the people to define them.[22] Anarchy, by promoting decentralization, freedom, justice, and equality, avoided the divisive trappings of the modern state.

Anarchists posit that the modern nation-state is a historically recent phenomenon that exercises institutional violence and social control over an arbitrarily drawn, confined territorial space, and concentrates authority in the hands of ubiquitous bureaucratic elites. It is but one of many possible forms of societal organization, one that has "partially effaced complex and overlapping webs of association with simpler, exclusive, hierarchical ones."[23] Anarchism should be understood, then, as a critique of the evolutionary and foundational (*archic*) mythology of the authoritarian model of politics born of the modern era. *An-arkhé*—etymologically the absence of all "government" but also of all "authority"—presupposed the infinite multiplicity and unending transformation of beings; it resisted the unification and ordering of society under the banner of a central power or the myth of an essential community.[24] Finally, anarchism distinguished itself from competing ideologies by the flexibility of its doctrine. "[We] consider as a definitive mistake," Kropotkin wrote, "a programme which demands full agreement among participants of all details of the ideal and, besides that, the organization of an extensive group of participants before proceeding to activity among the people."[25] While they condemned the state, anarchists did not focus their energies on its "overthrow"; their preferred use of the term "social revolution" suggests an aversion for direct confrontation with it, and a preference for the ongoing revolutionary transformation of social relations from below.

The movement also emerged as a counterpoint to capitalism and thus concerned itself with the freeing of labor from class domination. "[Anarchists] envisaged a post-revolutionary society built on a plurality of organizations based on free accord, the unions being only one such organization." For Kropotkin, "the aim of socialism was the full enjoyment of the fruits of labor."[26] Pietro Gori asserted that "[the] anarchist solution to the problem of liberty presupposes a socialist solution to the problem of property."[27] Thus, while anarchism is often, in the minds of historians, divorced from its socialist lineage, it is in fact a tradition of libertarian socialism with intellectual roots in the nineteenth-century quest for a utopian alternative to the capitalist state. It is worth recalling these words written by Karl Marx, who did not reject the term: "All socialists understand by *anarchy* this: once the goal of the proletarian movement, the abolition of classes, is achieved, the power of the State ... disappears, and government functions are transformed into simple administrative ones."[28]

Anarchists in the labor movement created associations and resistance societies that opposed capitalist forms of alienation and exploitation, defending workers' rights and strikers' platforms and spreading written propaganda; they sought to culturally and socially integrate civically disenfranchised workers, artisans, rural laborers, plebian urban sectors, and uprooted migrants into a collective subject—the "working people"—that they viewed as the insurgents of a coming revolution. The effectiveness of this endeavor was dependent on the existence of a much broader countercultural and pedagogical agenda that, in addition to the dissemination of nineteenth-century European anarchist traditions, involved their translation for Latin American audiences and the invention of a new cultural imaginary. The most salient characteristics of anarchist cultural productions, whether in music, theater, poetry, or literature, were an insistence on denouncing social injustice, raising consciousness, political mobilization, and the exaltation of virtue and beauty.[29] They framed, in the words of Kirwin Shaffer, the "diagnostic" and "prognostic" aspects of cultural militancy—their understanding of existing society and of their vision for the future—in popular, accessible, often festive, and always Promethean terms.[30]

Hence, by contributing culturally as well as politically to the creation of new collective subjects and expression of popular traditions, anarchists participated in the creation of modern "national" identities in Latin America while combating conservative, atavistic, racialized discourses of national belonging. Consider two examples to highlight this: Cuba and Peru. The 1895 outbreak of the independence war in Cuba posed a challenge to anarchist labor activists not because they were "foreigners" or lacked the conceptual tools to comprehend national movements but because the legacies of slavery, civil war, and working-class disenfranchisement had caused the "social question" to be framed in terms not yet anchored in a tradition of "the national." Over the course of the war, however, Cuban anarchists forged original forms of working-class organization, transnational relationships with émigré communities in the United States, and "class ties among people of diverse race, political sympathy, and origin."[31] When the cigar maker Enrique Roíg San Martín ironically described Cuba as having only three parties—"the Spaniards, the Cubans, and the blacks"[32]—he was identifying fissures in the edifice of national unity that were rooted in local historical conditions. The movement ultimately embraced the revolution and upheld national sovereignty while remaining critical of the exclusionary, economically dependent, and racially divisive regime that emerged from it. Shaffer has shown that postwar anarchists in Cuba, who participated in the rebellion and actively cultivated solidarity in labor and intellectual circles, "latched on to [the symbolism of independence leader José Martí], concluding that rather than allow the elite to adopt the war's symbolism for the purpose of the State, the anarchists would 'liberate' these symbols from State exploitation."[33] Carlos Rama and Ángel Capelletti argue that, "from the perspective of organization and praxis," the ideologically heterodox and mostly working-class protagonists of Latin American anarchism "produced forms hitherto unknown in Europe."[34]

The originality of Peruvian anarchism lay in its efforts to develop organic ties between urban and rural workers and indigenous peasants, a strategy that placed the "national question" at the heart of its propaganda.[35] Steven Hirsch has shown that provincial migrants extended the influence of anarchism to the indigenous peasantry in the rural areas of Cuzco and Puno through the Comité Central Pro-Derecho Indígena Tahuantinsuyo, founded in 1919. A Quechua-speaking "Indian-Mestizo," Ezequiel Urviola, helped organize indigenous self-defense organizations in Puno before participating in the Universidad Popular González Prada and advocating rationalist education and schools for Indians as well as pride in their race and in the Inca past; Urviola was a leader of the autonomous Federación Indígena Obrera Regional Peruana in the 1920s, in which he sought to impress the importance of workers' self-emancipation and rejection of government-backed paternalism.[36] Such initiatives had roots in earlier attempts by anarchists to advocate indigenous rights; it is, in this sense, illustrative that they participated between 1909 and 1916 in the educational and legal campaigns of a national organization with goals quite different from their own: the Asociación Pro-Indígena. Hence, voices within the anarchist and labor movements cast the Peruvian "national" question as a key dimension of their strategy for social emancipation.

Manuel González Prada, the best known anarchist in Peru, had become convinced that Indians themselves would be the architects of profound socioeconomic transformations of power and property in Peru. He advocated a radical, federalist reorganization of the agrarian economy by indigenous communes along the lines of collectivism and mutual aid (the village-based *ayllu*). These would work in close cooperation with resistance societies and anarchist groups in the cities, reproducing the idealized harmony of the precolonial state of Tawantinsuyo. It was, much like Kropotkin's embrace of the peasant *"mir"* in Russia, an idealized vision of the premodern past and an organicist utopia for the socialist future.[37] González Prada's vision translated two decades of anarchist thought and action into a real pan-ethnic movement of workers, peasants, and intellectuals to resolve social, agrarian, and national problems by means that were revolutionary for their time.

Writing the History of Anarchism in Latin America

Labor remains important to the historiography of anarchism. The rise of social history in the 1960s and 1970s ushered in a wave of historical research focused on organized labor activism in the late nineteenth and early twentieth centuries. Industrial capitalism (whether industrialized agriculture, manufacturing, shipping, or construction) impacted workers and anarchists on a daily basis, shaping their responses to an evolving economic system that, in Latin America as in the rest of the world, rationalized and bureaucratized labor processes, uprooted local communities, and transformed artisanal and agrarian societies. Anarchists also competed with socialists, revolutionary syndicalists, social Catholics, and later communist trade unionists, and resisted the rise of the "national-popular" state, which subordinated organized labor to the political and economic agenda of "populist" regimes in Mexico, Brazil, Argentina, and elsewhere.

Much of the labor-focused approach to the literature explores the links between anarchist groups and unions, the role of anarchists in labor and rent strikes, and the relationship of anarchist workers to the larger body politic of the nation, particularly their role in focusing attention on the "social question" and working-class welfare. To get a sense of the comparative successes and failures of anarchist involvement in organized labor, one might begin with John Hart, Rodney Anderson, Norman Caulfield, and John Lear (Mexico);[38] Diego Abad de Santillán, Yaacov Oved, Edgardo Bilsky, and Gonzalo Zaragoza Rivera (Argentina);[39] Anton Rosenthal and Rodolfo Porrini (Uruguay);[40] Edgar Rodrigues, Jacy Alves de Seixas, and Beatriz Ana Loner (Brazil);[41] Joan Casanovas, Evan Daniel, and Rebecca Condron (Cuba);[42] Luis Tejada R., Joël Delhom, Piedad Pareja Pflucker,

Ricardo Melgar Bao, David Parker, and Steven Hirsch (Peru);[43] Peter De-Shazo, Sergio Grez Toso, and Victor Muñoz Cortés (Chile);[44] and Alexei Páez (Ecuador).[45] Central to these studies is the role of anarchists in working-class formation and consciousness-raising as well as organization of strikes and boycotts against both international and domestic capital.

In the last two decades of the twentieth century, social historians branched out to study anarchists as more than just actors of organized labor. This approach, which found anarchists engaging with the larger society over social and cultural issues shaping the nation and the larger region, displayed two interlocking dimensions. First, historians began to explore anarchism as a "social movement" that was, while not entirely independent of the labor movement, propelled by its own set of goals and interests. Second, anarchists produced a plethora of cultural productions, including novels, plays, and short stories. They also organized schools, theater and music groups, and alternative health institutes. Historians began producing cultural histories of anarchism that illustrated how libertarians debated societal issues and addressed or challenged constituencies other than those of organized labor.

Cultural histories showcased anarchist efforts to create new schools and health initiatives that challenged the dominant societal institutions in education, health laws, and medicine. Social campaigns were reflected in the cultural productions of these movements, where theater groups staged anarchist plays and authors wrote fiction attacking social problems such as prostitution, promoting idealized visions of motherhood, seeking labor emancipation, sometimes celebrating revolutionary violence or disruptions of everyday life, organizing alternative schools, and denouncing exploitation in numerous guises. Culture allowed anarchists not only to critique the broader society but also to offer new ideas about what it meant to be Cuban, Mexican, or Argentine. In addition, anarchist-run schools, restaurants, and health institutes offered followers ways to live the revolution in the present.

Dora Barrancos' early work in Argentina (complemented by Juan Suriano's work nearly two decades later) pioneered the study of anarchist culture, especially education and the role of gender in the movement.[46] Kirwin Shaffer addressed the shortcomings and achievements of anarchist education in Cuba, noting that as in Argentina, its success was often predicated on the strength of organized labor.[47] Suriano, Shaffer, Jorell Meléndez, and Rubén Dávila Santiago explored anarchist theater and fiction as forms of popular education.[48] Finally, anarchist critiques of society often led libertarians to align with non-anarchists who shared similar goals on a particular issue. For instance, anarchists, spiritists, and freethinkers frequently worked together on issues of free speech and anticlericalism in Chile (Grez Toso) and Puerto Rico (Shaffer).[49]

The link between society, culture, and anarchism was especially prevalent when anarchists confronted national realities regarding race, ethnicity, and gender. While anarchists opposed racism and sexism, many often brought racialized and patriarchal attitudes to their projects and cultural productions. Historians have explored anarchist efforts to address issues surrounding gender and ethnicity, the difficulties they raised, and the ways in which they were overcome. Barrancos' study of gender was complemented in particular by Maxine Molyneux and Laura Fernández Cordero (Argentina), Shaffer (Cuba), Norma Valle Ferrer (Puerto Rico), and Elizabeth Quay Hutchison (Chile).[50] In countries dominated by indigenous peoples, anarchists reoriented their message to fit those specific ethnic realities. For example, Steven Hirsch's work on Peruvian anarchists mobilizing in both Spanish and Quechua speaks to the ways in which anarchists used culture, language, and ethnicity to promote their ideals. James Sandos illustrated how anarchists were not above engaging in ethnic violence along the U.S.-Mexico border.[51]

In addition to studies of labor and culture, biographies of individual militants long have played an important role in our understanding of the history of anarchism in Latin America. The men and women reflected in these portraits were the "faces of anarchism." It is true that anarchists preached the importance of communal or collective action in their schools, unions, and workplaces and embraced mutual aid to guide humanity in a spirit of cooperative evolution. Still, central to anarchist principles is the importance of individual autonomy. After all, to anarchists, it was the unholy troika of the state, church, and capital, with their manufactured, authoritarian institutions, that corrupted "natural man" and forced people to compete for survival. Once these institutions were abolished, cutthroat individualism would also disappear and individuals would be liberated to fulfill their true desires and freedoms.

As a result, the primacy of individual freedom has always been a key operating engine in the forces driving anarchist thought and actions. It is therefore only fitting that biographies of individual anarchists should play a central role in the historiography of anarchism. Historians have written biographical portraits of both well-known and less-well-known anarchists in the region. Some of the names are quite famous, such as Manuel González

Prada in Peru (Thomas Ward and Isabelle Tauzin), Ricardo Flores Magón
in Mexico and Los Angeles (Ward Albro, Juan Gómez-Quiñones, Salvador
Hernández Padilla, David Poole, and Claudio Lomnitz), Rafael Barrett in
Paraguay (Francisco Corral, Vladimiro Muñoz, Norma Suiffet, and Catriel
Etcheverri), and Luisa Capetillo in Puerto Rico (Valle Ferrer).[52] Other lesser
known figures have emerged in the historiography, such as Spanish anarchist José María Blázquez de Pedro, who was prominent in the Panamanian
movement (Hernando Franco Muñoz); the anarchist and rationalist school
teacher Blanca de Moncaleano, who traveled with her better-known husband, J. F. Moncaleano, from Colombia to Cuba and then to Mexico and
Los Angeles (Lina Marcela de Vito); Enrique Creci, an anarchist who died
in the Cuban War for Independence, and Alfredo López, who led the anarcho-syndicalist union in Havana in the 1920s (Olga Cabrera); or Práxedis
Guerrero, an anarchist active in Mexico and the American Southwest who
was overshadowed by his co-conspirator, Ricardo Flores Magón (Ward Albro and Eugenio Martínez Nuñez).[53]

Meanwhile, studies of transnational anarchism have grown in the past
decade, and biographies play a role here too. Biographies that trace the
international movements of anarchists—those whom Constance Bantman
calls "militant go-betweens"—put a face on the transnational and transregional networks that anarchists created throughout Latin America.[54]
Latin American revolutions and network operations have been central to
transnational histories of Latin American anarchism. The Cuban War for
Independence from 1895 to 1898 and the Mexican Revolution (both before
its "formal" launch in 1910 by Francisco Madero and through the 1910s)
have generated considerable research on transnational anarchism. Cuba
and Mexico were unique in Latin American anarchism since these were
the two countries in the Americas where strong anarchist movements operated in broader revolutionary contexts. Casanovas, Daniel, and Shaffer
have explored the role of organized labor in Havana and across the Florida
Straits to Key West and Tampa.[55] They illustrate how urban-based anarchists coordinated workers and pushed the labor movement to put aside
objections to "national" independence movements. Anarchists published
columns in Tampa supporting the war and raised money and fighters in
Florida to go to Cuba as part of a larger war against imperial tyranny. These
studies built upon Gerald Poyo's earlier research, which outlined the relationships between the nationalist José Martí and the Cuban- and Spanish-
born anarchists in Florida.[56] The War for Independence in Cuba was truly
transnational in scope and organization.

Anarchists throughout Mexico and the North American Southwest engaged in widespread transnational activism during the Mexican Revolution. While biographical portraits of Flores Magón and Guerrero illustrate these processes of agitation and armed uprising, other historians have focused on how the broader Partido Liberal Mexicano (PLM) movement operated on both sides of the border. In particular, W. Dirk Raat and Ricardo Cuauhtémoc Esparza Valdivia describe the PLM's operations into and throughout Mexico both before and after Madero's declaration of war against the regime of Porfirio Díaz.[57] The United States–based Industrial Workers of the World (IWW) operated in conjunction with different anarchist forces in the Revolution, including with the PLM in the occupation of Baja California in 1911, with PLM agitators to organize workers in Northern Mexico, and with the state-run Casa del Obrero Mundial to organize workers along the Gulf of Mexico. As noted earlier, Sandos outlines the controversial history of PLM clubs along the Texas-Mexico border and racialized violence in 1915. In addition, anarchists from outside this revolutionized border region worked with the PLM for an anarchist revolution in Mexico as noted by Jacinto Barrera Bassols' work on the link between the PLM and the Cuban anarchists running the newspaper ¡Tierra!.[58]

While scholars of revolutionary politics in Cuba and Mexico showed how anarchists mobilized transnational support networks, other historians focused more on how networks arose and were maintained outside of the "glamorous" events of revolution. The anarchist and anarcho-syndicalist press has been a key source for historians trying to unlock these networks. Using IWW and Caribbean newspapers, Anton Rosenthal and Shaffer trace the flow of the anarchist press throughout the hemisphere.[59] These exchanges spread ideas and money in ways that solidified the links within and between networks. Flows of people were equally important, especially European migrant anarchists who continuously reinforced anarchist groups and initiatives in Cuba (Sánchez Cobos), brought new languages and dimensions to Brazil (Toledo and Biondi) and Argentina (Miguelánez Martínez and Moya), and initiated a presence throughout the Caribbean, especially in Panama where few if any anarchists existed until they arrived to build and organize in the Canal Zone (Shaffer).[60]

Migration, communication flows, and organizing for international campaigns can be seen in research increasingly presented at international symposia and published in Latin American Studies journals. These include the work of María Miguelánez on Argentine anarchists reaching out into the Andes during the 1920s, David Struthers' work on how immigration into Los Angeles impacted anarchist internationalism in a multiethnic city, Anna Ribera Carbó's exploration of the Latin American anarchist process of myth-making following Francisco Ferrer y Guardia's execution in 1909, and Geoffroy de Laforcade's discussion of the 1929 anarchist and communist continental conferences in Buenos Aires.[61]

The authors represented in this volume frequently allude to transnational perspectives and methodologies. Transnationalism is not just the lens through which historians see the world they study; it was also how our historical subjects lived their "internationalist" ideals. They migrated across borders, shipped newspapers abroad, published news and communiqués from anarchists across the Americas, and translated ideals that were central to the global movement into local and regional variations in order to appeal for support and strengthen the resolve of local anarchists.

At a deeper level, anarchist transnationalism was structural. Anarchists created regional networks linking like-minded people, and these networks overlapped throughout the hemisphere. For instance, through their writings, publishing endeavors, and migrations, anarchists in the Caribbean created a regional network that linked the hub of Cuba with other nodes in Puerto Rico, Southern Florida, and Panama. This regional network was itself linked to a transatlantic network that stretched mainly to Spain but also to Italy, in which anarchists from southern Europe arrived in the extended Caribbean and information and money flowed both ways across the Atlantic. The network was also intimately linked to a network that stretched from the Caribbean north along the United States Atlantic seaboard to the New York metropolitan area. This Caribbean network also was linked to a Pacific network that saw anarchists from Peru traveling back and forth to Panama and working with Caribbean, Spanish, and Italian migrant anarchists in the Canal Zone and the Republic of Panama between 1911 and 1925. These same Peruvian anarchists were also linked to a network of anarchists in the Southern Cone, rooted principally in Argentina but encompassing the riverine environments of Uruguay and southern Brazil. All of these networks represented anarchist structures of material support. Just as importantly, however, they were structures of morale-building and consciousness-raising. They facilitated the interaction of people of different races, ethnicities, and genders, and in the process helped to forge the internationalist principles that were near and dear to anarchists.[62]

However, anarchists were not the only entities to operate transnationally. Governments, the Catholic Church, Jewish immigrants, and corporations, to cite only a few examples, also operated across geopolitical borders. In this context anarchists found themselves sometimes dealing with the same corporation in different countries (for example, the American Tobacco Corporation in Cuba, Florida, and Puerto Rico) or familiar government bureaucrats who were transferred to different sites (as was the case with American military administrators in Cuba, Puerto Rico, and the Canal Zone).

It should also be noted that the period ranging from the 1890s to 1920s, which represents anarchism's heyday in the region, coincided with the expansion of United States imperial presence, especially in the extended Caribbean Basin. Here and elsewhere, government intelligence agencies monitored the movements and activities of anarchists who moved along these various networks, sharing intelligence and working cooperatively to detain, imprison, or deport anarchists. In some ways the emergence of Operation Condor in the Southern Cone in the 1970s, which tracked leftists and dissidents around the hemisphere, was nothing new. Governments—in cooperation with the United States and European services—had done the same thing generations before. Indeed, continental conferences of anarchists and communists that were held in 1929 in Buenos Aires coincided with a continental congress of police departments that were tasked with antisubversive undertakings against movements that they correctly perceived as transnational in scope. Governmental belief in the need for international accords and transnational policing dated to the 1890s in Europe, and by the early 1900s that Italian government was launching a transnational surveillance network that stretched across the Atlantic to Argentina in order to monitor Italian anarchists there.[63] Hence, when anarchists traveled abroad, they not only interacted with like-minded radicals across the Americas but also encountered the trials, tribulations, and dangers that came with crossing borders at a time when governments increasingly cooperated with one another to repress anarchist activity and movement.

Such network arrangements were tricky things. After all, anarchists found themselves engaged in often illegal activity since several countries outlawed anarchists or strictly prohibited their entrance into the country. Resistance societies in the labor movement frequently were denied "*personería gremial*," or legal recognition, a status that they would have been loath to accept anyway. As a result, anarchists needed to be committed to the maintenance of solidarity, mutual cooperation, and information-sharing. Yet, more than just commitment was required. Networks such as those generated by anarchists were rooted in "trust," and their regional and transregional networks constituted what Charles Tilly calls "trust networks." By considering Tilly's ideas about the role of trust in these networks, we can see another dimension to how anarchist networks functioned and how the erosion of trust could adversely affect local and transnational organizing. For Tilly, trust networks connect people directly or indirectly, forming a network of multiple sites. These networks create ties that attribute to "one member significant claims on the attention or aid of another," and the united members collectively carry out "major long-term enterprises." The key, for Tilly, revolves around risk: "The configuration of ties within the network sets the collective enterprise at risk to the malfeasance, mistakes, and failures of individual members."[64]

Anarchist networks fit the description quite well. These were multisite networks in which activists worked for an assortment of causes, such as free thought, rational education, better working and living conditions, improved relations between racial groups and the sexes, and the sustained publication of newspapers, leaflets, and other proselytizing materials—in short, everything that was necessary to bring forth the "social revolution." But these networks, and the various groups that comprised them, were reliant on the dedication, veracity, and unrelenting persistence of individual anarchists. Would anarchists and their supporters get the newspaper out on time? Would people learn their lines for the weekly anarchist theater performance? Would people regularly dedicate part of their wages and salaries to purchase newspapers and books, or to support alternative health institutes, anarchist schools, or workers centers? Centrally important, especially for anarchists, was the issue of whether anarchists would be loyal to the ultimate goal of social revolution and would refrain from abandoning course or turning on one another. Betrayals, whether due to differences of opinion on theory and tactics or due to personality clashes, threatened to create internecine conflicts and disrupt good will and cooperation. When trust broke down, the larger long-term anarchist enterprise in a particular site, or even throughout a region or regions, was put in peril. Monetary contributions might dry up. Papers could fold. Local projects or international campaigns of solidarity ran the risk of being sidetracked. Networks helped anarchists organize and implement their internationalist, antiauthoritarian agendas. Subjected to constant surveillance and altered by changing political environments or fluctuating labor markets, they rested on personal relations and trust among fellow activists, and suffered when those were weakened.

Anarchism in Latin America

The chapters in this volume epitomize the breadth of methodological approaches and the expanding geographical dimension in the historiography of Latin American anarchism. While five chapters discuss anarchism in Argentina and Mexico—the traditional focus of much writing on anarchism—either by themselves or from a transnational perspective, one of our goals as editors was to include work that "decentered" the study of anarchism from Argentina and Mexico and to privilege the history of anarchism throughout the hemisphere to show its diversity, similarities, and interconnectedness. These chapters also illustrate how historians continue to find value in "nationally" focused studies but how the emergence of subnational and transnational perspectives expands our understandings.

The authors of the chapters in this volume contribute original angles and insights. While anarchists have generally been studied within the confines of national political borders, anarchists regularly crossed borders to agitate and find work. Evan Daniel traces the back-and-forth movements of Cuban cigar makers in Havana, Tampa, and New York City. This tale of migrant anarchist workers reflects the fact that even before the twentieth century the cigar industry was itself transnational, and these migrating radicals found social spaces that enabled them to organize transnationally to fight for Cuban independence from Spain. Anarchists traveled other migratory routes, including one leading to the Panama Canal Zone. As a United States possession, the Canal Zone was under North American control; thus, here anarchist politics took on a strident anti-imperialist flavor. As Shaffer illustrates, these anarchists developed and maintained transnational networks that linked the Canal Zone to anarchists in Cuba, Spain, and the United States. One tool anarchists used to maintain network linkages was their newspapers. In this vein, Anton Rosenthal illustrates how the anarcho-syndicalist IWW used its Spanish-language press throughout Latin America to coordinate a transhemispheric movement that was responsive to local demands but also united under the IWW goal of trying to create "One Big Union" in all of the Americas. Finally, while most people think about European anarchists arriving in the Americas, James Baer describes how anarchists in Argentina traveled to Spain to fight for the Republic against Franco and the Fascists. Transnationalism was multidirectional.

Considering the anarchist hatred for the state, it comes as a surprise whenever anarchists actually praise the state, as Lars Peterson illustrates in Uruguay during the Batlle Administrations of the early 1900s. Unlike

Raymond Craib's Chilean anarchists who were under constant threat from the state, some anarchists in Montevideo found themselves supporting Batlle's social reform agenda, reflecting another often overlooked dimension of the anarchist historical experience in Latin America. That is, despite their often rigid, doctrinaire public statements, they could cooperate with non-anarchists on issues of common cause, whether these were socialists, communists, naturists, freethinkers, spiritists, and even conservatives. Collective actions of anarchists were not limited to unions. As Shaffer shows for Cuba, activities beyond the union halls and the workplace were central for anarchist prefigurative politics. Anarchists used their cultural politics to guide and inform potential followers on how to interpret history and the present in order to march toward an imagined future. Before reaching that future new dawn, however, followers could partake in educational and health experiments to prepare them for the new era. Beatriz Loner's study on southern Brazil decenters traditional historians' focus on Rio de Janeiro and São Paulo and shifts to the south where anarchists operated in a regional context that itself spilled over political borders into Argentina and Uruguay. While Loner spins anarchist history away from the cities to the regions, Geoffroy de Laforcade goes beyond the "classical anarchist" period of the 1890s to 1920s to focus on the lingering libertarian activism in Argentine shipyards, and in the historically rebellious local community of La Boca del Riachuelo both before and after the fall of Juan Perón in the late 1950s.

Besides work on Farabundo Martí in El Salvador and Augusto César Sandino in Nicaragua, there are few studies on the pre-1960s political left in Central America. David Díaz-Arias not only explores the anarchist presence in Costa Rica but also highlights something fairly unique in the history of Latin American anarchism: anarchists being incorporated into the pantheon of national heroes. Only in Mexico and Cuba do we see similar state appropriation of anarchists into a national pantheon: Ricardo Flores Magón in Mexico and to a lesser extent Alfredo López and Enrique Creci in Cuba. Shawn England also illustrates the link between anarchists and their "homegrown" relationships by demonstrating how the *magonistas* in the U.S. Southwest and Mexico incorporated a version of Mexican *indigenismo* decades before the Mexican state and muralists like Diego Rivera made it popular. Steven Hirsch's chapter on race and ethnicity among Peruvian anarchists offers interesting comparative insights with Díaz-Arias and England on the importance of the "national" and the "subnational" shaping anarchist organizing and how anarchists reached out to indigenous peoples in Northern Peru—far removed from the ports and large cities of the country. While these chapters delve into anarchists tapping into the "local" and thus hybridizing the international anarchist message for local consumption and goals, Craib illustrates how the Chilean state stressed anarchists' foreignness as a means to delegitimize the anarchist agenda. Yet these "pernicious foreigners" were not necessarily migrants who willingly chose to leave home and settle wherever they could possibly find work. Many of these migrant anarchists had Chilean wives and children; they would have been happy to sink roots and become part of the body politic as opposed to placeless radicals. The state did all it could to prevent this. Finally, while several authors tackle themes of race, ethnicity, and national identity, Laura Fernández Cordero illustrates how women fought for their emancipation within the larger anarchist agenda to liberate humanity. After all, the anarchist agenda was first and foremost about "freedom." Still, female libertarians often encountered patriarchal ideas and assumptions from male anarchists. As a result, groups of female anarchists in Argentina pushed to liberate anarchism from such authoritarian ideas, resulting in anarchists fighting anarchists over the meaning of sexual politics and women's emancipation.

This collection is the first volume to sample the diversity of historiographical approaches and empirical case studies produced by the new wave of research on Latin American anarchism, and it does so with the largest geographical coverage of the hemisphere in the historiography. It touches on a plethora of themes that reflect a broad current interest in the renewed study of anarchism: organizational forms, working-class culture, labor movements, local-regional and urban-rural settings, transnational networks, race and national identity, gender, migration, exile, revolution, and education. We hope that this book will become a reference for scholars, students, and teachers of intellectual and labor history, the history of social movements and revolutions, and of Latin American history in general.

Notes

1. Rama, *Utopismo socialista*.
2. Nettlau, *Actividad anarquista en México*.
3. Vargas Martínez, *Colombia, 1854*, 29.
4. Rodrigues, *Os libertários*, 20–52; and Leuenroth, *Anarquismo*, 91 and 141–42.
5. Quiroule, *La ciudad anarquista Americana*.
6. Rodrigues, *Os libertários*, 85–101.
7. Nash, *Mayan Visions*; and Stephen, *Zapata Lives!*

8. Sitrin, *Horizontalism*; Sitrin, *Everyday Revolutions*; Almeyra, *La protesta social en la Argentina*; and Holloway, *Changing the World*.

9. See Lida and Yankelevich, *Cultura y política del anarquismo*.

10. See Hirsch and van der Walt, *Anarchism and Syndicalism*; E.I.A.L., 22, no. 2, (July–December 2011); and Delhom, *¡Viva la Social!*

11. Hirsch and van der Walt, "Rethinking Anarchism," liv.

12. Viñas, *Anarquistas en América Latina*; and Aricó, "Para un análisis."

13. Max Nettlau, "Antes del congreso continental Americano de mayo de 1929," *La Protesta*, May 3, 1929.

14. Reclus, *L'Homme et la Terre*, 527.

15. Lazarte, *Federalismo y decentralización*.

16. Proudhon, "Idée générale de la Révolution," 212.

17. Proudhon, "Du principe federative," 266–67.

18. Thompson, *The European Revolutions*, 7–8.

19. Bakunin, "Appeal to the Slavs," 34.

20. Bakunin, "Circular Letter to Friends in Italy" (1871), 42–43.

21. Bakunin, "Federalism, Socialism, Anti-Theologism," 38.

22. Nataf, *Des anarchistes en France*, 275–88.

23. Clark, *Living without Domination*, 94–96.

24. García, *L'Anarchisme aujourd'hui*, 112.

25. Kropotkin, *Fugitive Writings*, 50.

26. Qtd. in Levy, *Gramsci and the Anarchists*, 13–14.

27. Gori, "La questione sociale e gli anarchici."

28. Marx, "Les prétendues scissions de l'internationale," 103.

29. Andreu, Fraysse, and Golluscio de Montoya, *Anarkos*.

30. Shaffer, "Rebel Soul: Cultural Politics and Cuban Anarchism, 1890s–1920s" chapter 6 of the present volume. See also Shaffer, *Anarchism and Countercultural Politics*.

31. Casanovas, *Bread, or Bullets!*, 202.

32. Ibid., 182.

33. Shaffer, "Tropical Libertarians," 62–71.

34. Rama and Capelletti, *El anarquismo en América Latina*, x–xi.

35. Melgar Bao, *Sindicalismo y milenarismo*, 33–35.

36. Hirsch, "Peruvian Anarcho-Syndicalism," 262–64.

37. Álvarez Junco, *La ideología política*, 596–97.

38. Hart, *Anarchism and the Mexican Working Class*; Anderson, *Outcasts in Their Own Land*; Caulfield, "Wobblies and Mexican Workers"; and Lear, *Workers, Neighbors, and Citizens*.

39. Abad de Santillán, *LA F.O.R.A., ideologia y trayectoria*; Oved, *El anarquismo*; Bilsky, *La FORA*; and Zaragoza, *Anarquismo argentino*.

40. Rosenthal, " Arrival of the Electric Streetcar"; and Porrini, "Izquierda uruguaya y culturas obreras."

41. Rodrigues, *Os libertários*; Alves de Seixas, *Memoire et oubli*; and Loner, *Construção de classe*.

42. Casanovas, *Bread, or Bullets!*; Daniel, "Rolling for the Revolution"; and Condron, "The Sindicato General de Obreros de la Industria Fabril."

43. Tejada R., *La cuestión de pan*; Delhom, "El movimiento obrero anarquista en el Perú"; Pareja Pflucker, *Anarquismo y sindicalismo en el Perú*; Melgar Bao, *Sindicalismo y milenarismo*; Parker, "Peruvian Politics and the Eight-Hour Day"; and Hirsch, "The Anarcho-Syndicalist Roots."

44. DeShazo, *Urban Workers*; Grez Toso, *Los anarquistas y el movimiento obrero*; and Muñoz Cortés, *Sin dios ni patrones*.

45. Páez, *El anarquismo en el Ecuador*.

46. Barrancos, *Anarquismo, educación y costumbres*; and Suriano, *Anarquistas*.

47. Shaffer, "Freedom Teaching."

48. Suriano, *Anarquistas*; Shaffer, "Prostitutes"; Shaffer "By Dynamite"; Meléndez, *Voces libertarias*; and Dávila Santiago, *Teatro obrero en Puerto Rico*.

49. Grez Toso, *Los anarquistas*; and Shaffer, *Black Flag Boricuas*.

50. Molyneux, "No God, No Boss, No Husband"; Fernández Cordero, "Queremos emanciparos"; Shaffer, "The Radical Muse"; Valle Ferrer, *Luisa Capetillo*; and Hutchison, "From 'la mujer esclava' to 'la mujer Limón.'"

51. Hirsch, "Peruvian Anarcho-Syndicalism"; and Sandos, *Rebellion in the Borderlands*.

52. Ward, *La anarquía inmanentista*; Tauzin-Castellanos, *Manuel González Prada*; Albro, *Always a Rebel*; Gómez-Quiñones, *Sembradores*; Hernández Padilla, *El magonismo*; Flores Magón, *Land and Liberty*; Lomnitz, *Return of Comrade Flores Magón*; Corral, *Vida y pensamiento de Rafael Barrett*; Muñoz, *Barrett*; Suiffet, *Rafael Barrett*; Catriel, *Rafael Barrett*; and Valle Ferrer, *Luisa Capetillo*.

53. Franco Muñoz, *Blázquez de Pedro*; Marcela de Vito, "Siguiendo las huellas literarias"; Cabrera, "Enrique Creci"; Cabrera, *Alfredo López*; Albro, *To Die on Your Feet*; and Martínez Núñez, *La vida heróica de Práxedis G. Guerrero*.

54. Bantman, "The Militant Go-Between."

55. Casanovas, *Bread, or Bullets!*; Daniel, "Rolling for the Revolution"; and Shaffer, "Cuba para todos."

56. Poyo, "The Anarchist Challenge."

57. Raat, *Revoltosos*; and Esparza Valdivia, *El fenómeno magonista*.

58. See Caulfield, "Wobblies and Mexican Workers"; Raat, *Revoltosos*; Sandos *Rebellion in the Borderlands*; and Barrera Bassols, *Los rebeldes de la bandera roja*.

59. Rosenthal, "Radical Border Crossers"; and Shaffer, "Havana Hub."

60. Sánchez Cobos, *Sembrando ideales*; Toledo and Biondi, "Constructing Syndicalism and Anarchism Globally"; Migueláñez Martínez, "Atlantic Circulation"; Moya, *Cousins and Strangers*; Moya, "The Positive Side of Stereotypes"; and Shaffer, "Tropical Libertarians."

61. Migueláñez Martínez, "Anarquistas en red"; Struthers, "The World in a City"; Ribera Carbó, "Ferrer Guardia en la Revolución Mexicana"; and de Laforcade, "Dissonant Preludes."

62. Shaffer, "Latin Lines and Dots."

63. Jensen, *Battle against Anarchist Terrorism*, 105–8, 219–21.

64. Tilly, *Trust and Rule*, 4–6.

I

CROSSING BORDERS

Internationalism, Solidarity, and Transnationalism

1

Cuban Cigar Makers in Havana, Key West, and Ybor City, 1850s–1890s

A Single Universe?

EVAN MATTHEW DANIEL

This chapter examines Cuban cigar makers in Key West and Tampa, Florida, from the 1850s to 1895 with particular attention paid to the development of the Cuban émigré labor movement and the shift in its ideological orientation over time. Paralleling developments in Cuba, the Florida labor movement largely followed the realignment that occurred in Havana from anarcho-mutualism to anarcho-collectivism. The ease and quickness of steamship transportation between Havana and Key West enabled Cuban cigar makers to keep in touch with their friends and families and maintain links with labor, political, and social organizations back on the island.[1] This, in combination with the reading of periodicals like *La Aurora*, in Nancy Hewitt's words, "combined to make the world of cigar workers on both sides of the Florida Straits a single universe."[2] But there were important differences between the nodes of this transnational network.

The chapter concerns three dimensions of the separatist project and anarchist/working-class participation in organizations that supported armed struggle against Spain, and illustrates how these dimensions differed in Florida and Cuba. First, creole cigar makers largely supported the cause of separatism.[3] Although in Cuba this was punishable by prison, deportation, or even death, in Florida, Cubans were able to organize toward radical ends rather openly. Understanding how and why anarchist tobacco workers came to support separatism is rooted in how the separatist movement changed over time. At various points in its development, the separatist movement appealed to different participants for different reasons. During the annexationist period from the 1850s to early 1860s, the primary participants in the émigré community were middle-class intellectuals and property owners in New York. During the Ten Years' War (1868–78) the movement attracted more working-class proponents, and by the 1880s fissures developed in the movement between nationalists and anarchists.

Second, there were tensions between creoles and peninsulars in the Florida exile communities. In a major shift from the workplace demographic in Havana, creoles—and to a lesser extent Afro-Cubans—dominated the cigar-making professions while peninsulars continued to serve as managers and owned most of the cigar factories. This led to schisms in the separatist and labor movements and impeded both movements' efforts to organize in the émigré community.

Third, this research builds from Gerald Poyo's path-breaking work on Cuban separatist organizations and activities in Florida and to a lesser extent New York.[4] Poyo argues that Spain's repressive policies, plus the close connections between the Cuban labor movement and that of the émigré communities, prompted most Cuban labor leaders to join the separatists in the early 1890s.[5] This chapter aims to expand on those transnational relations, especially the close connections between labor leaders and the anarchist movement.

Anarchist Ideology and the Cuban Labor Movement

The Cuban labor organizations of the 1850s were informed by the gradualist mutualism of Pierre-Joseph Proudhon.[6] Utopian socialism and mutualism both advanced the notion that Cuban workers had the right to establish cooperatives and trade unions, to bargain collectively, to elect delegates for this reason, and to gain an education. Opposing strikes as a form of coercion, Proudhon and other mutualists advocated workers' education and self-organization in mutual aid societies and cooperatives.

Another early advocate of cooperatives was Spanish utopian socialist Fernando Garrido. Garrido was editor of the Fourierist newspaper *La Atracción* (1846) and eventually became friends with Mikhail Bakunin and a member of Bakunin's Fraternité Internationale.[7] After spending time in the United Kingdom and witnessing the development of the Rochdale Cooperative Society, Garrido became convinced that the emancipation of Spanish workers would result from free association in producers and consumers cooperatives.

Educational associations were another area of emphasis. In Cuba, *liceos* were associations where the peninsular and creole elite met, socialized, and debated the role of Spain in Cuba. In the early 1860s, the creole socioeconomic elite used these bourgeois cultural institutions and periodicals to create a political movement to foster colonial reform. While they began as an elite institution, workers adopted the *liceo* model for their own purposes.

One exemplar of the connection between the *liceo* and early working-class organization is Saturnino Martínez. Born in Sariego in the Asturias region of Spain, he served as an apprentice cigar maker shortly after arriving in Cuba at a young age.[8] Martínez was educated in the *liceos* at the same time as other members of the popular classes began to organize themselves into workers associations based around the *liceo* model. Shortly after observing strikes at the Cabanas and El Fígaro cigar factories in August 1865, Martínez founded the first Cuban labor periodical, *La Aurora: Periódico Semanal Dedicado a los Artesanos*. *La Aurora* promoted the establishment of workers associations, viewing its primary mission as educating and developing workers' intellects. The periodical placed great emphasis on the problems facing skilled workers and the formation of artisans' associations rather than explicitly political matters.[9] And *La Aurora* did not place an emphasis on workers as a class with common interests. Martínez was also instrumental in the development of the *lectura*, or cigar factory readers.

Cuba experienced an early war of independence, the Ten Years' War (1868–78), which was sparked by a combination of local and international factors. Spain's anti-Bourbon Revolución Gloriosa (Glorious Revolution) of September 1868, the shift toward a reactionary colonial policy on the island, and the accompanying crackdown on labor reformism all precipitated the collapse of the consensus developed between creole elites and the Spanish government. The Glorious Revolution dethroned Queen Isabella II in September, and in October Spanish workers' right to organize was restored. The following year a liberal constitution was written and adopted as the fundamental law of Spain.

Another important change in Spain and throughout Europe was a noticeable increase in strike activity. George Esenwein notes that, due to its support and promotion of the strike, "the International Working Men's Association especially benefited from this sharp rise in labor unrest, for its membership was soon swelled by the influx of more militant workers."[10] One month after the start of the Glorious Revolution, the revolutionary anarchist Mikhail Bakunin sent the French anarchists Élisée Reclus, Aristide Rey, and Alfred Naquet to Spain in order to contact the Spanish labor movement and, in Esenwein's words, "pave the way" for Bakunin's "principal emissary," the Italian anarchist Giuseppe Fanelli.[11]

Instead of a gradual, evolutionary, and peaceful shift toward socialism, Bakunin was an apostle of class struggle and violent revolutionary upheaval. He sought to establish an international federation of anarchist organizations dedicated to global revolt. Bakunin argued for the collectivization of private property and the means of production as opposed to the more moderate goal of organizing cooperatives to reform the capitalist system. In the future society, federations of agricultural and industrial collectives were envisioned as replacements for the state and capitalist economic relations.

Bakunin postulated an influential theory of political action that he described as revolutionary socialism or collectivist anarchism.[12] While critical of cooperatives as reformist, Bakunin viewed trade unions and strikes in a much more favorable light than Proudhon or Garrido did. Bakuninist influence on trade union ideology and organization is evident in Spain and Cuba, particularly the notion of the strike as an economic weapon to be used by workers against the capitalist class. Bakunin and the collectivists, like the later syndicalists, ultimately believed that a general or insurrectionary strike—rather than the seizure of political power—was necessary to overthrow capitalism.[13] In addition, Bakunin believed that "oppressed nationalities" (such as the Cubans) deserved anarchists' support in their struggle against imperialism and the state.

On September 24, 1881, Spanish anarchists affiliated with the First International established the Federación de Trabajadores de la Región Española (FTRE, Federation of the Workers of the Spanish Region). The collectivist ideas of the FTRE arrived in Cuba via peninsular immigrants and the Spanish press. For example, the Cuban typographer J. C. Campos, who fled to New York during the Ten Years' War, was instrumental in establishing contact between Cuban and Spanish anarchists when he returned to Havana.[14]

By mid-1882 Cuban labor leaders established the Junta Central de Artesanos (JCA) in Havana (which later changed its name to the Junta Central de Trabajadores). This new organization connected the early trade unions and mutual benefit associations into a unified labor movement.[15] Valeriano Rodríguez, a peninsular Asturian cigar maker, printer, and activist in the New York labor movement during the 1870s, became the JCA's first president.[16] While linked to the Havana labor movement, the JCA's ultimate goal was the creation of a much broader Junta Federal de la Región (Federal Board of the [Cuban] Region) that would serve as a national federation of Cuban workers, similar to the FTRE in Spain.[17]

After Rodríguez unexpectedly died in January 1883, the creole anarchist Enrique Messonier Álvarez became director of the JCA. Messonier previously served as interim secretary of the Centro de Artesanos in 1880 and then secretary of the Gremio de Obreros del Ramo de Tabaquerías (GORT) until early 1882 when he was promoted to vice president.[18] Messonier clashed with Martínez and the other mutualists on the direction of the labor movement and the role of electoral politics.

The challenge to Martínez's leadership came in 1885 from younger men promoting Bakunin's concepts of anarcho-collectivism. In July 1885 the Cosmopolitan Congress of Barcelona was held to "reinforce the position of the collectivist tendency, predominant in Spain, through public and open debate with the anarcho-communists."[19] Anarcho-collectivist ideas were circulated and promoted in large measure by peninsular workers who were active in the Spanish anarchist labor movement and then migrated to Cuba.[20]

Most prominent among the new collectivist anarchists was Enrique Roíg San Martín. The son of an army doctor and educated in the Colegio San Ancleto in Havana, he worked from 1860 to 1882 in the sugar mills, starting as a laborer, rising through the ranks, and eventually becoming manager. His twenty-odd years of association with black slaves, contract workers, and free laborers in the cane fields facilitated his willingness to work across racial boundaries. He studied the doctrines of Bakunin, Marx, and Engels and became an anarchist. He took a position as a *lector* in a tobacco factory and dedicated the remaining seven years of his life to revolutionary anarchism. Roíg's writings first appeared in 1883 in *El Obrero* (The Worker). He next wrote for *El Boletín del Gremio de Obreros* in 1884–86, which was directed toward tobacco workers.

Havana's cigar makers made many advances in 1887. They organized a successful strike in the fall that led to the creation of a new union, the Asociación Benéfica y Protección a los Trabajadores, also known as the Alianza Obrera. Headed by the anarchists Roíg, Enrique Creci, and Enrique Messonier, the Alianza called for a new federation that would join all existing tobacco worker organizations and demanded equality between creole, peninsular, and Afro-Cuban workers. Havana's workers also held a labor congress in the city and surrounding towns in November organized by peninsular members of the Spanish FTRE.

In another important development in 1887, Roíg and Messonier founded the influential Havana weekly *El Productor: Seminario consagrado a la defensa de los intereses económicos-sociales de la clase obrera* and a Bakuninist bimonthly titled *Hijos del Mundo* was also published.[21] In distinction from the reformist *La Aurora*, *El Productor* sought to extend the principles of

Bakuninist collectivism throughout Cuba.[22] Based in Havana, *El Productor* had correspondents in Santiago de las Vegas and Guanabacoa, Cuba, in addition to Tampa and Key West, Florida. *El Productor* included locally written pieces, letters to the editor, and translations of articles from European anarchist papers, including Élisée Reclus' *Le Revolte*, *La Acracia*, the similarly named *El Productor* in Barcelona, and *El Proceso de Paris*. The periodical covered strikes, demonstrations, and other political activities in Europe, Latin America, and the world while seeking to reach beyond just tobacco workers. In this vein, it was the first Cuban paper to outline the idea of class struggle as opposed to the reformist stance and craft workers' perspective of *La Aurora*, and it offered Cuba's workers anarchism as a clear alternative to Spanish colonialism and capitalism. An article titled "Evolucionomania," although it does not mention Martínez by name, takes aim at the reformist efforts he played such a major role in developing: "Anarchy is merely the absence of tyranny in the regime of society, and we are fighting any system that holds a bit of tyranny in the regime. We reject the idea of evolution that has invaded us in the likeness of some voracious epidemic."[23] Simply put, instead of evolution and slow reform, the authors called for class struggle and social revolution.

Key West: An Early Cuban Community in the United States, 1860s–1870s

The Ten Years' War led to a dramatic decline in domestic cigar production, which, in combination with the high duty on finished tobacco products entering the United States, led to an increase in unemployment among cigar makers in Cuba. A few entrepreneurs saw an opportunity for profit. In an early example of outsourcing, tobacco capitalists relocated their operations to Key West, Florida. The pioneer of employing Cuban labor and importing Cuban tobacco to the Key was the German émigré Samuel Seidenberg.[24] Key West offered easy access to the tobacco regions of western Cuba and the commercial centers of Havana. Havana is only ninety miles from Key West, which was about six to seven hours by steamboat. In 1869, as the war in Cuba deepened, the Spaniard Vicente Martínez Ybor left Havana and established a factory in New York followed by his El Príncipe de Gales (Prince of Wales) factory in Key West.[25]

In light of the economic situation in Cuba in the 1860s and with jobs readily available on the Key, cigar makers arrived in droves. In 1868 three thousand Cuban cigar makers arrived in Key West, and by 1870 approximately eighteen thousand made the tiny island their home.[26] The *Florida Union* described two thousand Cubans lining the Havana docks to leave the island.[27] The *Bangor Daily Whig & Courier* described the scene in Key West in the following manner: "Key West, Fla., is at present literally overrun with Cuban refugees, and every vessel, steamer, yacht, or smack arriving from Havana is generally crowded with them."[28]

The struggle for independence had been especially popular among creoles, leading many to leave the island for the United States. One was José Dolores Poyo, a journalist for *La Gazeta de la Habana* and supporter of the Cuban insurgency who relocated to Key West. Soon after arriving, Poyo found work as a *lector* at Martínez Ybor's factory. Juan María Reyes, a journalist affiliated with the printers' newspaper *El Siglo* and the cigar makers' newspaper *La Aurora*, was employed as a *lector* in Seidenberg & Company's La Rosa Española factory and the Samuel Wolf factory.[29]

Shortly after arriving in the United States, Cuban émigrés created political and social institutions that were similar to organizations in Cuba, with some important derivations. Émigré labor associations in Florida were closely connected with the Quesadistas, a prominent tendency of the Cuban separatist movement in the United States named after Gen. Manuel de Quesada, an abolitionist and revolutionary. The competing tendency, the Aldamistas, was named after plantation owner Miguel Aldama, who sought economic and political liberalization but not radical social change.[30] The Quesadistas received a large measure of support from cigar makers, founding organizations in the United States that provided material support for filibustering expeditions, and served as volunteers for the "Liberation Army" in Cuba.[31] They also created a variety of mutual aid associations and cooperatives that provided similar services to those in Cuba.

In 1870 the predominantly working-class Club Patriótico Cubano (Cuban Patriots' Club) of Key West provided a base of operations for émigré separatists whose leaders formed the Partido Radical Independiente.[32] Their newspaper, *La Voz de la Patria*, described the party's platform of political independence and representative democracy in Cuba and Puerto Rico. Over the next twenty-five years, forty-six small separatist organizations sprang up in Florida wherever there were émigré communities.[33]

In February 1878 the signing of the Pact of Zanjón codified an end to the Ten Years' War and enabled Cubans to travel freely from Cuba to the United States. However, the cessation of hostilities on the island did not spell an end to separatist organizing in Key West. Gen. Manuel de Céspedes held a meeting on March 11, 1878, where he implored Cuban exiles to continue raising money and readying men for a future revolt. On October 12, 1878, Dolores Poyo published a new periodical, *El Yara*, named after the town where Céspedes launched the Ten Years' War.

El Yara promoted the independence cause, adopted an explicitly nationalist perspective, and contained articles on Cuba and the Cuban émigré communities. The labor leader Carlos Baliño was a contributor to the newspaper. Born in 1848 in Guanajay, Cuba, he first studied architecture and bookkeeping and in 1868 entered the academy San Alejandro to become a painter. However, the family was forced to flee Cuba due to their support of the insurgency. Originally landing in New Orleans, the family relocated to Key West where Baliño found work as an *escogedor* (tobacco sorter) in the Key's cigar factories and was the leader of the revolutionary club Francisco V. Aguilera.[34] Along with Ramón Rivero y Rivero, Baliño emerged as one of the most prominent labor leaders in the Florida émigré communities, first in the Gremio de Escogedores (tobacco sorters union), then the Knights of Labor and Unión de Tabaqueros.

The late-1870s also witnessed a short strike in July 1878 and the emergence of a new labor organization in 1879, the Unión de Tabaqueros. Unlike the skilled craft unionism of the Cigar Makers International Union (CMIU), the Unión de Tabaqueros adopted an industrial or "general union" model, where all workers employed in the cigar industry—rollers, selectors, classers, and strippers—were members of the same organization. The union was open to creoles, Afro-Cubans, and mulattos. Despite this inclusive stance, the union prohibited peninsulars from joining. In addition to Baliño, the leadership included anarchist Rivero y Rivero, who was the organization's secretary, Oscar Martín, Eduardo Pajarín, and Afro-Cubans Francisco Segura and Guillermo Sorondo.[35]

As a recession deepened in May 1878, the Key's factories laid off two-thirds of their workers, and unemployed cigar makers numbered five thousand.[36] By July the situation had deteriorated to such an extent that the workers went on strike and threatened to leave for Havana en masse if their demands were not met.[37] The 1878 strike was the first time Key West's cigar makers successfully shut down production on a large scale. This led General García and fellow Comité Revolucionario Cubano activist José Francisco Lamadriz to travel from New York to Key West in an attempt to broker an agreement between the strikers and employers.

While creoles were largely united around the general cause of independence, divisions remained regarding tactics, personalities, and, perhaps above all, class. In essence, the interests of creole émigré elites and the interests of creole cigar makers often clashed. García recognized that the cause of independence relied on the support of all classes, and any rifts in the émigré communities would make it much more difficult to raise funds for future separatist endeavors. A settlement was reached after a few days, with employers recognizing the union and the establishment of a standard industry price list.[38] After the strike ended, García returned to New York and Lamadriz remained in Key West to assist the separatist cause.[39]

Key West in the 1880s: Economic Growth and Labor Conflict

After a short insurrection (Guerra Chiquita) was defeated in 1880, a number of revolutionary leaders and veterans arrived on the Key from Cuba, including Enrique Canals, Gerardo Castellanos, José Rogelio Castillo, and Fernándo Figueredo. Castellanos and Castillo opened small cigar workshops, and Castillo was employed as typographer for *El Yara*.[40] Figueredo founded a short-lived newspaper, *La Voz de Hatuey*, and gave a series of talks on his experiences during the Ten Years' War at the Club San Carlos. The lectures were later published as the widely read *La Revolución de Yara, 1868–1878*.[41] These veterans and other activists precipitated a proliferation of organizations dedicated to Cuban independence on the Key. A few continued their clandestine efforts at insurrection, including producing dynamite for insurgents and guerrilla fighters remaining in Cuba.[42]

Key West's émigré labor movement was greatly influenced by the emigrants who left Cuba in ever-increasing numbers. This demographic shift had a major impact on the character of the Key's labor movement. The cigar makers who arrived in the 1860s and 1870s were products of a movement shaped largely by the gradualist mutualism of Saturnino Martínez. By contrast, the workers of the 1880s were more swayed by the revolutionary ideology of anarcho-collectivism that was attracting more and more adherents in Havana. While the separatists were able to find common ground with the mutualists, their relationship with the collectivists was far more tenuous.

As mentioned previously, some of the key activists in this shift were the Cuban anarchists affiliated with La Alianza Obrera and the periodical *El Productor*, including Roíg, Creci, and Messonier. Messonier and other anarchists affiliated with *El Productor* traveled from Havana to Key West and helped to found the Federación Local de Tabaqueros on October 11, 1888. In this manner the regular movement of cigar makers between Havana, Key West, and Tampa during the 1880s contributed to the radicalization of

Cuban and Spanish labor in Florida.[43] La Alianza attracted more and more adherents among cigar makers in the émigré communities, and *El Productor* drew increasing numbers of cigar makers who demanded that it be read to them.

The increasing anarcho-collectivist influence on the Cuban and émigré labor movement in the 1880s led to a critical questioning among union leaders regarding labor's role in the separatist movement. Creole workers remained strongly committed to the separatists during the 1860s and 1870s even though the cigar manufacturers who were separatist benefactors actively opposed their efforts for a better life. Cigar makers did not see any results stemming from their political activism and monetary support of the separatist cause. Furthermore, Afro-Cubans and mulattos—who made up approximately 20 percent of the Key's population—were growing tired of the discrimination they faced in their own communities and in the broader Anglo-American society. They could see the contradictions in a separatist movement that called on all émigrés to support independence while creole separatist leaders continued to discriminate against them in their organizations and hiring practices. As Poyo notes, "by the late 1880s many Cuban blacks had withdrawn from active participation in the separatist movement and joined the anarchist groundswell."[44]

Labor organizations made gains in the 1880s as work stoppages and other disruptions became commonplace, and efforts were made to forge links between Cuban émigré labor organizations and American unions, in particular the CMIU and Knights of Labor. In 1880 Unión de Tabaqueros president Manuel Escassi named CMIU president Adolph Strasser an honorary member of the organization. Strasser replied with lengthy correspondence praising Cuban successes in Florida and calling for their affiliation with the CMIU.[45] He noted that the cigar makers in "New York and Key West must combine for mutual protection," but the CMIU never sent an organizer to the Key.[46]

In 1889 the Key's separatists reorganized as the Convención Cubana. The organization was committed to independence and armed struggle, but it placed emphasis on organizing revolutionary cells on the island rather than training émigrés for invading and ultimately overthrowing the colonial government. Unlike many other separatist organizations, whose activities were public, the Convención Cubana was an underground association also referred to as the Club Secreto.[47]

Despite their rigid class-struggle rhetoric, émigré anarcho-collectivists in the United States appeared flexible in their willingness to work with the separatists. As Shaffer notes, anarchists did not frame the anti-imperialist cause as synonymous with nationalism. Instead, they envisioned the struggle as one link in a chain of events that would lead to global social revolution.[48] However, many separatists were not quick to reciprocate. In Cuba the anarchist leadership was often just as dogmatic as separatist leaders in the émigré communities. This ultimately led to an ideological struggle between anarchists and nationalists in the Key.

During 1888 and 1889 the Key West correspondent for *El Productor* berated the local cigar factory owners for reorganizing the working-class Cuban community after the fire of 1886 as a "company town." The author noted the manufacturers "at very low cost monopolized large tracts of land around the factories, and like the large northern mining and railroad firms, built hundreds of small rooms, creating barrios in mosquito-infested areas lacking all hygiene, which they then rented to workers at inflated prices."[49] He continued, "of course the *burgués* cannot ignore the rest that is concerned with his feudatory and to provide for all its needs he installs the barroom, owned by the manufacturers and calculated to keep the workers in a constant state of moral decay and sociopolitical inactivity." These problems, he suggested, could only be eliminated by the creation of a militant labor organization dedicated exclusively to social revolution.[50]

The schism between anarchists and separatists reached a crescendo in early 1889, when anarchists led a strike at the Pino Brothers factory, demanding an increase in wages.[51] The strike was well organized and spread to the Seidenberg, Julius Ellinger, Trujillo and Sons, and Horace Kelly factories.[52] By the end of the year, only 1 of 179 cigar factories in Key West remained open.[53] As in previous strikes, workers threatened to leave for New York, Havana, and the new cigar factories in Tampa.[54] The Spanish consul in Key West made arrangements for the gunboat *Jorge Juan* to transport workers across the Florida Straits. A merchant steamer soon followed and then another sent by the Alianza Obrera.

The Key West newspaper *El Cubano*, edited by Pedro Pequeño and Néstor Leonelo Carbonell, expressed their solidarity with the workers, declaring, "all over the world the workers have served as cannon fodder in political revolutions; they have been the targets of all governments; they have served as the human ladder on which the ambitious of all time have risen to power and riches."[55] The nationalist *El Yara* took a different approach and rejected calls by labor militants to abandon compromise in labor-management relations. Dolores Poyo also condemned anarchism as a "pro-Spanish" ideology.[56] The creole cigar manufacturer Eduardo Hidalgo

Gato took things a step further, claiming the anarchists were operating in the pay of Spanish agents, "It seems a regular occurrence that when a Cuban cigar makers' strike occurs at Key West that a Spanish gunboat invariably arrives at the port. . . ."[57] Cigar makers and their anarchist leadership regularly responded by accusing the separatists of using the cause of Cuban independence to undermine the cause of Cuban workers.[58]

The conflict became so intense that Dolores Poyo rejected reading *El Productor* at the Ellinger Factory where he was employed and was subsequently dismissed by the workers.[59] By December 1889 most of the Key's factories remained closed. As the Christmas season brought an increasing demand for cigars, orders were again fulfilled by suppliers in New York and Tampa. In January 1890 the factory owners agreed to labor's demands. Anarchists in Key West, Havana, and Spain were buoyed by the success of their activism.[60]

Ybor City: Latin Paternalism in a Southern Company Town, 1885–1889

By the mid-1880s Martínez Ybor and other factory owners found the increasing militancy of the Key's cigar makers more than a nuisance. Strikes and other work disruptions were impeding production and, by extension, their profits. Therefore, several manufacturers launched a search for a new site for their factories. At the end of 1885 Martínez Ybor settled on a forty-acre tract of land east of Tampa that would be known as the Ciudad de Ybor, or Ybor City.[61]

Ybor City—despite being named after the factory owner—was not a one-company town but a one-industry town as fellow owners began relocating factories to Tampa, especially after an 1886 fire that incinerated half of the Key.[62] Dolores Poyo arrived in Tampa on April 12, 1886, aboard the *Mascotte*. The anarchist *lector* Rivero y Rivero made a similar passage where he eventually settled with his wife, Adelaide, and the rest of his immediate family.[63] Carlos Baliño and Ramón Rubiera—two experienced activists from the labor struggles in Key West and New York during the early 1880s—also moved to Ybor City in 1886 and took on leadership positions as organizers in the labor movement.[64] Baliño also helped to found the auxiliary lodge of the mutual benefit, Caballeros de la Luz, Provenir número 7, and founded two lodges of the Caballeros del Trabajo (Knights of Labor), including Tampa's Unión y Fraternidad.[65]

Cigar makers reconstructed the organizations and associations they brought with them from Cuba or Key West. This included the practice of cigar factory reading. In another similarity to their experiences in Key West, *lectores* in Tampa faced the difficulty of an absence of Spanish-language newspapers that were published locally. Spanish-language newspapers from Havana, New York, and Key West arrived at least two days after publication.[66] Therefore the *lectores* needed to translate English-language newspapers to Spanish to ensure cigar makers were hearing the latest news.

It was in this context that Dolores Poyo restarted *El Yara* shortly after arriving in Tampa.[67] As journalism took up increasing amounts of time, Poyo left his position as *lector* in Ybor's factory and was replaced by the anarchist Ramón Rivero y Rivero. At the end of 1886 Rivero started his own newspaper, *La Revista de Florida*, where he was assisted by Francisco Segura, José I. Izaguirre and Enrique Creci.[68] Rivero was an important propagandist in Tampa, responsible for the founding or editing of fourteen newspapers throughout his life, including, *La Revista*, *El Crítico de Ybor City*, and *Cuba*, the organ of the Cuban Revolutionary Party.[69]

La Revista carried a similar mix of news and opinion as *El Yara*. However, while the latter held an explicitly nationalist line regarding separatism and independence, *La Revista* was much more focused on the cause of labor and workers' issues, taking an ecumenical socialist position and openly declaring "the banner of socialism is our banner," equated with "Liberty, Equality and Fraternity . . . the recovery of honor."[70] Reflecting the waning but still persistent influence of gradualism on the Cuban labor movement, the newspaper's stated purpose was infusing "into its readers a love for study, economy and work as the only firm basis for advancement."[71]

In addition to the establishment of cigar factories, the growth of Cuban communities, and publication of Spanish-language newspapers, Tampa also witnessed an upsurge in labor organizing. Shortly after Martínez Ybor and Sánchez y Haya built their factories, the Knights of Labor successfully organized a lodge of creole and peninsular cigar makers, just as they had previously done in Key West.[72] The September 1, 1886, edition of the Tampa *Guardian* also makes reference to a chapter of "colored Knights of Labor in Tampa," and an organizer for the Knights made a trip to the city the following month.[73] However, the Knights were unable to completely bridge the ethnonational divisions between creoles and peninsulars.

In December 1886 creole cigar makers established a branch of the New York–based La Federación Cubana de Tabaqueros (Cuban Federation of

Cigar Makers) to counter the ethnically mixed local formed by the Knights. The Knights argued that the Cuban Federation existed simply to exacerbate tensions between peninsulars and creoles, while the Federation countered, "The only division that exists is a very natural one. The Spaniards who have controlled the cigar-making trade at New York and several other cities want to control it here, and we the Cuban cigar makers of Ybor & Co., are determined not to let them control a trade that has been created and enlarged by us in this country."[74]

In addition to his prolific publishing and journalistic endeavors, Rivero was active in the development of revolutionary organizations and clubs, including the Federación Cubana de Obreros (Cuban Workers' Federation), the Centro Independiente Cubano (Center for Cuban Independence), the Club Revolucionario, and the social and educational club Flor Crombet in 1887.[75] The following year Rivero established the cigar makers' secret society, La Liga Patriótica Cubana (Cuban Patriotic League). Known publicly as the Sociedad de Socorros Mutuos Hijos de la Fe (Sons of Faith Mutual Benefit Society), the league advocated armed struggle against Spanish rule and met at the Liceo Cubano.

If the separatist movement and its leaders were able to exert substantial ideological discipline on the Key's cigar makers, this was not the case in Tampa. In Key West, separatist leaders like Poyo, Figueredo, and Lamadriz vehemently opposed any club, organization, ideology, or movement that would move Cuban émigrés away from the cause of independence. Their fear of the potential for Cubans to be divided against each other resulted from their understanding of the squabbles and dissent that had plagued separatist endeavors between the 1850s and 1880s, and they were determined to do everything in their power to prevent this from happening again.

The working-class leadership in the Tampa émigré community disagreed. As labor activists and organizers influenced by anarcho-collectivism, they linked the cause of separatism and independence to the labor struggles taking place in Florida and Cuba. Rather than viewing the potential of their activism to take energy and resources away from the separatist struggle, they encouraged cigar makers and other workers to defend their rights as members of a working-class that shared common interests.[76]

Concurrent with the rise of anarcho-collectivism in Cuba and Key West, Cuban cigar makers in Tampa began to organize along collectivist lines, affiliating with the Alianza Obrera. Veteran labor activists including

Baliño, Martín, Pajarín, and Mateo Leal promoted Cuban labor radicalism in Florida with the local labor press assisting in the dissemination of anarchist ideas among the cigar makers and other workers.[77] The Florida-based Cuban writer José de C. Palomino had a regular (anonymous) column in *El Productor*, which indicates that the transmission of ideas was not exclusively from Havana to the émigré communities but also flowed from Florida back to the island.[78]

Like their comrades in Cuba, some anarchist labor editors and activists were not staunch ideologues. These radicals promoted a flexible form of revolutionary militancy rather than a rigid ideology, stressing the socialists' common rejection of the gradualist mutualism that dominated the early years of the Cuban labor movement as well as the liberal creole émigré separatist movement. Writing in *El Productor*, Morúa Delgado defined socialism as "the leveling, not of riches, but of the rights of man to acquire them, to possess them, to enjoy them."[79] Poyo notes that "most Cubans in Tampa" regarded socialism as a "vaguely defined commitment to justice, equality and dignity."[80] However, the same could not be said for the labor leadership, who largely considered themselves "revolutionary socialists," which was a popular euphemism for anarchism.

El Productor regularly challenged the nationalist tendency in the separatist movement and argued nationalism was contrary to the workers' collective interests. The newspaper emphasized the contradictions between socialism and nationalism and proffered the former was always preferable for workers than the latter. Nevertheless, most labor activists continued to support independence even as they acknowledged that political independence would not result in the social revolution they longed for. In the words of one labor activist, "I am a Cuban and I desire independence . . . because I believe with independence we will have more liberty, and enjoy absolute freedom of the press and [labor] association."[81]

In the late 1880s, links between Florida and Havana labor organizations were clear to those living in Cuba and in Florida's émigré communities. This worried separatists like Manuel P. Delgado, a cigar maker and staff member of *El Yara*. He attempted to forward a resolution that prohibited any formal relations with the Cuban labor movement. However, the resolution was voted down.[82] Tension in the Florida émigré communities between anarchists and separatists—and the separatist leadership in Key West and Tampa—remained high throughout the 1880s as each vied for the allegiance of working-class Cubans in Florida. These debates ran parallel to a sequence of strikes in Ybor City and Key West that came close to paralyzing the separatist movement.[83] One especially intense strike occurred in Ybor City in January 1887 that involved ethnonational schisms as well as ideological divisions.

While creoles dominated the profession of cigar rolling, and both creoles and Afro-Cubans were a majority among Florida's cigar makers, they were scarce in the white-collar administration as well as factory ownership. As creole and Afro-Cuban cigar makers increasingly began to frame their relationship with factory owners as exploitation, their class-consciousness was often conjoined with an underlying and preexisting antipeninsular and anti-Spanish bias.

The January 1887 strike is emblematic of this tension. It started when a peninsular worker was fired by Santos Benítez, a creole foreman, apparently without any justification beyond the worker's nationality. In response workers organized by the Knights of Labor walked out and demanded that Martínez Ybor fire Benítez for abusing his authority as foreman. Representatives of the union arranged to meet with Martínez Ybor and the factory management on the evening of January 20. Shots were fired, and four men, "apparently all Knights or their supporters," were struck.[84] Five workers were wounded and one eventually died. A week later the management agreed to fire Benítez, but this led to creole cigar makers walking off the job, as he was a very popular foreman.[85] Eventually Benítez offered to leave of his own accord and the strike ended.

In 1889 Carlos Baliño launched *La Tribuna del Trabajo* to further unify anarchist efforts on both sides of the Florida Straits. The newspaper was both a voice of the Cuban working class in exile and on the island and an outspoken proponent of Cuban separatism. Havana's *El Productor* heralded the arrival of the newspaper as contributing to "the progressive march of all workers organizations in the world."[86] In the article "This Is the Road to Take," Baliño outlined his perspective and opposition to the new form of "industrial slavery" that had supplanted chattel slavery.[87]

Lastly, Florida strikers began to receive the support of a young nationalist from New York named José Martí. Unlike the vast majority of creole intellectuals—and even working-class nationalists like Poyo—Martí thought critically about the requisite steps to create an alliance between workers, intellectuals, and capitalists in the separatist movement. How could these often competing classes unite around the cause of independence? Martí deduced if the cigar makers and other Cuban émigré workers could be convinced that the struggle for independence was also a struggle for economic justice, labor radicals would be allies of the separatist movement rather than adversaries as Poyo believed.

Tampa and Key West in the 1890s: The Broadening Appeal of Martí's Inclusive Separatism

It was the anarchists who provoked or at least precipitated the reason for Martí's momentous trip to Florida in November 1891. On May 1, 1891, Tampa's Cuban anarchists organized a demonstration in support of the Haymarket martyrs. Marching down the street carrying red flags while singing songs, the demonstrators included both creoles and peninsulars who largely supported Cuban independence. However, in the tense atmosphere that prevailed between Spaniards and Cubans, it is reported that a peninsular shouted "Viva España!" in front of the home of a creole veteran of the Ten Years' War.[88]

The separatists responded within a week with a rally and demonstration of their own. Cuban independence flags were flown instead of red flags, and the manifestation combined a similar mix of pomp and revelry.[89] Within days the patriotic marchers formed the militant Los Independientes de Tampa as well as the longer-lasting El Club Ignacio Agramonte. Néstor Leonelo Carbonell, a veteran of the Ten Years' War; his son, Eligio; cigar makers; and journalists established the club as a revolutionary organization that served to raise money for the next Cuban war of independence.[90] Starting with membership dues of ten cents, the club soon began collecting larger donations at cigar factories and by throwing large parties.[91] Originally open and ecumenical, the club soon passed a resolution banning members of anarchist organizations.[92] It was in this tumultuous situation that Martí made his first trip to Florida.

Members of the club planned on holding a large event on October 10, the holiday commemorating the "Grito de Yara." Unable to raise the necessary funds, the group settled upon a parade the next month, November 27, which would include a guest speaker.[93] The guest, at Nestor Carbonell's request, was José Martí. Carbonell invited Martí to speak as a guest of El Club Ignacio Agramonte. At this time, Martí was not popular among creole cigar makers who had some familiarity with his writings. And Martí was aware of the cantankerous debates concerning separatism and anarchism by reading émigré newspapers. Martí viewed the cigar factories and cigar makers' communities in Key West and Tampa as "civilian camps" of the revolution.[94] Yet many cigar makers felt he was a New York intellectual and journalist who was out of touch with working-class concerns and aspirations.

Martí's speech, which is today known as "With All, and for the Good of All," delivered on November 26, 1891, roused both creoles and Afro-Cubans. Martí emphasized in his opening lines that all Cubans must be galvanized if the independence movement were to succeed, "Cubans: For suffering Cuba, the first word. Cuba must be considered an altar for the offering of our lives, not a pedestal for lifting us above it."[95] He linked the cause of independence and revolution to individual liberty and equality between Cubans of all races, ethnicities, and classes. After his speech, Martí, Carbonell, Rivero, Baliño (who relocated from Key West to Tampa in 1891), and other independence leaders met at the Hotel Duval where they began to construct a draft for a new organization that would centralize and direct all revolutionary activities.[96]

Martí traveled around Ybor City accompanied by cigar makers and veterans of the Ten Years' War. El Yara publicized Martí's experiences in Tampa, describing the welcome Martí received and his talks at various clubs and cigar factories.[97] He returned to his hotel as he had the previous evening to continue working on his revolutionary masterwork, "The Tampa Resolutions," which was accepted by the Tampa clubs on November 28.[98]

On July 8, 1892, Martí journeyed to Key West aboard the steamer Mascot. Compared to the small reception he received in Tampa in November 1891, less than a year later he was treated as a revolutionary hero and greeted at the wharf by representatives of the Key's revolutionary clubs and organizations, a brass band, and a throng of supporters carrying Cuban flags and banners, who followed him to the Club San Carlos.[99] Insurrectionary General Rodríguez arrived the same day as Martí and was preceded a few weeks earlier by Gen. Carlos Roloff. For many émigrés, this signaled that a new attempt to overthrow the Spanish government was imminent.[100]

On July 18, 1892, Poyo, Rivero, Roloff, and the veteran Serafín Sánchez accompanied Martí on his return trip to Tampa. When the delegation arrived they were greeted with a similar throng of supporters as in Key West. The revolutionary organizations and Cuban clubs held three days of celebrations.[101] The next day the group visited the cigar factories of Martínez Ybor, Sánchez y Haya and Sons, and Fernández y Sabby, and in the evening met with Afro-Cubans affiliated with the Liga Cubana de Instrucción and the Club Ignacio Agramonte.[102] On the 20th the delegation visited more cigar factories and the homes of Tampa's separatists. The roster of speakers in the cigar factories represented a major shift in the separatist movement's approach and showed the influence of Martí's endeavors to unify the disparate strands of the movement.

Nationalists like Poyo, military veterans Roloff and Sánchez, and labor leaders Rivero and Ramón Rubiera, were joined by Afro-Cubans Joaquín Granados and Cornelio Brito as well as the peninsular anarchists Silverio Gómez and José Pérez Molina.[103] After the speeches, a group of approximately 1,500 separatists and their supporters gathered at the Círculo de Trabajadores and marched to the Liceo Cubano. A correspondent for *Patria* who covered Martí's visit described how the group represented "the unity of the oppressed" and was impressed with the diversity of "Spaniards and Cubans, glorious military figures and prominent émigrés, distinguished journalists and eminent public men, whites and blacks, poor and rich."[104]

A similar event occurred in Tampa on October 10, 1892, in commemoration of the Grito de Yara. Carlos Baliño, one of the keynote speakers, encouraged the unity developing between separatist and anarchist cigar makers, socialists, and reformists who were all working toward the cause of Cuba Libre. Baliño's oratory borrowed from the writings of anarchists Justus H. Schwab and the Catalonian Pedro Esteve, who criticized the Spanish government for turning Cuba into a "hacienda."[105]

Martí's preliminary tasks were now largely accomplished. His vision of Cuban unity had effectively cut across class lines, appealing to capitalists and workers alike. Unlike previous creole separatists—especially the annexationists of the 1850s and the leadership of the New York junta during the 1860s and 1870s—he was inclusive of and appealed directly to Afro-Cubans and mulattos as well as creoles. In the pages of *Patria*, Martí explicitly linked the fates of Afro-Cubans, creoles, and mulattos in the struggle for independence. For example, his article "Mi Raza" (My Race), contended, "A Cuban is more than mulatto, black or white. Dying for Cuba on the battlefield, the souls of both Negroes and white men have risen together."[106]

He also had the support of veterans of the Ten Years' War whose military expertise would be necessary for the next phase of his plan, a second Cuban insurrection. By 1893 revolutionaries in the Florida émigré communities were openly training and drilling for an assault on the island. In March *The Galveston Daily News* reported 250 men on Key West and 100 in Tampa "armed with repeating rifles" who did not make any attempts to conceal their motives and "could be seen going through the manual of arms under an instructor any night of the week if one passed the theater of San Carlos on Duval Street."[107] In April the *Bangor Daily Whig & Courier* reported, "the revolution is near at hand. Many believe it will come within the next few days. No one places it more than two weeks in the future."[108] Fighting broke out in May with the insurgents mobilizing close to two thousand men at arms.[109]

Despite the ethnonational and ideological divisions in the Florida émigré communities, by the 1890s anarchists and separatists managed to heal some of the antagonism that was previously rampant in Key West and Tampa. Martí's leadership and conciliatory approach represented a major shift in the separatist attitude toward the labor movement and especially their anarchist leaders. This led to reciprocation and the willingness among the anarchist leadership in Cuba, Key West, and Tampa including Creci, Roíg, Messonier, Sandalio Romanelle, Francisco Segura, Guillermo Sorondo, and many others to work with Martí. As evidence of this shift, I conclude with two examples. By January 1893 a separatist club named after Roíg was organized by Baliño in Tampa, something that would have been unthinkable the previous decade when the cigar factory strikes and debates between *El Yara* and *El Productor* fomented rancor between separatists and anarchists. Even more astonishing, after a short stay in Tampa in the summer of 1895, the anarchist Creci returned to Havana in early 1896, served as an officer in the Cuban revolutionary army, and was wounded. He was murdered in a field hospital while recovering from his injuries.[110]

Notes

1. James, *Holding Aloft*, 236–37.

2. Hewitt, *Southern Discomfort*, 14.

3. "Creole" refers to Spaniards born in Cuba while "peninsular" refers to Spaniards born in Spain.

4. Poyo, *"With All, and for the Good of All."*

5. Ibid.

6. Recent scholarship argues that in the early 1890s anarchist cigar makers' organizations in the émigré communities of South Florida and New York City were key actors in the struggle for independence, working-class formation, and the construction of Cuban identity. See Casanovas, *Bread, or Bullets!*; Poyo, *"With All, and for the Good of All"*; and Shaffer, "Cuba para todos."

7. Esenwein, *Anarchist Ideology*, 12. See also Lehning, "Bakunin's Conceptions."

8. Rivero Muñiz, "La lectura en las tabaquerías."

9. *El Siglo*, May 6, 1866.

10. Esenwein, *Anarchist Ideology*, 13.

11. Ibid., 15.

12. Maximoff, *Political Philosophy of Bakunin*, 75.

13. Ibid., 55.

14. Fernandez, *Cuban Anarchism*, 19.

15. Alexander, *A History of Organized Labor in Cuba*, 10.

16. Casanovas, *Bread, or Bullets!*, 151.

17. *El Obrero*, July 11, 1883.

18. Casanovas, *Bread or Bullets!*, 152.

19. Casanovas, "Pedro Esteve," 62.

20. Alexander, *A History of Organized Labor in Cuba*, 10.

21. The newspaper maintained a close relationship with Barcelona's *El Productor*.

22. *El movimiento obrero cubano*.

23. *El Productor*, September 22, 1892.

24. Westfall, *Key West*, 22.

25. Browne, *Key West*, 117–18. Also see Westfall, *Key West*.

26. Thomas, *Cuba*, 291.

27. *Florida Union*, September 16, 1869.

28. *Bangor Daily Whig & Courier*, March 25, 1869.

29. Poyo, "Key West and the Cuban Ten Years War," 289–90; Poyo, "Impact of Cuban and Spanish Workers," 48; Mormino, "The Reader and the Worker"; and Westfall, *Key West*, 15.

30. Casanovas, *Bread, or Bullets!*, 111–13, 125.

31. See *La Revolución*, July 21, 1870, February 12, 1873, March 8, 1873; Casanovas, *Bread or Bullets!*, 112; Castellanos, *Motivos De Cayo Hueso*, 122, 160, 205; and Poyo, "With All, and for the Good of All," 35–51.

32. *El Demócrata*, November 17, 1870.

33. Mormino and Pozzetta, *Immigrant World*, 79.

34. Steffy, "Cuban Immigrants," 32.

35. Ronning, *José Martí*, 30.

36. *Weekly Floridian*, May 5, 15, and 25, 1878.

37. Ibid., July 9, 1878.

38. Ibid., November 18, 1879.

39. For more on the strike, see the *Cigar Makers' Official Journal*, December 10, 1879, and February 10, 1880; *Tobacco Leaf*, November 8, 1879; *Weekly Floridian*, November 18, 1879.

40. Poyo, "Cuban Patriots in Key West," 26.

41. Socarrás, *La Revolución de Yara*, 25–26.

42. The *Galveston Daily News*, June 13, 1884, reports Federico Marero was arrested at Key West for having "fuse, detonating caps and books of instructions upon the manufacture of dynamite."

43. Poyo, "Impact of Cuban and Spanish Workers," 52.

44. Ibid. Also see Poyo's, "Cuban Émigré Communities in the United States," 78–105.

45. Poyo, "Cuban and Spanish Workers," 54.

46. *Cigar Makers' Official Journal*, February 10, 1880.

47. See Archivo Nacional de Cuba, Fondo Secretaria de la Exterior, Legajo 6540, No. 047, "Constitución del Club Secreto."

48. Shaffer, "Cuba para todos," 46.

49. *El Productor*, November 22, 1888.

50. Ibid.

51. *Tobacco Leaf*, February 27, 1889.

52. Ibid., November 27, 1889.

53. *Tampa Journal*, November 7, 1889.

54. Ibid., December 5, 1889.

55. *El Cubano*, May 12 and July 26, 1889; and Poyo, "With All, and for the Good of All," 89.

56. *El Yara*, December 18, 1888.

57. *The Picayune's Key West Florida Special* (New Orleans), October 1889; and *Tobacco Leaf*, October 23, 1889.

58. *Cigar Makers' Official Journal*, January 1886 and February 1887.

59. *El Productor*, December 19, 1889, and February 16, 1890.

60. *Tobacco Leaf*, January 15, 1890.

61. Westfall, *Key West*, 43.

62. *Weekly Floridian*, April 8, 1886.

63. Tinajero, *El Lector*, 87.

64. Poyo, "Tampa's Cigarworkers," 95.

65. See "Our Havana," *Tampa Tribune*, May 25, 1894.

66. Tinajero, *El Lector*, 87.

67. Ibid., 88.

68. *El Productor*, November 1, 1888, April 13, 1890; Rivero Muñiz, "Los Cubanos en Tampa," 74; Poyo, "Tampa's Cigarworkers," 95; James, *Holding Aloft the Banner*, 241; and Cabrera, *Alfredo López: Maestro del proletariado*.

69. Steffy, "Cuban Immigrants," 32.

70. *El Productor*, July 28, 1889.

71. *Tampa Journal*, August 17, 1888.

72. McLaurin, *The Knights of Labor*, 48–49. Ingalls notes the Knights also had two other mixed locals in Tampa. See Ingalls, *Urban Vigilantes*, 35.

73. *Guardian* (Tampa), September 1, 1886.

74. *Tampa Journal*, February 2, 1887, cited in Ingalls, 36.

75. Tinajero, *El Lector*, 89.

76. Poyo, "Tampa's Cigarworkers," 95.

77. Ronning, *José Martí*, 30.

78. See *El Productor*, 1888–89; and Poyo, "With All, and for the Good of All," 87.

79. Delgado qtd. in Poyo, "With All, and for the Good of All," 87.

80. Poyo, "Tampa's Cigarworkers," 95.

81. *El Productor*, April 13, and June 8, 1890.

82. Ibid., December 27, 1888; January 20, 1889; and November 3, 1889.

83. For descriptions of the strikes, see ibid., October 1889–January 1890; *Cigar Makers' Official Journal*, November 1889–January 1890; and *Tobacco Leaf*, October 1889–January 1890.

84. *Tobacco Leaf*, January 29 and February 5, 1887; and *Florida Times-Union*, January 28 and 29, and February 2, 1887.

85. Ingalls, *Urban Vigilantes*, 36.

86. *El Productor*, March 3, 1889.

87. Baliño, "This Is the Road to Take," *La Tribuna del Trabajo*, March 1889, 24.

88. Rivero Muñiz, "Los Cubanos," 47; and Carbonell y Rivero, *Tampa*, 15.

89. Steffy, "Cuban Immigrants," 86.

90. Tinajero, *El Lector*, 90.

91. Rivero Muñiz, "Los Cubanos," 48 and 53.

92. Poyo, "Tampa's Cigarworkers," 97.

93. Steffy, "Cuban Immigrants," 38.

94. Martí, *Obras Completas*, 1:712.

95. Martí, "Our America," *El Partido Liberal* (Mexico City), March 5, 1892.

96. True, "Revolutionaries in Exile," 38.

97. Tinajero, *El Lector*, 77.

98. True, "Revolutionaries in Exile," 40.

99. *Daily Picayune*, July 9, 1892.

100. Ibid.

101. Poyo, "Tampa's Cigarworkers," 100.

102. Ibid.

103. Ibid.

104. *Patria* July 30 and August 6, 1892.

105. Falk, Pateman, and Moran, *Emma Goldman*, 555; and Steffy, "Cuban Immigrants," 63.

106. *Patria*, April 16, 1893.

107. *Galveston Daily News*, March 11, 1893.

108. *Bangor Daily Whig & Courier*, April 5, 1893.

109. *New York Times*, May 3, 1893; and *Rocky Mountain News*, May 3, 1893.

110. *El Esclavo*, September 11, 1895; García, *La Aurora y El Productor*, 121–50; and Casanovas, *Bread or Bullets!*, 227.

2

Panama Red

Anarchist Politics and Transnational Networks in the Panama Canal Zone, 1904–1913

KIRWIN SHAFFER

At the beginning of the twentieth century, anarchist groups arose throughout Latin America to challenge an array of social forces, including the Catholic Church, capitalists, and politicians. These groups usually were forged by a combination of native and foreign-born anarchists—the latter mostly from Spain—riding the waves of Spanish migration to Argentina, Brazil, Uruguay, Cuba, and elsewhere in the Americas. Throughout the hemisphere, international anarchists responded to changes incurred by the growing industrialization of Latin American economies; protested living and working conditions of the laboring poor; and confronted the politicians, priests, school administrators, and other representatives of official society who anarchists distrusted as deceivers at best, oppressors at worst. Yet, with the widespread uptick in anarchist activity in the early 1900s, one part of Latin America remained relatively free of anarchist penetration: Central America and the Western Caribbean. This began to change as a result of two interrelated events: Panama's independence from Colombia in 1903 and the construction of the Panama Canal by the United States, which required employing thousands of migrant workers. Spanish-speaking anarchists followed this stream of laborers into the Canal Zone where they created a vibrant anarchist presence, complete with a newspaper, workers' center, cultural events, and two rival movements. Just as the canal created transnational linkages by drawing workers, Protestant and Catholic religious organizations, and political administrators from around the world, these canal anarchists likewise participated in vast trans-Caribbean and trans-Atlantic networks.

The limited presence of anarchists in Central America is reflected in the paucity of historical research on them in the region.[1] Anarchists in the Panamanian isthmus have received better coverage than their Central American counterparts, but that too has been limited. Traditional studies of anarchism in Latin America analyzed anarchists by examining their relationships within a country's larger organized labor movement. That also has been the case with Panama and the Panama Canal Zone where historians have studied anarchists as part of the isthmus' labor history generally and in relation to canal construction specifically.[2]

While anarchists in Central America and the Western Caribbean were scarce, they were less so in the Eastern Caribbean, especially in Puerto Rico and Cuba. In the former, anarchists maintained a presence within the island's labor movement from the 1890s to early 1920s, founding short-lived newspapers, leading worker education initiatives, authoring plays and short stories, and providing anarchist critiques within the reformist labor federation that dominated the island. In Cuba anarchists forged the largest, longest-lived anarchist movement in the Caribbean Basin. From the 1890s when they fought for Cuban independence through the 1920s, they created nearly thirty newspapers, dozens of schools for workers and children, alternative health institutes, vegetarian restaurants, and a plethora of cultural productions including plays, theater companies, short stories, and novels.[3] Because of Cuba's importance within the Caribbean anarchist network and its role linking the Caribbean network with a trans-Atlantic network rooted in Spain, the island came to play a central role in the development and machinations of the anarchist presence in the Panama Canal Zone.

The Panama Canal Zone presented a unique environment for global anarchists. First, this was not a sovereign country with a national labor movement but a territory owned and run by an expanding power: the United States. Despite early attempts by the United States to prohibit anarchists from the Canal Zone, Spanish and Cuban labor radicals slowly began to appear among the canal builders. It is not a stretch to say that anarchists sailed into the isthmus on the backs of U.S. expansionism, despite U.S. efforts to prevent this. Second, unlike anarchists anywhere else in the Americas, there was no "native" anarchist presence in the Canal Zone. This was entirely an immigrant anarchist endeavor in which anarchists operated as a completely foreign entity within a neocolonial context. As such, anarchists had to rely exclusively on their transnational contacts, which in turn often rested on their own personal international experiences. Thus, their influence and relations went far beyond the isthmus. For a brief period, these Canal Zone anarchists maintained links in an international anarchist network that stretched across the Americas and the Atlantic Ocean. In fact, they were at times the main financiers of anarchist initiatives and newspapers in Cuba and Spain. This chapter examines Canal Zone anarchists in this transnational context, illustrating how they maintained and expanded their transnational linkages that stretched to Argentina, the United States, Spain, and Cuba. In short, these Panama Reds played a key role in creating a global anarchist *red* (network).

Yet, while this transnational anarchist presence in the western Caribbean was vital for the flow of people, information, and money along trans-Caribbean and trans-Atlantic networks, the networks themselves helped to undermine anarchist initiatives in the Canal Zone. Personality conflicts, ideological schisms, and a form of "anarchist policing"—even anarchist persecution of fellow anarchists—resulted in the creation of two rival movements in the Canal Zone, with each movement linked to different anarchist allies along the networks. This in turn led to the collapse of the anarchist press, the flight of several anarchists, and a series of international anarchist internal investigations that resulted in widespread discussions about what it meant to be an anarchist and what global causes were worthy of anarchist support. Consequently, even though they were a relatively small, short-lived, immigrant presence, the anarchists in the Panama Canal Zone provide an exceptional look at how early twentieth-century anarchism operated along regional and transregional networks.

Anarchist Networks in the Caribbean

Since the beginning of this century, scholars of anarchism have been developing transnational and transregional approaches to study a movement that until recently has been dominated by country-specific histories—that is, the history of anarchism in Spain or Cuba, and so on. This new methodological focus allows historians to better situate anarchists in the ebb and flow of migration that these radicals tended to ride around the world at a time when global capitalism opened new frontiers of exploitation and ever-larger and quicker steam ships facilitated the migration of workers and radicals into these zones.[4]

The anarchist press played a key role in maintaining informal transnational linkages. The anarchist weekly newspaper *¡Tierra!* from Havana, which ran from 1902 to 1915, was not only the most important movement newspaper in Cuba. It was also the most widely read in the Caribbean network, especially among small, often isolated anarchist groups that developed in Puerto Rico, southern Florida, and—as will be seen in this chapter—in the Panama Canal Zone. The "go-betweens" in these locations collected money and sent it to ¡Tierra! to finance propaganda events and international causes, as well as to purchase newspapers and pamphlets. Often ¡Tierra! included reports and analyses from native-born or migrant anarchists in these other locations. When published, these regional accounts helped Cuban anarchists understand their situation in a broader regional context. When the accounts were sent to Puerto Rico, Florida, and the Canal Zone, readers could read about not only Cuban events but also events from throughout the region and even their own location. At times when these places lacked their own media, this transnational newspaper became the local tool for consciousness raising.[5]

The Caribbean transnational network was centered in Havana, which was the key "nodal city" of the Caribbean regional network.[6] There migrating anarchists found a large, diverse movement of anarcho-communists, anarcho-syndicalists, and anarcho-naturists (all of whom interacted with one another) with different newspapers from the island and abroad, a library and reading room, vegetarian restaurants, and a cultural apparatus of plays, weekly readings and recitals, and fiction. The Caribbean regional network did not operate in global isolation but overlapped with other regional networks. The Atlantic seaboard network stretched from the Eastern Caribbean to the New York City area, and a trans-Atlantic regional network linked Spanish-speaking anarchists in the Caribbean with Spain. Beginning in the 1890s, Havana functioned as a pivot point where anarchists could travel before heading across any of the three regional networks.

The victory of the United States against Spain in 1898 ushered in a wave of U.S. economic, military, and political intervention in the Caribbean, resulting in the construction of a canal through Central America to facilitate the flow of U.S. goods and military personnel. Between 1904 and 1914, workers migrated to the U.S.-owned Canal Zone to build the canal. Anarchists from Spain and Cuba joined this migrant workforce, creating groups, publishing a magazine, sending money for global campaigns, and communicating with fellow anarchists throughout the three regional networks in order to keep linkages alive and raise consciousness.

The Origins of Anarchism in the Panama Canal Zone

In 1901 an anarchist assassinated U.S. president William McKinley. This was the latest in a series of attacks and assassinations against prominent political and business elites on both sides of the Atlantic Ocean as elements of the international anarchist movement continued their "propaganda by the deed" campaigns to rid the world of those who they saw as bringing undue misery and repression upon the globe's working peoples. The assassination heightened U.S. vigilance against anarchists in the United States and abroad. Three years later Washington was preparing to build the Panama Canal through the middle of the newly formed Republic of Panama. Due to increased anarchist activity in the United States, Spain, Cuba, and elsewhere, Washington feared the emergence of an anarchist presence in the newly liberated Panamanian isthmus. North American officials wanted nothing to stand in their way that could prevent or slow down the canal project, which they envisioned as key to expanding U.S. economic and military power on the world stage. As a result, the government outlawed the migration of anarchists to the Canal Zone. On May 9, 1904, President Roosevelt's executive order authorized the Isthmian Canal Commission (ICC)—the Canal Zone's authority—to restrict immigration. To gauge how the U.S. administration viewed anarchism in the wake of McKinley's assassination, one only has to see how anarchists were placed in a category with other undesirables banned from the zone. The order banned the entry of felons, people "with loathsome or dangerous contagious diseases," "anarchists," and "those whose purpose is to incite insurrection." At its February 20, 1905, meeting, the ICC granted Canal governor George Davis the power to enforce this prohibition as he saw fit.[7]

By 1905, though, a handful of anarchists had slipped through the immigration restrictions and had begun to establish cross-Caribbean connections.[8] Then, in the wake of a series of strikes in early 1907, Canal Zone–based anarchists such as A. Córdoba, A. Sans, R. Fernández, and others began collecting money to send to Havana in order to receive copies of ¡Tierra! to distribute among their fellow workers. With the monetary donations came the occasional letter outlining labor issues in the zone. The first published communication from Panama to Havana occurred in September 1907 when one writer described a recent meeting urging Canal Zone workers to demand the eight-hour, ten-dollar workday, with sixteen dollars for work on holidays. Just as important was the writer's denunciation of U.S.

control and working conditions. As he put it, canal employment recruiters deliberately lied to workers in Spain by painting scenarios of excellent working conditions in order to lure cheap workers whose arrival would drive down wages even more. He also described police abuses of workers who were arrested and fined for doing nothing more than being suspected of "disturbing order or throwing an orange peel into the street." In addition, some U.S. foremen fired workers from the job for doing nothing more than smoking a cigar while working. Thirty-seven men signed a letter to ¡Tierra!, urging its editors to notify Spanish anarchist papers to spread the word to Spaniards thinking of coming to Panama that if they did, then they should expect poor conditions and abuse from North Americans.[9]

While Canal Zone anarchists began to develop Cuban connections in 1907, they also reached across the Atlantic to Spain. Over the coming years, they regularly wrote to Spanish anarchist newspapers to describe workplace conditions and social issues arising in the construction zone as well as to send money to support newspapers in Barcelona and other Spanish cities. As early as January 1907, anarchist workers in the Canal Zone again warned colleagues in Spain of the deceptions awaiting them in Panama: illness, danger, death for the least fortunate, poor food, insufferable living quarters, and legal thievery by those who charged outrageous prices for workers who escaped death or dismemberment.[10] Anarchist denunciations were joined by similar warnings to the Spanish liberal and Socialist press. Spanish leftists faulted the Spanish government for its complicity with U.S. labor recruiters. They viewed this complicity as a scandalous means whereby the government in Madrid could rid the peninsula of workers (besides those already shipping out to Cuba and Argentina in great numbers) rather than come up with an effective agrarian reform and employment policy. The criticisms became so profound and unending in the Spanish press that in 1909 the Liberal government prohibited further contracted emigration to the isthmus.[11]

As a result of the Spanish government's new stance, fewer Spanish workers arrived in Panama, and thus fewer anarchists could be found there. For two years Canal Zone–based anarchists had little organizational strength. This lack of organization resulted in only the occasional letter or rare monetary contribution between anarchists in Panama and Cuba. Thus, from 1909 to 1911 the trans-Caribbean linkages between Panama and Cuba were extremely tenuous. While the link with Cuba weakened, isthmus-based anarchists still maintained contact with Spain. The key agitator sustaining this open flow of information and money was M. D. Rodríguez—a man who would develop the first anarchist periodical in the zone, and who would help to undermine the anarchist cause at the same time.

The Rise of Transnational Anarchist Organizing in the Canal Zone

Rodríguez went by several names in the zone, such as M. D. Rodríguez, Bernardo Pérez, and Intransigente.[12] Hailing from northwest Spain, Rodríguez epitomized the wandering anarchist so crucial for establishing networks and living the anarchist ideal of "internationalism." After leaving Spain, he worked for anarchist causes in Rosario, Argentina, from 1906 to 1907. In November 1907 authorities deported him from Argentina and he moved to Havana, working in the emerging Cuban anarchist movement by 1908.[13] In early 1910 Rodríguez left Havana for the Canal Zone and immediately wrote to Barcelona's anarchist weekly *Tierra y Libertad*. In his first letters in May he offered a full social and political critique of Panama and the Canal Zone.

Besides the familiar descriptions of poor living and working conditions, he lamented the near complete lack of anarchist ideas and questionable working-class consciousness throughout Central America, including Panama. This was particularly evident when anarchists in the Canal Zone tried to get workers to boycott Spanish products earlier in the year to protest Spain's execution of radical educator Francisco Ferrer in October 1909. To make matters worse, Rodríguez continued, the isthmus was so full of churches and religious dogma that even a Panamanian university professor was forced to resign after expressing anticlerical remarks. Rodríguez matched his attacks on the Church with equal derision about U.S. employment policies in the zone. Canal administrators had brought workers from around the globe—a move that anarchists saw as a plot to keep workers divided by race, ethnicity, and language. As Rodríguez reminded readers, all foreign workers were suffering from the policies of "Uncle Sam," especially black workers from throughout the Caribbean, who were the poorest paid and lived in the worst conditions.[14]

Month after month Rodríguez's columns were regular features in Barcelona's anarchist press. He continued to decry conditions in the zone and did not tire from criticizing what appeared to be a constant wave of clergy arriving in Panama, urging everyone to fight against their dogma. He was particularly fond of heaping scorn upon the United States. He condemned how the U.S. administered the canal, the separate hospital wards for Ameri-

cans, the higher pay for Americans, the severe exploitation of black workers who labored for next to nothing, and the practice of officials illegally
opening mail and destroying radical newspapers. Rodríguez also critiqued
conditions in the United States itself, such as the lynching of black Americans. As he facetiously concluded in one of his columns, "This justifies that
America *is civilized*."[15]

Perhaps the biggest shock for Spanish and Cuban workers was the realization that they were not considered "white" in the Canal Zone. The situation was truly weird. One of the reasons that employers had sought Spanish
workers was the view that they worked better and were smarter or more
civilized than "lazy" Antilleans. In Cuba, Spaniards had been encouraged
to migrate to the island in order to whiten the population. But in the Canal
Zone, Spaniards officially became "semiwhite." More important than any
psychological torment that this might have brought on was the fact that
being listed as "semiwhite" meant that Spaniards and most nonblack, non–
U.S. citizens were relegated to the "silver roll" with black Caribbean workers. The "silver roll" was a second-class pay system in which "nonwhite" and
"semiwhite" workers received lower pay and labored in worse conditions
than mostly white North Americans while doing the most dangerous de-
molition and construction work.

In July 1911 worker "insubordination" spread throughout the Canal Zone
as laborers protested conditions, low pay, their American overseers, and
the perceived replacement of workers with West Indians. Sympathy strikes
emerged in other parts of the zone, especially among Spanish workers who
became targets of increased anarchist propaganda.[16] This anarchist militancy had been coordinated by the Federación de Agrupaciones e Individ-
uos Libres del Istmo de Panamá. The federation, founded in June, claimed
groups with names like Los Egoistas in Gatún, Gente Nueva in Punta del
Toro, Los Deseos in Corozal, Los Invencibles in Culebra and Los Sedientos
in Balboa, and elsewhere—in short, towns lining the canal construction
route. In August nearly 120 individuals signed a communiqué published
in Havana. Rodríguez was the driving force behind this surge in anarchist
agitation in mid-1911.

The federation also launched its first transnational initiative: raising
funds in the Canal Zone to create a print shop in Spain that would be dedicated to publishing only anarchist newspapers and propaganda.[17] Such
initiatives were vital to the global anarchist cause. Anarchist newspapers
regularly moved between print shops, either due to legal harassment or
more likely due to running up such large debts to the shop that owners

refused to publish new issues. This was a common problem throughout the Spanish-speaking anarchist world. Suddenly, here in the zone was a group of anarchists who pledged themselves to be the financial backbone of anarchist publishing efforts half way around the world.

Considering that Spanish, Cuban, and Italian workers were considered semiwhite and thus received lower pay than "white" workers, anarchists had to deal not only with the traditional lack of working-class consciousness among the workers but also with people who received low pay and thus who had only limited amounts of money to spend to support anarchist organizing. Fundraising for the Spanish print shop was to be coordinated through three publications—one in Spain, one in Cuba, and a new venture in the Panama Canal Zone. The Cuban link would not be through the seemingly logical venue of the widely read ¡Tierra!. Rather, it would go through a new Havana publication Vía Libre. Rodríguez's shutting out the most important and widely disseminated anarchist publication in the Caribbean reflected a growing anarchist schism in the region. In Cuba the anarchist movement had begun to fracture in 1910 and 1911 as anarchists in Havana alone began publishing three newspapers at once. This fracturing rested on personality and ideological disputes that pitted ¡Tierra! against La Voz del Dependiente—the anarcho-syndicalist newspaper of the restaurant and café workers in Havana—and issues revolving around teachers in and financing of the new Ferrer schools.[18]

The internal disputes among anarchists in Havana resulted in a shifting of this network. While ¡Tierra! and the anarchist groups who published it had been early recipients of Panamanian money and correspondence, some of those who split but stayed in Cuba began to publish the anarchist newspaper Vía Libre in 1911. Rodríguez linked himself to Vía Libre. He and others began collecting money for anarchist causes such as an anarchist press in Spain and financial support for Vía Libre. In fact, Panamanian-based anarchists became crucial financial backers of Vía Libre in its early issues. For instance, in August, Cubans in Havana and Manzanillo contributed 7.54 pesos, but anarchists in Panama contributed nearly 27 pesos.[19]

While the links between the Canal Zone and ¡Tierra! were nonexistent in the summer of 1911, by late summer internal conflicts within Cuba had been resolved. Once again anarchists representing different groups and newspapers on the island began to speak with a more unified voice. This reunified movement—made possible by the Cuban government's deportation of several divisive anarchists in Havana—found ¡Tierra! reemerging as an important mouthpiece of the circum-Caribbean's anarchist network and an important venue for some of Panama's anarchists—but not Rodríguez or the federation.[20]

The Panamanian Anarchist Press and the Schism in the Zone

While some canal-based anarchists resumed their relations with ¡Tierra!, a closer look reveals something disastrous developing in the Canal Zone. As Panamanian money and correspondence began to appear again in ¡Tierra!, those connections were not linked to Rodríguez's Federación Anarquista de Panamá. Rather, a schism in the anarchist movement in the Canal Zone was about to tear apart the isthmian efforts, and Rodríguez—a man responsible for so much movement development since 1910—would crash the ship into the locks.

In September Rodríguez launched El Único, the first anarchist publication in the Panamanian isthmus. Ideologically, the magazine reflected "individualist anarchism" and proclaimed itself the publication of the Federación Individualista Internacional (FII)—an international organization composed of groups in Spain, Cuba, Panama, Argentina, and Canada. Individualist anarchism had a strong following in northwestern Spain, from where many Spanish laborers on the canal originated, including many of the writers for El Único. As individualists, Rodríguez and his comrades followed the writings of Max Stirner, one of the more controversial anarchist figures to impact the global movement. While Stirner condemned the state and all forms of religion, his ideas differed markedly from anarcho-communists and anarcho-syndicalists. He challenged the anarcho-communist belief in reason and natural progress as almost "religious" in nature. In addition, he believed that communism and syndicalism were unacceptable forms of organization and hierarchy that crushed the individual, stifled initiative, and discouraged dissent. Rodríguez adapted Stirner's ideas into his own individualist program for the FII and El Único. The magazine quickly became noted for its rabid antistate positions, its criticisms of religion, and its condemnation of what Rodríguez considered the unseemly worship of fallen anarchist heroes. For Rodríguez, these tenets, combined with a fervent rejection of authority, served as the basis for his "anarchic individualism." Even the magazine's name—El Único—came from Stirner's book The Ego and His Own, translated as El Único y su propiedad.[21]

From October 1911 to April 1912, the staff printed 2,500 copies of El Único each month, except for January 1912 when 4,250 copies were printed and distributed through the Canal Zone, Spain, Cuba, and beyond. Rodríguez and his columnists used the magazine for three purposes: to raise money and awareness, to agitate against conditions and foreign representatives in the Zone, and—in its most controversial role—to function as a "policing" journal targeting anarchists with whom Rodríguez disagreed.

First, *El Único* devoted much of its goal to raising awareness and money for anarchist projects. Money arrived from throughout the Americas and Europe for the magazine and its causes, such as the Comité Pro-Presos Internacional and the continued campaign to purchase a printing press.[22] To facilitate fundraising, the editors resorted to a bit of coercion as well as consciousness raising. The editors pressured restaurants, saloons, and barber shops to prominently display and sell *El Único*. Otherwise, those places would be boycotted.[23]

Second, the magazine focused much of its writing on Panama and the Canal Zone where the main readership worked and resided. Earlier columns from the zone to *¡Tierra!* and *Tierra y Libertad* focused largely on workplace conditions, pay, and health concerns. Through the pages of *El Único* and at regular public meetings, Rodríguez and his associates joined these critiques with blatant political challenges to the ICC, foreign consuls in the zone, and Catholic priests. For instance, the prevalence of disease and workplace injuries filled Canal Zone hospitals with stricken workers. The chief medical officer, William Gorgas, reported how Spanish patients in the canal's hospitals always had anarchist reading materials, which arrived directly from Cuba and Spain.[24] When the ICC banned the anarchist press in the hospital at Ancón, *El Único* asked "Where is freedom of opinion so often mentioned by the North Americans? One doesn't even see this in Russia."[25]

True to general anarchist principles, the magazine and its anarchist contingent remained faithful to their anticlerical roots as well. As already noted, anarchists in the zone had long complained about the presence of churches in the zone—a presence urged by the ICC as a way to undermine radicalization of the labor force.[26] Antireligion statements occurred in the first issue of *El Único* when Rodríguez published a column entitled "Flee Monk" by the Colombian anarchist educator J. F. Moncaleano, who was then leading rationalist schools in Cuba. The column, along with the magazine's antistate writings, clearly articulated *El Único*'s sentiments expressed humorously under the magazine's mast head: "READING PROHIBITED BY CLERGY, POLITICIANS, EXPLOITERS, AND GOVERNMENT OFFICIALS." In the spirit of these antireligious and antistate appeals, Rodríguez recognized those workers who refused to succumb to religion. For instance, he praised an unnamed anarchist in Las Cascadas when he and his wife refused to baptize their baby or record its birth in the civil regis-try.[27] Catholic priests in the zone were outraged at these anticlerical stands, and they complained bitterly to U.S. officials. Father D. Quijano could not believe that the ICC allowed anarchists to hold meetings in the Canal Zone, where they could freely proselytize to "some innocent boys. . . . Of course the few good men that there are among the laborers are intimidated, and obliged to join the anarchists." Father Henry Collins debated religion with anarchists, who considered Collins to be a spy for the ICC. Certainly Collins had frequent contact with ICC officials. He expressed his outrage in October 1911 when anarchists planned a rally commemorating the execution of the Spanish educator Francisco Ferrer. Rodríguez announced that the meal at the rally would consist of, among other items, "Fried Priest Heart" and "Iced Jesuit's Blood." Father Collins denounced Rodríguez and the event to ICC chairman George Goethals, claiming that *El Único* and the anarchists in the Canal Zone were part of "an international conspiration [*sic*]" that, if left unchecked, would result in a large number of anarchists capable of toppling the weak government of the Republic of Panama.[28]

Rodríguez also practiced the time-honored tradition of anarchists adopting religious titles when they wrote anticlerical tracts. Rodríguez went by various pseudonyms, including Fray B. P. Pérez (Father B. P. Pérez) and E. Fraile (E. Friar). But this adoption of a religious title had a sinister side too. In late 1911, soon after the magazine began to appear, a schism split *El Único*'s editorial board. Rodríguez began an inquisitorial campaign against fellow anarchists in the Canal Zone and abroad. Over the next six months the magazine became Rodríguez's monthly tool to attack and belittle anarchists who strayed from his individualist orthodoxy. In the campaign that followed, the anticlerical zealot Rodríguez used his pulpit to "excommunicate" anarchists from the Federación de Anarquistas de Panamá and urged anarchist readers abroad to deny their support to anarchists with whom he disagreed. Rodríguez's holy war quickly would be met by a transnational campaign against him—a campaign that linked anarchists in Argentina, Cuba, Spain, the United States, and Canal Zone. The controversy would illustrate how anarchist networks could coordinate movements for growth as well as turn inward and become self-policing networks that wreaked havoc within these movements.

Excommunicating the Wayward: Rodríguez's War and the Global Response

By mid-November 1911 Rodríguez launched his campaign to purge provocateurs and false anarchists both locally and abroad. In the Canal Zone, a rivalry was developing between two different anarchist camps. One camp was represented by anarchists like Braulio Hurtado, José Novo, Antonio Sanz, and Serafín G. González, who had been in the zone for many years and initiated, then continued, correspondence with Havana's ¡Tierra!. Meanwhile, Rodríguez urged readers to boycott ¡Tierra! and only give money and readership to Havana's Vía Libre. Because ¡Tierra! and those who supported it were primarily anarcho-communists, Rodríguez saw them as "authoritarians" and not true anarchists. He thought that only his brand of individualist anarchism was worthy of the name "anarchism."

Then Rodríguez turned inward and publicly condemned those who had worked to help bring forth El Único. He called one anarchist a former Rural Guardsman in Cuba, and another a former Civil Guardsman in Spain. When he announced a meeting of the Anarchist Federation in late January 1912, he unilaterally prohibited the group "¡Germinal!" in Río Grande from sending a delegation because of disputes he had with members of the group. He also turned his sights on the Italian anarchist Salvatore "Sem" Campo, who had written for the magazine in its October and November issues, charging Campo with being a work gang foreman who forced those under him to contribute twenty-five cents gold coin to sustain a small chapel where mass was pronounced in English and Spanish.[29] In a most unusual move for an anarchist—one that merely added to Rodríguez's scorn—Campo filed a libel suit against Rodríguez and El Único in U.S. superior court in Cristóbal, Canal Zone. Despite the efforts of his English-speaking lawyer, C. P. Fairman, Rodríguez was convicted of libel, fined fifteen dollars, and had to pay court costs.[30] The trial and conviction only intensified his witch hunt and the internal policing of the Panamanian anarchist scene. In February, March, and April, Rodríguez lambasted his former El Único colleague Aquilino López, charging him with not only being a bad anarchist but also a freeloader who refused to pay back Rodríguez and others who had loaned López money and clothes upon arriving in Panama from Cuba in mid-1911. Ultimately, in his increasingly paranoid worldview, Rodríguez saw López as a troublemaker and probably a spy sent by Rodríguez's enemies in Cuba.[31]

While Rodríguez stridently attacked these individuals in his midst, he also turned his anger on bigger foes, especially Ricardo Flores Magón and the Partido Liberal Mexicano (PLM) based along the U.S.-Mexico border who were fighting an anarchist battle within the Mexican Revolution. From the start, Rodríguez took a contrarian stance to widespread international anarchist support for the PLM. Papers in Spain, Cuba, the United States, and elsewhere were establishing fund drives to raise money for the PLM; but not Rodríguez. On a monthly basis, he lampooned the Magonistas and their Los Angeles, California–based newspaper, *Regeneración*, referring to it as "Degeneración" (Degeneration, not Regeneration).[32] The Rodríguez-PLM controversy actually had begun just as *El Único* appeared in September 1911. That month Flores Magón warned international readers (especially subscribers to *Regeneración* in the Canal Zone) about Rodríguez. He was a bit of an enigma, Flores Magón noted. While Rodríguez was quick to profess the highest ideals, he was also the bitterest enemy of the Mexican proletariat because he attacked the PLM for its supposed lack of true anarchism. In fact, Flores Magón suggested that Rodríguez was "nothing more than an 'organizer'" who preferred to live the good life off the backs of the workers. Equally bad, while just as the PLM was actively taking up arms to do something concrete for the anarchist ideal, along came Rodríguez to say take it slow. Just when funds were being collected to help the Mexican anarchists in their revolutionary struggle, Rodríguez cast a chill by urging people not to send such money. Taking a swipe at *Vía Libre* in Havana, the U.S.-based Flores Magón charged that the paper lived under the tutorship of Rodríguez.[33]

In November Rodríguez responded by condemning the PLM and all "liberal" parties. While promising Mexicans a better future if the "Mexican" Liberal Party won the revolution, what about everyone else, Rodríguez asked? "We know that the foreman of Magón Company aspires to conquer . . . the lands for Mexicans and the gallows for foreigners and natives who violate the [PLM] slogan 'Tierra y Libertad.'"[34] Later Rodríguez clarified why he did not think it wise to send money to the PLM: "While modern schools are closing, advanced newspapers disappear, prisoners are deprived of needed solidarity and the free diffusion of newspapers and pamphlets is forgotten, anarchists invest their few cents to sustain a battle denying Anarchy, which is the liberal Mexican *revolution*."[35] Indeed, as anarchists in the Americas began fundraising campaigns for the PLM, donations to other anarchist causes suffered. One could only tap the pockets of workers so far. There was not an endless supply of money available to support families of prisoners, newspapers, legal defenses of political prisoners, schools, and revolutions. For instance, the Mexican Revolution occurred just as the modern school movement in Cuba was sputtering forth. Cuban donations to the PLM cause in 1910 and 1911 did, in fact, take money away from the modern school movement on the island. As donations to the PLM rose, donation levels to the schools fell.[36]

Anticipating this kind of response, *Regeneración* reached out to the international community. In late November 1911 Flores Magón published a page-one exposé of Rodríguez by Enrique T. Chas from Spain. The article aimed to unmask the real Rodríguez by people who knew him before his Panama days when he agitated in Argentina. It was not a pretty picture. According to Chas, Rodríguez's infamy emerged during the general strike in Rosario, Argentina, in 1906 and 1907. It was a tense atmosphere. Two police informants had been shot dead by the strikers. Tensions ran high. But rather than aid the strike in solidarity, Rodríguez at that crucial moment took it upon himself to write a column for a bourgeois newspaper, claiming that the strike was really sponsored by certain politicians, that the strikers had amassed three hundred rifles, and that they intended to burn down the piers at the Port of Rosario. The resulting police crackdown led to a mass jailing where at least one comrade died. Knowing that the strikers would want revenge upon him, Rodríguez organized his own deportation from Argentina to Cuba before heading to Panama. There, Chas warned, he would set out to organize groups, intending to use his new heightened position to disparage comrades.[37]

Cuban anarchists joined the attack against Rodríguez. In early December, Osvaldo Nola—another "agent provocateur," according to Rodríguez—praised the PLM and attacked Rodríguez. Regarding the PLM and the Mexican Revolution, Nola represented the official line of *¡Tierra!*, the New York–based *Cultura Obrera*, and the Barcelona-based *Tierra y Libertad*: anarchists had to support the PLM's revolutionary work because "supporting it is a duty and denying it our help is a renunciation of the struggle for human emancipation, for what we fight and what the Liberal Party fights." As Nola put it, the PLM had long made it clear that while it was the "Mexican" Revolution and the Partido Liberal "Mexicano," the PLM was not a nationalistic, antiforeigner venture. But then again, as Nola concluded, Rodríguez's misstatements and attempts to undermine the noble work of those in Los Angeles and on the Mexican battle fields was understandable if one knew the true history of Rodríguez's exploits in Argentina and Cuba.[38]

Soon after, in January 1912, in an open letter to the Anarchist Federation in the zone, *¡Tierra!*'s editors noted some of the things Rodríguez had done in Cuba between 1908 and 1910. They charged him with giving information to the secret police that led to the deportation of anarchist newspaper publisher Abelardo Saavedra. Rodríguez was accused of breaking a construction workers' strike, having no problem selling religious trinkets, and more. "He, in the end, had to leave Cuba, despised by all dignified men who feared coming in contact with his filthy slobber." The editors hoped that this trans-Caribbean information sharing would help reconnect the majority of anarchists in Cuba with those in the Canal Zone.[39]

Throughout all of this, one voice in the controversy had remained silent: that of Aquilino López, an original ally and then bitter enemy of Rodríguez. In mid-February 1912 López joined the debate. In a letter addressed to Cuban and Panamanian anarchists, he offered his version of events. Rodríguez was as big of an egomaniacal phony as had been described, wrote López. The man even saw himself as "a new Christ." When people asked Rodríguez to substantiate his charges that certain anarchists in Panama were spies, or informers, or worked as policemen before coming to the Canal Zone, Rodríguez could offer no proof.[40] Then *¡Tierra!* published Teófila Rebolledo's letter to the international anarchist community in which she attacked Rodríguez and his followers—"these people with their fanaticism" and Rodríguez who "portrays himself as the persecuted when he is the persecutor of all the anarchists in Panama."[41]

In mid-April López published yet another scathing critique of Rodríguez in *¡Tierra!*. López's letter offered the best insight yet as to the chaotic and destructive situation that had unfolded the previous eight months. Recalling the spirit of solidarity throughout the zone in mid-1911 when the Anarchist Federation set out to launch its own publication, he lamented how quickly that spirit disappeared. The whole point had been to raise consciousness and a movement in the zone while generating money for a printing press in Spain so that *Tierra y Libertad* could publish daily and escalate the propaganda war for anarchism in Spain and wherever the paper was read. But quickly *El Único* fell into debt and not as much money could be sent to Spain. Even worse, the federation had spent a large amount of money to publish "a newspaper that only served to fight against the purest initiatives and to defame *compañeros* domestically and internationally" while making Panamanian anarchists look like a joke to their comrades around the world. If the federation and the magazine had only stayed true to its original mission, concluded López, "we would have had the printing

press and a daily newspaper in Spain." Instead, a leading Spanish paper—
Acción Libertaria—had folded, no daily newspaper existed, the movement
in Panama was divided and in turmoil, and countless potential followers
had been lost. In response all Rodríguez could do was decry the charges
and condemn López as "an agent provocateur."[42]

In mid-1912 *El Único* folded. In agreement with comrades in Vigo and
Gijón, Spain, all pending columns and articles were sent to Gijón to be
published in a new newspaper there, *El Libertario*, which began in August.
By November the Spanish paper had become the official organ of the FII,
succeeding *El Único* in that role.[43] Over the next year the Anarchist Federation of Panama, in conjunction with the FII, regularly sent money to
El Libertario. While some of the money was for copies of the paper or to
support political prisoners, large proportions of these regular contributions
from throughout the zone continued to be dedicated to purchasing a Spanish anarchist printing press. In one important way *El Libertario* was similar
to *Vía Libre* in Havana. Both papers were intimately linked to and significantly dependent on the Canal Zone. While *El Libertario* did not publish
a full financial list of donations, the only contributors who were regularly
published were representatives of the zone-based FII and the Anarchist
Federation of Panama. Panama's value to the anarchist cause was celebrated
by one writer when he suggested in early 1913 that "without exaggerating,
we can say that the Anarchist Federation of Panama is at the vanguard of
the global movement for human emancipation."[44] This was overstating the
case, to be sure, but this Spanish paper was funded mostly by Panama-
based anarchists.

Throughout 1912 and 1913 numerous groups continued to pledge their
loyalty to the Anarchist Federation of Panama in such towns as Bas Obispo,
Pedro Miguel, Emperador, Corozal, Miraflores, Gatún, and Culebra. During meetings one could usually count on at least one speaker to condemn
fellow "renegade" anarchists. For instance, Jesús Loúzara (a.k.a. Rudolf
Lone) was a regular correspondent to Spain from the canal, writing under
the pseudonym "Sin Dios." In January 1913 he lamented that so many self-
professed anarchists in Panama were really not anarchists. While understanding how the religious and the unthinking still rejected them, "what
one cannot admit to oneself is that the so-called anarchists deny our libertarian ideals and conduct themselves like perfect castrators of an individual's energy, as authoritarian agents."[45] Clearly, the federation and its
leaders remained committed to individualist anarchism and any anarchist

who professed syndicalist or communist tendencies was simply not good enough to be called an "anarchist."

Despite the Panama federation's continued hard-line stance, in early 1913 there appeared some movement at reconciliation within the overlapping anarchist networks that linked Panama, Cuba, and Spain. For some time two rival anarchist groups had coexisted in the small Canal city of Pedro Miguel: "Libre Examen" linked itself with the FII and federation, and "Los Nada" maintained good relations with ¡Tierra! thanks to its long-time resident anarchist and correspondent to the Havana newspaper Braulio Hurtado. Then in March "Los Nada" sent over 130 pesos to the rival Spanish newspaper El Libertario for copies of the newspaper and to fund the FII's printing press project. It is notable that they sent the money straight to Spain and not via the federation in Panama. At the same time, the editorial group of ¡Tierra! also sent money to El Libertario for pamphlets. A week later, the two rival anarchist groups in Gatún ("Los Egoistas" with the federation and "Libre Pensamiento") joined forces and ordered copies of ¡Tierra! from Havana.[46] While these were small efforts at reconciliation, they were the first steps in a growing reconnectedness over the coming year as one Canal Zone group after another in 1913 began ordering former rival newspapers from Spain and Cuba, competing groups in the same town began working as one, and the heated rhetoric began to cool during talks at public gatherings.[47]

But two questions remained: why the rapprochement and why by mid-1913? Both questions can be answered simply. M. D. Rodríguez had disappeared. Rodríguez had a long history of fleeing the scene when situations became dicey. He fled Argentina in 1907 as the government cracked down on strikers in Rosario. He fled Cuba as the internecine conflicts erupted there in 1910. But each time he had left, he very publicly reemerged somewhere else, as he had done in 1910 in the Panama Canal Zone. However, by mid-1913 even his allies in Spain and Panama feared the worst, and the "worst" did not mean death but betrayal.

Following the closing of El Único in June 1912 after publishing fourteen editions, Rodríguez had made arrangements with anarchists in Spain to create El Libertario in order to carry on propaganda efforts and the campaign to raise money for a printing press. He noted that he had balanced El Único's books and was in possession of over 800 gold pesetas for the new newspaper and campaign.[48] Overall, the efforts to fund a press had been successful. In May 1913 Acción Libertaria (the successor to El Libertario and now published in Madrid), recorded that since October 1912 the campaign had raised nearly 2,200 pesetas, almost all of it from the Anarchist Federation of Panama.[49] But a nagging question remained. Where was Rodríguez and the money? In June 1913 *Acción Libertaria* asked this very question. "Several months have passed without any notice regarding our revered *compañero*, notwithstanding the efforts we have made to find out." Giving him the benefit of the doubt, the editors feared he might have become a victim of "some disgrace or illness." Ultimately, they asked if anyone in the network knew where Rodríguez was.[50]

The last word came from Rodríguez's strongest individualist ally in the Panamanian federation, Jesús Loúzara. In August he seemed to confirm the worst. Just as Rodríguez had never expressed qualms about "exposing" supposed anarchists and "excommunicating" them from the federation, now Loúzara was forced to do the same:

> We earnestly beg *compañero* M. D. Rodríguez, *Intransigente*, to get in touch with us upon reading this notice. By not doing so, and since his silence toward this F of A [Federación de Anarquistas] can only increase our doubts, we advise him to be aware of the consequences that we will have to adopt against him. If *Intransigente* wants to continue to merit the title of *compañero*, we hope that this notice will be enough for him to tell us where he currently resides.[51]

Rodríguez did not respond. In fact, he seems to have not only dropped out of the anarchist campaign (at least under his own name) but also from the historical record.

The divisions among anarchists in the Canal Zone resulted largely from the work of one man, Rodríguez. To be sure, he had help. However, it makes sense that the growing rapprochement between anarchist groups in the zone as well as between the FII in Spain and Panama with Cuba's *¡Tierra!* could have only happened with Rodríguez out of the way. Where did he go? Did he take the money and run? Was he only in the project the whole time to siphon money for his final escape? Did he go off to found a "colonia libertaria," as he once proposed?[52] Like his former comrades, we are left to wonder the answers to those questions. But with him gone, new trusting relationships arose and the trans-Caribbean and trans-Atlantic networks began to merge in a new spirit of unity. Unfortunately, the timing was too late. The Panama Canal was about to open and there was less need for workers in the zone. Undoubtedly, the conflicts generated by Rodríguez (whether for personal gain or due to ideological purity and rigidity) undermined the movement in the short span of time it had to develop before new workers were no longer required. Rodríguez had been at the forefront of forging a consolidated anarchist presence in the zone from 1911 to 1912 and developing transnational ties between anarchists across the Caribbean and Atlantic. Yet his actions and the global anarchist response—a response that likewise traveled along regional networks—also undermined that presence and created disastrous divisions while wasting precious anarchist resources.

Conclusion

When the United States chose to build a canal through Central America, it did so with the goal of expanding its global economic and military reach. The Panama Canal became a central point for global U.S. expansion. When anarchists set off for the Panamanian isthmus between 1904 and 1914—the years of construction—their goal was less about creating a Pan-American anarchist movement centered in the heart of the Western Hemisphere or even a long-term anarchist movement in the Canal Zone. After all, everyone knew that as construction wound down, fewer and fewer employees would be needed. Most of those already there would repatriate to their home countries or migrate to some other emerging global capitalist outpost to work and agitate. So, unlike anarchist movements in other Latin American countries that were forged by immigrants and natives alike to develop a permanent presence in their countries, all anarchists in the Canal Zone were immigrants who had come in part to raise consciousness among workers and money for the international movement with few illusions about sustaining a long-term presence. Thus, anarchists in the zone were less interested in developing an anarchist social movement and more interested in working within the Canal Zone labor force to raise consciousness and money for short term projects like newspapers and printing presses—projects that would have larger, long-term ramifications. This was more than a few men and women propagating a "set of ideas," but it was not a full-fledged social movement campaign either. Rather, the Panama Canal Zone experience illustrates a sort of middle ground.

Because of the temporary and transitory nature of anarchism on the Panama Canal, anarchists were forced to rely on their international connections for money, activism, publications, and supporters. Also, these anarchists used their location to initiate transnational activities. Funds were raised in the canal not only to buy newspapers from abroad but also to finance newspapers in Cuba and Spain. Similarly, for a period of time, the Canal Zone radicals were the primary international financial backers of anarchist efforts to create an anarchist printing shop in Spain. As traveling radicals, these anarchists from Spain and Cuba spearheaded radical agitation and activism against the United States by challenging Canal Zone authorities and helping to organize strikes, meetings, and a magazine that directly attacked the United States. The zone's only anarchist publication, *El Único*, not only challenged North American control but also turned inward and lambasted anarchists with whom the editor and his supporters disagreed. M. D. Rodríguez and his fellow individualists used the magazine to condemn anarcho-communists in the Canal Zone, in Cuba, and in the Mexican Revolution. Via the magazine, these criticisms spread to subscribers who belonged to FII groups in Panama, Cuba, Spain, and Canada. However, anarcho-communists had their own networks of activists that formed rival groups in the Canal Zone, Cuba, Spain, Argentina, Mexico, and the United States. When attacked by Rodríguez and the FII from their base in the Canal Zone, the overlapping Caribbean, Atlantic, and broader hemispheric anarcho-communist networks responded in kind.

Historians of anarchism rely heavily on the anarchist press to recreate the histories of these often illusive and lightly documented men and women. Yet we have to recall the central importance of the anarchist press for our historical subjects. These newspapers were the heart of propaganda campaigns designed to reach new audiences in the working class while reaffirming the beliefs of committed anarchists. Beyond this propaganda role, though, the anarchist press was vital in maintaining linkages across far-flung networks and to raising money internationally for projects that anarchists deemed important. Certainly, the Panama case illustrates these roles of the press: the Cuban and Spanish papers were distributed far and wide among the plethora of anarchist groups sprouting up throughout the Canal Zone while such groups could place copies for sale in shops, cafes, and barber shops to appeal to workers during their down time. Meanwhile, *El Único* collected money from Panamanian workers for numerous international campaigns such as starting a printing press and financing a newspaper in Cuba. But the Panama case clearly illustrates a third role of the anarchist press: as an enforcer of anarchist ideas that exposed potential troublemakers. Thus, the transnational campaign that played out in the pages of newspapers from Spain, Los Angeles, Cuba, and Panama illustrates how the anarchists used their newspapers to police their networks.

Ultimately, the Panama Canal anarchists provide a unique view of how anarchists moved around the Caribbean and beyond, how anarchist funds were raised and distributed around hemispheric and trans-Atlantic networks, and how anarchists communicated with each other to share ideas and information along and between regional networks. The canal anarchists also illustrate how those communication networks could be used to cause dissention in the anarchist ranks as well as to investigate and repudiate troublemakers. The internecine conflict from 1911 to 1912 ruptured the trust that was crucial for anarchist networks to operate. However much Rodríguez's actions were designed to prop up his anarcho-individualist network associated with the FII, his actions undermined several years of cautious, tenuous network building between the Canal Zone, Cuba, and Spain—work, ironically, in which Rodríguez had played a large role. It took the efforts of the anarcho-communist network stretching from Spain to Havana to Los Angeles to the Canal Zone to return fire and reconnect the individualists and the communists in these regional networks—and in the end, to reestablish a level of trust within global anarchism.

Notes

1. Rama and Cappelletti, *El anarquismo en América Latina*; Cappelletti, *Hechos y figuras del anarquismo hispanoamericano*; Viñas, *Anarquismo en América Latina*; and Marshall, *Demanding the Impossible*. Also see David Díaz-Arias' research on Costa Rica in this volume.

2. See Greene, *Canal Builders*; Greene, "Spaniards on the Silver Roll"; Marco Serra, *Los obreros españoles*; Franco Muñoz, *Blázquez de Pedro*; Turner Morales, *Raíz, historia y perspectivas*; and Gandásequi, *Las luchas obreras en Panamá*.

3. For works on Cuban anarchism, see Shaffer, *Anarchism and Countercultural Politics*; Casanovas, *Bread, or Bullets!*; Sánchez Cobos, *Sembrando ideales*; and Poyo, "Anarchist Challenge." For Puerto Rican anarchism, see Shaffer, "Havana Hub"; Shaffer, "By Dynamite"; as well as Valle Ferrer, *Luisa Capetilla*.

4. For excellent theoretical and historical discussions of migration, global transformations, and anarchist transnationalism, see Kirk, MacRaild, and Nolan, "Introduction: Transnational Ideas"; Turcato, "Italian Anarchism"; Bantman, "Militant Go-Between"; Bantman, "Internationalism without an International?"; and Berry and Bantman, *New Perspectives on Anarchism*.

5. Shaffer, "Havana Hub," 45–81.

6. Khuri-Makdisi, *Eastern Mediterranean*, 19–29.

7. *Proceedings of the First Canal Commission*, 372–73. See also Viñas, *Anarquistas en América Latina*, 99.

8. *¡Tierra!* (Havana), July 8, 1905, 4. Luis Prats was the first to make contact when he sent money to *¡Tierra!*.

9. *¡Tierra!*, September 7, 1907, 3. See also, Shaffer, "Tropical Libertarians," 273–320.

10. *Tierra y Libertad* (Barcelona), January 31, 1907, 2.

11. Marco Serra, *Los obreros españoles*, 26–40.

12. I use the name M. D. Rodríguez. While ICC informants used "Bernardo Pérez," he was mostly referred to as Rodríguez in the international press, especially by the Argentines, Cubans, and Spaniards who knew him best.

13. For some of his correspondence from Argentina to Spain, see *Tierra y Libertad* from June through July 1907. See *Acción Libertaria* (Gijón, Spain), March 31, 1911, 4, for his account of his deportation from Argentina.

14. *Tierra y Libertad*, May 19, 1910, 3; and June 8, 1910, 4.

15. *Tierra y Libertad*, September 21, 1910, 3–4. Using only ICC records, it has been argued that Canal Zone anarchists never developed an antiracism agenda. In fact, looking at their letters published abroad, antiracism as expressed in terms of drawing attention to the plight of black workers was a frequent, if not constant, theme. See for instance, Greene, *Canal Builders*, 175, for the ICC records-based interpretation.

16. Greene, "Spaniards on the Silver Roll," 90–92; and Greene, *Canal Builders*, 172.

17. *Acción Libertaria*, June 30, 1911, 4.

18. Shaffer, *Anarchism and Countercultural Politics*, 180–84; and Shaffer, "Freedom Teaching," 151–83.

19. *Vía Libre*, August 5, 1911, 4. For an official view of the anarchist impact, see Report by Zone Policeman No. 5 to the Chief of Police in Ancón, Canal Zone, September 19, 1911, Record Group 185 General Files of the Panama Canal 1905–1914 [hereafter referred to as ICC 1905–1914], 2-P-59, NARA, College Park, MD.

20. For the overall history of these Cuban divisions and the end of the divide, see Shaffer, *Anarchism and Countercultural Politics*, 178–83.

21. *El Único* (Panama Canal Zone), March 12, 1912, 91.

22. See the inside front and back covers of *El Único* for this information.

23. Report on Meeting of European Laborers at Mireaflores [*sic*], September 17, 1911, to the Ancón Chief of Police, ICC 1905–1914, 2-P-59.

24. Greene, *Canal Builders*, 175.

25. *El Único*, January 12, 1912, 61–62.

26. Conniff, *Black Labor on a White Canal*, 38.

27. *El Único*, September 12, 1911 Suplemento, 14; and October 12, 1911, 7. Capital letters in originals.

28. See letters from Quijano and Collins from August to October 1911 in ICC 1905–1914, 2-P-59.

29. *El Único*, November 12, 1911, inside front and back covers; and January 12, 1912, 61–62, 64–65.

30. Ibid., January 20, 1912 Suplemento, 2; and March 12, 1912, 95.

31. Ibid., March 12, 1912, 94.

32. Ibid., March 12, 1912, 88.

33. *Regeneración* (Los Angeles, California), September 30, 1911, 3. López also spoke against the Mexican Revolution at a public meeting in Ancón, Canal Zone, in September. See the police report to ICC Secretary Bishop, September 25, 1911 in ICC 1905–1914, 2-P-59.

34. *El Único*, November 12, 1911, 28.

35. Ibid., January 12, 1912, 58–59. Italics in original.

36. Shaffer, "Freedom Teaching," 173; and Shaffer, "Havana Hub," 60.

37. *Regeneración*, November 25, 1911, 1.

38. *¡Tierra!*, December 2, 1911, 3.

39. Ibid., January 20, 1912, 2.

40. Ibid., February 17, 1912, 3–4.

41. Ibid., February 24, 1912, 3.

42. Ibid., April 27, 1912, 4; and *El Único*, May 10, 1912, 4.

43. *El Libertario* (Gijón, Spain), August 10. 1912, 4.

44. Ibid., January 25, 1913, 3.

45. Ibid., January 18, 1913, 4; and January 25, 1913, 3.

46. Ibid., March 22, 1913, 4; and March 29, 1913, 4.

47. See weekly editions of *El Libertario* and, beginning May 23, 1913, its successor *Acción Libertaria*.

48. *El Libertario*, August 10, 1912, 4.

49. *Acción Libertaria*, May 23, 1913, 4.

50. Ibid., June 27, 1913, 4.

51. Ibid., August 15, 1913, 4.

52. *El Único*, May 10, 1912, 4.

3

Moving between the Global and the Local

The Industrial Workers of the World and Their Press in Latin America

ANTON ROSENTHAL

The Industrial Workers of the World (IWW) was an early-twentieth-century organization with a truly global reach, filled with activists who eagerly crossed international borders in support of causes that they sometimes strategically framed as local but which clearly fit into a broad plan of worldwide syndicalist revolution linked with anarchism. This goes against the grain of much of the historiography of the organization, which is tied to nation-based studies and often misses the internationalist orientation of the syndicalist movement. Founded in Chicago in 1905 as an alternative to the reformist, craft-union-based American Federation of Labor, the IWW spread globally through its industry-based unions, particularly the Marine Transport Workers Union (MTW), and through a varied and vibrant press aimed at the "unorganizable"—European immigrants, blacks, Chinese, Mexicans, the unskilled. In the first three decades of the twentieth century, the IWW was able to establish chapters, meeting halls, or newspapers in places as disparate as London, Stockholm, Antwerp, Hamburg, Vancouver, Sydney, South Africa, Los Angeles, Tampa, New Orleans, Arizona, and Minnesota.[1] Its history in the United States has been well documented.[2] The "Wobblies" were vilified, beaten, tortured, tarred and feathered, sentenced to long prison terms under conspiracy laws, and occasionally murdered.[3] They continued to publish their vision of a new society, write songs to inspire action, and recruit new members, even as their offices were ransacked and their members forcibly removed from plazas, camps, and trains. They inspired such fear in those with property that they were run out of towns and sometimes forcibly abandoned in deserts without food, water, or clothing.[4] They earned the reputation of being dangerous and persistent.

Such a mobile and storied organization should not have gone unnoticed in Latin America, but historians of that region have largely relegated it to a sidebar of labor history, if they have noticed it at all.[5] The most detailed treatment we have is a three-decades-old master's thesis on the IWW in Chile, which tends to rely more on Wobbly newspapers in the United States than on those published in Chile for accounts of strikes, meetings, and repression. The author later published a more general book on the history of organized labor in Chile, but the IWW does not feature prominently in that narrative. There have been a handful of articles published on the IWW in Mexico, but little of its overall story has been unearthed.[6] One reason for this lacuna may be that the activities of the IWW do not fall neatly into narratives of radicalism driven by workers in export industries or ones in which anarchism is seen as a primitive stage on the path to stronger forms of unionism tied to political parties. In short, the IWW is a missing chapter in Latin American labor history, and the IWW in Latin America is a missing chapter in the global history of the Wobblies.

The geography of the IWW in Latin America is remarkable for its breadth, and the organization is also notable for its longevity, sometimes extending into the 1930s. It took root most extensively in Chile, with locals or newspapers established in the northern mining town of Iquique, the main port of Valparaíso, the capital city of Santiago, and the secondary cities of Concepción, Talcahuano, and Talca beginning in 1918. By 1925 the IWW had an estimated ten thousand members in the Andean country.[7] The confederation was also active in a number of other Latin American nations during the 1910s and 1920s. Pushed by the open ideological space created by the Mexican Revolution of 1910, the IWW was able to maintain a significant presence in the textile city of Orizaba, the oil town of Tampico, the Pacific Coast of Baja California, and Mexico City. Militants who had been active in the American Southwest were key contributors to this cross-border organizing effort. The IWW also found adherents and sympathizers in the ports of Puerta de Tierra in Puerto Rico, Guayaquil, Callao, Mollendo, Rio de Janeiro, Buenos Aires, and Montevideo. The two most interesting points about this geography are that it demonstrates a mobility of both people and ideas across the seas in the 1910s and 1920s and that it is primarily urban in nature, precisely the characteristics most conducive to creating a vibrant alternative press dedicated to disseminating the theory and practice of revolution from around the globe.

The organization's varied press provides a useful and underutilized window on its activities, aspirations, and limits in many parts of Latin America.

Often the target of violent repression by the state and vigilantes, a surprising number of papers survived for over a year. They documented boycott campaigns and strikes while disseminating anarchist and syndicalist tracts from Europe and the United States. Chile featured the IWW organs *La Voz del Mar* and *Mar y Tierra* of Valparaíso, *Acción Directa* and *Hoja Sanitaria* of Santiago, *El Productor* of Iquique, and *Bandera Roja* of Concepción—the most extensive IWW press in a nation outside of the United States. Another IWW press took root in Mexico and along the U.S.-Mexico border. It included *El Rebelde* and *Huelga General* of Los Angeles, *La Unión Industrial* of Phoenix, *El Obrero Industrial* of Tampico, *Palanca Obrera* of Torreón, and *El Comunista de México* of Mexico City. The most consistent publication among these was *Acción Directa*, which published from 1920 to 1927, but *Mar y Tierra* published intermittently over a longer period (from 1911 to 1921), and *La Voz del Mar* published over a six-year period (1924–1930) with a significant interruption.[8] Some of these papers served as the organs for specific occupational groups that published them, such as oil workers in Tampico, seamen in Valparaíso, and taxi drivers in Montevideo. Circulation was usually in the thousands, which suggests that the IWW had an influence that was greater than its modest membership numbers would indicate.[9] In general, these papers were four to eight pages, published bimonthly or monthly, and featured news of local actions and meetings, descriptions of poor workplace conditions and exploitative treatment, news of IWW activities throughout the Americas, and calls to improve support for the organization through the regular payment of dues. With the exception of *El Rebelde*, they did not generally feature the visionary graphics and mobilizing cartoons that made the IWW in the United States famous, but they did document the cultural aspects of the organization, including inspirational poetry, notices of picnics and funerals, advice on hygiene, and information on worker libraries.[10]

The IWW sought to organize workers from all backgrounds across the globe into industrial unions that crossed national borders, much in the same way as capital organized investment and the forms of production. The general trend of historiography on the IWW has been to view it as a U.S. organization and concentrate on describing local activities such as strikes, free speech fights, and repression, within the limited context of the first Red Scare. Peter DeShazo and Robert J. Halstead complained in 1974 that "historians have generally paid little attention to IWW internationalism."[11] Three decades later, Franklin Rosemont detailed the small amount of attention that key IWW histories devoted to the Mexican Revolution in which hundreds of Wobblies played a role.[12] Scholars have been reluctant to take the IWW at its word and treat it as a decentralized organization with global aspirations. Viewed with a broader lens, it is clear that the Wobblies had effective and extensive networks that took advantage of local opportunities and conditions, and arose in a variety of locales at different times.

This chapter explores three key interrelated themes in IWW strategy and ideology and sets them within an international, rather than a national, context: (1) the increasing geographic mobility of the modern worker in the early twentieth century, especially under the pressure of state repression; (2) the rhetoric of direct action, including dignity of the worker and the unifying notion of solidarity that countered state and employer authority; and (3) the organization's creation of spaces of resistance which enabled it to have an influence that went well beyond its membership rolls.

Mobility and the Geography of the IWW in Latin America

The IWW was an eminently modern organization. It put forward innovative work rules, and it argued rationally for a reorganization of society along syndicalist lines. In 1919 the official IWW organ, *The One Big Union Monthly*, summarized the union's vision.

> Most every intelligent worker now-a-days recognizes as a fact that capitalism is going to pieces, and that a new system of owning and operating the means of production and distribution is going to take its place. The IWW claims to have discovered that system and is now perfecting it as fast as it can, with the hope of having the structure of the new society ready to take the place of capitalism, when the latter no longer can perform the functions of society.[13]

One of the most compelling aspects of its modernist ethos was its promotion of mobility as a strategic response to the actions of employers and government agents. It used the U.S. railroad system to mobilize hundreds of workers from around the country to the sites of major strikes or free speech fights. In Latin America, the mobility of IWW militants often paralleled the mobility of capital. Towns that were structured by foreign capital, such as the oil town of Tampico or the mining town of Iquique, attracted IWW followers who recruited migrant workers and engaged in the strategy of direct action. Latin American IWW locals were neither accidental in origin nor centrally orchestrated from the United States, emerging instead from a combination of local necessity and external intellectual and political influences. The appearance of the IWW in Latin America postdated and was more haphazard than its history within the United States. The areas of Latin America where the IWW was most visible were Chile and Mexico, where industrialization occurred somewhat late and the organization of labor confederations was consequently delayed.

In Chile the IWW began forming unions just at the close of World War I. Its members were often pushed from the ports into other regions of the country, thus contributing to the organization's growth. In the eight years following its first nationwide convention in 1919, the IWW established locals in nineteen different cities and towns in Chile. Besides dockworkers and seamen, the Chilean IWW also attracted to its ranks streetcar workers, bakers, teamsters, shoemakers, railroad freight handlers, printers, construction crews, and female factory workers.[14] It also gained many sympathizers among students.[15]

The main stronghold of the IWW in Chile was the port city of Valparaíso. Juan Onofre Chamorro, a Wobbly who worked as a sailor and a butcher, gained experience organizing a general strike there in 1913 and eventually went on to publish *Mar y Tierra* in 1917. IWW sailors brought literature into the port and made contacts with port workers. The MTW, one of the strongest unions in the IWW, was composed of a large contingent of Spanish-speaking sailors who created an effective information network along the Pacific and Atlantic Coasts during this period.[16] These sailors were joined in Valparaíso by a small group of Wobblies who had been deported from Australia during World War I.[17] The IWW in Australia attracted an estimated two thousand members in Sydney, Melbourne, Adelaide, and other cities and towns and became perceived as a threat when it launched free speech fights, parades, and mass meetings that drew over ten thousand participants. It stressed antimilitarism in its publications, which were seized in raids by the government, though some copies were sent to sister publications in Latin America. Those deported were convicted of being members of the IWW and advocating antiwar policies. At least twenty-nine Wobblies were deported as part of the suppression of the organization, and at least thirteen of them were put ashore in Chile in 1918. These included Tom Barker, one of the most important leaders of the IWW in Australia; two Danes, one of whom had joined the IWW in Seattle; a Russian Jew born in London; two Americans; Alexander Rosenthal, an Englishman; and T. Dillon, an Irishman. This group landed in Chile in August 1918 and discovered that the Valparaíso IWW already had about three hundred members and a newspaper. The deportees, who were without spare clothing and had few resources, made their way as best they could, some going to Buenos Aires, some to Santiago, while others stayed in Valparaíso. The British subjects were given a small amount of money upon landing and then were harassed by the local police to the point that they were unable to find jobs.[18] Their fortunes followed different paths: "[Tom] Barker wrote again on 16 December to Laidlaw to say that Rosenthal was earning 300 Chilean dollars working on the local tramway, [Julius] Muhlberg was boat building, Barker was about to take a job as an assistant to a consulting engineer and Tom Dillon, unfortunately, was in hospital recovering from attempted suicide owing, said Barker, 'to the villainous treatment here.'"[19] This coalition of itinerant Wobblies, foreign merchantmen, and Chilean anarchists had a startling impact on a relatively late developing labor movement.[20] By 1920 Barker and Muhlberg were back in Europe, but in May 1921 the Second Regional Convention of the Chilean IWW was held in Valparaíso and drew delegates from ten cities, nearly one-third of whom worked in the ports or on ships.[21] By the early 1920s the IWW virtually controlled the docks of Valparaíso and had attracted some nine thousand members.[22] In this decade the Wobblies organized mass strikes, May Day rallies, boycotts, and demonstrations in a variety of cities from Santiago to Iquique and the northern nitrate fields, and from Valparaíso to southern ports such as Punta Arenas and Concepción. *La Voz del Mar* regularly ran boxes in large bold type admonishing its readers to boycott one or another of the shipping companies that were involved in labor disputes. Most interestingly, it linked the IWW to a tradition of resistance in the port city that predated the union's existence and harked back to the infamous uprising of May 1903.[23] The IWW engaged in the struggle to establish the eight-hour day on board steamships that frequented Valparaíso. This was waged ship by ship, with a three-day strike in May 1925, until the union won an agreement with the Compañía Sud América to pay overtime for work outside of the regular workday.[24] The IWW also fought blacklisting by the shipping firm of Gonzalez Soffia and Co.[25] In 1922 in Santiago the IWW became involved in a lock-out of the tile firm Roberto Matta and Company, initiated by a partner who became frustrated with his workers when they did not respond positively to his offer to give them a football and boxing gloves if they left the union.[26]

Not all of the resistance activities in Chile were focused on workplace issues. In Valparaíso the IWW organized a campaign against the exportation of staple foods such as potatoes and grains during a time when the rising cost of living was creating misery among workers' families, and in Concepción the IWW local mobilized against poor housing conditions that contributed to tuberculosis in working-class neighborhoods.[27] The IWW was also involved in organizing a protest in 1926 in Santiago against the planned execution in the United States of Nicola Sacco and Bartolomeo Vanzetti.[28]

These activities brought the Wobblies to the attention of the authorities, for which they paid a heavy price. A letter from the Chilean IWW to the Chicago paper the *One Big Union Monthly* in January 1921 described the police crackdown in these terms:

> We are passing through a period of repression which for savage ferocity has never been equalled [*sic*] in this country. . . .
>
> There are large numbers of our comrades and fellow workers in the jails of Chile; over 100 in Santiago, 25 in Valparaiso, as many more in Concepcion, Iquique, Caleta Buena, Antofagasta, Tocopilla, Punta Arenas and other localities. . . .
>
> In the face of the acquiescant [*sic*] police, a mob of clericals [*sic*] and patriots, made up of students of the religious colleges and military in civilian clothes, with the national flag and a portrait of the president at their head, proceeded to destroy all that stood for enlightenment and freedom for the workers and producers. They beat up our Fellow Worker Juan Gandulfo, a student, most cruelly, because he would not obey their demands that he kiss the flag they were carrying. . . .[29]

The motif of forced flag-kissing or destroying the flags of the IWW while preserving Old Glory was also a favorite of vigilantes in the United States when they raided IWW meetings or abducted Wobblies during free speech fights.[30] It suggests that the internationalism of the Wobblies was recognized as antithetical to nationalist sentiments, especially during and after wars. Issues of *La Voz del Mar* began to carry a box stating "This newspaper is submitted to and revised by MILITARY CENSORS," lines were blacked out in mid-sentence, and large parts of columns were covered with the word "censored" placed vertically on the page.[31]

The IWW took the struggle into working-class neighborhoods as well, organizing rent strikes in Valparaíso and Santiago in 1925.[32] It maintained this presence for another decade, opening another newspaper in 1936 in the port with help from comrades in the United States and providing a free health clinic, library, and theater to workers in the capital well into the 1940s.[33] Thus the Wobblies contributed to the maintenance of a working-class culture in Chile long after they had passed their prime as an international organization. The intense repression of the 1920s also affected the geography of the IWW in the Southern Cone by forcing the staffs of newspapers to relocate. For example *Acción Directa* of Santiago, the most important vehicle for the dissemination of IWW ideas and activities in Chile, published its fiftieth issue in February 1928 from Buenos Aires with a new tag line in the masthead: "Edición de los deportados, emigrados anarquistas e IWW de Chile."[34]

The case of IWW involvement in Mexican politics is better known. While Mexico had arguably the most advanced labor movement in the 1870s, it had mostly collapsed under the dictatorship of Porfirio Díaz and was in a rebuilding phase when the Mexican Revolution broke out in 1910.[35] Anarchists made use of the relative lack of state surveillance during the revolutionary period to establish labor organizations in Mexico City and in other urban areas. Although a Mexican branch of the IWW was not formally organized until September 1919, at the end of the violent period of revolution, American Wobblies did play a small role in the fighting it-self.[36] The U.S. IWW had supported the Mexican Liberal Party (Partido Liberal Mexicano, PLM), organized by Ricardo Flores Magón, as early as 1906 while both groups were in their infancy. When the PLM attempted to set up an anarchist commune in Baja California in 1911, scores of Wobblies from California and other border states, many bearing European nationalities, joined to defend the seized land.[37] They were led by a truck driver of German descent from Sonora who was raised in Los Angeles.[38] The commune lasted six months before it was destroyed by government troops, with much of the PLM leadership going into exile in California.

In the period between the fall of the Baja commune and the establishment of a central IWW administration within Mexico, the Wobblies carried out a concerted propaganda campaign through their press, which was established in ports and border cities such as Los Angeles, Phoenix, and Tampa. Mexican workers who had migrated to work in Arizona mines had already encountered the IWW, and many of them returned to work in Northern Mexico, bringing syndicalist ideology home with them. The key newspapers in this group are *El Obrero Industrial*, a four-page "*semanario sindicalista*" published in Tampa from 1912 to at least 1914 (an organ of Local 102, whose benefactors had mostly Spanish surnames but which also received aid from IWW locals as far away as Des Moines, Kansas City, Sacramento, San Francisco, and Salt Lake City);[39] *Huelga General* from Los Angeles, which published a simultaneous bilingual edition and which folded in its second year for lack of funds;[40] *El Rebelde*, which succeeded it, edited by José B. Corona, beginning in 1915 and lasting at least until 1917, a four-page bimonthly; and *La Unión Industrial* of Phoenix, edited by M. R. Cuellar, another four-page bimonthly newspaper that came out at the opening of the Mexican Revolution of 1910 and lasted at least two years.[41] A number of these publications shared members of their executive boards and the interaction with the PLM was significant. According to Josef Barton, "Through the short-lived but aggressive newspapers of the Mexican Liberal Party and the Industrial Workers of the World—thirty-nine of them appeared between 1907 and 1913—these fragile groups [of migrant workers in Texas] not only maintained connections but even coordinated defense campaigns."[42]

IWW ideas were also brought in to the port of Tampico on the Atlantic Coast by the ever-present MTW. According to historian Dan La Botz, Herman P. Levine (a.k.a. Martin Paley, a.k.a. Mischa Poltiolevsky), a former socialist who turned to anarcho-syndicalism, moved to Tampico around 1919 and found that the Spanish-speaking crew of the "C. A. Canfield" had arrived three years earlier and had started recruiting members to the IWW. Levine proceeded to ally with other American and Mexican militants and to edit the union's newspaper, *El Obrero Industrial*, before being deported in 1921.[43] Within a short time, IWW organizers were leading strikes against both oil companies and shipping companies. According to historian Norman Caulfield,

> The IWW's actions and the state's use of military force fueled the organizational development and militant character of the region's working-class movement. In late 1916 Mexican IWW organizer Pedro Coria arrived in Tampico from Arizona, where he had been organizing miners and distributing IWW literature. In January 1917, Coria helped establish Tampico IWW union, MTW Local #100.[44]

The IWW also benefited from the fact that Tampico was located on a railroad line that connected it with the United States. In the small town of González, two hours north of Tampico, the union established a farm that housed as many as sixty members as a "way station" to the port. The U.S. Consul reported in 1923 that many of these men were from Los Angeles, including some important leaders.[45]

While the IWW counted approximately eight hundred members in Tampico in the early 1920s, it had grown strong enough to lead a strike of an estimated ten thousand workers in the port. This power stemmed in part from its organizational ties to the Casa del Obrero Mundial, the anarcho-syndicalist organization that emerged in Mexico City during the Revolution. A leader of the Casa, Lázaro Gutiérrez de Lara, had previously been an IWW organizer in San Diego, California, the site of a free speech fight.[46] The Casa worked in opposition to the reformist Confederación Regional Obrera Mexicana (CROM). In the late 1910s CROM and the American Federation of Labor formed an alliance in opposition to the IWW in Mexico. The cooperation between the Casa and the Wobblies, which dated from 1916, allowed the IWW to be effective in a variety of industries, from oil and shipping to mining and construction in Tampico. Thus, the IWW extended its influence across the international border, and the Casa was able to build a significant base outside of its stronghold in Mexico City.

Mexican Wobblies were a diverse group. Besides the occupations already mentioned in Tampico, the IWW attracted railroad workers, printers, streetcar operators, coffee processors, textile workers, bartenders, and even police and soldiers before 1920.[47] Nationwide, these probably did not exceed six thousand at any one time. As in the case of Chile, a number of these occupations featured mobility as part of their daily practice, and traditional societal controls were often absent. One writer observes that "Tampico was a city of great tolerance. The usual censors of manners were almost absent. The extended family, the most effective watchdog, hardly existed among the working men, most of whom had migrated to Tampico alone, and church pressure could hardly be felt."[48]

Perhaps the most famous of the Mexican IWW's to cross the border was Primo Tapia de la Cruz. Tapia grew up in the state of Michoacán and left home as a young man for Los Angeles where he began his ten-year U.S. sojourn in 1910. There he worked for the Flores Magón brothers, who were producing the newspaper *Regeneración*, and from them he learned both English and anarchism. He also became acquainted with the IWW in Los Angeles and served as a Wobbly organizer, eventually working in construction, mines, a sugar beet refinery, and the railroads across an area that ranged from the Rockies to Nebraska and Texas. Tapia had great skills as a bilingual orator, but the IWW in the United States had been severely crippled by the Red Scare. After a failed strike in 1921 he returned to Mexico and joined the Communist Party. He helped to organize the League of Agrarian Committees and eventually led an insurrection that seized land in the region of Michoacán. In 1926 he was tortured and then executed by Mexican *federales*.[49]

Although Chile and Mexico witnessed the lion's share of IWW activity in Latin America from 1910 to 1930, there were other zones of IWW organizing. The taxi drivers of Montevideo seem to be an unusual case within the Uruguayan labor movement, not tied to the export sector of the economy, though their affiliation with the anarchist Federación Obrera Regional Uruguaya provided them with an effective network. Their own informal daily interactions involving the city's vibrant café culture may have had the effect of spreading the idea of industrial unionism to waiters and their assistants who formed a union that adopted IWW principles in 1921.[50] The taxi drivers' monthly newspaper, *Hacia la Libertad*, had a press run of five thousand copies, which must have been several times their union membership, suggesting a disproportional influence in the capital city.[51] It is unclear how the taxi drivers came to be familiar with the IWW; as a port, however, Montevideo surely had members of the MTW drifting in and out of its downtown area on a regular basis, probably with newspapers in hand. This was the mechanism for spreading the organization to Peru as relayed in the pages of *La Voz del Mar*, an IWW newspaper published in Valparaíso and carried by seamen up the Pacific Coast. A letter and a story printed in this newspaper in 1925 noted that sailors on two ships of the Compañía Sud Americana de Vapores joined with railroad workers and formed a local of the IWW in the port city of Mollendo.[52] A strike in support of two fired workers of the Peruvian Corporation, which owned the railroad, was carried out at some risk but local and global solidarity was central to the workers' motivating ideology: "Dear comrades, you will give us the honor of carrying our embrace of friendship to all the brothers of the coast of Chile as our greatest desire of the uniting of worker with worker, because, he that lives by the sweat of his brow should not know borders nor flags. For this reason we should not remove ourselves from the I.W.W. which we consider the greatest tree in the world."[53] The Peruvian workers also sent money to *La Voz del Mar*, which responded by requesting that Peruvian port workers solicit IWW newspapers from crews in transit and that crew members headed for Peru stop by the union local in Valparaíso to pick up packages of the newspaper for transport to the north.[54] Two years earlier the IWW struck the Peruvian Central Lines in support of a fired veteran railroad worker. They won his reinstatement with an industrial action that cut across craft lines on the railroad.[55]

Another site of IWW activity in South America was Ecuador. Alexei Páez maintains that Wobbly ideas circulated from the Chicago newspaper *Solidaridad* and were frequently discussed on Guayaquil's "*malecón*" (boardwalk), the primary public space of the port city.[56] The IWW local in the port of Guayaquil was raided by police in 1924, resulting in the wounding of an IWW newsboy, the burning of some eight hundred anarchist papers and ten thousand copies of the IWW declaration of principles, and the destruction of a printing press and furniture.[57] This account confirms that IWW ideas continued to be discussed, debated, and violently opposed some two years after the greatest massacre of workers in the city's history, which is commonly thought to have paralyzed the national labor movement for a full decade. Páez reprints a letter from the leader of the IWW in Guayaquil, suggesting that the organization continued to have a presence in the port until at least 1926.[58]

Many of the IWW locals that emerged across Latin America were in touch with each other. Some exchanged newspapers and made copies available to members while others reprinted letters of greetings and solidarity, including one sent from Tampico to Chile in 1924 announcing the founding of a stevedores' local and another from the "Grupo para la propaganda internacional" in Buenos Aires asking for copies of periodicals to be sent from neighboring countries.[59] Ships' crews also carried information about the IWW from port to port, including details of repression, which were sometimes reported in the Wobbly press. In response to one of these incidents, *Mar y Tierra* could not resist a bit of anti-imperialist rhetoric mixed with the motif of class struggle: "And in spite of all the persecutions, the workers always go forward in their work of emancipation without being intimidated by the danger of being lynched or jailed by the brutal orders of the government and kings of the yankee gold."[60] But not all ship crews were welcomed with open arms. Jon Bekken writes that in 1925, following a strike called by the MTW along the eastern U.S. coast in solidarity with British seamen, "the Baltimore MTW forwarded the names of scabs who shipped out to Latin America to the MTW affiliates there, so they could be greeted appropriately."[61]

There was also some interchange among activists from different regions, either through the reprinting of their essays or in person. Raúl Haya de la Torre, the Peruvian student leader who later would lead the populist American Popular Revolutionary Alliance party (APRA), visited the editors of *Acción Directa*, and they sent him home with an open letter to the workers of Peru from Luis Castro, the secretary general of the IWW in Chile, which they also published. It was filled with fraternal sentiments of international solidarity.[62] Pedro Esteve, who had published the New York–based IWW newspaper *Cultura Obrera* from 1913 to 1914, had one of his essays serialized by *Bandera Roja* the following decade beginning with their first issue.[63] Santiago's *Acción Directa* showed an interest in Mexican politics by reprinting on its front page an interview given by Enrique Flores

Magón after he arrived back in Mexico from his exile in the United States in 1923.[64] The Valparaíso IWW also maintained contact with the *Federación Marítima* of Callao, and the Chilean IWW sent two delegates to the first meeting of the *Asociación Continental Americana de Trabajadores* in Buenos Aires in 1929, which included representatives of the labor movements in Argentina, Brazil, Uruguay, Bolivia, Paraguay, Mexico, and Guatemala.[65]

What set the IWW apart from other labor organizations was its signature physical mobility and its social fluidity. Many Wobblies moved between a number of occupations during their lives. Some were anchored firmly in work that was connected to the street or to movement of some sort—streetcar operators, taxi drivers, teamsters, seamen, and railroad workers. Others used the railroad or the ship to move across national borders to take advantage of revolutionary opportunities as they arose or to flee harassment and repression at the hands of police or vigilantes. In many cases they allied with comrades from different nationalities in the pursuit of a new syndicalist society. Paul Buhle notes the solidarity among "Finnish-American, Hungarian or Russian immigrants" and migrant workers in Mexico and Canada: "The Wobblies, facing the emerging problem of working people at the dawn of the twentieth century, saw the international mobility of labor as well as capital as inevitable; . . . the IWW embraced every worker as a basic principle of solidarity."[66]

Solidarity and the Appeal of Direct Action

On a Sunday evening in March 1922 in downtown Montevideo, hundreds of taxi drivers attended a union meeting, spilling out "halfway into the street." After three hours of discussion, members voted to go out on strike for thirty-six hours. Some twenty carloads of workers drove through the city and its suburbs in the early morning hours informing those workers who could not attend the meeting about the impending strike with the result that by four in the morning, no vehicles remained in service and the city, in the eyes of one observer, became "a desert." The major labor organization of Uruguay, the anarchist FORU, threw its support to the strike in a gesture of solidarity. But here is the unusual part: the strike was called not for an increase in wages or for an improvement of working conditions. Rather, it was provoked by the threatened detention and extradition to neighboring Argentina of a chauffeur, Ramón Silveyra, by Uruguayan authorities in the border town of Carmelo. The fugitive had been condemned to prison for twenty years for an unspecified political crime. The union that called the strike, the Sindicato Único del Automóvil, subscribed to the principles of the IWW, and it took quite seriously the motto "An injury to one is an injury to all." The taxi drivers employed the strategy of direct action, favored by the IWW, to influence a government whose existence they disdained, in defense of a fellow driver fleeing harassment in a neighboring country. But they also engaged in the action as a demonstration of working-class solidarity in support of a social revolution that crossed national lines and had the power to disrupt daily life in one of the largest capital cities in Latin America.[67]

One of the keys to understanding the IWW as a global network is the universal appeal of its rhetoric and its strategy. Itinerant organizers such as Tom Barker, Pedro Coria, Primo Tapia, and Lázaro Gutiérrez de Lara, crossing oceans, borders, and cultures to reach new recruits and aid the actions of established locals, needed a rhetoric that could be easily translated to different situations and that would be inclusive in its appeal. Direct action was simple to understand and attractive because it did not require years of political groundwork and party organizing before it could be deployed. Eschewing partisan politics, direct action focused attention squarely on a range of responses to employer abuse: sabotage and slowdown, boycott and strike. The short-term goal of these actions was self-defense and the amelioration of intolerable workplace conditions while the long-term goal, particularly in the case of the general strike, was the abolition of the wage system and the elimination of states that protected capitalism. But before the instruments of direct action could be launched, workers had to be mobilized through concepts that were easily shared across borders, often through the medium of the IWW press. The key concepts in this mobilization were dignity, respect, and solidarity.

Perhaps the primary way that the IWW connected with workers was to talk about exploitation and authority in its newspapers, and here is where it is most clearly linked to anarchism. In the face of the modernist currents of the time that stressed the general progress of society in the machine age, the IWW press frequently referred to workers as "wage slaves" who were abused by capitalists and in need of emancipation, thus bringing imagery from centuries long past to the campaign of contemporary class struggle. The humanity of workers was constantly juxtaposed to the "tyranny" of employers or government employees who abused authority. "It is absolutely undeniable that the conditions of work on board the ships large and small were characteristically inhuman and bestial," begins a typical call for ship crews to join the IWW.[68] Taxi drivers facing hunger as a consequence of the lifting of their licenses by the city of Montevideo were admonished: "This has to be given up. Either we are men and we proceed as such, or we are nothing."[69]

Beyond the notions of capitalism as a new form of servitude and revolution as emancipation, the rhetoric of the IWW press also questioned the idea of authority flowing naturally from social hierarchy. In cases when the IWW launched boycotts of particular businesses or sought to put public pressure on an employer, the owner was often taken to task for an abuse of authority that undermined the human dignity of the workers he oversaw. The front page of an issue of *La Voz del Mar*, for example, described the poor conditions under which a crew worked on the steamship *Luisa* owned by W. James and Co.: "The crew members tell us that their food is comprised only of potatoes, grated, whole, crushed, fried, in short, potatoes and more potatoes."[70] It then turned its readers' attention to the engineer. "His abuse consists in maintaining on board the most criminal scarcity of water, to the point that his zeal is recognized by the Management as the most economical Engineer of the coast."[71] This notion of dignity, and its twin of freedom, was not confined to the workplace but expanded into the private lives of workers as well. In 1925, at a time when the IWW had been severely weakened in Chile by harsh repression, a tenant league was formed in Santiago to combat the high cost of living through a movement to pay only 50 percent of the charged rent on housing. It was led by an IWW militant.[72] This movement originated a few weeks earlier in Valparaíso with a demonstration by some thirty thousand workers that resulted in a campaign to create a "rational school" to be built in a neglected neighborhood.[73]

The concept of solidarity was explained to readers of the IWW press, though, given the early history of general strikes in the region, it was not entirely new.[74] Still, during the time that the IWW was active in Latin American cities, many of them experienced strikes that crossed occupational lines or demonstrated mass support for nonworkplace issues. In time the IWW's strategy and ideology reached workers in traditionally artisan trades who were not its primary targets for recruitment. One writer finds that the union "exercised some influence over the unions of the shoemakers and the Federation of Print Workers.[75]

On occasion, solidarity was also expressed internationally by the IWW. A case in point is the demonstration that it staged in Tampico in 1926 in support of the Italian anarchists Sacco and Vanzetti, who had been condemned to death in the United States.[76] Solidarity, of course, is not unidirectional, and the wide influence of IWW organizing in Santiago was demonstrated by the funeral of a Wobbly student and poet, José Domingo Gómez Rojas, who had been tortured in his prison cell and died in 1921. "His funeral brought out forty thousand people, of all ages and both sexes, paralyzing the industrial and commercial activities of the capitol [*sic*] city of Chile for the day, and tying up local transportation completely."[77] Solidarity was also expressed ritualistically in annual May Day rallies. These were jointly planned by the IWW and its rival labor confederation, the La Federación Obrera de Chile, in Chile in 1922 and 1923, with the IWW continuing to participate through 1926. The two organizations had previously combined to shut down Santiago and Valparaíso in 1921 with general strikes in support of bakers.[78]

Lastly, solidarity was also central to the conception of the IWW as an international movement: "For this organization there are no borders, no local or regional interests but only collective and general interests. An injury made to one worker is an injury done to all workers, and it aspires to create ties of solidarity that unite all the efforts of the workers in support of their liberation from the North Pole to the South Pole."[79] The General Defense Committee of Chicago asked workers in Latin American port cities to organize demonstrations at the docks where ships carrying North American passengers disembarked. They were instructed to carry placards and flags with messages in English protesting the continued incarceration of sixty-one IWW prisoners in the United States.[80]

Creating Spaces of Resistance and Progress

One way to envision the IWW in Latin America is to see it as an effective creator of spaces of resistance to capitalism and as a promoter of alternative forms of social progress. Its press certainly served as a space of resistance to the pervasive workplace control exercised by abusive employers and to the widespread repression unleashed by governments on their national labor movements following World War I. IWW papers not only served as sources of news about local organizing activities and boycotts, they also put their readers in touch with an international syndicalist movement, and in that sense the space they created offered a broad vision of the future. The editor of *La Voz del Mar* laid out the lofty goals of his paper: to have workers acquire knowledge of sociological facts, to study multiple means of struggle, and to create conscious fighters for social demands.[81] The U.S.-based *Industrial Pioneer* noted that "the press and the organization are each vitally necessary to the other. We strengthen the organization when we build up the press. It is our chief point of contact with the unorganized whom we must reach to succeed in our revolutionary task of overthrowing capitalism. As we push the press among the unorganized, making it their spokesman, they will give power to the organization until it shall be invincible."[82] In 1921, after a wave of repression, the *One Big Union Monthly* proposed the creation of an international IWW press service and a daily press in order to better convince the working class that it should follow the path of industrial unionism.[83] The IWW in Latin America certainly benefited from the network of members who carried newspapers from port to port. In one case, besides the request for English and Spanish-language papers from the United States, there was also the plea from the MTW in Valparaíso to send a printing press the size of the ones that produced *Marine Worker*.[84] Seven months later the union had collected eight hundred dollars to buy a printing press with the goal of making each ship "a library or a center of propaganda" with everyone on board contributing to meetings and discussions.[85]

The IWW press in Latin America was a key element in the construction of a counterculture. This alternative to capitalist culture was inclusive of a variety of ideological perspectives, demonstrating the flexibility of the organization in the face of shifting political currents, repression, and competition from other labor groups. On one level it sought to educate and reform workers to become model citizens of a new society, in many ways drawing on the earlier efforts of anarchist artisans in Latin America for inspiration. So, for example, carpenters, painters, bricklayers, and other construction workers donated their time to rebuilding an IWW local in an abandoned theater in Santiago, where they remodeled offices, created a night school, a library, and a clinic.[86] Similarly, in Valparaíso the IWW held its first literary musical assembly in the Novedades Theatre, which featured poetry readings and a musical performance. Such cultural gatherings did not always take place peacefully. During the rent strike in Valparaíso, a benefit show for the strike committee featuring dramatic and musical performances ended with a fistfight between attendees and performers on one hand and two drunk policemen and a navy sailor on the other. The Wobblies suffered a destroyed guitar, and several were detained by the police.[87]

While constructing a counterculture, the IWW also fought against aspects of the existing working-class culture that had developed on board ships and in tenements, especially drinking. A lawyer who was portraying a group of IWW prisoners to a judge as respected citizens who were making a useful contribution to society highlighted their sobriety as a means of undercutting the stereotype of workers as inebriated ruffians.[88] The IWW press also occasionally campaigned against drinking and pointed to the ruination caused by the neighborhood tavern.[89]

Perhaps the most interesting intersection of the IWW press with cultural development was the newspaper *Hoja Sanitaria IWW*, published monthly from 1924 to 1927 in Santiago, which consisted of four pages and was distributed for free. Much of its work was devoted to combating communicable diseases, including those transmitted sexually. It ran articles describing tuberculosis and its treatment, warning of the dangers of untreated syphilis, promoting the vaccination against rabies, and discussing the proper care and feeding of babies.[90] It also discussed the dangers of lice found in the homes and schools of the poor, particularly in regard to typhus.[91] Hygiene was its byword, and it serialized a book about the subject with anatomical drawings. At the same time it extolled the benefits of sunlight as a killer of microorganisms. *Hoja Sanitaria* also carried ads for a clinic, located next door to a print shop, which was open six evenings a week, and a dental clinic at the same location that gave a 10 percent discount to Wobblies. The newspaper firmly tied the IWW in Santiago to modernism and foreshadowed the emphasis on cleanliness that was to be one of the elements of populism.

Conclusion

The IWW was a truly international organization, able to move people and ideas across borders and to influence a wide array of workers, many of whom were previously among the unorganized. A key instrument in the propagation of its ideas and strategies was a decentralized but well-connected press that emerged in small and large cities throughout Latin America and that was linked in a variety of ways to its predecessors in the United States and Australia. The press itself was transnational in its orientation, nearly always promoting class solidarity above national identity and crossing borders either in the hands of Wobblies on ships or relocating in exile.

By adopting a historical perspective that privileges space over chronology we have been able to reposition the IWW as an international movement within syndicalism, which opened up new ways of thought and behavior for workers from Santiago to Sydney and from Mexico to Minnesota as they confronted the mobility of capital, the Great War, and repression that was both bloody and effective. Their newspapers were destroyed far more frequently than they died naturally, though the latter certainly did happen when financial support dwindled.[92] Still, some papers weathered the storms of destructive raids, deportations of staff, and legal banishment to reemerge later, at least briefly.

The IWW in Latin America was a flexible and tolerant organization that had an inclusive orientation, ready to recruit those workers seen as marginal to the labor movement and open to working with anarchists, socialists, and communists if their joint efforts could be seen as furthering the goals of working-class solidarity and did not involve ties to political parties.[93] Its connections to anarchism appear to have been stronger than they were in the United States, where the IWW tended to avoid identification with those currents. Anarchism in Latin America was stronger at a later date than in the United States, playing a key role in the Mexican Revolution and deeply influencing the labor movements of Chile, Argentina, Uruguay, Brazil, Cuba, Ecuador, and Peru. In some ways it was more respected in the southern region as a cultural force. The IWW press often discussed anarchist ideas or historical personages such as Peter Kropotkin in its pages and occasionally ran ads that suggested linkages with local anarchists.[94] Yet histories of anarchism have consistently marginalized or ignored the contributions of the IWW.[95]

The extraordinary mobility of the Wobblies was their strength, allowing them to mobilize for defense, push open new spaces, extend their recruitment efforts, and dodge some of the repressive tactics that they confronted. But it also worked to their detriment. Their very ability to appear seemingly out of nowhere engendered fear among local business owners and their allies. Though at times borders were permeable for them, at other times Wobblies got caught in tightening zones. The Magonista newspaper *Regeneración* relates the account of Wobblies branded as insurrectionists for their alliance with Flores Magón's PLM who were trapped between Mexican *rurales* who wanted to shoot them if they ventured south of the Río Grande and vigilantes who burned down their headquarters when they remained in the United States.[96] Like the pirates and gauchos who preceded them, the Wobblies found that the mobility that they most cherished came under attack by governments that deemed them intolerable and sought to eliminate their free spaces of activity.

Notes

A longer version of this chapter appeared in *Estudios Interdisciplinarios de América Latina y el Caribe*, 22, no. 2, Julio–Diciembre 2011. The author would like to acknowledge the research assistance of Jessica Stites Mor and Alison Bruey and the staff of the International Institute for Social History in Amsterdam. Support for research was provided by the University of Kansas General Research Fund.

1. DeShazo, *Urban Workers*, 315; Bekken, "Marine Transport Workers," 20; and Gambs, *Decline of the I.W.W.*

2. Renshaw, *Wobblies*; Dubofsky, *We Shall Be All*; Conlin, *At the Point of Production*; Salerno, *Red November*; Bird, Georgakas and Shaffer, *Solidarity Forever*; and Buhle and Schulman, *Wobblies!*

3. The term "Wobbly" has origins in various legends, none of which are particularly convincing nor apparently produced by members of the IWW. The first known use of the term was by an enemy of radicalism, Harrison Gray Otis, publisher of the Los Angeles Times. See Renshaw, *Wobblies*, 1–2.

4. *The One Big Union Monthly* II:2, no. 12 (February 1920): 46.

5. Bergquist, *Labor in Latin America*, 61 and 64; Hall and Spalding, "Urban Labor Movements," 216; Poblete Troncoso and Burnett, *Rise of the Latin American Labor Movement*, 61; and González Casanova, *Historia del movimiento obrero*, 96.

6. DeShazo, "Industrial Workers of the World in Chile"; DeShazo, *Urban Workers*; Caulfield, "Wobblies"; Blaisdell, *Desert Revolution*; and La Botz, "American 'Slackers.'"

7. DeShazo, "Industrial Workers of the World in Chile," 91 and 109. A much higher estimate of twenty-five thousand members is given by Trachtenberg and Glassberg, *American Labor*, 346.

8. DeShazo, *Urban Workers*, 336–37; and Arias Escobedo, *La Prensa Obrera en Chile*, 45–81.

9. *La Voz del Mar* had a subscriber base of 1,272 and a print run of 2,000 in 1925; I:12 (March 24, 1925): 6; I:13 (April 8, 1925): 6. *Acción Directa* had a press run of 2,000 in 1922; no. 13 (Segunda Quincena del Julio 1922); and *Hacia la Libertad* had a press run of 5,000; II:3 (January 1923): 1. These numbers can be compared with those of the well-known anarchist daily paper in Buenos Aires, *La Protesta*, which printed 4,000–8,000 copies until 1909 when it began to greatly expand its readership, Suriano, *Paradoxes of Utopia*, 123.

10. Salerno, *Red November*, 5.

11. DeShazo and Halstead, "Los Wobblies del Sur," 1.

12. Rosemont, *Joe Hill*, 88n1. Paul Avrich notes that the Baja insurrectionists "included hundreds of American anarchists and Wobblies, among them Frank Little and Joe Hill, the most celebrated martyrs to the IWW cause." Avrich, *Anarchist Portraits*, 209. Mitchell Verter estimates that one-fifth of the "500 soldiers assembled for battle" and provisioned by John Kenneth Turner and the IWW were actually Wobblies. Bufe and Verter, *Dreams of Freedom*, 78.

13. *The One Big Union Monthly*, 1, no. 1 (March 1, 1919): 24–25; see also Bergquist, *Labor in Latin America*, 61.

14. DeShazo, *Urban Workers*, 154, 190; and Arias Escobedo, *La Prensa Obrera en Chile* 63–81.

15. Alba, *Politics and the Labor Movement*, 250.

16. Cole, *Wobblies on the Waterfront*, 160.

17. This interpretation differs from that of Patrick Renshaw, who likens the work of U.S. and Australian seamen in the region from Peru to Uruguay to tree planters, sowing IWW ideas into undisturbed earth that took root later on. See Renshaw, *Wobblies*, 235.

18. Cain, *Wobblies at War*, 262–70.

19. Cain, "Industrial Workers of the World," 61.

20. DeShazo notes that the claim by the major confederation FORCh that it had twelve thousand members in Santiago in 1919 was exaggerated, while Sergio Grez Toso writes that the anarchists in Santiago and Valparaíso were still disorganized and divided among themselves as late as 1913 before beginning a period of growth. DeShazo, *Urban Workers*, 154; and Grez Toso, *Historia del comunismo*, 247–49.

21. *The One Big Union Monthly* II:6, no. 16 (June 1920): 57; and DeShazo, "Industrial Workers of the World in Chile," 48.

22. Trachtenberg and Glassberg, *American Labor*, 346; DeShazo, *Urban Workers*, 320; and Brignardello Valdivia, *Valparaíso Anarquista*, 79.

23. *La Voz del Mar* II:29 (May 1, 1926): 2.

24. Ibid., I:15 (May 20, 1925): 1.

25. Ibid., I:13 (April 8, 1925): 1.

26. *Acción Directa* IV:19, Primera quincena (December 1922): 3.

27. *Bandera Roja* I:2 (April 1926): 3.

28. Ibid., I:6 (July 1926): 4. Sacco and Vanzetti were two Italian immigrants who were tried for the murders of two payroll clerks in Massachusetts. Their anarchist sympathies led to their case becoming an international cause célèbre in the years leading up to their execution. See Watson, *Sacco & Vanzetti*.

29. *One Big Union Monthly*, January 1921, pp. 12–13.

30. Miller, "The IWW Free Speech Fight: San Diego, 1912," 225.

31. *La Voz del Mar* I:18 (July 17, 1925): 6.

32. DeShazo, *Urban Workers*, 206–23.

33. Bekken, "Marine Transport Workers," 20; and Lagos Valenzuela, *Bosquejo histórico*, 42.

34. *Acción Directa* (Buenos Aires, Argentina), no. 50 (February 1928): 1.

35. Spalding and Hall, "Urban Working Class," 338–39.

36. Trachtenberg and Glassberg, *American Labor*, 349.

37. DeShazo and Halstead, "Los Wobblies del Sur," 23.

38. Blaisdell, *Desert Revolution*, 48.

39. *El Obrero Industrial* (Tampa) III:2 (April 30, 1914).

40. *Huelga General* (Los Angeles) II:26 (March 7, 1914).

41. A second incarnation emerged in 1911, edited by Jose Sousa, but it is unclear if it lasted longer than its first issue. *La Unión Industrial* (Phoenix), Segunda Época, no. 1 (October 7, 1911).

42. Barton, "Borderland Discontents," 173.

43. La Botz, "American 'Slackers,'" 580; and DeShazo and Halstead, "Los Wobblies del Sur," 29–31.

44. Caulfield, "Wobblies and Mexican Workers," 57.

45. Zogbaum, *B. Traven*, 2.

46. DeShazo and Halstead, "Los Wobblies del Sur," 25.

47. Ibid., 28–29; and La Botz, "American 'Slackers,'" 580.

48. Zogbaum, *B. Traven*, 20.

49. Friedrich, *Agrarian Revolt*, 58–77 and 128–30; and Buhle and Schulman, *Wobblies!*, 217–29.

50. *El Productor* (Iquique, Chile) I:1 (August 21, 1921): 4.

51. *Hacia la Libertad*, I:1 (November 1922): 1.

52. *La Voz del Mar* 1:12 (March 24, 1925): 5.

53. Ibid.

54. Ibid.

55. Renshaw, *Wobblies*, 235–36.

56. Páez, *El anarquismo en el Ecuador*, 48–49.

57. *La Voz del Mar* I:6 (primera quincena de Noviembre, 1924): 2.

58. Páez, *El anarquismo en el Ecuador*, 161–63.

59. *La Voz del Mar* I:8 (December 20, 1924): 4; and *Acción Directa*, no. 13, Segunda quincena (June 1922): 4.

60. *Mar y Tierra* I:2 (April 17, 1920): 4.

61. Bekken, "Marine Transport Workers," 20.

62. *Acción Directa*, no. 13, Segunda quincena (June 1922).

63. *Bandera Roja* I:1 (March 1926): 1.

64. *Acción Directa*, no. 25, Primera quincena (July 1923): 1.

65. *La Voz del Mar* I:7 (November 30, 1924): 4; and Godio, *Historia del movimiento obrero latinoamericano*, 163.

66. Buhle, "Legacy of the IWW," 17–18.

67. This account is based on a broadsheet flyer inserted in the March 1923 issue of *Hacia la Libertad* II:5, Montevideo, Uruguay.

68. *La Voz del Mar* I:7 (November 30, 1924): 2.

69. *Hacia la Libertad* I:1 (November 1922): 2.

70. *La Voz del Mar* I:9 (January 15, 1925): 1.

71. Ibid.

72. DeShazo, *Urban Workers*, 223.

73. *La Voz del Mar* I:13 (April 18, 1925): 1.

74. *Mar y Tierra* I:3 (May 1, 1920): 4. *Acción Directa* ran a small box with a drawing of a man's face behind prison bars with the text: "RECUERDE COMPAÑERO Los presos de la IWW de Santiago y Concepción claman: SOLIDARIDAD!!" *Acción Directa*, no. 13 (Segunda quincena de Julio de 1922).

75. Pizarro, *La Huelga Obrera en Chile*, 68.

76. Salazar, *Historia de las luchas*, 242.

77. *Industrial Pioneer* 1:2 (March 1921): 55.

78. DeShazo, *Urban Workers*, 187 and 207; and *Bandera Roja* I:4 (June 1926): 5.

79. *Anarkos* (Montevideo), January 8, 1922.

80. *Hacia la Libertad* II:5 (March 1923): 3.

81. *La Voz del Mar* I:15 (May 20, 1925).

82. *Industrial Pioneer* (July 1926): 20–21.

83. *The One Big Union Monthly* III:1, no. 23 (January 1921): 44.

84. Letter from Juan Leighton, General Secretary Treasurer of the Marine Transport Union to Anon., May 21, 1924, Wayne State University Archives of Labor and Urban Affairs and University Archives, IWW Collection, Box 17, Folder 32.

85. *La Voz del Mar* 1:9 (January 15, 1925): 2.

86. Torrealba Z., *Los Subversivos*, 8–9.

87. *La Voz del Mar* 1:13 (April 8, 1925): 1.

88. Torrealba Z., *Los Subversivos*, 7.

89. *La Voz del Mar* I:8 (December 20, 1924): 6; *Hoja Sanitaria* I:8 (April 1925): 1; and *Acción Directa* IV:14 (August 1922): 3–4.

90. *Hoja Sanitaria* I: 5 (January 1925): 1; I:8 (April 1925): 1 and 3; and II:16 (May 1926): 3.

91. *Hoja Sanitaria* II:16 (May 1926): 4.

92. *Huelga General* (Los Angeles) 2:26, Suplemento (March 7, 1914): 1.

93. "Summary of Minutes of the International Congress of Marine Workers," March 20, 1926, Montevideo, Wayne State University Archives of Labor and Urban Affairs and University Archives, Collection IWW, Box 70, Folder 19.

94. *Bandera Roja* ran an ad from the Librería Libertaria in Santiago that listed a book for sale by the French anarchist E. Reclús, I:5 (July 1926): 6. The IWW local of taxi drivers in Montevideo characterized itself as "anarchist communist" at its founding, *Hacia la Libertad* I:1 (November 1922): 3. But there was occasional confusion as to whether the IWW was anarchist in orientation. A notice for a book about the anarchist movement led by Nestor Makhno in Russia carried the headline: "Compañero anarquista o IWW" in *Acción Directa*, no. 48 (February 1927): 4.

95. A recent history of anarchism in Buenos Aires fails to mention the IWW, its press, or Tom Barker in its discussion of the anarchist press of that city: Suriano, *Paradoxes of Utopia*. Alexandre Skirda, in *Facing the Enemy*, ignores both the IWW and Latin American anarchism. Colin Ward mentions the IWW twice in passing but does not discuss its activities or importance (*Anarchism*). In *Demanding the Impossible*, Peter Marshall devotes a paragraph to the IWW in Chile but fails to see its operations elsewhere in Latin America. David Miller refers to the IWW as an American union and characterizes it as "a curiosity" (*Anarchism*, 135).

96. *Regeneración*, No. 72 (January 13, 1912): 4.

4

The FACA and the FAI

Argentine Anarchists and the Revolution in Spain, 1930–1939

JAMES BAER

The jail at Villa Devoto on the western edge of Buenos Aires is an ugly block of concrete, six stories high. Many anarchists were arrested and jailed in Villa Devoto after the September 6, 1930, military coup in Argentina. In 1931 several hundred prisoners held a clandestine congress in their cell block in an effort to unite their many disparate factions. The goal was to overcome contentious disagreements that had resulted in the futility of organized resistance to the military regime. José Grunfeld, Jacobo Maguid, Jesús Villarías, Danilo Berisso, and Enrique Balbuena began a series of discussions to analyze the difficulties faced by the anarchist movement under a military dictatorship. Many of the political prisoners remained in the Villa Devoto jail throughout 1931. Other inmates were sent to the prison in Ushuaia, Tierra del Fuego. Foreign-born detainees were deported by the hundreds to Italy, Romania, Germany, and Spain. As the prisoners of Villa Devoto came to a consensus about the necessary changes, they transcribed and adopted an agreement to be sent to comrades around the country. Finally, in February 1932, when Gen. Agustín P. Justo became president in elections marred by fraud, most political prisoners were freed. Maguid, Grunfeld, and the others continued their activities in support of the faction of the anarchist movement that had become increasingly critical of the movement's historic standard-bearers.

The meeting of prisoners in a dingy cell block in 1931 was a moment of transition from the decline of Argentina's once-powerful anarchist federation, the FORA (Federación Obrera Regional Argentina), to the emergence of the FACA (Federación Anarco-Comunista Argentina), a movement that has endured to the present as the FLA (Federación Libertaria Argentina). The FACA became an important organization in the second half of the

1930s in Argentina, specifically due to its close ties with the anarchist organization in Spain, the FAI (Federación Anarquista Ibérica). The anarchist movements of Spain and Argentina each drew on the experiences of the other. Events in Argentina had an impact on the anarchists in Spain, and the activities of Argentine anarchists in Spain motivated the FACA in Argentina.

Members of the FACA became significant contributors to the Spanish Revolution that occurred during the civil war in Spain, serving in critical posts and helping to influence the history of Spanish anarchism throughout the war. At the same time, support by the FACA for the Spanish Republic in the civil war became a central focus for the anarchist movement in Argentina. This chapter seeks to highlight the importance of Argentine anarchism in the 1930s and the critical nature of the transnational connection between the anarchist movements in Spain and Argentina.[1]

The decade of the 1930s is often ignored in the historiography of Argentine anarchism.[2] The FORA lost much of its influence after the military coup in 1930, conveniently marking the end of the anarchist era for many historians. Yaacov Oved states categorically, "As an active movement, with its own institutions and publications, anarchism existed uninterrupted in Argentina for about fifty years, between 1880 and 1930."[3] However, the years between 1930 and 1943, often referred to as the "infamous decade" in Argentine history, were productive years for the anarchists in Argentina and need further study. The creation of the FACA, the sustained efforts to free political prisoners, and the ever-closer links with the Spanish anarchist movement mark this as an important period for Argentine anarchists.

Two books about the 1930s demonstrate some of the questions studied and ignored. Fernándo López Trujillo suggests that the creation of new groups to challenge the moribund FORA resulted in a form of politicized anarchism.[4] López Trujillo discusses the important transnational connections between Argentine and Spanish anarchists, but only within the broader context of a relationship with world anarchists in Cuba, Chile, Peru, and France. In an earlier work, Ernesto Goldar writes to answer a nationalist perspective that claims it is best when Argentines look within to find the source of their strength.[5] He counters with a study of the 1930s, when Argentines of all ideologies were drawn into the conflict in Spain. However, rather than advancing a transnational approach, Goldar uses the Spanish Civil War as an external event that affected the people and history of Argentina. His argument ignores the fact that the anarchist movement was transnational by its very nature and active in both countries. This chapter shows how anarchists were involved with the Spanish movement before, during, and after the civil war and how that has affected the trajectory of the FACA.

The FORA and the CNT

The FORA originated in 1904 as the successor to the anarchist FOA (Federación Obrera Argentina). Italian and Spanish immigrants were important sources of anarchist thought at the turn of the twentieth century. The organizational ability and oratory skills of Italian anarchists such as Errico Malatesta and Pietro Gori blended with the ideological mix and editorial talents of Spanish anarchists Antonio Pellicer Paraire and Gregorio Inglán y Lafarga, among others, to create a powerful anarchist movement in Argentina.[6] By the early twentieth century, Argentine anarchists controlled the largest federation of labor unions in Argentina and threatened the state with massive strike movements throughout the first decade. In response the Argentine government passed a residency law in 1902 that allowed the government to deport foreigners who were involved in strikes. In addition, the government enacted the Law of Social Defense in 1910 that prohibited anarchists from entering the country and identified penalties for engaging in what were viewed as the subversive activities of anarchist labor unions.[7]

The deportations of immigrant anarchists began in 1902 and continued throughout the first four decades of the twentieth century. These deportations forced anarchists to return to their native lands, where many continued their involvement in the anarchist movement. The Spanish weekly anarchist newspaper *Tierra y Libertad*, founded in 1906, had among its editors Antonio Loredo, who had been deported from Argentina in 1905. Loredo took an active part in the events of the Tragic Week in July 1909 in Spain when violence erupted in Barcelona. The Spanish government called up army reserves to fight in North Africa. In response, anarchist and socialist workers in Barcelona and throughout Catalonia called for a general strike, and confrontations with the army led to dozens of deaths. Loredo was jailed for several months and, upon release, was expelled from the country. "You can deport me," he told the police as they shipped him off to Montevideo, "but I will return to Spain."[8] From Montevideo Loredo moved back to Buenos Aires, where he served on the editorial board of the Argentine anarchist daily *La Protesta* before being arrested and deported once again from Argentina, thus fulfilling his promise to return to Spain with the help of Argentine authorities.

The significance of immigration for the anarchist movement has been well documented in many studies.[9] The focus here is on the continuing links between the anarchist movements of Spain and Argentina, which were strengthened by the deportation of prominent figures. However, there were also important connections between anarchist organizations in both countries. The anarchist newspaper in Spain, *Solidaridad Obrera*, commented on Argentina's anarchist organizations in February of 1910, and in October of that same year Spanish anarchists met to establish a national federation in part inspired by the Argentine example, the CNT (Confederación Nacional del Trabajo).[10]

The organizations in Argentina and Spain supported each other, but there were conflicts due to ideological differences. In 1915 the FORA faced opposition by a syndicalist movement more focused on issues of trade unionism and social reform than on social revolution. The anarchists and syndicalists separated, each taking the name FORA but adding a Roman numeral to designate its allegiance to the fifth congress in 1905, which had adopted anarcho-communism, or the ninth congress in 1915, which embraced trade union apoliticism and the organization of industries nationally by branch rather than of localities across crafts. The tension between anarcho-communism and syndicalism was echoed in controversies over organization in Spain.

Political circumstances led to differences between Spanish and Argentine anarchists as well. In 1916, four years after the promulgation of universal male suffrage, Argentines elected Hipólito Yrigoyen from the Radical Civic Union, a reformist party, as president of the Republic. Yrigoyen was dependent on a broad base of support and attempted, by professing the neutrality of the state in conflicts with employers, to bring organized labor into his coalition. The application of repressive laws diminished and new opportunities for organization allowed anarchist, syndicalist, and socialist labor federations to operate freely despite important periods of conflict at the end of the decade. In Catalonia, a massive strike in 1919 against a power company, La Canadiense, ushered in an era of violence that eventually led to the wholesale repression of labor under the dictatorship of Gen. Miguel Primo de Rivera in 1922. In Argentina the unfettered FORA-V mounted a campaign in the 1920s to push its revolutionary ideology as the standard for international anarchism, criticizing the Spanish CNT, along with the Unión Sindical Argentina (USA), for their embrace of syndicalist members. At the second meeting of the newly reconstituted International Workingmen's Association (AIT) in Amsterdam in 1925, the Argentine representative, Diego

Abad de Santillán, a prominent figure in *La Protesta*, argued vociferously with the Spanish representative, Eusabio Carbó, accusing the Spanish CNT of supporting the rival syndicalist federation in Argentina. "Santillán noted that Carbó, as a representative of the CNT in Spain, could not remain impartial due to the public and private polemic between the comrades of the FORA and those of the CNT."[11]

A dramatic turn of events in the early 1930s changed the fortunes of both Spanish and Argentine anarchists. In 1930 King Alfonso XIII of Spain asked Primo de Rivera to step down as dictator. General elections in early 1931 culminated in the rejection of the monarchy and the abdication of the king. The newly formed Spanish Republic ended most restrictions on labor unions, and anarchists in Spain found opportunities to expand their organizing and their power. In Argentina, however, a military coup by Gen. José Félix Uriburu in September 1930 ushered in an era of repression that severely limited anarchist organizations in Argentina. The military coup and subsequent repression closed the most widely circulated daily newspaper *La Protesta*, as many hundreds of anarchist militants were jailed or deported, and the FORA was nearly destroyed. That same year also saw the creation of a powerful new national, centralized labor confederation of syndicalists, socialists, and independent unions, the General Confederation of Labor (CGT), which eventually became the most powerful labor movement in the nation. A new era of industrial organization had begun, and the anarchists, who had once dominated the labor movement in Argentina, found themselves eclipsed and in disarray. Manuel Villar and Abad de Santillán, two of the editors of *La Protesta*, fled to Uruguay to avoid arrest. Rodolfo González Pacheco, editor of the rival *La Antorcha*, was arrested but permitted to go into exile in Uruguay. During the 1930s anarchists focused on getting their members out of prison and defending themselves from prosecution. Unlike the anarchists and the FORA, the leaders of the CGT cooperated with the regime in return for a modicum of control over organized labor. Attempts to restart the anarchist movement were largely unsuccessful. Villar and Abad de Santillán returned surreptitiously to Argentina and attempted to publish *La Protesta* in 1932, but their franking privileges were rescinded and the daily paper languished. For a time they did publish a new periodical, *Nervio* (meaning nerve or strength), but Villar was arrested and deported to Spain in 1933 and Abad de Santillán abandoned Argentina for Spain in 1934.[12]

Those imprisoned in the Villa Devoto jail, however, did attempt to unify the anarchist movement and overcome some of its divisions. When freed from jail these anarchists organized a national anarchist conference in Rosario that began on September 13, 1932. Fifty-three delegates representing thirty different organizations attended. It was a difficult meeting because the older FORA comrades disagreed fundamentally with suggestions that the organization represent industrial unions as well as distinct craft-based and locally federated anarchist groups.[13] They argued against what they called "specificism," which posited that trade unions should be organized along the lines of specific industrial branches, and argued in favor of a strong umbrella organization that would inherit the role played by the FORA-V for several decades prior to 1930. The fear of those opposed to "specificism" was that affiliated groups within each industry would engage in political alliances with non-affiliated unions or other labor organizations.[14] Grunfeld and the younger members of the anarchist movement had created a Provincial Workers' Federation in Rosario that included sixty unions, only twelve of which were affiliated with the traditional FORA. Grunfeld believed the new era called for new tactics and that the older FORA leadership did not understand the need for cooperation beyond the ranks of craft-based resistance societies and local anarchist federations.[15]

Divisions within the FORA led to the creation of the Regional Committee of Anarchist Relations (CRRA) in October 1932, with its national headquarters in Buenos Aires. The leadership group included Jacobo Maguid, Ángel Geracci, Natalio Saltarelli, Arón Cupit, and Enrique Balbuena. Grunfeld and Alberto Balbuena were sent on a nationwide tour to meet with comrades and encourage them to establish additional groups, "to spread the ideals of anarchism and participate in working-class activities, modernizing the language of propaganda and increasing the range of activities to include all the problems faced by these communities."[16] Their efforts met with some success; the original six area committees grew to sixteen by 1933 and eventually reached thirty.[17] However, when the next regional FORA congress met in Rosario in September 1934, the leadership of the federation and those representing the CRRA were unable to reconcile their differences. The critical issue was whether to maintain a purely apolitical stance, at the risk of becoming marginalized within the Argentine labor movement, or to accept forms of trade union organization that were not wholly anarchist while working within the unions as anarchists, as was the case in Spain with the CNT.

The CRRA continued its campaign to make inroads within the labor movement and fostered close relations with Spanish anarchists of the FAI.

Among those Spanish anarchists who sided with the Argentine concept of revolutionary anarcho-communism were those who had met and created a National Federation of Anarchist Groups in April 1923. This new federation, alongside a Regional Committee in Catalonia, helped lay the groundwork for the foundation of the FAI in 1927 by establishing relationships among small groups of anarchist militant cells known as affinity groups. The concept of affinity groups was inherited from the nineteenth century and the Alliance for Social Democracy created by Mikhail Bakunin. The Russian founder of anarchist communism wanted such groups to provide leadership and maintain ideological purity among anarchists. The CRRA wrote to the Peninsular Committee of the FAI in 1934 to indicate that Abad de Santillán, who had left Argentina for Spain and joined the FAI, was to be considered an intermediary between the movements of the two countries. In addition, the CRRA asked for information about the structure of the FAI to be used at an upcoming conference.[18] López Trujillo notes the link between the Argentine FACA and FAI-CNT in Spain in the creation of "specificism" in the Argentine movement.[19] The CRRA met to create a new organization, separate from the FORA in October 1935: the Argentine Anarcho-Communist Federation (FACA), a name that harkened back to the principles of the anarchist movement at the beginning of the twentieth century and attempted to take the mantle of revolutionary anarchism away from the aging FORA.

The immediate goals of the FACA were similar to those of the FORA: expand its influence among workers and defend those threatened with prison or in jail. Three prominent imprisoned anarchists in Argentina were members of the car drivers union: José Santos Ares, Florindo Goyoso, and José María Montero, all arrested in September 1930 and threatened with the death penalty under the state of siege. The three had their sentences reduced to penal servitude in Ushuaia, where they served two years until released. All three were eventually deported from the country, although they managed to return to Argentina where they had families. The other group, Pascual Vuotto, Reclus de Diago, and Santiago Mainini, were arrested in 1931, tortured, and imprisoned in a penitentiary in Bragado, southwest of Buenos Aires. The campaign for the release of the "prisoners of Bragado" united many disparate groups and provided a focus for Argentine anarchists, who were increasingly marginalized within the labor movement.[20] The other emphasis for Argentine anarchists after 1936 was the revolution and civil war in Spain.

The revolution that erupted in Barcelona as a consequence of the military uprising signaled the greatest hope for anarchists worldwide for a proletarian revolution expressing the goals of anarchism. The military uprising occurred in July 1936 when Gen. Francisco Franco rebelled against the republican government in Spain. Franco's troops secured nearly one-half of Spain but were unable immediately to take over the capital of Madrid or Barcelona. As the workers triumphed in Barcelona, they began to lay the groundwork for the anarchist revolution for which they had long dreamed and planned. The mixture of factory seizures, civil war, political chaos, and rivalries among socialists, communists, and anarchists produced fear among many supporters of the Republic, but encouraged anarchists to take control of the anti-Franco resistance. Nearly forty years after those first days of revolution, Diego Abad de Santillán enthusiastically recounted the excitement he felt. "The leadership [of the revolution] was everywhere," he said; he indicated that, for him, it was the beginning of a new world where anarchist ideals of participation, experimentation and change would liberate the working class.[21] After discussing the merits of taking power and imposing their will, anarchists decided to cooperate with other groups fighting for the Republic. In Barcelona they joined the Central Antifascist Militias Committee that, for a time, was the virtual government of Catalonia.[22] Abad de Santillán was the committee member responsible for coordinating the economy. Buenaventura Durruti organized a column of soldiers to fight at the front that was established between the forces of Franco and the Republic. For the next ten months, until May 1937 when fighting between communists and anarchists led to a restructuring that weakened anarchist power, Catalonia experienced a dramatic social revolution. Remnants of that revolution persisted until the collapse of the Spanish Republic in April 1939, and anarchists were a significant part of the war effort throughout the period. They served as a beacon of hope for anarchists from around the world, as Emma Goldman visited to show her support, and anarchists came from all over Europe to observe and fight. But the anarchists from Argentina, although not numerically important, were among the most significant participants in the anarchist movement and helped to shape this period of Spanish history.

The FACA in the Spanish Civil War

In 1936 the FACA sent several members to Spain to participate in the anarchist-led revolution and to fight in the civil war. José Grunfeld remembered:

Many libertarians came from Argentina: Ingeniero Jacobo Maguid, Professor José María Lunazzi of La Plata, Laureano Riera Díaz and Arturo Tomás García from the capital; Jacobo Prinzeman (Prince); Villamor, I can't remember his first name, from Rosario; Doctora Anita Piacenza, my wife, from Rosario; the playwright Rodolfo González Pacheco from the capital. There were others, but I don't remember their names. Of those listed Maguid, Prince, Villamor, Grunfeld and García, stayed until the end, some in Catalonia and the others in the South-Center.... Lunazzi, González Pacheco and others only stayed a few weeks. Anita Piacenza returned to Argentina in 1938 due to heart problems. Laureano Riera Díaz arrived much later than the rest of us. I am forgetting another compañero, Antonio Casanova Picado, who was born in Galicia but lived a long time in Argentina. The same was true of Riera, who arrived in Argentina as a child.[23]

Jacobo Prince (Prinzman) had edited *Pampa Libre* in Argentina during the period of the 1920s when anarchist groups formed around opposing periodicals. In 1924 anarchists from a rival group broke into his office and shot him, wounding him severely. Prince survived, but his right arm was permanently affected. In the 1930s he belonged to the FACA and was one of the three representatives the organization sent to Spain. Prince took responsibility for sending CNT/FAI information to Argentina to be distributed.[24] Prince also joined the FAI in Spain and represented the FAI at several important meetings in 1937. In May 1938 Prince joined Germinal de Sousa, secretary of the Peninsular Committee of the FAI, at a meeting of the National Committee of the CNT in Barcelona in which the CNT pressured the FAI to sign an agreement to join the Popular Front.[25] This was a delicate and important moment for the Spanish anarchist movement, and that an Argentine was included in these decisions demonstrates the influence of Argentine anarchism in Spain. Another Argentine who held important posts during the Spanish Civil War was José Grunfeld. The FACA authorized Grunfeld, Prince, and Maguid to go to Spain in the fall of 1936. Grunfeld traveled with his *compañera*, Anita Piacenza. Their arrival in revolutionary Catalonia thrilled them. "At last, we were living the long-awaited revolution, in whose cause we were so immersed."[26]

Grunfeld and Piacenza were taken to the Hotel Oriente, where they met other foreign anarchists, among them the French-born Gastón Leval, who had lived many years in Rosario, Argentina. "We did not form a separate group," wrote Grunfeld. "We were integrated with the Spanish in various anarchist groups in Barcelona. My compañera and I belonged to 'Grupo C' [of the FAI]. I joined the construction union, painters section, of the CNT in Barcelona."[27] Leval took Grunfeld immediately to the regional offices of the CNT-FAI in Catalonia and that first evening he was appointed provisional secretary of the FAI in Barcelona. Grunfeld was surprised that he was incorporated so quickly into the leadership of the Spanish anarchist movement.[28] Grunfeld's immediate acceptance into the Spanish movement was probably due to his close association with Abad de Santillán, Gastón Leval, Manuel Villar, and other militants who had returned from Argentina to Spain. Grunfeld continued as secretary of the FAI in Barcelona for several months, until replaced by a Spanish militant who had returned to the country. In early 1937 Grunfeld was chosen, again with the insistence of Gastón Leval, as one of the members of a newly formed Secretariat of Defense of the CNT-FAI regional in Catalonia. There were four members of the secretariat: Domingo Ascaso, a man named Huix from the textile union representing the CNT, another man named Picas representing the FAI, and Grunfeld. Since the others were already occupied with many duties, Grunfeld was designated secretary. His principal duties were to oversee the provisioning and support of troops, and to coordinate volunteers, publicity, and records for the Aragon Front in what was called the War Commission. Grunfeld continued in this post throughout the rest of the war, resigning in 1939 in disagreement with García Oliver over foreign volunteers that made him feel he was becoming isolated from Spanish comrades as a foreigner himself. Instead he transferred to the peninsular subcommittee in Valencia to coordinate relations among regional committees in that zone. This tension between a universal anarchist ideal and a Spanish movement rarely occurred among Argentine anarchists in Spain. Instead the most significant incident highlighting this tension occurred in February 1939, near the end of the war, when Juan Negrín, then head of the Republican government, asked to meet with representatives of the anarchist movement. Juan López represented the CNT; Lorenzo Iñigo, the Libertarian Youth; and José Grunfeld, the FAI. Grunfeld, at that time secretary of the FAI, described the meeting: "We were received by Negrín in a standard sized room. I was the last to shake his hand and just as we were about to begin the discussion, which was the point of our visit, he asked me my nationality. I replied that I was a citizen of Argentina but that I had come as the representative of the FAI. As if it was something that he had planned, Negrín told me that he could not discuss matters of state with a foreigner and that I should leave the room."[29] Grunfeld allowed his colleagues to continue with the meeting, although Negrín did not accomplish his goal of gaining strong support from the anarchists.

It is unclear whether Negrín's reaction was due to Grunfeld's role as an anarchist, his foreign birth, or his Jewish heritage. Other foreigners in Spain included anarchists from Russia, Italy, Germany, and South America. These were welcomed but regarded with some suspicion by Spanish anarchists.[30] Nevertheless, in the face of some resentment, only Argentine foreigners achieved positions of authority: Grunfeld in the FAI, Prince with *Solidaridad Obrera*, and Jacobo Maguid as the editor of the principal newspaper of the movement, *Tierra y Libertad*.

Like Grunfeld, Maguid was greeted in Spain by friends from Argentina. Abad de Santillán put Maguid up with his family in a home commandeered from a wealthy businessman who had fled. Maguid marveled at the original paintings and artwork, which were covered by Abad de Santillán to avoid damage. "'Now,' [Abad de] Santillán said, 'they belong to the people.'"[31] In Barcelona a surprised Maguid was informed that he had already been chosen to edit the weekly newspaper *Tierra y Libertad* and to serve as a member of the FAI Regional Committee of Catalonia. Maguid had not assumed he would have any leadership role in Spain; on the voyage by ship from Argentina he had been brushing up on his engineering books, expecting to participate in a technical capacity in the rebuilding of Spain.[32] He might not have been as surprised with his appointment as editor, however, if he had known that one of the men he was joining was Adolfo Verde, a Spaniard he had worked with on *La Protesta* in Buenos Aires. This network among Argentine and Spanish anarchists was based on personal relationships developed in Argentina and now put to use in Spain.[33]

In his columns in the newspaper, Maguid continuously supported the cause of Spanish anarchism and counseled against divisions that could weaken the movement. This seemed to be a common theme among the Argentines and Spaniards who had returned from Argentina. Other anarchists, including Emma Goldman, with whom Maguid met were more critical of cooperation with other groups in Spain.[34] "We must make judgments calmly and put aside preconceptions," Maguid wrote.[35] He also suggested that *Tierra y Libertad* ought to focus more on the fundamentals of anarchism rather than just war news.[36] Maguid held an important role in the revolution and sought to further its goals. He joined the "Nervio" group of the FAI, which included many who had lived in Argentina and dedicated himself to the Spanish cause. He lived with Grunfeld, Anita Piacenza (who also worked for *Tierra y Libertad*), and Jacobo Prince, who was the editor of the influential daily newspaper *Solidaridad Obrera*.

Jacobo Maguid continued as the editor of *Tierra y Libertad* from late 1936 through 1938, traveling widely around Republican territory and meeting many distinguished foreigners, including Camillo Berneri and Emma Goldman. However, as divisions within the movement became more intense, Maguid, who sided with the FAI militants against the more labor oriented CNT, resigned his position so as not to become embroiled in these battles. Instead he took on an assignment to collect and organize the archives of the CNT-FAI. He was still working on these documents in January 1939 when Barcelona fell and he, along with tens of thousands, fled into France.

José Grunfeld and Jacobo Maguid, along with Jacobo Prince, served as representatives of the FACA in Spain but also held positions of trust and authority in the Spanish movement, an integration of Argentine and Spanish anarchism that worked for the success of the anarchist revolution in Spain. This reflected a unity among the militants of both countries, and they focused their energies on the anarchist revolution they wanted to succeed. Unfortunately, revolution and war were difficult to sustain. Most of all, anarchists wanted to win the war and expand their revolution. Those anarchists who decided to join the government did so to further the war effort. Those who opposed participation believed that anarchists would be more effective as a fighting force without government constraints. Still others, including Jacobo Maguid, wrote that there should be a greater focus on the fundamentals of anarchism.[37] They all realized that their revolution would fail if the war were lost. The irony is that anarchist cooperation with other groups supporting the Republican government also meant that, in the event of victory, their revolution would be in jeopardy. Anarchist workers continued to operate their factories, shops, and farms while anarchist soldiers continued to fight in the ranks. The course of the war, however, became ever grimmer.

In July 1936 the Republican government controlled approximately 50 percent of Spain, including most of the Mediterranean coast, Madrid and La Mancha in the center, and Asturias, in the north. General Franco and the army controlled parts of the south and a swath from Vigo in the northwest to the Pyrenees along the French border. In the early stages of the war Madrid was the prize, and the battle for the capital was intense in November 1936. Franco's army was supported by German airplanes and an Italian army, but he was unable to break through the defenses of the International Brigades, the militias, and the Republican army in Madrid. The Republican government evacuated Madrid and left for Valencia, but its defenses held until 1939. Instead Franco's army concentrated on taking the mineral-rich north, which was cut off from the rest of Republican territory, and consolidated its hold on the south in Andalusia. By October 1937 the Republican government controlled a little more than one-third of Spain. Working-class morale remained high, however, especially in areas transformed by the anarchists.[38]

A year later an offensive by Franco's forces caused Republican forces to give up more territory. Although the pace of Republican withdrawal was slow, it lost seventy thousand men and eventually the battle, dooming the region of Catalonia to the north. Franco then focused on capturing Catalonia and its industries in Barcelona. His forces continuously bombed the city, and thousands of refugees fled north toward France. By January 1939 Barcelona fell to Franco's forces. The Spanish Republican government remained in control of the Levante along the Mediterranean, La Mancha and Old Castile in the center, and Madrid. With these events, the Republic's leaders knew they had lost the war, and many in the region—especially those most closely associated with the anarchist revolution—knew they had to flee.

Refugees, the FACA, and the End of the War

In Argentina, the FACA "founded, in agreement with the Spanish CNT and FAI, the *Servicio de Propaganda de España*, published the *Documentos Históricos de España* magazine, and pushed for the creation of the Solidaridad Internacional Antifascista (SIA)," an organization to aid victims of fascist aggression.[39] Affiliated groups were established in France, Great Britain, and in the United States. A section opened in Buenos Aires, probably in April 1938, and another was created in Rosario in July 1938.[40] In September 1939, a few months after the civil war had ended and a time when much work needed to be done to assist refugees in France who wished to leave for Latin America, a Comisión de Ayuda a Exiliados Antifascistas, or Commission to Assist Antifascist Exiles (CAEA), emerged in Buenos Aires. Laureano Riera Díaz, a Spanish immigrant and a member of the FACA who had returned to Spain during the war and was now back in Argentina, served as its secretary. Another organization created in Argentina was the Patronato Español de Ayuda a Las Víctimas De Agresión, or Office to Assist

Spanish Victims of Aggression (PEAVA). One of its founders was a Spanish anarchist, Orencio Conesa, who had immigrated to Argentina in 1925. During the civil war these groups raised money to send to Spain and, after the war, attempted to assist refugees. In August 1939 PEAVA indicated that it had secured the release of Juan José Villamor, an anarchist militant, from a French concentration camp. He was returned to Argentina on board the ship *Formosa*, arriving on August 19, 1939.[41]

The archives of the Argentine Libertarian Federation (FLA), the successor to the FACA in Buenos Aires, contain correspondence regarding these organizations. A document dated August 3, 1939, specifies what assistance will be provided by the CAEA to refugees arriving from Spain: "a) Refugees will be welcomed at the port; b) Each one will have a file created; c) Attention will be focused on those still incarcerated in Europe; d) Housing, food and medical assistance will be provided; e) Refugees will be referred to local unions for jobs; f) Refugees will have access to the press; g) Refugees will receive help with government forms, documentation and family assistance."[42]

The SIA also contacted its counterpart in France, remarking on the disturbing news that the French government had ceased returning Argentines fleeing Spain due to lack of funds. The Argentine SIA suggested a campaign in France to push for more government funds and for French unions to devote a sum of money to assist Argentine refugees from Spain.[43] Other activities of the organization included assisting Spanish refugees petitioning the Ministry of Foreign Affairs for legal residency, and tracking individuals fleeing Spain at the end of the war for friends and relatives in Argentina.[44] Argentine anarchists in 1939 were more involved in efforts to repatriate Argentines who had fought in Spain and to assist refugees from Spain than in any specific issue regarding labor in Argentina other than freeing the Bragado prisoners.

Tens of thousands of Spaniards fled the advancing forces of the Nationalist Army as it conquered Catalonia in January 1939. Republican leaders and anarchist militants also sought to escape the forces of General Franco. Abad de Santillán, José Grunfeld, Pedro Herrera, Germinal de Sousa, and Jacobo Maguid were among those who managed to escape. The experiences of Maguid and Grunfeld shed light on the circumstances in which many anarchists were forced to migrate at the end of the civil war. Maguid lived in Barcelona throughout the war and in January 1939 went to the CNT-FAI offices to find a means to escape Spain. There he saw a truck filled with men already pulling out. Maguid was too late. He went home and burned any documents that might prove incriminating, hoping he would not be forgotten. A colleague called on the telephone to tell him that a vehicle would come to pick him up and to be ready quickly. On January 26, 1939, he began his long journey. Maguid got as far as Gerona on the road to France but was unable to find a vehicle to take him over the border. He took a train north to the town of Figueras, where he got off and boarded another train to take him closer to the border. Finally he began walking toward the border but found that the Senegalese soldiers guarding the French border would not let anyone through except the wounded. Changing his plans, Maguid traipsed into the Pyrenees Mountains, looking for a way to cross surreptitiously into France. Suddenly he fell from the path and landed below, unconscious. He was found, loaded onto an ambulance, and permitted to cross the border into France as an injured refugee.

Once in France, Maguid attempted to contact the SIA in Paris. However, he was interned in the concentration camp at Argelès-sur-Mer in Southern France just north of the Spanish border. Maguid revealed himself to other anarchists in the camp, and they helped plan his escape. He was assigned to accompany the water bearer who brought water from the nearby village every day and was given an armband to wear so he would be allowed outside the camp. Then, in the village, as the water bearer returned to the camp, Maguid was picked up by a car that took him to Marseilles. There he was reunited with other anarchist leaders, among them Pedro Herrera. Maguid began working with a clandestine organization preparing false documents to enable Spanish anarchists to leave France. However, since his arm, which had been hurt in the fall in the Pyrenees, had never healed, the others persuaded Maguid to leave France and return to Argentina. He received money from Buenos Aires to pay for his voyage, and, with a new passport from the Argentine consulate, he set sail from Cherbourg, returning to Buenos Aires after more than two years in Spain. In Argentina Maguid continued to work with the FACA and the FLA until his death in 1997.

José Grunfeld's story is less harrowing. Grunfeld was one of the last anarchist militants to leave Madrid. He and a colleague obtained an automobile and set out for Valencia, about two hundred miles to the east. In Valencia they found that the port of Alicante, already crowded with fifteen thousand militants, was their best hope for escape from Spain. As they drove south along the coast, they stopped in the town of Gandía. They heard that a British warship lay off the coast and was prepared to take on refugees. Grunfeld managed to board the vessel and was taken to Marseilles. There the English Committee to Aid Refugees put him on a train for Paris. From

Paris Grunfeld continued to the English Channel, crossed to Dover, and arrived in London. In London he met with colleagues from the local SIA and received some money from the British. After a short stay in Britain, Grunfeld returned to Paris, where he worked with Spanish exiles to help those interned, like Maguid, in Argelès. Finally, Grunfeld left France and returned to Argentina at the end of July 1939, where he remained active in the FACA and the FLA. Grunfeld served on the Cultural Commission of the National Council of the FLA and in 1980 helped organize a national congress of the labor movement, despite threats from the military dictatorship. The June 1980 meeting created the National Standing Committee for Free Trade Unionism (COPENASILI).[45]

Hugh Thomas estimates that approximately 20,000–25,000 Republican refugees were transported to Mexico and to other Latin American countries, including the Dominican Republic, Venezuela, Panama, Chile, and Argentina, while 140,000 remained in France.[46] Before the end of the war, Manuel Villar was asked by the CNT to serve as a representative in Mexico, where Republican exiles were warmly welcomed by the government of Lázaro Cárdenas. However, he chose to remain in Spain and oppose the Franco dictatorship. Villar was jailed twice in Spain, once for twenty years, before leaving and returning to Argentina. Abad de Santillán fled to France, then to Argentina, where he continued his participation with the FACA and its successor for more than three decades.

Conclusion

The anarchist movement in Argentina never recovered the influence in the labor movement that it had before World War I, and the ideological splits of the 1920s and 1930s further contributed to the marginalization of anarchists generally. However, the actions of the militants who served in Spain during its war and revolution and those of the FACA who supported them gave renewed vigor to the anarchist movement in Argentina. Efforts to aid refugees from Spain and fascist Europe, hope that World War II would bring the downfall of Franco's regime in Spain, and renewed determination in the campaign to free the "prisoners of Bragado" energized anarchists. This chapter has shown that the transnational nature of the anarchist movement is an integral part of its history. One cannot isolate events in Argentina or in Spain, and that link has been the focus of this chapter. The interconnectedness of anarchists in Spain and Argentina, the impact on their respective movements, and their effect within Argentina has important consequences for our understanding of the anarchist movement in Argentina. Hopefully more studies on this period and on these relationships from a transnational perspective will yield additional insights.

The increasing political influence of Col. Juan D. Perón also brought anarchists and the FACA into active opposition. After the discredited government of Ramón Castillo was overthrown by a military coup in 1943, the military government that followed appointed Juan Perón as head of the Labor Department. Perón used his position to curry favor with organized labor, much to the disgust of anarchists in the FACA. One of the areas that sparked opposition was Perón's attempt to control organized labor and bend it to his political goals.[47] The FACA and other anarchist movements in Argentina opposed the emergence of the populist colonel, who was elected president in 1945. In 1946 the newly published anarchist newspaper *Reconstruir* strongly criticized the government and policies of Perón.[48] Government reaction led to arrests and a temporary suspension of the paper. Abad de Santillán joined the opposition and was instrumental in organizing another anti-Peronist periodical, *Americalee*, in the mid-1940s. In 1947 Jacobo Prince, on behalf of the FACA, edited a pamphlet entitled "One Year of Peronismo" that criticized the regime.[49] The FACA opposed not only the regime of Perón but also the military governments that replaced it after 1955.

In February 1955 the fourth congress of the FACA changed the name of the organization to the Federación Libertaria Argentina (FLA). Throughout the 1950s and the rest of the twentieth century, the FLA supported civil, political, and human rights through its publications and its Atheneum on 1551 Brasil Street in Buenos Aires. Anarchist traditions have influenced other contemporary groups in Argentina as well. Marguerite Guzmán Bouvard, for example, identified the Mothers of the Plaza de Mayo, who championed the cause of the disappeared in the 1980s, as anarchists. "What characterizes the Mothers as anarchists is their rebelliousness and their aim of a complete transformation of Argentine society" through direct action.[50] The Argentine protesters who took to the streets to denounce government policies that led to an economic implosion in late 2001 also exemplified anarchist practices and principles. While the anarchist movement in Argentina reached a low point in the 1930s, it did not disappear. The FACA and its participation with the FAI in Spain gave Argentina's anarchists a second wind, and they remain active to this day.

Notes

1. See Migueláñez Martínez, "Anarquismo argentino transnacional."
2. A classic work on Latin American labor is Spalding's, *Organized Labor in Latin America.* Spalding identifies a formative period in which anarchists in Argentina are powerful as lasting until 1914. In the post–World War I era, Spalding sees the Argentine Radical Civic Party as one of the reasons for the decline of anarchist unions. Horowitz, in his article "Argentina's Failed General Strike of 1921," argues that anarchist unions, weakened by decreasing immigration and ideological divisions, were stunned by government actions in the early 1920s.
3. Oved, "Influencia del anarquismo español."
4. López Trujillo, *Vidas en rojo y negro.*
5. Goldar, *Argentinos y la guerra civil española.*
6. Oved, "Influencia del anarquismo," looks at the relationship between Spanish and Argentine anarchism at the end of the nineteenth and the beginning of the twentieth century. Nido's (pseudonyn of Amadeo Lluan) *Informe general del movimiento anarquista de la Argentina* was originally a report submitted at a conference of anarchists in Rosario, Argentina in 1926. See also Zaragoza, "Anarquistas españoles en Argentina," where he also refers to the fusion of Italian and Spanish anarchism in Argentina. Osvaldo Bayer discusses the importance of Italian anarchists in "The Influence of Italian Immigration on the Argentine Anarchist Movement," accessed on January 4, 2013, https://libcom.org/library/influence-italian-immigration-argentine-anarchist-movement-osvaldo-bayer.
7. See Costanzo, "Inadmissible Turned History."
8. *Tierra y Libertad* (Barcelona), March 29, 1916.
9. Many books have focused on the importance of immigrants in the Argentine anarchist movements. See Zaragoza, *Anarquismo argentino*; López, *La FORA en el movimiento obrero*; Penelas, *Los gallegos anarquistas en la Argentina*; Abad de Santillán, *La F.O.R.A., ideología y trayectoria*; and Abad de Santillán, *El movimiento anarquista en la Argentina.*
10. *Solidaridad Obrera* (Barcelona), February 19, 1910.
11. From the minutes of the opening day at the Amsterdam conference of the AIT, March 21, 1922. Abad de Santillán Archives, file 4, International Institute for Social History, Amsterdam.
12. See also Abad de Santillán, *Memorias 1897–1936.*
13. This perspective comes from José Grunfeld, *Memorias*, 141. See also Atán, *Cuatro historias de anarquistas.* Atán, a reporter, asks Grunfeld many questions about his militancy and his ideas.
14. For a defense of the FORA see López, *La FORA en el movimiento obrero*; and Solomonoff, *Ideologias del movimiento obrero*, 194.
15. Grunfeld, *Memorias*, 139.
16. Ibid., 152.
17. See Pérez, "Anarchist Movement."
18. Letter from the CRRA (Argentina) to the Peninsular Committee of the FAI, May 8, 1934. The FAI responded on August 1, 1934, with the requested information. Archivo FAI, Comité Peninsular, Paquete 20, International Institute for Social History, Amsterdam.
19. López Trujillo, *Vidas en rojo y negro*, 103.

20. Vuotto, *Vida de un proletario*.

21. "La cabeza estaba en todas partes." Abad de Santillán to author, personal interview, Buenos Aires, July 21, 1973.

22. José Peirats, in *La CNT en la revolución española*, Vol. 1 names the anarchist members of the Committee: Juan García Oliver, Aurelio Fernández, José Aséns, Diego Abad de Santillán, and Marcos Alcón (160).

23. Letter from José Grunfeld to author, April 27, 1992.

24. A letter from Prince on FACA letterhead to the secretary of the Peninsular Committee of the FAI on October 8, 1937, indicated that the FACA had distributed FAI information in Argentina. Archives of the FAI, Comité Peninsular, paquete 15, microfilm 150, number 6 B3. International Institute for Social History, Amsterdam.

25. Peirats, *La CNT en la revolución española*. Vol. 3, 97.

26. Grunfeld, *Memorias*, 174.

27. Grunfeld to author April 27, 1992.

28. Grunfeld, *Memorias*, 176: "In one of the halls there was a compañero who, if I am not mistaken, was called Traball, who accused me of not making a revolution in Argentina, like anarchists in Spain were doing."

29. Ibid., 223.

30. Letter writer Pablo refers to animosity against Grunfeld and other foreigners. Letter dated November 8, 1938. Archives of the FAI, Comité Peninsular, paquete 15, microfilm 150, number 6 B3. International Institute for Social History, Amsterdam.

31. Cimazo, *Recuerdos de un Libertario*, 42.

32. Cimazo, *La Revolución Libertaria*, 132.

33. Cimazo, *Recuerdos de un Libertario*, 43.

34. In *Recuerdos*, Maguid (Cimazo) writes of his meeting with the famous Emma Goldman when she visited the offices of the newspaper *Tierra y Libertad*. "The dialog began in English, in which I could barely jabber, stringing together poorly-worded sentences. I found the solution when I suggested that we speak in Yiddish, a language she understood quite well and one I could manage passably" (48).

35. Cimazo, *La Revolución Libertaria*, 118.

36. Letter to the Peninsular Committee of the FAI, February 1937. Archives of the FAI, Comité Peninsular, microfilm 213, Paquete 48, number 4 A. International Institute for Social History, Amsterdam.

37. Archives of the FAI, Comité Peninsular, Microfilm 213, Paquete 48, February 1937. International Institute for Social History, Amsterdam.

38. See González, "Politics of Betrayal."

39. Translated from the Federación Libertaria Argentina (FLA) history. http://www.federacionlibertaria.org/home.html.

40. The archives of the Federación Libertaria Argentina (FLA), Buenos Aires, successor to the FACA, contains an "Informe de la Comisión Organizadora Nacional" that lists the date April 27, 1938, and a letter from José María Lunazzi in Rosario indicating that a local section is being formed, dated July 16, 1938.

41. "Relación con el Patronato Español," August 21, 1939. In the archives of the FLA.

42. Letter from Laureano Riera Díaz to Dr. Manuel Martín Fernández, August 3, 1939. Archives of the FLA.

43. Letter from Laureano Riera Díaz to the French Section of the SIA, August 17, 1939. Archive of the FLA.

44. Letter from Laureano Riera Díaz to the Secretary of the Local Committee of the SIA in Rosario, August 15, 1939, indicating assistance to Marcelino Fernández and Leonor González with the Ministry of Foreign Affairs. Archive of the FLA; and Letter to Compañera Matilde, delegate to the SIA in France from the SIA, CAEA in Argentina, August 11, 1939: "Family members are looking for Manuel Tur, who has disappeared. . . . Señora Monserrat Avis de Gelaver is searching for Anita Imbers Gelaver, single woman from Catalonia, who is a kindergarten teacher." Archive of the FLA.

45. *Tierra y Libertad* (Madrid) No. 210, January 2006.

46. Thomas, *Spanish Civil War*, 758.

47. *Reconstruir* No. 20, agosto de 1947.

48. Cimazo, *Recuerdos de un Libertario*, 64.

49. Grunfeld, *Memorias de un anarquista*, 279.

50. Bouvard, *Revolutionizing Motherhood*, 226.

II

HARNESSING THE COLLECTIVE

Labor, Culture, and Counterhegemonic Movements

5

From Anarchists to "Anarcho-Batllistas"

Populism and Labor Legislation in Uruguay

LARS PETERSON

In mid-1905, the Sociedad de Resistencia Obreros Sastres (Tailors' Resistance Society) of Uruguay found itself embroiled in controversy. The anarchist labor union had just ended a twenty-one day strike aimed at forcing employers to honor a labor agreement won (also through a strike) two years earlier. And though the 1905 strike also ended largely in success, the circumstances of the negotiations drew criticism. The anarchist newspaper *El Libertario* attacked the tailors' union for allegedly using the "office of the [Montevideo] chief of police to meet with the bosses, [and] having [the chief] act as arbiter or judge over differences that emerged during the discussion." The tailors adamantly denied the charges. According to them, "the union of the 'Obreros Sastres' never asked for the intervention of the Chief of Police." Instead, "during the strike, we were invited to a 'conversation' by the mentioned Police Chief, who invited us, not in an official capacity, but as an ordinary citizen." The tailors had accepted the arrangement and did indeed meet their employers at the police station. At the conclusion of the strike, the union petitioned to hold a celebration including a band and a banquet. And yes, the police chief had been in attendance but, again, solely "as an ordinary individual" and only because he had invited himself; though anarchists, the tailors stated that it would have been rude and contrary to their principles to have asked him to leave. Besides, Colonel Bernassa later wrote them a note apologizing for having invited himself.[1]

The tailors' side of the story did little to sooth anarchist worries that one of their unions had been compromised by state intervention. In fact, the editors of *El Libertario* used the tailors' scandal as an egregious example of what they saw as a larger dangerous trend: that of "a complete misunderstanding of what is or ought to be the struggle between capital and labor amounting to fundamental errors which, unfortunately, are taking shape among many workers." What was that "complete misunderstanding?" Reformism. As further proof of creeping heterodoxy, El Libertario dressed down El Obrero—a fellow anarchist labor newspaper—for neutrally reporting the mediated end to the tailors' strike rather than joining the criticism.[2]

Argument and Literature

In his contribution to El primer batllismo—a work that attempts to capture José Batlle y Ordóñez's lasting influence on Uruguayan politics—historian Carlos Zubillaga proposes that Batlle was a populist. His two presidential terms (1903–7, 1911–15) did come far before Latin American historiography acknowledges (with one important exception[3]) the appearance of populism as a broad regional trend. Nonetheless, Batlle fits the characteristics of a populist including his (selective) charismatic leadership, his appeals to labor as a new constituency including efforts to enfranchise them, and his attempts to build progressive and often vertical cross-class alliances through the Colorado Party.[4] I build on that argument by defining a central paradox unidentified by all of the Uruguayan historiography: at the turn of the twentieth century, organized workers—those most likely to receive the kinds of social provisioning we associate with populism—were largely organized around anarchism, an ideology completely at odds with statist politics. The other critical component that validates claims of Batlle's populism—and which Uruguayan historiography has been most hesitant to acknowledge—is that the president was in competition with a radical camp, which he in fact attempted to channel, co-opt, and neutralize. How, then, did the state colonize anarchism?

While a few labor histories have mentioned a peculiar anarchist faction—anarcho-batllismo—that, in varying degrees, pragmatically supported Batlle during his second presidency, no one has explored its roots;[5] neither has it been examined comparatively or placed within the context of early-twentieth-century labor-state reforms. The incident described earlier of police mediation in a strike highlights the change in relationship workers in general would come to have with Uruguay's government. It points to the early presence of an ideological flexibility among anarchist unions that appears to have grown over time. Specifically, it indicates avenues of rapport some state officials could develop with a segment of those workers most hostile to political and economic reforms. Early populism in Uruguay

coupled with the domestic and foreign context of repression pushed seg-
ments of anarchism to ally with the most progressive elements of the political elite. This experience in turn resonates with the histories of changing
dynamics between state officials and anarchists in other parts of the world.

Labor and Politics in Early-Twentieth-Century Uruguay

In 1900 Uruguayan society was experiencing serious changes in its social
and economic relations. Migration, especially from Italy and Spain and
heaviest just before and during most of the period in question, brought
people anxious to live and prosper amid the attendant restructuring of
political economies during the second industrial revolution. Anarchism
traveled with immigrants to Uruguay during the late nineteenth century,
took root, and flourished. By the early 1900s it was the dominant ideology among workers, followed by Catholic unionism (including Christian
democracy) and then socialism. Influenced by anarcho-syndicalism, anarchist unions followed a particular model of organization known as resistance societies (of which the tailors' union was but one), patterned after
the society they hoped to build following the revolution against state and
capital. Resistance societies attempted to include all workers of a particular
trade and empowered members to shape their association through direct
democracy (though they often empowered liaisons to manage the day-to-
day affairs of the organization and serve as representatives to larger labor
associations). Explicit in their abhorrence of authoritarian institutions, resistance societies recognized no arbiter between themselves and employers.
After decades of trial and error, Uruguayan anarchists in 1905 managed to
establish an umbrella federation to coordinate solidarity and struggle in
resistance societies. Named the Uruguayan Regional Workers' Federation
(Federación Obrera Regional Uruguaya, or FORU), it had counterparts in
Argentina, Chile, and Paraguay.[6]

Transformations were also taking place among state officials. Since independence and for most of the nineteenth century, the Blancos and Colorados—Uruguay's two traditional parties—engaged in brutal and often
long-lasting wars for political control. In 1904 the Blanco Party, smarting
from decisive military defeat, looked away from saber and lance to workers and saw a new potential electorate and client base. The Colorado Party,
especially within the faction headed by José Batlle (known as the batllistas),
responded by promoting a degree of support, protection, and ultimately

advanced labor legislation (accident compensation, maximum work hours, retirement pensions, etc.) in an effort to retain their political dominance and pacify growing labor militancy.

Labor Legislation, 1903–1905

Beginning in 1903 massive action on the part of Catholic workers brought a petition directly to Parliament for a national day of rest; it was the first labor bill to reach the legislature. The following year, this time with official support from Blanco representative Oriol Solé y Rodríguez, the proposed law was discussed at length but never came up for a vote. During the deliberations, Representative Areco, a Colorado, presented a hastily prepared labor bill of his own—in effect bidding on behalf of his party for workers as a constituency. Then in 1905 Blanco representatives Carlos Roxlo and Luis Alberto de Herrera presented a new labor bill, this one lengthy, well thought out, and comprehensive.[7]

The proposed law provided a range of protections and provisions, all of which matched and responded to almost every labor grievance expressed in the working-class press. Compliance with the law would be ensured by the police or by hygiene specialists with the power to inspect and fine. Of special interest, the legislation would have also created a "committee of social questions" composed equally of industrialists and workers; labor representation on the committee would be selected by unions registered with the state. This committee would enjoy the power of arbitration, should all parties accept its intervention. It would also have the power to propose additional labor laws and have those considered speedily, even ahead of comparable ones proposed by parliamentarians or even the president. Such powers would have offered to workers—through the filter of representatives and the possible veto by their own employers—an indirect voice in the introduction of labor bills. In an age when few workers even had the right to vote in Uruguay (or elsewhere), this form of enfranchisement could have been very seductive.

In his presentation to colleagues, Roxlo addressed a particular source of likely opposition to the bill: workers. He acknowledged deep distrust among workers but was confident that, with time and the state's favorable disposition toward them, workers would eventually come around. Roxlo stated poetically, "Doctor Luis Alberto de Herrera and I have cast a seed in hopes that it will bear fruit and show that, despite the distrusts of the working class, they—seeing how the State and the legislators worry about their destinies—may repeat one day [José] Martí's beautiful phrase: 'the world is not evil: for every worm two roses spring.'" As for his party, he denied that all conservatives were indifferent to the plight of workers. "There is a great error," he said, "in the manner the proletarian classes reason: there is the error of believing that bills for labor reforms solely come from those truly close to workers such as liberals."[8] Labor law was an act of good faith that would reconcile workers with their representatives both liberal and conservative.

After three months of inaction, within the context of a peak year for labor unrest and during the prolonged port workers' strike, de Herrera demanded immediate passage of his cosponsored bill, which was still tied up in committee. He also broke Parliament's silence on strikes, referencing the recent wave afflicting the country. Right before his speech, it appears that a group of workers had entered Parliament and had jeered the legislators, presumably for not having passed a labor law; they had to be forcibly removed before the session could continue.[9]

Three weeks later Roxlo and de Herrera introduced a new bill that said nothing about workplace safety standards, accident compensation, retirement pensions, or a weekly day of rest. The eight-hour day was reserved for night work; everyone else (except domestic workers) would work ten hours. The Committee on Social Questions had also been removed. Instead resistance societies were empowered to speak for workers collectively, but regulation of them had also expanded. Some protections for workers had been added, including safeguards on their wages and their civil-political autonomy. In short, the new bill protected workers less and circumscribed their actions more.[10]

Why the partial about-face? Historian Milton Vanger argues that after the prolonged port strike—with eleven thousand participants, it was "the largest strike in Uruguayan history," and struck directly at the country's export economy—Roxlo's and de Herrera's "pro-labor sympathies wore thin," and their revisions reflect that shift in disposition.[11] It was a time of strikes and rumors of strikes. To the coauthors, perhaps, any labor bill needed as much coercion as concession.

Early Anarchist Reactions to Labor Law

Although the Catholic workers' Sundays-off campaign caused quite a stir in the mainstream press, anarchist newspapers were tight-lipped about it.[12] Anarchists usually despised labor legislation for one or more of the following reasons. First, it was seen as a Machiavellian and authoritarian imposition intended, under the pretense of neutrality, to rig (through state regulation) labor relations further in favor of employers. Second, by design or by consequence, reforms would lull workers into a state of complacency, leading them to surrender to state officials—no matter how well-meaning—any self-determination in matters regarding their own employment. The official newspaper of the FORU, echoing Peter Kropotkin, put it bluntly: "The emancipation of the workmen must be the act of the workmen themselves."[13] Third, it was seen by some (especially anarchists opposed to bread-and-butter labor politics) as a zero-sum game, since capitalist employers, merchants, and landlords—sometimes seen as consciously in league—would compensate for higher labor costs by either deteriorating work conditions, raising the costs of goods or rent, or both.[14]

In 1905, when legislators from both political parties introduced labor bills, the editors of *El Obrero* were particularly dismissive of the proposed legislation. "How is it possible," they asked, "that persons so removed from the people, that know nothing of their sufferings, their miseries and privations, should take so much interest in the proletarian mass? The people, dear legislators, do not need laws of any kind, they have enough [trouble] with the absurdity of maintaining parasites." They further warned of the danger inherent in having people who did not work regulating the workplaces of others.[15] *El Libertario* opined similarly, lamenting that "we men who every day leave a part of our body and our *soul* in the dungeons of industry, in the fields, see ourselves more persecuted by the ambitious idle who consume the product of our labor." Among those "idlers" figured legislators (including Representatives Roxlo and de Herrera, both mentioned specifically)—who were responsible for the recent civil war, a struggle for "ambition" and "the right to live as layabouts." "If they wanted to speak on behalf of workers, they should stop collecting [their salaries]" and become workers themselves. "We want to rid ourselves of everything that is unjust, inhuman and anti-social: we want to get rid of all the indolent; we want to proclaim productive work as an exclusive virtue so we cannot countenance work laws fashioned by those who do not know that elemental virtue."[16] If solutions to the myriad wrongs inherent in industrialization were to be found, anarchists believed those would originate with victims themselves.

Others engaged with specific pieces of the proposed laws rather than dismissing them out of hand. *Despertar* denounced the bills but took pains to scrutinize them point by point. They did so in a seven-part series, covering both parties' proposals. Blancos, they said, would only cater to workers long enough to become the majority party and rearrange the political system to their benefit, at which time they would "toss the Labor Law to the ground and the worker will remain a slave." Colorados, on the other hand, had only proposed a bill of their own so as to prevent Blanco ascendancy, expecting to disregard the law thereafter.[17] However, the columnist's largest criticism was that the proposed regulations were rife with loopholes, contradictions, and inadequacies. Even if passed, the law could not possibly be enforced. Better to constrain capital through workers' own efforts rather than put any hope on the magnanimity and competence of political elites.[18] Although the resistance society that published *Despertar* had recently informally accepted state arbitration, not even they were willing to entertain formal state intervention. Nor were any other anarchists at the time.

Police Matters

If legislators at the turn of the twentieth century were experimenting with new kinds of state intervention, so too were the police. In fact, police policy was a reflection of the coercive, co-optative, and conciliatory modernist project then being elaborated by Parliament and presidents—incentives and disincentives given to labor within a managed and populist reform process.

In 1904 police chief Colonel Bernassa y Jerez sought to professionalize security forces by compiling a thick police manual full of laws and norms to be enforced; a smaller second volume appeared in 1906. His occasional annotations are of special interest. Under "Instructions Concerning the Strike" Bernassa y Jerez wrote that "the frequency of labor strikes produced, which occasion the consequent social perturbations, requires the preferential attention of police authority, by nature of their institution charged with maintaining public order, liberty, property, and individual security." Acknowledging the political power of radicalized workers, Bernassa y Jerez cast them as antidemocratic. Police were promised that if they followed his instructions they would "contribute to the maintenance of the free exercise of all rights within order, encouraging the spirit of workers with the deep conviction that they may fully exercise their faculties so long as they do not infringe upon the rights of others; and to the producer and industrialist classes the full confidence that authority keeps vigil over their property, guaranteeing the functioning of their industry or commerce." However, and above all else, precinct commanders were to remember "the fundamental principle of all good Police that 'it is better to prevent than to repress.'"[19]

The colonel's shift in tactics demonstrates the changing and complex nature of labor conditions in Uruguay at the time, requiring a more varied and sophisticated toolbox on the part of police. Bernassa y Jerez included arbitration and intelligence work among the new implements in this expanded toolbox. Good police preparation for a strike involved infiltration. The police chief recommended that "you should not neglect [labor] meetings because, even though the Law protects and regulates them, often from these emerge perturbing rumors that sow disquiet and anxiety." Because of this "your presence or that of your subordinates is indispensable at every meeting where the law permits . . . to prevent by all means possible that these degenerate into tumultuous assemblies."[20]

Batlle himself, as head of the executive, also demonstrated a range of dispositions toward labor during his first term in office. In a well-known case, the president interceded on behalf of an anarchist denied entry by the police at the port in Montevideo. No law existed barring anarchists from the country—the Uruguayan police had just been colluding with counterparts in Buenos Aires. When Batlle heard about the expulsion, he immediately contacted the man and paid his fare back to the capital. As Milton Vanger put it, "this sort of legalism hardly endeared Batlle to employers but it reminded the unions, anarchist-led, that they had a friend at the top."[21]

But Batlle could just as easily use switch as he did bait. During the port strike, he issued orders that the police give equal protection to strikers and strikebreakers; he claimed to only be enforcing the law but it may have given employers the edge they needed. In late June the police opened fire on strikers as they moved to fight a group of strikebreakers. They wounded four and killed a striker by the name of Andrés Soto. The port strike ended in defeat.[22] Like Bernassa y Jerez, Batlle also attempted mediation. In early 1905 railroad workers went on strike; the president appointed his vice president and soon-to-be successor, Claudio Williman, to negotiate on behalf of workers. The government had more leverage here than in the port strike (the railroad had just petitioned to extend its railroad lines), and the strike was won.[23]

In October 1907 an open letter in the form of a pamphlet appeared in Montevideo detailing police offenses. Entitled "¡Yo Acuso!" the pamphlet self-consciously referenced Émile Zola's 1898 open letter "J'accuse," written to the president of France and charging government officials of wrongdoing in the Dreyfus case.[24] In this instance, however, the writer was Leoncio Lasso de la Vega, famous journalist and anarchist, and the letter was directed to Claudio Williman early in his presidential term. Lasso de la Vega accused the police chief, Colonel West—Bernassa y Jerez's successor—of a range of offenses. West, also reflecting the prerogatives of the new president, had pushed the police back to tactics of repression. The most grievous of these charges involved a recent incident at the International Center of Social Studies (Centro Internacional de Estudios Sociales), an important anarchist meeting place and think-tank of sorts. West had successfully infiltrated anarchist circles and planted several police agents, one a would-be assassin. This hit man discharged a revolver in an attempt to kill the famous anarchist poet Ángel Falco as he gave a speech; miraculously no one was injured.[25]

Over the years, the police had physically assaulted workers, infiltrated the labor movement, prevented peaceful assembly and free speech, sent agent provocateurs, carried out mass arrests, engaged in wrongful imprisonment, and so on. He also colluded with Argentine authorities in persecuting anarchists that sought refuge in Uruguay. "All of these facts," noted Emilio Frugoni, Uruguay's first elected Socialist member of Parliament, "demonstrate that while we pretend to serve as an example to all the other South American Republics for the liberty and modernity of our laws, in practice we walk in the footsteps of the Argentine Republic."[26]

Anarcho-Batllismo

Issues of tactics had always fueled rivalries within the anarchist community. But at the end of 1910 an even greater polemic broke out with the appearance of a new and peculiar ideology we may call anarcho-batllismo. Adherents of the faction looked to Batlle's second presidency as a propitious moment to guide and radicalize expected labor reforms. In early 1910, toward the end of Williman's administration and Batlle's anticipated return from Europe to preside over the country a second time, whispers of heterodoxies emerged. *La Nueva Senda*'s first reaction was to issue a stinging critique of any notion that Batlle might be a different kind of politician or that supporting him could be tactically opportune. Their position was unequivocal: "Understand that even in the case of an immediate utilitarian idea, [supporting Batlle] can set a bad precedent (exploitable by any pretentious person with the vocation of shepherd of the proletarian masses), constitutes a weakness, an inconsistency, a supposition than what History and Science teach could not be true." This was unshakable faith in the tenets of anarchism.[27]

Shortly thereafter the newspaper hosted at the International Center a debate on the subject of anarchist political participation. Two long-time anarchists—Leoncio Lasso de la Vega (author of the pamphlet ¡Yo Acuso!) and Ángel Falco (survivor of the assassination attempt by the police agent)—figured prominently in those debates. There, Lasso de la Vega first openly declared his heterodoxy, stating his intent to support Batlle's new candidacy. Falco vacillated, so Lasso de la Vega received the brunt of outrage, though both were heavily criticized.[28]

Anarcho-batllismo emerged clearly as a political ideology in the pages of the newspaper *Salpicón*, edited by Lasso de la Vega. Appearing on October 13, 1910, to coincide with the first anniversary of Francisco Ferrer's execution, the short-lived newspaper embraced Batlle as the champion of progressive forces in Uruguay. Lasso de la Vega explained why, despite his hostility toward politicians, he was supporting Batlle: "I wished for divorce, and he provided it; I hoped for the abolition of the death penalty and he proved it; I desire the divorce from the Church [by the government]—submissive within a truly popular State—and he is the only one that, today, deigns consider the problem and solve it. This figure, whom I present you, is not the *national politician*, but the *Man* that advocates solutions of a global character." Consistent with the general conviviality between socialists, anarchists, and some liberals, one of Batlle's major qualities to Lasso de la Vega (and several other anarcho-batllistas) was his staunch anticlericalism.

Casting a wide ideological net with his entreaties, Lasso de la Vega said this: "Whenever I hear [Batlle] being called an *anarchist* by his enemies, as if that were a terrible insult, I exclaim within: 'I am glad; I wish he could be one through and through, but scientific anarchism—let us be clear here—that of Bakunin; that of Kropotkin; that of Reclus." To Lasso de la Vega the lines were clearly demarcated: "In these moments, there should only be two parties clearly delineated in Uruguay: those that love progress, with Batlle; those that hate it, against Batlle. Choose your post: with the owls in shadow or with the eagles in the light of the sun, flying to lofty heights." His Manichean rhetoric went further. While defending a recent article in *El Día* by Ángel Falco (who was now giving Batlle his unequivocal support), Lasso de la Vega suggested that "if at any time armed struggle on the part of workers were justified—in order to fortify the triumph of their ideals—that moment is now."[29]

Following this article, cracks began to appear in anarchists' cohesion with regard to parliamentary politics. In fact, workers' relationship to the state became one of the areas of strongest contention for anarchists in Uruguay. Quite accidently, the newspaper *Tiempos Nuevos* became the standard-bearer of antipolitical anarchism against a tide of defections. Its first issue reminded Uruguayans to abstain from voting even as they announced FORU's upcoming third congress, crucial "in these moments where the participation or abstinence in politics of a conscious labor element is under debate."[30]

A confluence of at least two events appears to have attracted some anarchists to electoral politics. The first was the worldwide movement in solidarity with Francisco Ferrer, imprisoned in the infamous Montjuich fortress and executed in 1909 by Spanish authorities. This event united Uruguayan radicals and reformists then in abeyance and pushed them into the streets, rekindling labor and radical action.[31] Second, and coinciding with that resurgence, a major reshuffling of electoral politics led some anarchists to view the political moment as exceptional and propitious to radical infiltration. In 1910 a failed Blanco uprising, aimed at preventing a second Batlle presidency, provoked the National Party's total abstention from the election. This led to a political scramble as batllistas attempted to extend their control over Parliament, and Socialists and Liberals (running on a coalition ticket) saw their first viable opportunity to each gain a seat. Political elites were deeply divided; radical politics was on the rise. For some, the revolution could not be too far behind.

Tiempos Nuevos sardonically reported that

> the inhabitants of Uruguay are traversing a period worthy of study by the best psychologists in the world. For some time now, we have been noting great novelties among all individuals affiliated with the various political and philosophical ideas. Batlle, who will cure everything as his admirers say, has been the cause of all the mental disorder among said individuals; beginning with some priests, liberals, socialists, and even a few so-called anarchists, all have weakened in their convictions and have embraced the situation as a lifesaver. There was a bit of everything. One deputy that a few days earlier had resigned as a Blanco announced his candidacy as a liberal; a man of letters that up until yesterday had been an anarchist, seeing that deputy seats were up for grabs, said that he had "evolved" and declared himself a liberal, presenting his candidacy.[32]

The novelty of anarcho-batllismo was such that *Tiempos Nuevos* republished a column from the Chilean newspaper *Luz Astral* that had heard of the development. It read in part: "ANARCHISTS—A telegram from Uruguay informs us that the anarchists of Montevideo have agreed to support the presidential candidacy of Batlle y Ordóñez." The newspaper appeared incredulous, saying that they had also recently received an anarchist pamphlet by the libertarian group *Nuevos Rumbos* announcing the imminent end of "all the nobles and bourgeoisie, including the politicians."[33] Ironically, anarcho-batllistas were arguing that they were supporting Batlle's candidacy precisely because it would spell the imminent end of the landed aristocracy, the bourgeoisie, and (at some point down the road) the politicians. Still, the internal conflicts of Uruguayan anarchism appeared to be raising some eyebrows abroad. Ten days before the presidential election, *Salpicón* devoted its nineteenth and final issue to Batlle, with laudatory articles, a poem, and a full-cover portrait of the Colorado leader. Contributors to the issue formed a *Who's Who* of anarcho-batllismo. The most important essay was the opening column by Leoncio Lasso de la Vega himself. Far less argumentative than in his earlier article, Lasso de la Vega abandoned himself to unrequited emotion. "This time—only time in my life—" he declared, "a politician has *completely* captivated me. Yes, completely; because the great conductors of peoples have only fascinated my mind. . . . That *good man* has captivated me, because he has taken possession of my mind and heart at the same time." Batlle's second presidency was a Second Coming, the advent of social redemption, and it beckoned, "suffer the proletarians to come unto me!"[34]

Alberto Lasplaces was a poet, educator, and journalist who contributed to libertarian newspapers such as *La Acción Obrera* and *Solidaridad*. Living in Spain at the time of Francisco Ferrer's arrest, Lasplaces interviewed the political prisoner a mere six days before his execution. Arrested shortly thereafter by Spanish authorities for allegedly inciting opposition to the government, he left for France as soon as charges were dropped.[35] Presumably his article, entitled "My Creed," was written abroad and reflects a language very similar to that of Lasso de la Vega. "I have never had political convictions," he began. "Politics, with its love of lies and hypocrisies, with its elevation of mediocrities; with its foundations based on violence and brutishness, causes me—simply put—revulsion. I cannot understand how certain people that claim to be honorable dedicate themselves to it." But just like Lasso de la Vega, Lasplaces reaffirmed that Batlle was a different sort of politician. "And all of us partisans of those new horizons and promising futures should be with that man, all enemies of stagnation and stasis. We, the youth, that still have our eyes fixed on a marvelous ideal, should form a brilliant honor guard to surround Batlle—not with a ring of iron but with a circle of hearts and a crown of minds."[36]

Ovido Fernández Ríos was another heterodox radical. Also a poet and journalist, Fernández Ríos mingled with anarchist intellectuals and, beginning in 1910, edited *La Semana*, a magazine dedicated to literary and cultural critiques. Several anarchist intellectuals (including Lasplaces and Lasso de la Vega) made a part of their living publishing in such bohemian and liberal (but not radical) publications. About the time he took up *La Semana*'s editorship, Fernández Ríos drifted toward batllismo. Enlisting in Batlle's camp proved to be financially beneficial. He became co-editor of *El Día* and later embarked on a long career in national politics; he served as secretary to President Feliciano Viera (Batlle's successor in 1915) and was elected several times to the Chamber of Deputies. Also employing religious language and symbolism, Fernández Ríos used his article to preempt (or perhaps respond to) charges of being a sell-out, saying, "And this is what happens to Strong men that, carrying the truth on their lips and enthusiasm in their hearts, cannot applaud nor defend Batlle without having their ears buzzing with the sound of injurious darts and angry murmurs coming from tattered and impotent souls."[37]

Without necessarily imputing the personal motivations for their switch to anarcho-batllismo, it is an inescapable conclusion that most high-profile defectors experienced career advancement and often upward economic mobility. Froilán Vásquez Ledesma Jr. was apparently one of the only exceptions. He had a long history of journalistic endeavors in liberal, anticlerical, and anarchist publications both in Montevideo and the countryside including *La Reforma*, *El Baluarte*, *Despertar*, *La Acción Obrera*, *La Nueva Senda*, and *El Surco*. His journalism ran him afoul of the law twice (one sent him to prison), both times for possible libelous accusations of priestly sexual misconduct. Also a poet, Vásquez Ledesma contributed to the *Salpicón* issue verses welcoming Batlle's return from Europe and (expected) second presidency: "Because if yesterday you knew how to expand your fame / As sincere warrior, the people today beg / For liberation which motivates and exalts you!"[38]

The final and most distinguished contributor was, of course, Leoncio Lasso de la Vega. At the time of this controversy he was in his late forties, a member of radical intellectual circles in Europe, Argentina, and Uruguay. In Uruguay, he was a famous writer, poet, and journalist, contributor to several important literary, anticlerical, and political newspapers and magazines. Anarcho-batllismo would be his final political adventure; he passed away in 1915 just prior to passage of the eight-hour law.[39]

In most cases anarcho-batllistas were highly visible and respected anarchists, which made their departure all the more painful and surely attracted others to the new faction. Lasso de la Vega certainly falls in this category. So too did Ángel Falco, a celebrated poet and orator and a prominent propagandist for the libertarian cause, whose efforts earned him the title "paladin of anarchism." He pledged his support for Batlle's presidency during the 1910 electoral campaign. Other defectors included Edmundo Bianchi, a poet and prolific journalist. Even Adrián Troitiño, a long-time anarchist militant in both Uruguay and Argentina, while not won over to anarcho-batllismo, departed the libertarian ranks in 1913 by advocating that workers enter the electoral arena to support the most progressive politicians; he published these opinions in Batlle's privately owned newspaper, *El Día*. He eventually became a member of the Socialist Party. Even the highly regarded writer, orator, and militant Virginia Bolten—veteran of libertarian struggles in Uruguay and Argentina and perhaps the most famous anarcha-feminist in the Río de la Plata region—also expressed sympathy for batllismo although she never abandoned radicalism.[40]

In terms of experience in and knowledge about labor politics, Francisco Corney Plana was arguably anarchism's greatest defector and a boon to Colorados and Uruguay's police apparatus. Corney had risen to prominence as the general secretary of the FORU in 1906. But his authoritarian behavior precipitated the formation of a committee in 1910 to circumvent his direction of the federation.[41] In 1915 or 1916 Corney began working for the notorious Montevideo chief of police, Virgilio Sampognaro, informing on individuals who had once been his comrades. He also used his influence to steer workers toward José Batlle and the Colorado Party. The first instance of such political shepherding took place during the 1911 general strike. Then, in January 1917, Corney appears to have given a speech encouraging workers to give their support in the upcoming elections to President Feliciano Viera, the Colorado Party, and its head, José Batlle. A handwritten copy of the speech, signed by the author, wound up among Sampognaro's reports and letters from Corney. Other archival evidence suggests a high degree of coordination with the chief of police to infiltrate labor unions and guide workers over to batllismo. Overcome with guilt, Corney took his own life in 1921.[42]

Orthodox anarchists reacted initially through *Tiempos Nuevos* and, after that paper closed in 1911, through *Anarkos* in 1912. But the greatest response to anarcho-batllismo was the newspaper *El Anarquista*, born in 1913. The paper was founded by Antonio Marzovillo and Juan Borobio, two anarchists who had been involved in the early polemics around political participation within the libertarian community. Nearly every single article in its surviving nine issues references the factional split within anarchism. The newspaper decried the flirtations of many anarchists with batllismo and even reported that some had wandered into the Blanco camp! The paper argued, with some hyperbole, that anarcho-batllismo threatened to extinguish anarchism in Uruguay altogether. Columnists reported with alarm that those who had been "steadfast anarchists" now take part in "demonstrations in favor of the Constitutional Reform; anarchists are visible in political clubs; anarchists proclaim loudly the advantages of legal reformism."[43] Some were even gaining employment through their new political connections.[44] As for the issue of reform, the newspaper restated what had long been anarchist positions: politicians, including Batlle, were either incapable of or unwilling to seriously challenge capitalism. Even if labor protections passed, they would not be enforced; labor movements would demobilize in anticipation that progressive politicians would force compliance with the law, only to be chronically disappointed. Reformism was a chimera—a delusion and a monstrous distortion that threatened working-class organization.

Eschatology and "Revolutionary Urgency"

Why this sudden and dramatic split between orthodoxy and pragmatism? Certainly there had been incentives and early signs of tension over anarchist cooperation with the state. A faction of state officials from both parties—under duress at times given the increasing acuteness of the social question—had for some years attempted to give substantial protections and improvements to workers. After comparative freedom of organization and struggle during the first Batlle administration, President Williman and Colonel West had, at least for a few years, quashed the labor movement. The extraordinary constraints radicals faced in Argentina during 1910 may have also factored into the anarcho-batllistas' calculus. Could Uruguay ever become Argentina? Now Batlle was coming back for a second term and with him greater potential for activism. All of that might have been incentive enough. But given that examples exist of similar accommodations between anarchists and state officials—all within about thirty years of each other—from Europe to the Middle East to Latin America, perhaps something more was afoot.

During the Mexican Revolution, Mexico City anarchists associated with the Casa del Obrero Mundial made a critical alliance with Venustiano Carranza; in exchange for promises of a favorable postrevolutionary political environment (including some labor protections) anarchists joined, fought alongside, and, most importantly, held Mexico City for the *caudillo*. In fact, they organized "Red Batallions" and contributed over ten thousand troops to the Constitutionalist forces. Carranza kept his side of the bargain until he felt his position secure and no longer in need of anarchist support. In late 1915, when anarchist unions went on strike in opposition to the Constitutionalist government's new restrictive and inadequate labor laws, Carranza responded with a heavy hand: he repressed anarchists and patronized new government-friendly unions. Mexico's welfare state, then, developed as the government stifled the more radical elements of the working class.[45]

In Argentina, the scholarly literature provides two examples of an anarcho-batllista-like faction. Historian Juan Suriano speaks of a "revolutionary urgency" among radicals that at times pulled some into mainstream politics. He also points to the larger problem of intellectuals defecting from anarchism in the early twentieth century, especially with the possibility of upward mobility through a government job, a post at a mainstream newspaper, or an academic appointment. Despite the prominence of intellectuals as orators, leaders, and the public face of anarchism, such frequent defections created "an extremely weak link between intellectuals and the anarchist movement" that probably hurt the latter in the long run. There were similar disconnections in Uruguay at the time.[46]

In 1916, just as state reforms had begun to pass in Uruguay, newly enfranchised workers in Argentina propelled the Radical Party to power. Populist Hipólito Yrigoyen won the presidency and, like the traditional Uruguayan parties, sought to pacify labor conflicts and build a political base among workers by extending protective legislation. As Joel Horowitz discovered in Argentina, anarchist-influenced syndicalists became the faction Yrigoyen most preferred to negotiate with, since both the president and these workers were pragmatic and preferred "informal relationships." Moves toward a welfare state came to a halt when Yrigoyen found it politically difficult to continue supporting labor during the post–World War I strikes. He quickly turned to repression, which culminated during the Semana Trágica (or Tragic Week), when police and right-wing gangs killed hundreds of workers. In 1923, when Argentina's second Radical president, Marcelo Alvear, and his allies attempted to establish a pension system, most workers, including syndicalists, actually joined employers in opposing state-sponsored pensions and went on strike. The Semana Trágica, perhaps, had taught workers to be wary of government intervention; workers rejected a pension system using arguments very similar to those made by orthodox anarchists in Uruguay against labor reforms.[47]

In Palestine, the kibbutz movement of the first (and even the second) Aliyah were heavily influenced by anarchism, especially by the writings of Gustav Landauer and Leo Tolstoy. Libertarian values have remained central to the internal organization of the *kibbutzim*. However, as historian James Horrox explains, while egalitarian and solidaristic values have persisted in kibbutz life, such communities did not extend this treatment to neighbors; members of the *kibbutzim* participated in the creation of the Israeli state with all the accompanying atrocities. It would be a stretch to say that anarchists participated in the creation of the Israeli state. But it is fitting to claim that the explicitly anarchist-influenced kibbutz movement colluded, at a moment of crisis, with a project of occupation—a tragic departure from libertarian socialist values.[48]

Far less controversial, one can see the alliance anarchists made with the Spanish Republic during the civil war against fascism as a pragmatic decision made in a moment of crisis. Given these examples, we can conclude that, in Uruguay as in other countries, anarchism in the early to mid-twentieth century proved to be a malleable ideology responsive to exigency, extraordinary need (revolution, resettlement), or opportunity (populism). Like Marxism (and even early radical republicanism), anarchism was a product of the Enlightenment—a movement that, as Richard Day has pointed out, was given to apocalyptic and eschatological politics: politics of the moment.[49] Perhaps we can push further and argue that the Enlightenment itself drew inspiration from thousands of years of Christian, Jewish, and Islamic eschatological traditions: Judgment Day, the Day of Redemption, the Second Coming. These theologies posited a moment when the just and unjust would be separated as wheat from chaff, sheep from goats, and so on. Similarly, Marxists and anarchists held vigil for the Revolution, a final reckoning with landlords, employers, the clergy, and the state; it was a more or less linear progression toward a moment when the poor would inherit the earth, a moment to mark the permanent end of struggle. But after decades of waiting in expectation, with constant failed predictions of the imminent end of capitalism and the state, anarchists in Uruguay, Argentina, Mexico, Palestine, and Spain attempted to hasten the Revolution by making tactical exceptions to basic ideological tenets. In this context, we should not see an alliance between anarcho-batllismo and the government of Batlle as an anomaly.

A typical pep talk illustrates the eschatological character of anarchist discourse. In 1905, from the pages of *El Obrero*, Virginia Bolten tried to fan the flames of insurrection. "To destroy is to create!" she said. "Smash without fear of going too far; give blow upon blow to the terrible Babel that contains in itself all degenerations and crimes. Your perseverance is your only possible salvation and will soon give you triumph; if you lose heart in the work, the setbacks will multiply."[50] The anxiety of an activist leaps from the pages: Bolten fears that, even at a time of extraordinary labor agitation and relative success, workers will squander the opportunity. She fears burnout. And the politics of the moment coupled with the images of "Babel" versus "salvation" match the general apocalyptic message of a revolutionary eschatology. It is hard to imagine sustaining energy and determination of this level for too long. It is perhaps no wonder that less than a decade later one could count Bolten, as at least, a cautious anarcha-batllista.

Mediation and Intercession

In late June 1910 *El Día* made the surprising announcement that the Labor Office had been charged with drafting a bill to create a pension system for all workers; the draft would be submitted to the Executive Branch and then on to Parliament. Bureaucrats sought feedback on details such as how deductions would be made to workers' wages. And in order to address these important issues, "nothing has seemed more appropriate than to consult about the unknowns with union delegates who represent the interests of the working classes." The newspaper reported that the Labor Office had already held a preliminary meeting with the Construction Workers Resistance Society (Sociedad de Resistencia Obreros Albañiles). "These delegates proved to be decided supporters of the proposed law although they stated their opinion that [the bill] should not be written with the character of absolute obligation since they believe that the most ample liberty should be given on this matter, giving workers the freedom to take advantage of the benefits of this law if they [individually] consider it advantageous."[51]

A week later the Construction Workers Resistance Society, through *El Día*, called for a summit involving all resistance societies to be held two days later at their center in order to formulate a response to the Labor Office's request.[52] Following the meeting, the societies issued a statement saying that "considering that the Labor Office is a dependency of the State which in turn is a ramification of capital—fruit of the labor of the dispossessed and which in consequence eternally perpetuates the exploitation of man by man—[resistance societies] should not attend the gathering [with the Office] because it would imply intervening in the creation of laws that have no other object but to legalize the exploitation from which we want to emancipate ourselves."[53] On its surface, there is nothing surprising about the declaration. But a second glance reveals two powerful concerns. One, what happened to the construction workers? They had eagerly (and unilaterally) answered the Labor Office's call but after meeting with the other resistance societies decided not to break ranks. Two, aside from the orthodox antistatist rhetoric, the societies assembled expressed a new concern: that they did not wish to "legalize exploitation." In other words, at this historic moment when the state was extending its social duties, anarchists worried that new labor laws would give their own exploitation the additional force of law.

Interestingly, a few days later *El Día* printed a letter to the editor from a tailor, identified only as a "wage worker." He explained: "With great confusion I have read about . . . a resolution taken by a group of workers assembled in the secretariat of the Tailors' Union." By calling it a mere "group of workers," the tailor begins a process of discrediting the summit. Referring to the statement issued by the resistance societies, "I ask these titled delegates of the labor organizations if there have been any meetings of the different unions called so as to know the opinions of the majority of workers in order to operate with them in mind." He added that to his knowledge the only such meeting held to solicit such dispositions from the general membership was actually through the construction workers—the very group now being shut down by the other resistance societies. The respondent asked that the Labor Office ignore "such an unconsulted resolution through which the sacred right which exists equally for all of us [to have a voice] is denied."[54]

Questions abound about this submission to *El Día*. Who was this worker? Why did he not identify himself by name? Did he fear intimidation? And, of course, was this a real letter from a disgruntled union member at all? The letter could be genuine in the sense that it called out what appeared to be authoritarian tendencies among anarchist leaders eager to stamp out reformism within resistance societies. However, it could have been a forgery, attempting to marginalize opponents of mediation.

Officials ultimately drafted the bill without any input from labor representatives, resistance societies, other labor unions, or workers in general.[55] A valuable story in itself, the debacle over pensions illustrates yet another instance of state attempts to bring workers to the negotiating table. It was subtle, benevolent sounding, not pressured (meaning it did not come during a strike), and one resistance society took the bait. But the state could still act unilaterally and demonstrate, as Representative Roxlo had put it in 1905, that "the State and the legislators worry about [workers'] destinies." Later *El Día* covered for the Labor Office by arguing the benefits of benevolent state tutelage, preparatory to more democracy.[56]

By early May 1911 labor organization had finally recovered from its three years of stagnation. FORU celebrated its third labor conference around May Day, holding an enormous parade and demonstration. Meanwhile, major discontent between workers and management at the British- and German-owned street-car system brewed, leading to a strike on May 12 that—following the betrayal of the companies once the strike ended in negotiation—in turn provoked Uruguay's first general strike. All resistance societies within FORU immediately pledged support for the trolly workers and most initiated solidarity strikes. One day after FORU's third conference and eighteen days before the general strike (also a full two months and four days after his reelection), Batlle requested from Parliament a copy of his original labor bill introduced in the dusk of his first administration. He wanted to make some revisions to it before asking Parliament to reconsider it. He resubmitted it to the General Assembly on June 11, following the largest labor action to date in Uruguay's history.[57]

The general strike of 1911 has been touted as a pivotal demonstration of labor's power. And it certainly was. Solidarity was at an all-time high and most resistance societies came to the aid of the trolley workers. The city was shut down for three days. As the press reported, there was an air of general awe felt by workers, city residents, and the government. Batlle expressed his support—within the bounds of law—for the strike, provoking a critical moment of rapprochement between president and workers, a moment facilitated by an anarcho-batllista.[58]

On May 22, after the thirty-seven resistance societies that made up FORU formally declared the general strike, a large group of workers jubilantly marched through the city. A contingent of about one thousand people broke off and made their way to the presidential palace, chanting "Long live the general strike!" and "Long live Batlle!" The president appeared on the balcony, receiving thunderous applause. It was at this moment that Ángel Falco climbed a tree near the palace and entreated Batlle on behalf of workers. "The people that know you," he said, expect that you will maintain your customary attitude during this emergency before the battle taking place between the strikers and the corporations; from you, who has led the country down the paths of liberty, . . . you cannot remain indifferent to this movement. [FORU], genuine representative of workers . . . , has declared the general strike, not against the government and the authorities that have remained neutral as in other countries, but rather against the companies who have not respected agreements made with employees. And so this rally salutes you . . . shouting Long live Batlle y Ordóñez!

The president responded diplomatically, illuminating the limits of labor struggle.

The laws and the order that I am obligated to maintain due to my position do not allow me to participate in your struggle. I am charged with safeguarding order and the rights of all citizens. . . . And so, the Government will guarantee your rights so long as you stay within the confines of legality. Organize yourselves, unite and try to conquer the betterment of your economic conditions with the assurance that you will never have an enemy in the Government so long as you respect order and law.[59]

Batlle's indication that he blessed the strike added the critical caveat that his support for it (police "neutrality" in this case) would end at the first sign of disorder—attacks on property, violence, and so on. And in order to make that threat patent, he mobilized three battalions of the military (one infantry, one cavalry, and even one artillery), deployed at every major intersection of the city, especially along the main stretch—18 de Julio—fully armed and accompanied by machine guns. On May 23 striking workers attacked with rocks one trolley operating in defiance of the strike. Police responded violently and wounded several in the scuffle. Though the resistance society gained important concessions (including the eight-hour workday and union recognition), the costs of the strike in the long run to trolley workers were enormous. The managers of the trolley companies maintained a level of hostility that translated into constant maneuvering against workers, heightened surveillance, and punitive firings. Solidarity strikers fared worse as dozens of them lost their jobs, and eighty-five workers were jailed by police and faced legal prosecution.

It was within these limitations that the state deployed mediators; the media also attempted to provide arbitration. Representative Héctor Gómez was the main negotiator during the strike. He was the vice president of the Círculo de Prensa (the Press Circle). FORU accepted the mediation, for which it was heavily criticized after the strike ended. The stakes were very high and perhaps most were willing to put principles aside for a major tactical victory.[60] Reformism within anarchist circles, which had first appeared in 1905, had taken firm root ideologically among anarcho-batllistas and tactically among resistance societies.

The Consequences of Reform

These reformist tendencies, among anarchists and workers generally, would persist as legislators started passing labor laws beginning in 1914. In 1918 universal male suffrage became part of the new constitution. But conservative elements had generally regrouped and further reforms became politically difficult, though not impossible. The election of Feliciano Viera, a moderate Colorado, in 1916 constituted what historians have termed "Viera's halt," though this is somewhat overstated. Labor laws continued to pass, even if at a slower pace. As orthodox anarchists predicted, the newly passed laws were ineffectual, at least at first. Sometimes labor legislation actually hurt workers. For instance, the eight-hour workday law passed in 1915 had so many defects that it provoked, on implementation, the largest and bloodiest strikes Uruguayans had witnessed up to that time. In some cases the law contained ambiguities that employers could and did exploit. Then again, when the industry was too powerful—as was the case with the meat packing plant Frigorífico Uruguay—the state could not enforce the law. In other cases the law was effectively enforced but, since legislators had failed to pass an accompanying minimum wage law, many workers lost a substantial percentage of their daily earnings. It took unprecedented action by workers to enforce the law, make up for its inadequacies, or raise wages to compensate for it. In other words, workers, uneasy as they might have been about statism, strove to make law work for them, thus developing an even greater stake in the state. One aspect of Uruguay's state reforms stands out from many counterparts in Latin America: unions, even workers in general, did not become tied to a particular political party.[61] I suggest that we attribute this peculiarity to Uruguay's complex anarchist heritage, still strong while the ink dried on the first labor laws.

Notes

1. *Despertar*, July 1905, 7–8; *El Libertario*, May 20, 1905, 4; *El Libertario*, July 10, 1905, 2–3 (small portions of this column are damaged and illegible); and *El Libertario*, July 14, 1905, 2–3.

2. *El Libertario*, May 20, 1905, 4; and *El Obrero*, May 20, 1905, 3.

3. Joel Horowitz argues that Argentine president Hipólito Yrigoyen was a populist in the way that we think of presidents Lázaro Cárdenas (Mexico), Getúlio Vargas (Brazil), and Franklin Delano Roosevelt (United States) as populists. He served his first term as president from 1916–1922 and attempted to establish informal alliances with labor unions. He also attempted to pass modest labor reforms. Horowitz, *Argentina's Radical Party*.

4. Carlos Zubillaga, "El batllismo."

5. Fernándo López D'Alesandro uses "anarco-batllismo" to describe this anarchist faction. It is unclear, however, whether López D'Alesandro coined the term. López D'Alesandro, *Historia de la izquierda uruguay*, 105–13; Rodríguez Díaz, *Los sectores populares en el Uruguay*, 24–28; and Suriano, *Paradoxes of Utopia*, 197–99.

6. Zubillaga, *Pan y trabajo*, 37–38.

7. See also Barrán, *Los conservadores uruguayos*, 101n49.

8. *Diario de Sesiones*, Tomo 175, May 3, 1904, 326–27.

9. *Diario de Sesiones*, Tomo 180, February 23, 1905, 81–89.

10. *Diario de Sesiones*, Tomo 182, June 24, 1905, 86–95.

11. Vanger, *José Batlle y Ordóñez*, 207–8.

12. The following anarchist newspapers were known to be in operation: *La Rebelión* (1902–3), *El Obrero Panadero* (1901–3), *El Obrero Sastre* (1903), and *Resistencia Gremial* (1903). *El Obrero* was in existence since 1904 but only 1905 was available for viewing at the Biblioteca Nacional.

13. *La Federación*, June 15, 1911, 1. Their translation of Kropotkin's famous phrase incorporated a religious term: "Que vuestra *redención* ha de ser de vosotros mismos" (emphasis added). The socialist newspaper *La Voz del Obrero* borrowed a different rendition of the quote for their masthead. The original comes from "Act for Yourselves," *Freedom*, January 1887, as quoted in Kropotkin, *Act for Yourselves*, 32.

14. For some iterations of these positions, see *La Acción Obrera*, September 20, 1908, 1; and *El Anarquista*, April 16, 1913, 1–2.

15. *El Obrero*, March 11, 1905, 2.

16. Emphasis in the original. *El Libertario*, March 5, 1905, 1.

17. *Despertar*, August 1905, 3–4.

18. *Despertar*, July 1905, 5–6; "La Ley del Trabajo," *Despertar*, August 1905, 3–4; *Despertar*, October 1905, 3–4; *Despertar*, February 1906, 5–6; *Despertar*, April and May, 1906, 9–10; *Despertar*, June 1906, 6–7; and *Despertar*, August 1906, 3–4.

19. *Departamento de Policía de la Capital: Prontuario Consultivo Policial*, Tomo I, 358–64.

20. Ibid.

21. Vanger, *José Batlle y Ordóñez*, 207.

22. *El Obrero*, June 24, 1905, 1; and Vanger, *José Batlle y Ordóñez*, 207–11.

23. Vanger, *José Batlle y Ordóñez*, 205–7, 210–11.

24. The Dreyfus Affair centered around French Army officer Alfred Dreyfus who, in 1894, was found guilty of treason. The case ignited worldwide condemnation of the French political system by those who saw in the affair scapegoating, anti-Semitism, and rampant judicial injustice. Dreyfus was eventually acquitted.

25. Lasso de la Vega, ¡Yo acuso!.

26. *Diario de sesiones*, Tomo 208, February 18, 1911, 39–48.

27. *La Nueva Senda*, April 8, 1910, 1.

28. Lopez D'Alesandro, *Historia de la izquierda uruguaya*, 90–91; and Zubillaga, *Perfiles en sombra*, 115. This chapter owes much to Carlos Zubillaga's biographical sketches of hundreds of radicals, most of them otherwise lost to history.

29. Emphasis in the original. *Salpicón*, November 9, 1910, 2–3.

30. *Tiempos Nuevos*, December 10, 1910, 1, 8.

31. López D'Alesandro, *Historia de la izquierda uruguay*, 30–42.

32. *Tiempos Nuevos*, December 23, 1910, 3.

33. Ibid., January 15, 1910, 5.

34. Emphasis in the original. *Salpicón*, February 19, 1911, 1–2.

35. In his interview with Ferrer, the soon-to-be martyr paid Uruguay this compliment: "It is a beautiful Republic. Its sons are very advanced in the social sciences. . . . It must be a great people." Zubillaga, *Perfiles en sombra*, 113–14.

36. *Salpicón*, February 19, 1911, 4.

37. Ibid., 4; and Zubillaga, *Perfiles en sombra*, 87.

38. *Salpicón*, February 19, 1911, 4; and Zubillaga, *Perfiles en sombra*, 189–90.

39. Zubillaga, *Perfiles en sombra*, 114–16.

40. Ibid., 45–49, 68–71, 177–80.

41. Rodríguez Díaz, *Los sectores populares en el Uruguay del novecientos: Segunda Parte*, 43–45.

42. Archivo General de la Nación, Archivo de Virgilio Sampognaro, Caja 216, Carpeta 21. Hojas 1-7 are a copy of the speech; and Zubillaga, *Perfiles en sombra*, 81–84.

43. *El Anarquista*, April 16, 1913, 1.

44. Ibid., April 16, 1913, 3–4.

45. Hart, *Anarchism and the Mexican Working Class*, 126–41, 150–52, 154–55.

46. Suriano, *Paradoxes of Utopia*, 44, 86–89, 171.

47. Horowitz, *Argentina's Radical Party*, 96–117, 128–29.

48. Horrox, *A Living Revolution*.

49. Day, *Gramsci Is Dead*.

50. *El Obrero*, May 20, 1905, 3.

51. *El Día*, June 22, 1910, 4.

52. Ibid., June 29, 1910, 5.

53. Ibid., July 2, 1910, 6.

54. Ibid., July 6, 1910, 5.

55. Ibid., September 8, 1910, 4–5.

56. Ibid., September 30, 1910, 3.

57. *Diario de Sesiones de la H. Cámara de Representantes*, Tomo 207, May 4, 1911, 258; and ibid., Tomo 211, July 4, 1911, 2.

58. Rosenthal, "Streetcar Workers"; Rodríguez Díaz, *Los sectores populares*; and Vanger, *Model Country*, 122–40.

59. *El Siglo*, May 23, 1911, as quoted in Rodríguez Díaz, *Los sectores populares en el Uruguay*, 107–11.

60. Rodríguez Díaz, *Los sectores populares en el Uruguay*, 106, 114–15, 119–22.

61. Collier and Collier, *Shaping the Political Arena*, 453–56.

6

Rebel Soul

Cultural Politics and Cuban Anarchism, 1890s–1920s

KIRWIN SHAFFER

Cuban society and culture were in a state of flux just before, during, and following independence from Spain in 1898. Anarchists were one segment in a multigroup contested terrain in which people from across the political spectrum and from all classes took to the streets, workplaces, newspapers, halls of government, the page, and the stage to debate how a free Cuba should develop. This chapter explores how both Cuban- and Spanish-born anarchists from the 1890s to the 1920s waged a series of cultural battles via use of political symbolism, creation of alternative health and educational institutions, and production of novels, plays, and short stories. They used culture and focused on cultural issues in hopes of creating a new anarchist-defined Cuba in the decades following independence when other groups likewise struggled to put forth their vision of *cubanidad*, that is, what it means to be Cuban. Two leading activists—the Spanish-born Adrián del Valle and Cuban-born Antonio Penichet—were the principal literary warriors shaping the anarchist agenda in these culture wars.

Anarchists long have been known for their work within labor unions and as a voice of working-class agitation. But leadership roles in strikes, boycotts, and union organizations were just one dimension of the anarchist-led working-class struggle. Rather, by looking at anarchist cultural politics in Cuba, we see how limiting a focus on workplace actions and agendas can be in defining anarchist politics specifically and working-class politics generally. Instead, anarchist cultural struggles—aimed primarily though not exclusively at workers—illustrate the wide array of tactics that this segment of Cuba's working class engaged in to shape a new Cuba that would benefit laboring men and women.

The Cultural Politics of Cuban Independence and Identity

Anarchist internationalism was an important variant of a broader social-ist internationalism emerging around the world at the turn of the twenti-eth century. Anarchist internationalism did not mean an abandonment of "Cuban" reality for the implementation of some foreign defined concept. Rather, to anarchists, especially those following the reasoning of Russian revolutionary Mikhail Bakunin, one should support all local struggles try-ing to break free from outside domination. The local customs, language, and history were important features of local and regional autonomy. This "nationality," as Bakunin referred to it, had to be preserved.[1] To destroy it in the name of some outside notion of "internationalism" would be to impose yet another outer system of control and deny local autonomy and free decision making. Anarchists, then, adapted internationalist goals to fit the cultural realities of the island and thus "Cubanized" anarchism. To this end anarchists engaged in the cultural politics of independence-era Cuba, specifically focusing on the role of anarchists in the anticolonial war versus Spain, the postwar symbolic use of the war and its leading figure José Martí, the role of immigration, and how all should contribute to an anarchist defi-nition for a new Cuba.

First, many anarchists (whether born on the island or the peninsula) in the 1890s joined the war for independence. They believed it was the first step to liberate a people from colonial tyranny and hopefully the begin-ning of a social revolution that would promote freedom and equality for all peoples. In their famous 1892 "Manifiesto del Congreso Obrero," Havana's anarchist leaders placed the movement squarely on the side of separatist forces. The manifesto argued that there was no contradiction between the fight for anarchist freedom and the fight for independence from Spain be-cause one could not reject a collective people's desire to break free from colonialism.[2] While some anarchists would remain ambivalent about align-ing themselves too closely with what they saw as José Martí's largely bour-geois, nationalistic Partido Revolucionario Cubano, anarchists both on the island and in Florida rallied to the separatist cause, including the tobacco worker Enrique Creci. In 1895 Creci published pro-independence articles in *Archivo Social* and then joined the rebel army. He achieved the rank of captain before being captured and executed by Spanish forces.[3] While Creci had openly joined the rebel army, other anarchists worked clandestinely by smuggling arms, collecting funds, creating underground communications networks, and plotting assassinations of Spanish officials.[4]

In January 1899, shortly after the formal US military occupation of Cuba began, del Valle and his colleague Luis Barcia returned to the island from New York and began publishing the first post–Spanish era anarchist newspaper, *El Nuevo Ideal* (1899–1901), in which they criticized the US occupation, charging the United States had no intention of allowing Cubans to freely pursue their own freedom.[5] *El Nuevo Ideal* and its long-running successors *¡Tierra!* (1902–15, 1924–25), *Rebelión!* (1908–10), *La Voz del Dependiente* (1907–11), *El Dependiente* (1911–17), and *Nueva Luz* (1922–25)—along with two dozen shorter-lived papers—came to serve as the nerve centers of the movement where every aspect of Cuban politics and culture were scrutinized. In these papers, on tours, and in weekly meetings, anarchists focused on what they saw as the Cuban elite's abandonment of the social and land reforms promised by independence, the selling off of the island to international concerns, and the suppression of workers. In such an environment, anarchists asked just what was the meaning of independence and thus the meaning of a new Cuban "nation" when those who had fought for freedom were being repressed and ignored by the new government. When Cuban leaders repeatedly arrested or deported anarchists as "pernicious foreigners" throughout the three decades following political independence from Spain, anarchists claimed that they were the true representatives of the ideals of independence, having fought and died during the war while continuing to struggle to implement those ideals in the midst of government policies that sold off Cuba to international capitalists.[6] By the 1920s anarchists openly referred to Cuba as a feudal outpost of the United States that undermined Cubans' original goals for autonomy and social reform and further questioned the meaning of an independent Cuba.[7]

Creators of anarchist culture incorporated the important symbolism of the independence war and its aftermath into their fiction and cultural critiques of postwar Cuba. Del Valle used the war as a central backdrop in three short stories while the war played a prominent role in Penichet's two novels. In 1907 del Valle published his collection of short stories, titled *Por el camino*, which included "Amor del padre." The story centers on the conflict between a father (who is a colonel in the Spanish army) and his son (who is a captain in the revolutionary forces). An encounter between the two leads the father to ask his son how he could possibly betray Spain. The son, Carlos, responds that he was born in Cuba. The colonel rises, folds his arms and responds, "Yes, you were born in Cuba, but Cuba is part of Spain and my blood, Spanish blood, runs through your veins." Echoing the dominant anarchist position about the war dating from the 1892 "Manifiesto,"

Carlos responds, "Spanish blood! . . . blood has no nationality; it's human, only human. If I struggle against Spain, it is not because I hate her, but because I love freedom for the place where I was born. . . . I fight for Cuba's freedom just as I would fight for the freedom of any oppressed people."[8]

However, over the decades, as anarchists found themselves increasingly persecuted by one Cuban government after another, both del Valle and Penichet would create characters and scenarios that were less supportive of a war that had helped to usher in politicians who repressed anarchists. In both his novella *Tiberianos* and his short story "El fin de un marinero," del Valle revisited the war and railed against patriotic militarism. For instance, in *Tiberianos*, the main character, Miguelillo, is a Spaniard by birth but supports the separatist cause. He flees to New York in the early 1890s (just as del Valle did) but comes to anguish about the war. While Miguelillo supported "those who aspire for a society of truly free and equal men, united by ties of solidarity," and while he is happy that Spain ultimately lost the war, he says the true losers were Cuban, Spanish, and North American mothers who lost sons in the service of patriotic violence.[9] This same sentiment echoes through "El fin de un marinero," set during the first major battle of the war after US forces intervened. Del Valle's narrator laments the death of a young Spanish soldier who dies in a US army hospital bed, "villainously murdered by that insatiable monster called national honor!" but also reflects on the fact that some poor mother sits "in some ignorant Spanish village," waiting in vain for a son she will never see again because he too died serving a state's nationalist pride.[10]

Penichet adopted a similar approach to the war in his novel *¡Alma Rebelde!, novela histórica*, which opens in 1895 with the beginning of the war. A young boy, Rodolfo, sits with his proseparatist mother, who tells him that one day he will grow up to obey a new Cuban government. When Rodolfo asks his mother what is the government, she responds that "the government is that which can; that which decrees, which controls the mayors and the judges and the soldiers and the police." Rodolfo responds, "OK, then the Spanish government orders them to kill and they have to obey, right?" "Yes, little one." "Ah, then we don't have to kill because we don't have a government. Right, mamá, that the Cubans don't have a government?" "Yes," his mother replies. "The Cubans have no government, but that is why the Cubans are fighting now—to have their own government. The Cubans want their own government, but the Spaniards won't let them." "But why do the Cubans want a government, mamá? So that they can order Cubans to kill just like the Spaniards?"[11] This opening exchange reflects not only how anarchists had evolved by the late 1910s to incorporate the symbolism of the war for independence into their cultural work but also how anarchists—after decades of government repression in which the state had come to dominate independence symbolism for its own political agenda—came to question the war and the abandonment of egalitarian and liberating goals that earlier anarchists had believed justified their support for separation from Spain.

A second component of Cuban anarchist culture and the cultural politics of independence revolved around how to use the image of independence forefather José Martí. Within a decade of his 1895 death, Martí had become a "national" symbol in Cuba. Different social sectors began referring to him as the "apostle," and most political factions in Cuba tried to link themselves to the political ideals and cultural image of Martí. His work in the Florida cigar factories in the early 1890s helped to bring the anarchist-dominated working class into the Partido Revolucionario Cubano, thus solidifying working-class Cuban support for the struggle versus Spain. His stated goals of social revolution following Spain's defeat were goals that anarchists saw as their own. Yet, in the years immediately following independence, anarchists asked in their newspapers and meetings whether Martí should be celebrated as one of their own. For instance, in response to the 1905 unveiling of the famous statue of Martí in Havana's Central Park, the editors of ¡Tierra!, while praising Martí as a good revolutionary, nevertheless questioned what might have happened had he lived. As one writer speculated—thus reflecting the general anarchist mistrust of all politicians—that since all governments and politicians were tyrannous, Martí probably would have become a tyrant too, if he had lived. Maybe it was better that Martí survived in marble as a cultural symbol of the war's ideals rather than if had he survived and proceeded to abandon those ideals like anarchists accused Cuban politicians of doing. At least as a statue he could serve as an inspiration for (not a repressor of) the masses.[12]

As years went by, anarchists adopted Martian symbolism as their own. They came to the conclusion that, rather than allow the elite to adopt the war's symbolism for their own purposes, anarchists would "liberate" these symbols from state exploitation. After all, anarchists argued, Martí's stated goals of liberation were more in accordance with anarchist goals of equality than with the policies of hierarchy, use of spies, and attacks on workers that the government waged in Martí's name. As one speaker told an audience in the town of Colón in 1907, "if Martí had lived, he would have been an anarchist."[13] In ¡Alma Rebelde! Penichet incorporated this symbolism.

As the boy Rodolfo grows into adulthood in the early 1910s, he begins to wonder if anarchist ideals might somehow be implemented through the government. Following the departure of the second US occupation government (1906–9), Rodolfo enters politics but quickly becomes disillusioned by politicians who he sees as working for their own financial interests while publicly stating that they labor for the electorate in the name of Martí. In the end, Rodolfo leaves politics to return to his job in a shoe shop. The narrator laments that the state and its treasury had become little more than a means for some Cubans to make a living rather than as a tool to improve society as Martí had intended.[14]

As Penichet became a leading anarchist figure in the growing labor movement of the late 1910s, he and others increasingly pursued antimilitarist agendas in their cultural productions, and sometimes Martian symbolism was employed against such state-sponsored militarism. As noted, successive Cuban governments had adopted José Martí to fit their various political agendas. However, in 1923 anarchists had enough of what they saw as deceptive uses of Martí in the island's political culture when one day Havana's public school children marched through the streets of the city. The anarchist weekly *Nueva Luz* (for which Penichet wrote) condemned the government-required, hours-long marching by children to honor Martí. As one columnist put it, this obligatory militaristic exercise forced upon children was less to honor Martí and more to honor Marte (Mars), the god of war.[15]

A third component of anarchist cultural politics and independence revolved around immigration. Cuba's leaders generally supported immigration for numerous reasons, including a desire to divide the workforce between Cubans and foreigners, flood the island with cheap labor, and whiten or "civilize" the workforce, as employers frequently expressed their beliefs that Spanish workers were better than Cuban.[16] While Cuban-born workers resented employers' preferences to import and hire foreign (especially Spanish) workers, anarchists urged caution. They noted that Spanish workers were like workers in most countries: generally powerless and doing what they could to put bread on the table. Anarchists urged Cuban workers to refrain from attacking Spanish workers for taking "Cuban" jobs.[17] Instead, Cuban workers needed to focus their anger first on the government, which encouraged labor migration into an environment with an inadequate number of jobs, and second on businessmen, who willingly hired foreign workers desperate to work for wages lower than those that Cubans demanded.[18] Ultimately, anarchists charged that the real threat to workers came from the elite in Cuba, and by fostering intra–working class conflict around false notions of "nationalism" (i.e., Cuban vs. foreign workers), the elite also undermined the social goals of better working conditions and equality promised by the war for independence.

During this time immigration became a small but important theme in anarchist cultural productions on the island. Penichet first addressed the anarchist understanding of immigration in his fiction in 1919. In that year immigrants to Cuba reached a high of over eighty thousand (with over thirty-two thousand of those coming from the peninsula) and nearly all of these came to work in fields, shops, and factories.[19] Yet the Cuban elite, as represented by the views of Joaquín Aramburu, longtime editor of the main daily newspaper, El Diario de la Marina, promoted another kind of immigrant: one with money who represented an expansion of business internationalism on the island.[20] These latter migrants became the nemesis in Cuban anarchist fiction while the average migrant day laborer became a noble worker in the cause of anarchist internationalism.

During the 1919 general strike in Havana, the government—increasingly feeling threatened by a rise in labor militancy—deported twenty-five labor leaders, including fourteen Spaniards, as "pernicious foreigners." Penichet escaped arrest by going into hiding, where he wrote La vida de un pernicioso. The novel's central character, Joaquín, criticizes government manipulation of patriotism and immigration, noting how Spanish workers are both desired by employers but also used to sow seeds of discord between Spanish- and Cuban-born workers on the island. Joaquín questions the whole concept of the "foreigner" since he himself had been born in Spain but also had fought against Spanish colonial rule during the war. He asks why so many working-class residents of the island—people who had actually fought for Cuban independence—were constantly harassed and abused while wealthy Spaniards with large amounts of capital were frequently heralded as heroes. As he recalls, "Of these Spanish descendants who still remain after independence, many appear to support liberty but have not at all reformed their feelings. However, the new arrivals [i.e., anarchist workers] bring with them influences of freedom. They come to help others be free; to help remove the economic yoke that asphyxiates Cubans."[21] Throughout the novel Penichet portrays elite Spanish residents in Cuba and exposes them along the way: one sells contraband, one runs a US corporation's interests and exploits workers, and another is a speculator. Which type of Spaniard did Cuba need, Penichet repeatedly asked: these types of "degenerates"— people like Lores, the speculator who gains his early fortune by plundering the pockets of dead soldiers during the war for independence and who now sleeps with other men—or Joaquín, the noble worker who strives to bring freedom to the popular classes while living with his former prostitute girlfriend?[22]

While anarchists never seriously challenged the state for control in post-war Cuba, they nevertheless continuously put forth their own radical inter-nationalist positions central to the evolving political culture on the island. The evolution of that political culture involved a series of battles over im-portant Cuban issues relating to the meaning of the war for independence, the manipulation of Martian symbolism, and disputes over immigration. Anarchist authors and movement leaders used these issues to frame a spe-cific anarchist interpretation of postindependence Cuban reality and in the process portrayed their movement as the true inheritors of the spirit of independence and even the ideals of José Martí. To this end, anarchists adapted the international movement's ideals to fit specific Cuban contexts and, they hoped, attract more followers by creating an anarchist-defined sense of *cubanidad* that would be egalitarian, internationalist, and commit-ted to all of the island's working masses, not just those born in Cuba.

The Cultural Politics of Health

The first US occupation of the island witnessed important improvements in health and sanitation, particularly a decline in malaria and yellow fever. Yet anarchists believed that "real" health reforms had to begin with the elimination of poverty. They stressed that the best approach to creating a healthy Cuba was to focus on improving living and working conditions, not treating symptoms with pills or injections after the fact. Consequently, health became a prominent issue in framing the ideological, institutional, and imaginative struggles that anarchists waged against Cuba's postwar leaders. They condemned what they saw as owner and state negligence re-garding unhealthy working conditions in the urban factories, cafés, restau-rants, and the expanding rural-based sugar complexes. According to this anarchist interpretation, the owners refused to spend the money necessary to improve lighting, airflow, and all-around quality of conditions. In the same vein, they argued that politicians and state agency functionaries were either powerless or unwilling to force owners to make such improvements, reflecting one more time how native and foreign capitalists had hijacked the social goals of independence.

Anarchists often infused their critiques of Cuba's health situation with descriptions of suffering women and children. For instance, they lamented how primarily Spanish owners of restaurants and cafés often hired children to work long hours in smoky, unclean conditions, with little to no fresh air or sunlight.[23] The blatant link to Spanish owners was designed to illustrate a recurring anarchist argument: that little had changed since the 1890s and that once again the Spanish bourgeoisie continued to exploit workers on the island. But when they also charged that current governmental health departments refused to play a more active role in regulating the health and sanitary standards of these establishments, they sought to show how the Cuban government was little better than the previous colonial regime. Young women and adolescent females often played important roles in the island's tobacco industry. They dominated the position of *despalilladora* (leaf stripper). Anarchists used health critiques here as well, claiming that conditions were so poor that many young women were forced to bend over barrels of leaf all day, thus "knotting up" their insides, which, they claimed, would lead to later problems bringing pregnancies to full term.[24] Thus, anarchists portrayed owner and state negligence as harmful not only to male workers but also to female and child laborers who would give rise to new generations of unhealthy Cubans, should changes not be forthcoming.

While some anarcho-syndicalists by the 1910s came to call for revolutionary parties and union-based direct action like boycotts and sabotage to force health reforms, anarcho-naturists emerged, urging Cuba's working poor to do what they could in the present to make themselves and their loved ones healthier. They promoted simple living, getting in touch with nature, vegetarianism, and an array of alternative therapies designed to maintain or regain one's health. To this end, anarchists created vegetarian restaurants. The most prominent one in Havana was next door to the offices of *¡Tierra!*. Many on the newspaper staff also worked in and held meetings at the restaurant, which was located in the heart of working-class Havana.[25] For those unable to make it to a restaurant, newspapers carried articles on vegetarianism and the health effects of different vegetables. Interestingly, del Valle edited the leading naturist newspaper, *Pro-Vida*, and Penichet wrote "vegetable columns" for *Nueva Luz*. Besides efforts to improve Cubans' diet, anarchists—in conjunction with non-anarchists—helped to create low-cost health institutes where individuals and families could get spa treatments, mild electric stimulation, hot and cold shower treatments, and solar therapy. The idea was to use such treatments to counter the effects of industrial civilization, which anarchists were convinced was taking humanity (and Cuba) ever further from what they viewed as nature's harmonious balances.[26]

Finally, anarcho-naturists led the challenge against the official medical establishment. Regular doctors had to be officially licensed by a government health board, but anarchists, being anarchists, hated all aspects of state bureaucracy, seeing officially licensed doctors as little more than scam artists who often refused to help the poor if they couldn't pay and sought to inject people with all kinds of serums rather than suggest better lifestyle changes.[27] When anarcho-naturist health practitioners suggested cheaper, more natural approaches to health care that average people could perform on their own, these doctors ran the risk of jail time. The best example was the anarcho-naturist homeopath Julián Magdalena. In 1911 local authorities in the western city of Pinar del Río arrested him for practicing medicine without a license. In such circumstances, Magdalena and others resorted to an assortment of political and religious rationales to justify their actions. Magdalena saw his persecution as similar to that of Jesus by the Romans or those targeted by the Inquisition in the Middle Ages.[28] Others saw themselves as victims of state-sanctioned centralization that impinged on freedom. All rejected the growing legal medical establishment's uses of required inoculations, not only because they saw them as unnatural but also because they saw such requirements as infringements on civil liberties and freedom of choice.[29]

As a leading figure in Cuba's anarcho-naturist movement, del Valle expressed interests in alternative health care and criticisms against urban industrial civilization in his fiction as well. Like many anarchists framing the poor health conditions on the island, del Valle portrayed cities like Havana as degenerate while praising the supposed transformative qualities of a simple, rural life, working the land in the fresh air and under the sun—all "natural" qualities lost when people toiled away 10–14-hour days in cramped, claustrophobic, dark factories and shops where fresh air was a luxury. In his stories del Valle suggested that if people fled the cities and began anew in the countryside, they would grow healthy both in body and spirit. A healthy Cuban would be a healthy revolutionary.

Del Valle's novella *Cero* is a prime example of this belief in nature's regenerative powers. The title character Cero lives a simple existence in the hills of rural Cuba. One day he encounters a disoriented man who has forgotten his name, so Cero names the stranger Cero-Cero. For the next thirteen years, the two men live and work side by side on Cero's small farm.

One day Cero-Cero recalls that he is Alonso Castillejos, president of a Havana bank and worth over $10 million. Yet when Alonso returns to Havana, his long-lost family, friends, and business partners keep their distance, causing him to have a nervous breakdown. Alonso writes to his old friend Cero about the disastrous return to urban, bourgeois life. Cero urges him to return to their little farm. Alonso fakes his own suicide and flees to the countryside where he resumes the name Cero-Cero. In the end, the elite capitalist banker is reborn a noble, simple Cuban *guajiro* (peasant).[30]

This regenerative life one could supposedly find in rural Cuba is central to del Valle's novella *El tesoro escondido*. Set on the fictitious island of "Bacuya"—fictitious but easily recognizable as Cuba—the story early on revolves around a pair of independence war veterans: Bertín and Bertón. Bertín regularly criticizes how the postindependence governments have sold off Bacuya's best lands to foreign capital, thus depriving residents of what he sees as an important goal of independence: "The land should be owned in common by the nation, given to those who wish to cultivate it, with the right only to those products derived from his labor."[31] He not only attacks the growing industrialization of rural Bacuya but also assaults the island's urban conditions. For instance, the two men travel to the capital city to visit Bertín's four grandsons. One is in the military, another is a priest, a third is a government lawyer, and the fourth is a medical official. Critical of both their chosen "bourgeois" professions and the urban decay he sees around him, Bertín unsuccessfully appeals to the medical official, Anselmo, to relocate his unhealthy-looking family to the health-inducing environs of the countryside. After all, he tells Anselmo, "What is the city but a dung heap? Every evil of the body and soul accumulates in the city. Here, one cannot think, breathe, nor live healthy."[32] Five years pass, and Bertín dies. His longtime companion Bertón sends all four grandsons letters, claiming that a buried treasure exists on the land; the first to find it can have it. All four soon arrive and begin to dig up the farm. After several days of honest manual labor, they uncover a box with a letter telling the four that the land now belonged to them since they had "labored" on it. However, only Anselmo expresses interest and accepts the contents of the "treasure chest." As the story concludes, he turns to Bertón and says "you will teach me to cultivate the land. You will be my *compañero*." In both short pieces, the land retains a mythical quality.[33] Laboring on it and deriving one's livelihood from such labor will rejuvenate and "baptize" the former urbanites into harmony with nature.

Both syndicalists and naturists framed their critiques and actions in order to help Cubans in the present while their "nemeses" in business, government, and religion ignored their earthly travails. At the same time, they portrayed Cuba's leaders as having abandoned a way of life that was in harmony with the natural order of the world, which anarchists saw as based on cooperation, mutual aid, and simple living. To this end, anarcho-naturists, led by their institutes and the literary endeavors of Adrián del Valle, framed a Cuba idyll that they believed should have existed following independence if those in power had followed the original goals of anarchist-defined social revolution. As a result, del Valle and his associates created an imagined Cuba for their readers, holding it up as a measure by which to judge how far removed from nature Cuba's postwar leaders had taken the island.

The Cultural Politics of Education and Gender

Following liberation from Spanish rule, education became an important cultural and political initiative on the island. Two waves of postwar US military occupation (1899–1902 and 1906–9) stimulated public school reforms, Protestant and Catholic religious schools expanded, and the Cuban government began taking an active role in the public educational system. During the first US occupation, the number of children enrolled in public schools grew from 30,000 in 1899 to 177,000 two years later.[34] The system—and its later modifications by Cuban governments—sought to provide both manual trades training designed to meet the different needs of rural and urban employers and civics training to make good republicans out of Cuban children. Yet not all parents were pleased with the overcrowded classrooms, the unmotivated and poorly paid teachers, or the lack of religious instruction. Thus, the number of private schools, mostly religious, grew from 316 in 1909 to 606 by 1925.[35]

Anarchists rejected both the religious and public school systems on a number of fronts. Founded on their traditional distrust of organized religions, anarchists attacked religious schools, portraying Catholic schools in particular as the embodiment of mysticism that frequently attacked sound, rational, scientific-based education. In his anticlericalist magazine *El Audaz*, del Valle suggested that Catholic schools fostered an increase in crime by the youth who attended such schools and portrayed these schools as being subservient to Rome.[36] In addition, anarchists saw Catholic schools as holdovers from the pre-independence era that reinforced an earlier form of educational tyranny.[37] They also had no love for public schools. They portrayed the Cuban state as using public education to indoctrinate students into a particular form of patriotic nationalism, that, according to anarchists, was merely a means to strengthen the rule of the capitalist elite, preserve a hierarchical system inherited from Spanish colonialism, and at the same time fashion in students an elite-defined sense of *cubanidad* reinforced by such symbolic practices as saying the pledge of allegiance, singing the national anthem, or saluting the Cuban flag. These *antibanderistas* further condemned public education, arguing that children were not helped to understand their rights nor did they receive effective training. While criticizing the curriculum, they also condemned the overcrowded classrooms and the bored, uncaring student bodies emerging from their schoolhouses every day.[38]

It was one thing to frame Cuban schools as upholders of an elite agenda for the island, but anarchists went beyond these critiques to create their own schools. Building on worker-run schools dating from before independence and the educational experiments of Francisco Ferrer in Spain, Cuba's anarchist-run schools went through two phases—the first a haphazard affair loosely organized by anarcho-communist groups from 1906–12, the second more coordinated and better financed by the anarcho-syndicalist influenced labor unions of the early 1920s. In both eras, schools followed Ferrer's coeducational model with a curriculum designed to allow students the freedom and flexibility to follow their interests and passions, coupled with occasional field trips to the countryside to study nature and to workplaces to see what could lay in store for their futures.

In the first phase, no formal process of rationalist education occurred until 1906, when workers founded the Centro de Estudios Sociales in the port city of Regla across the bay from Havana.[39] A Ferrer school was created there in 1908, with Miguel Martínez Saavedra soon arriving from Spain to direct the school at the urging of Ferrer.[40] Over the next four years, anarchists struggled to develop schools in Havana and elsewhere. Personal disputes, factional divides, and a large percentage of workers' limited contributions being directed to support the Mexican Revolution and other causes resulted in the Havana-area schools closing by late 1912.[41] By the early 1920s, as the labor movement surged under anarcho-syndicalist control, a new era of schools emerged. Anarchists, particularly Havana Workers Federation member Antonio Penichet, began working closely with socialists and communists to create an island-wide network of rationalist schools funded significantly by contributions from workplaces and unions such as the Havana Electric Workers Union and the Havana Workers Federation. To Penichet, the schools were central to creating a new Cuba, and in his influential *Tácticas en uso y tácticas a seguir*, the founding of rationalist schools was the final (and arguably his most important) strategy for revolutionaries: "While we do not have our own schools," wrote Penichet, "we will continue to see our future obstructed. We must save our children from becoming social debris. We must save the future with our cause."[42] Nevertheless, schools struggled for lack of stable funding, and they also suffered the same problems associated with the larger public school system, especially difficulty finding appropriately trained teachers. Furthermore, while the Federation school in Havana had nearly one hundred students in 1923, most schools did not attract enough children and their tuition.[43]

Consequently, anarchists created and staged alternative educational mediums to reinforce the schools' lessons while also reaching larger audiences. This revolutionary culture of novels, plays, poetry recitals, short stories, and songs was designed to put forth the movement's ideals and critique the larger social forces that impacted people's daily lives. Because women played a key role in the anarchist imagination, authors explicitly targeted women with their literary and performance culture. Anarchist authors portrayed women as victims and victimizers, depending on the particular message of the piece. But most importantly, authors held up women as "revolutionary mothers" who embodied an anarchist-defined natural harmony. Although it was questionable as to how successfully anarchists attracted women to the movement (few women served in leadership roles around the island, though some did serve on boards, in theater groups, and as teachers), their efforts were designed to portray a working mother who could function strongly and equally with men both inside and outside the home where she would further serve as a symbol of an emancipated humanity.

Women and children regularly took lead roles in weekly anarchist social gatherings, where audiences came to see them sing revolutionary anthems, recite poetry, and put on plays. The most frequently performed play was del Valle's "Fin de fiesta." This short, seven-scene play captured many anarchist themes, including worker solidarity, exploitative capitalists, and attacks on traditional religious or social customs, particularly regarding marriage. Elena, the daughter of wealthy factory owner Don Pedro, is in love with Julián, a worker from that factory. When her father arranges a marriage for his daughter, she seeks advice from the family priest who proceeds to tell her that she must accept her fate. Meanwhile, Julián and his coworkers go on strike, setting fire to Don Pedro's factory. When Don Pedro, with pistol in hand, confronts Julián outside the burning factory, Elena intervenes. In the ensuing struggle, Don Pedro accidentally shoots and kills his daughter. The female actors of this drama illustrated to female audiences the anarchist vision of bourgeois paternalism and the enslavement of marriage. Elena's character reflects more, though: a female martyr inspired by love and justice who sacrificed herself to save a worker.[44]

Penichet's play ";Salvemos el hogar!" continues the critical look at marriage and the conflict between a worker filled with anarchist consciousness and his children and wife, who relish vice, consumerism, and religious dogma. When Matías goes to hear working-class lectures, his family derides him for wasting his time. The workers at his factory soon go on strike, but the owners violently suppress it. Matías' wife and children are conceitedly pleased because they see strikes as foolish, but the wife, Magdalena, is also angry at the absence of wages coming into the home during the strike: "now I will not be able to buy the ribbons and scalloped lace to adorn my dress for the dance." Matías is distraught and considers abandoning the family until his friend Domingo intervenes. Domingo cautions Matías: "No, don't drive yourself to despair, Matías. Calm down. What is happening to you is happening to the majority of workers." Domingo urges him to bring home information on the workers' cause and take the family to the Workers Center to hear talks or see plays.[45] Thus, the play centers on the importance of bringing women into the anarchist cultural environment so that they can be enlightened on their proper roles in the family in order to create a revolutionary society.

While Cuban anarchists despised marriage, most nevertheless celebrated the importance of family and motherhood. As Penichet wrote in *Tácticas en uso y tácticas a seguir*, "First, it is necessary to triumph in the home and then triumph in society." Penichet viewed the home front as the basis for all social relationships, referring to the home as "the most pronounced origin of communism and its best field for experimentation."[46] Within this home, women played a revered role and anarchists regularly portrayed women as "revolutionary mothers" who would be necessary to lead the next generation into a new dawn of anarchist egalitarianism and freedom. This revolutionary mother imagery could be seen in cartoons, on newspaper mastheads, and particularly in del Valle's and Penichet's fiction. Take, for instance, del Valle's short story "En el mar; Narración de un viaje trágico." Survivors of a shipwreck wander the open sea in a small lifeboat. One of the survivors is an infant who is slowly starving due to lack of food on board and its mother having died in the wreck. A single woman, responding to her own maternal instincts and in a motherly moment, bares her breasts and offers her milk-less nipples to placate the child.[47]

While it was one thing for a woman to act "motherly," other anarchist fiction focused more directly on motherhood—both noble and otherwise. In *La mulata Soledad*, del Valle describes the independent, selfless Soledad, a young mixed-race mother. The daughter of anarchists, Soledad rejects dominant strands of island thought such as religious dogma, marriage as an institution for social advancement, and the related theme of black or mulatto women seeking to marry white men in order to "improve" the race and their own social standing. When Soledad becomes pregnant out of wedlock, she leaves her sewing job and takes on piecework in her home. Ultimately, her child's white father, Carlos—a young doctor-in-training who is being tutored by an anarchist doctor—returns to Soledad and the child after divorcing his wife. He dedicates himself to offering medical services to the poor and working class with Soledad by his side. Meanwhile, though never marrying, the couple lives together in an anarchist-defined "free union," with Soledad functioning as the family's revolutionary mother. The novel ends with their child pulling the three of them together with his arms around their necks. Soledad exclaims, "Look, Carlos, the knot that unites us. Stronger than the sacredness and legality of marriage," exemplifying Penichet's focus of the family as the basis for communism.[48]

In *¡Alma Rebelde!*, Penichet plays on this notion of revolutionary motherhood with a working-class woman doing what she can for the sake of her children. This is particularly evident in his character Rosa, the mother of Miguel, who is the main character Rodolfo's best friend. Miguel gets his girlfriend pregnant, and they consider an abortion. However, Rodolfo the anarchist says no, as does Rosa. She tells her son that once she too had considered having an abortion, but she is thankful that she carried the child to term because Miguel was that child. Abortion signifies an important issue concerning the anarchist paternalist notions of women's natural roles as mothers. As Penichet expresses through Rodolfo, no one has the right "to commit those mysterious murders that frequently occur with impunity. The child ought to be preserved for nobody knows what its designated mission is on the earth."[49] To these anarchists, abortion is murder and a violation of a woman's obligation to motherhood. Children have the same rights as adults, anarchists believed, and a mother's "persecution" of the fetus is equal to the government's persecution of innocents in society.

In fact, the woman who commits abortion is on par with other mothers who sell their young daughters into prostitution—another theme of women abandoning their roles as mothers. This becomes very evident in Penichet's short story "La venta de una virgen." The mother Jacinta embodies nearly every quality of a bad mother. After giving birth to her daughter Lucía, Jacinta denies her daughter fresh breast milk in order to sell herself as a wet nurse to the rich. To continue her "enterprise," she has more children. But she knows it would be impossible to continue this, so she schemes some more. Jacinta enters into a business arrangement with a wealthy man named Godínez. He pays her for the opportunity to take the young, prepubescent Lucía's virginity, which he ultimately does in a violent rape scene. Lucía is understandably distraught, and throws herself off the Malecón seawall on the edge of Havana harbor. Her suicide destroys Jacinta, but not because Jacinta has lost her only daughter; rather, she has lost her money-making enterprise.[50] Ultimately, such mothers—those who have abortions, those who sell their own children into slavery, those who mock their husbands and urge their children to mock their fathers for striving to build a better future—these women are the antithesis of anarchist revolutionary motherhood as represented by Penichet's Rosa or del Valle's Soledad. The latter are the models that women readers of these stories or attendees at performances would hopefully emulate in order to bring forth the new era of anarchist social relations in Cuba.

Conclusion: Anarchist Culture and Popular Intellectuals

Studies that focus on the culture of anarchism provide a more rounded view of anarchists, their relationships, and their missions than traditional approaches that look at anarchists mostly as one segment of the labor movement involved in strikes and other labor actions. Culture includes those aspects of a collective's lives that link or bond a society together through social interactions, intellectual inquiry, morality, and aesthetics at any given time. Daniel Levine calls for locating "critical social spaces . . . [that] provide arenas in which important events are remembered and, in some form, reproduced: parades, meetings, commemorations. This is where abstractions of 'human agency' take on concrete form in the work by men and women who, by their actions, make and remake culture: real people, not 'the people.'"[51] This is particularly relevant for understanding the anarchists who rejected participating in politics. Meetings, schools, health clinics, plays, and literature became useful cultural arenas for anarchists to challenge Cuba's hegemonic forces. Consequently, by studying the political conflicts surrounding larger cultural issues, we can better understand the discourses surrounding the evolution of a larger society's culture and how anarchists engaged in those cultural debates.

As Richard Sonn notes, anarchists worked extensively in the cultural environment where they found themselves "spreading the word by all possible means: by words, songs, and the personal example of a superior life, as well as by deeds."[52] Because anarchists throughout the international movement refrained from organizing mass political parties or even attacking the state by force of arms (or the ballot), cultural work was crucial. Fiction and theater became important tools to entertain and to educate. The creation of anarchist schools and health institutes offered real alternatives to state and church institutions. As Sonn further points out, sometimes "anarchist culture was a substitute for formal organization. Anarchists expressed their solidarity at a grassroots level, in the cafés and union halls, in anarchist libraries and schools, and through the anarchist press. In fact they were sometimes suspected of being more involved in living the revolution than in making one."[53] Cuba's leading anarchists believed that one had to live and work in the here and now to prepare the masses for that future revolution. Cultural work was basic to this preparation.

To best understand anarchist culture and its role in anarchist challenges, I suggest that we see the anarchists more as a "social movement" and less as part of the labor movement. Since the 1980s scholars have turned their attentions to how social movements "frame" their activities and agendas, or, put another way, how they assign meaning to and interpret themselves, their actions, and the worlds in which they operate and seek to make change. Taking from David Snow's definition of "framing processes," Doug McAdam and his colleagues refer to this process as "the conscious strategic efforts by groups of people to fashion shared understandings of the world and of themselves that legitimate and motivate collective action." The culture of social movements plays a key role in this approach because culture links "social construction and dissemination of new ideas." In this sense, how a movement and the movement's larger social context are framed is key to understanding the vision that movement leaders have of the present and their goal-oriented future.[54]

A central component of framing process analysis concerns the roles of popular intellectuals like del Valle and Penichet. While framing implies interpretation and a movement-defined construction of reality, it is mostly individuals who are responsible for putting forth these central frames. In Cuba, Penichet and del Valle were the main framers through their leadership of different strands of the movement, their roles as leading editors of major movement newspapers, and their preeminent positions as the leading literary figures of the movement. As much as anyone else, they articulated the goals of the anarchist movement in Cuba, helped to frame the agenda, and shaped the anarchist response in the culture wars to define what it meant to be Cuban. These frames not only cast an anarchist vision on the cultural, political, and social realities of early-twentieth-century Cuba but these frames were also "diagnostic" and "prognostic," giving Cuba's working-class readers and viewers ways to explain their lives and suggestions on how to rectify problems they experienced. While anarchists played key roles in Cuban labor unions and workplace actions in the two decades after independence from Spain, their cultural work was every bit as vital as strikes and other traditional labor tactics in redefining working-class politics and visions on the island.

Notes

1. Dolgoff, *Bakunin on Anarchism*, 401–2.

2. *El movimiento obrero cubano*, 81.

3. Cabrera, "Enrique Creci," 148–49; and Casanovas, *Bread, or Bullets!*, 227.

4. Fernández, *El anarquismo en Cuba*, 42–45.

5. *El Nuevo Ideal*, February 4, 1899, 1.

6. *¡Tierra!*, November 26, 1914, 1; *El Dependiente*, November 26, 1914, 2; and Cabrera, *Los que viven*, 157–64.

7. *Nueva Luz*, February 15, 1923, 11; *El Progreso*, November 29, 1924, 3; and *¡Tierra!*, November 27, 1924, 1.

8. del Valle, "Amor de padre," 111.

9. del Valle, *Tiberianos*, 21–28.

10. del Valle, "El fin de un marinero," 67–69.

11. Penichet, *¡Alma Rebelde!*, 14.

12. *¡Tierra!*, March 4, 1905, 2–3.

13. Ibid., June 12, 1907, 2.

14. Penichet, *¡Alma Rebelde!*, 65–68.

15. *Nueva Luz*, February 1, 1923, 2.

16. Clark, "Labor Conditions in Cuba," 30–31, 685, 788–89; Naranjo Orovio, "Trabajo libre," 751, 760–63; and García Álvarez and Naranjo Orovio, "Cubanos y españoles," 109–14.

17. *¡Tierra!*, June 20, 1903, 3; June 27, 1903, 4.

18. Ibid., June 25, 1904, 1; October 29, 1904, 2; February 11, 1905, 2; February 8, 1908, 2; and November 14, 1908, 3.

19. *Censo de la República de Cuba. Año de 1919*, 173–76.

20. *El Diario de la Marina*, January 6, 1909, 3.

21. Penichet, *La vida de un pernicioso*, 37.

22. Ibid., 133.

23. *Luzbel*, July 15, 1904, 7.

24. *El Nuevo Ideal*, February 25, 1899, 3.

25. *Pro-Vida*, January 1915, 1–2; March 1917, 6–7; June 16, 1917, 4; and September 16, 1917, 6.

26. Ibid., February 1915, 1; and June 1915, 4.

27. Ibid., June 1915, 3–4.

28. *La Voz del Dependiente*, May 11, 1911, 1; June 1, 1911, 2–3; and June 6, 1911, 2–3.

29. *Pro-Vida*, February 1915, 1–2; and March 1915, 4.

30. del Valle, *Cero*, 1–25.

31. del Valle, *El tesoro escondido*, 7–8.

32. Ibid., 18–19.

33. Ibid., 30.

34. *Civil Report of Brigadier General Leonard Wood*, 184–85.

35. de la Fuente, *A Nation for All*, 143–46.

36. *El Audaz*, June 7, 1913, 2.

37. Johnston, "Cuban Nationalism," 30–31; *Nueva Luz*, October 19, 1922, 1–2; January 25, 1923, 1; and February 15, 1923, 1.

38. *¡Tierra!*, June 30, 1906, 1; September 24, 1910, 1; *Rebelión!*, July 3, 1909, 2; and *Nueva Luz*, February 15, 1923, 1.

39. Gómez Luaces, "Monografía histórica," n.p.

40. *La Voz del Dependiente*, October 8, 1908 (insert); and *¡Tierra!*, October 31, 1908, 3.

41. *La Voz del Dependiente*, June 24, 1909, 3; October 28, 1909, 3; November 18, 1909, 3; January 31, 1910, 3; February 14, 1910, 3; February 24, 1910, 2–3; March 3, 1910, 2; March 24, 1910, 3; *¡Tierra!*, December 4, 1909, 4; December 11, 1909, 4; January 15, 1910, 1; June 8, 1912, 3; and January 14, 1913, 2.

42. Penichet, *Tácticas en uso*, 45.

43. For a discussion of anarchist education and the challenges it faced during the 1920s, see Shaffer, "Freedom Teaching."

44. de Lidia (a.k.a. Adrián del Valle), *Fin de fiesta*, 5–16.

45. *Nueva Luz*, April 10, 1925, 5.

46. Penichet, *Tácticas en uso*, 38–41.

47. del Valle, "En el mar," 127–65.

48. del Valle, *La mulata Soledad*, 159.

49. Penichet, *¡Alma Rebelde!*, 91–92.

50. Penichet, "La venta de una virgen," 193–210.

51. Levine, "Constructing Culture and Power," 21–22.

52. Sonn, *Anarchism*, 52.

53. Ibid.

54. McAdam, McCarthy, and Zald, *Comparative Perspectives on Social Movements*, 6.

7

From Workers' Militancy to Cultural Action

Brazilian Anarchism in Rio Grande do Sul, 1890s–1940s

BEATRIZ ANA LONER

In Brazil anarchist ideas penetrated the southern state of Rio Grande do Sul more strongly and for longer than in most other places. In the Brazilian context, Rio Grande do Sul had the third strongest and most active working-class movement, keeping a reasonably constant organizational level throughout the Old Republic period (1889–1930) and even beyond. Here libertarian ideas grew, finding expression in union struggles as well as cultural and educational activities that often engaged the broader local community. It was also in this state, better than most others, that the movement survived waves of repression that undermined anarchist militancy elsewhere. Another striking characteristic was the interchange between Rio Grande do Sul libertarian ideas and militants and their counterparts in the two most important cities of the River Plate region: Montevideo and Buenos Aires. In this region where the borders of Argentina, Brazil, and Uruguay merge, anarchists could travel and communicate transnationally with one another. This chapter explores the main activities and accomplishments of the anarchist movement in Rio Grande do Sul in the first decades of the twentieth century.

In Brazil libertarian ideas spread during the late nineteenth century—a time of great change in Brazilian society with the end of slavery (1888), the proclamation of the Republic (1889), and growing European immigration. Some libertarians had arrived in country earlier as they fled the tide of repression following the Paris Commune, or to participate in utopian rural communities. Primarily restricted to small isolated groups, these European radicals gathered in cities and ports where they disseminated anarchist ideas in factories and transport sectors.

One area where anarchists organized was Rio Grande do Sul, the southernmost state of Brazil. Rio Grande do Sul has wide borders with Uruguay toward the south and with Argentina to the west, forming the Río de la Plata River watershed. Since the early settlements, when both man and cattle wandered randomly through the region's plains, up until the wars that formed the South American nations during the imperial period (1822–89), Rio Grande do Sul always stood out as a unique feature of Brazil's territory. Some of the first immigrant settlements in the country were established there beginning in 1824 when European migrants settled in the northern part of the state. These settlers introduced small properties and subsistence production in a place frequently marked by large landed estates, an African enslaved workforce, and extensive cattle ranches.

The Brazilian government had a long history of employing Rio Grande do Sul's inhabitants in various military campaigns waged by the nineteenth-century Brazilian Empire, in bloody episodes against the empire (Farroupilha's Revolution), and in internal oligarchic disputes in 1893 and 1923. By the beginning of the twentieth century, the gaucho state of Rio Grande do Sul was a military society, of an agro-pastoral imprint, with production centered on supplying the internal market (cattle, jerked beef, and colonial products), and integrated into the Brazilian nation-state.[1]

Rio Grande do Sul also began a wave of industrialization characterized by a diversity of offices and manufacturers in Porto Alegre and Pelotas, and major factories such as textile mills, cigars, and food in Rio Grande. The labor movement developed in those three cities, and it is where the first anarchist militants appeared. Many anarchists arrived from harbors in Montevideo or Buenos Aires while others came from the Brazilian cities of Santos and Rio de Janeiro.

This chapter explores some of the regional variations in Brazilian anarchism by examining the movement in Rio Grande do Sul. It examines the impact of outside influences as well as Rio Grande do Sul's own dynamics in terms of oligarchic politics in relation to the national pattern upon the state's anarchists. I am especially interested in two interconnected points: the lower repression that anarchists suffered in the 1920s in comparison with militants from other regions of Brazil, and the consequences of this situation reflected on the direction of the movement. Paradoxically, despite the relative greater freedom of assembly and discussion, anarchist unions almost disappeared by the late 1920s. The decline in anarchist union activities has reasons much deeper than governmental repression. Thus, the state of Rio Grande do Sul provides a good measure of comparison for other regions of the country because one can observe a libertarian development less fragmented by repression.

The First Emergence of Anarchists and Early Activities

Libertarian ideas first entered the region as a result of the weakening of the Cecília Colony. The colony was a collective agricultural experiment developed in the state of Paraná to the north by the libertarian Giovanni Rossi and other Italians from 1890 to 1895. Following the colony's collapse, anarchists scattered throughout southern Brazil.[2] Some dedicated themselves to a discreet propaganda of their ideas, settling in small country towns and taking part in study groups of little influence. Others went to Porto Alegre and participated in the foundation of a newspaper. They saw an anarchist newspaper as an important tool to spread the word of anarchism, especially since the city only sporadically received Argentinean or Portuguese revolutionary newspapers. A few of the Cecília anarchists fought in the armed oligarchic disputes, joining an "Italian-Brazilian battalion" in the so-called Federalista's revolution of 1893.

Anarchists in Rio Grande do Sul were frequent targets of police repression. Local newspapers dedicated considerable space to news about "dangerous anarchists" and their deeds in Europe or the Plate. As a result, no matter how discreet one's activities, anarchists came under suspicion. From time to time the press reported news about "undesirable foreigners" found living in Pelotas, forced to board a ship, and deported as demanded by Uruguay in 1902, or arrested, like the two Frenchmen who celebrated anarchist assaults in Europe in a hotel in Rio Grande in 1894.[3] In this town, the only seaport in the state, dissonant voices demanded to be heard, praising anarchy through the streets in 1892 and generating conflicts with the supporters of the Republican Party of Rio Grande do Sul (PRR) and its adversaries. To the state's governing members, such dissonant voices were a warning that an even bigger danger than the internal rural oligarchic fights existed: growing militancy in the factories and working-class neighborhoods of the cities.

In 1898 the First Southern Rio Grande Workers Conference (I Congresso Operário Sul-Riograndense) was held. Many delegates came from a broad socialist background. Besides helping to support the approval of a proposal to use boycotts, some leftists were incorporated into the emerging structures of organized labor, including one member of the "Libertarian Group" who served on the central committee of the Southern Rio Grande Worker's

Confederacy (Confederação Operária Sul Rio Grandense), created by this congress.[4] However, neither the confederacy nor the early harmony between socialists and anarchists lasted for long. In 1902 anarchists created the International Worker's Union (União Operária Internacional) in Porto Alegre as a way to counter socialist influences among workers. The same goal would be present in 1906 with the creation of the newspaper *A Luta*, which engaged in a running controversy with the socialist paper *A Democracia* run by Francisco Xavier da Costa. Xavier da Costa would become one of the greatest adversaries of the libertarian group in Porto Alegre.

In that same year anarchists played a key role in leading workers in the state capital of Porto Alegre on strike for twenty-one days. On the heels of that successful mobilization, the Left founded the Federação Operária do Rio Grande do Sul (Rio Grande do Sul Labor Federation, FORGS). While socialists dominated FORGS until 1911, a group with libertarian influences led it afterward.

Government leaders and their allies portrayed the strikers as foreign workers who were not integrated into the lifeblood of the nation. But as the movement survived and grew, a class identity started to form among workers, eroding much of the ethnic bonds that had divided workers, such as the previous "German" unity whereby German workers and industrialists saw their interests in mutually supportive ethnic terms.[5] In a state with high immigration, this was a decisive step for the spread of libertarian internationalist ideas that until then had been primarily linked to Italian immigrants in the capital. During the 1910s anarchists built on these successes and came to dominate the state's workers movement. This growing link between labor and anarchism helped to propel libertarian propositions in everything from everyday union battles to cultural activities.

While anarchists made headway in the cities, libertarian ideas began to flourish in rural Rio Grande do Sul. In 1909 Ukrainian peasants settled in Erebango (then Erechim) beside Jewish settlers in nearby older colonies (Quatro Irmãos, Philipson) in the state's northern rural zones. They started a commune that continued throughout the 1910s and was reinforced after 1918 through contacts with the Russian Workers Federation in South America, periodically receiving its newspaper, *Golos Truda*, and other Russian-language newspapers from Canada and the United States. Discussing their common experience and educating themselves in anarchist theory, they then launched a new organization, the União dos Trabalhadores Rurais Russos do Brasil (Rural Russian Workers of Brazil Union—UTRRB), and joined forces with Russian trade worker unions in cities across the south and southeast of Brazil from the late 1910s to the 1920s.[6] In the 1920s the youth in these agrarian communities created the anarchist-leaning Rural Workers Youth. According to Mauricio Tragtenberg, who lived in one of those settlements in his childhood, they used anarchist egalitarian principles in their activities, with everyone acting as students and teachers, carrying out chores collectively, and sharing knowledge and ideas during evening talks.[7] The settlement of mainly Russian peasantry formed one of the few successful examples of an agricultural community based on libertarian principles in Brazil.

Anarchism's Second Blossoming

During the 1910s anarchist ideals spread throughout Rio Grande do Sul. As in São Paulo and Rio de Janeiro, anarchist ideas particularly penetrated the state's labor movement. Much of the growth in Rio Grande do Sul was a direct result of actions in the countries bordering the River Plate. For instance, in 1902 Argentina passed the Residency Law that allowed the government to deport foreigners who were considered agitators. As a result, anarchists arrived in southern Brazil. As the Argentine state celebrated that country's independence centennial in the early 1910s, anarchists were persecuted and the workers movement faced waves of repression. Many militants then relocated both to Montevideo and around Rio Grande do Sul.[8] Besides entering the state through the port of Rio Grande, anarchists clandestinely passed through any of the many towns along the Uruguay River on the border with Argentina or across Uruguay's dry land borders. As has already been noted, many anarchists who took residence in Rio Grande do Sul around the nineteenth century, preferred to live in small border towns or in Rio Grande since those places were better suited to contact the movement in other Latin American countries.

The 1910s witnessed the greatest successes for libertarian ideas and actions, especially beyond the workplace. Anarchists launched schools, worker's athenaeums, social study centers, and women's centers. Theater groups multiplied, different strands of libertarian thought were discussed, and anarchists published several newspapers. Such efforts led to large-scale campaigns for the eight-hour day and the great Campaign for Peace in 1914 and 1915. These were accompanied by increased worker militancy, with constant strikes and mobilization that peaked during the general strikes of 1917 to 1919.[9] Perhaps the most symbolic episode in this situation was the victory of militants affiliated with anarchists in the 1911 FORGS elections.

As their influence grew in 1911 and 1912, anarchists joined with revolutionary unionists and other militants in Porto Alegre and Pelotas to exercise their growing strength. Workers were increasingly attracted to the anarchists for a couple of reasons. First, workers began to see reformist and moderate socialist ideas from the first decade of the century as fruitless, and reformist and moderate socialist leadership as eroded and with few new ideas to offer. Second, socialists grew increasingly frustrated with the turn to electoral politics of some of their leaders. For instance, in Porto Alegre the socialist leader, Xavier da Costa, joined with the governmental party, PRR (Rio Grande do Sul's Republican Party), and was elected as town councilman in 1912. This was a disappointment to many of his party fellows, bringing them closer to their anarchist rivals while in turn serving to discredit the socialists.

As anarchists came to heavily influence the state labor movement and reorient FORGS in Porto Alegre and the Liga Operária (Worker's League) in Pelotas toward revolutionary unionism, this new conquered space started to attract anarchist militants from the center of Brazil. These internal migrants helped to develop the cultural and organizational framework in Rio Grande do Sul, increasing the dispersion and influence of these ideas to other organizations and cities in the state.

In those years Rio Grande do Sul received a considerable contingent of anarchists who would settle in the state. A key reason for the arrival of anarchists from around Brazil was the 1913 Second Brazilian Workers Gathering, organized by the Brazilian Labor Confederacy (Confederação Operária Brasileira, COB) in Rio de Janeiro. A group of anarchist gaucho delegates attended and spoke of their efforts in Rio Grande do Sul. In Pelotas these men played a special role developing anarchism between 1914 and 1917. As a result, anarchists clearly dominated that city's labor movement. Such activity surpassed anarchist organization in Porto Alegre where FORGS delayed a complete turn toward revolutionary unionism until 1918.[10]

In Porto Alegre, the same Pelotas-style unanimity wasn't reached in the labor movement, and the anarchists were less able to centralize the movement under libertarian principles as FORGS went through many different directions, some of them not particularly committed to unionist ideas. Even so, FORGS and its newspaper, *A Voz do Trabalhador*, started to disseminate their positions and union concerns to all of the state's labor associations. By the end of 1913 FORGS had twenty affiliated entities and another fifty-two with which they maintained friendly relations.[11] In the coming years, this influence tended to increase throughout Rio Grande do Sul.

As for the trajectory of anarchist groups in Porto Alegre, their objectives were centered on actions at FORGS, especially between 1913 and 1916. At the same time, though, they neglected the União Operária Internacional and the newspaper *A Luta*. In fact, a 1914 report emphasized that there was no autonomist anarchist group in the state capital.[12] Yet, while the Porto Alegre anarchists focused their organizational work on the FORGS, they continued to promote anarchist culture in the city through the creation of schools, like the Modern School, the Elisee Reclus School, and others, besides study centers and theater groups. Later on the International Worker's Gathering (UGT) played an important role in the 1917 general strike and relaunched its newspaper, *A Luta*. In 1918 they founded the UGT to oppose FORGS, which had fallen under the control of their rivals. A few months later the two organizations united under the statutes of the UGT but remained under the name FORGS, keeping the association throughout that decade and the next under anarchist influence.[13]

Throughout these developments, anarchists worked as transmitters of ideas, actions, and attitudes that influenced wide numbers of workers and other leaderships. In fact, what we call the "workers movement" always comprised a wide range of men and women, from those who were willing to collaborate with the bosses and the government to those who were more radical and everything in between. Sometimes the same militant could take different positions over time and according to the situation and specific opportunity. The worker who wasn't affiliated with any association but who may have consented to participating in a strike at other times refused to even participate as a spectator in the assemblies. Still, such a person was as much a part of the workers' movement as the veteran leader who engaged in all mobilizations. In this perspective, the strong libertarian presence in the movement meant that their ideas and actions influenced a wide range of militants, leaders, and associations.

In the early 1900s unions adopted a policy of political neutrality, allowing revolutionary unionist ideas a space to expand within the union environment where anarchist militants worked side by side with other militants who did not have a commitment with anarchist ideals. The "option for political and ideological neutrality in the unions appeared as an appropriate tactical solution to prevent opponents to use it for such means" and it also provided a good space of development for libertarian ideas.[14] However that did not mean there were no contradictions among the several internal groups.

In Brazil revolutionary unionists tended to work in mutual tolerance and acted with other ideological currents considered integral to anarchism so that this large group included everything from individualist anarchists to revolutionary unionists. In the 1920s the differences between the groups became important in Rio Grande do Sul's movement, but in the 1910s there was great complement between the activities of the groups, according to their own leaders: "Anarchists in this capital, since the beginnings of their propaganda, started to propagate Unionism in the workers environment. . . . The main current among anarchists here is communism and its propagators find the anarchist intervention in the laborers' movement very useful, not only for the publications that they can bring to the working-class organization but also for providing a wide field of action to develop and spread the ideal that shall place free men on free land."[15] Pelotas is a prime example of the potential unleashed when anarchists controlled the main union and libertarians of different tendencies were allowed to emphasize whatever seemed better: education, culture, unionism, or any combination thereof. Between 1914 and 1918 libertarians developed theater groups and created a dramatic arts course. They founded a band, music group, and music school for the workers. Educationally, union members developed an athenaeum and an elementary school, besides creating the Rationalist School in 1918. There were women's night classes linked to the Women's Center for Social Studies, which also promoted educational conferences. The Center for Social Studies and the Iconoclastic Group were in charge of discussions and philosophical or political thought. They published two newspapers, *A Luta* and *Terra Livre*, and combined these cultural tasks with other political activities such as fundraising for the Local Federation, the Tenant's Association, the Pro-peace Center, and the Youth Anti-Militarism Group. They developed the Peace Campaign and fights against hunger in which they used public urban spaces downtown and in local neighborhoods for parades and rallies to mark their presence.

Throughout the state, there was a spread of initiatives that gathered diverse sympathizers and militants for union and cultural work. In that decade gaucho union members participated actively in the 1913 Congresso Operário Brasileiro and the Congresso Internacional Pela Paz as well as the Congresso Anarquista Sul Americano in 1915, besides being affiliated with the COB. They also sent representation to the official congress of 1912 in Rio de Janeiro, but they retreated immediately after it opened, denouncing the congress as a political maneuver since it was being promoted by the government. They released several short-lived newspapers, which were edited on portable graphic printers like the one belonging to Zenon de Almeida, who edited *Terra Livre* (1915) and *A Luta* (1916) in Pelotas and then *Nosso Verbo* (1920) in Rio Grande. Meanwhile, in the capital, FORGS published *A Voz do Trabalhador*, *O Sindicalista*, and *Der Freie Arbeiter* from 1920 to 1930.

With the growing influence of revolutionary unionists among the working class, strike actions spread. The strikes at the end of the decade emerged through a combination of the effects brought by the First World War, such as unemployment and growing scarcity. If, in the two initial years of the conflict, there were few strikes, the situation began to change in 1916, when miners in São Jerônimo and stoneworkers and urban paving workers in Porto Alegre went on strike. In 1917 railroad workers struck throughout the state. The leaders of those actions were not always anarchists, but in this general atmosphere workers' radicalization ended up boosting anarchist ideas.

The 1917 General Strike in Rio Grande do Sul sought a wide array of goals: better wages and fewer working hours, the fight against scarcity of life, and an end to increasing rents. In Porto Alegre, FORGS' directors were not in favor of the strike. As a result, non-FORGS associations played a bigger influence.[16] There the strike lasted five days, reaching factory workers, public service workers, longshoremen, dockworkers, and typographers. The city practically came to a halt due to a walk-out of the transportation service workers, with the Popular Defense League deciding who was allowed to circulate on the streets as strikers searched for more workers to persuade into the movement. Ultimately, authorities considered many of the demands to be reasonable and some workers' wages were raised, defusing the strike's radicalism.[17]

Anarchists in Rio Grande did not take part in the 1917 general strike. But by 1918 Rio Grande workers were growing increasingly militant, especially following the mobilization of ice box plant workers. Workers then founded the UGT. One of its first actions was to lead the 1918 general strike. In 1919 the UGT was a main actor in an even bigger labor mobilization. The strike that took place between May 5 and May 17 began at the construction site for the new port, but it soon spread. Trade workers joined, and firemen and sailors refused to suppress them. The strike coincided with a national maritime workers movement, which amplified the movement in town. The workers, who in 1918 had sponsored the sabotage of an electric power plant, did not do the same in 1919 due to the unpopularity of such a measure. However, they did use picket lines twice, and many of them carried guns.[18]

Worker radicalism inspired repressive actions. Since the beginning of the movement, military troops as well as a war ship were sent to Rio Grande. The fear of an insurrection led to the closing of factories and commerce. Authorities prohibited unions from opening, banned assemblies, and censored the press and mail. Using guns and horses, police broke down picket lines, resulting in two deaths and several injuries as well as large numbers of arrests.

The Porto Alegre unions also felt the change in the government policy in 1918 when authorities frustrated a new strike attempt by closing FORGS and arresting its leaders. But such repression actually propelled anarchists in Rio Grande and Porto Alegre toward greater, not lesser, radicalism and a growing disposition to confront employers. As Frederico Bartz notes, "Borges de Medeiros and the Republican power attitudes in 1918 would also help to create a spirit of radicalization that would translate, among other things, in the search for inspiration in more radical models to the labor associations."[19]

Something that helped the radical current in Rio Grande was the number of libertarians that were in the city during those years, many deported from Rio de Janeiro and São Paulo and who ended up getting involved in Rio Grande's associations and unions.[20] Worker radicalization also resulted from the intransigence of the state government that used force as a way to repress these movements, closing themselves to negotiate, as some other cities had done. In Rio Grande, workers continued to agitate through strikes and strong association, a condition that did not begin to decline until early 1922 when the UGT leaders were arrested and put on trial.

The general strike of 1919 in Porto Alegre was led by FORGS, which lay now in the hands of anarchists, and started to proclaim the need for a "revolutionary general strike." Their newspapers clarified its objectives:

We are at war against private property, the State and the Church, in a war in which the greatest goal is the complete annihilation of those institutions.

We fight for an anarcho-communist society, which is a social state that allows the unobstructed unfolding of individual freedom for every man. . . . This general refusal from work will reach its end with the passing of the means of production to the working people. . . . [21]

The Russian Revolution began to impact the militants, spreading the idea that social revolution was just ahead. The labor and even anarchist press from 1917 to 1919 defended maximalism, seeing no difference between it and anarchism. International news of radical events, uprisings, and mobilizing movements were promising, and there was a great identification with the German Spartacist League. As for the news about Russia, libertarians in Rio Grande do Sul considered the news too imprecise since it was filtered by news agencies, which had very little credit among libertarians. Therefore, it took a long time until the differences between anarchists and communists were established. In the meantime, "communist" associations appeared that were, in fact, of anarchist militancy and conception. What was most important is that the Russian Revolution's emergence convinced militants about the imminence of revolution.[22] As a result, they began their preparations, which included dating their pamphlets and papers to reflect the era of revolution. For instance, they labeled 1919 as "III Year of Social Revolution."[23] According to Bartz, in 1919 Rio Grande do Sul surpassed all other states in worker-led paralyzations of the economy.

The 1919 general strike in Porto Alegre ended after a failed attempt to rally in front of City Hall on September 7, Brazilian Independence Day. In a confrontation in which one of the workers' leadership was killed, police stormed the FORGS' headquarters and arrested two foreign leaders of the movement, held them in prison, and threatened to deport them as a means to prevent the rally. The imprisonment of foreigners was part of the policy of all governments, in an effort to delegitimize the movements. But the fact that these two leaders were never deported shows a clear distinction between the state government of Rio Grande do Sul and all other states that did deport foreign militants.[24]

Despite government crackdowns, infrequent strikes continued into the early 1920s throughout Rio Grande do Sul. Beginning in 1922 increased repression reduced the number of militant organizations, placing anarchists in a delicate situation. As repression increased against workers, the rest of Brazil began to suffer from military instability, leading to a cycle of army uprisings from the young lieutenants against the oligarchic national government, which they considered corrupt and inefficient. Yet within this chaos a new entity was born. In 1922 the Communist Party of Brazil (PCB) formed, solidifying a long, suppressed rupture between the leaderships of the workers movement.

Regrouping in the 1920s

The crisis in the 1920s was provoked by the increase of repression against the anarchist movement. Within the workers movement, this led to much debate regarding anarchist methods. Such methods led many to see anarchist tactics as wasted efforts with inconsistent results that created weak associations. As a result, many workers were disillusioned and found other paths in life, leaving militancy or, at least, avoiding union activities. Some were drawn to other political forces, whether from the left or the right.

Incredibly, twenty-one of the twenty-two founders of the PCB in 1922 had been anarchists at one time of their activist lives. This exposed the biggest internal problem of anarchism in this decade: many of its militants were attracted to and seduced by Bolshevism, some of them permanently. However, for those who craved the supposed guarantee of a "scientific" answer for revolution and then found it to be a mere ephemeral temptation, the way back to the libertarian path was not always open as rivalries and antagonisms unfolded in those moments. As a result, many quit militancy all together, returning to their private lives.

Torn apart by internal disputes, they were also under siege. Hundreds of anarchist militants across Brazil were arrested. Some were deported. Others were sent to the concentration camp Clevelândia at Oiapoque in the Amazon. From there, half of them did not return. Some escaped, some died from tropical diseases caught in the camp.[25] Repression only subsided around 1927, with the end of the siege. Then anarchists unsuccessfully tried to reorganize in São Paulo and Rio de Janeiro, states hit hardest by repressive measures. One reason they failed was that they now faced competition with communists for the heart of the labor movement.

Rio Grande do Sul was an exception to the national trend of political repression. While anarchists suffered under the weight of police action, it was far less intense than in other states. In the south there were practically no deportations to Oiapoque or permanent "vanishing" of militants. Many of them, when caught by the police, were taken to the border and released into Uruguay, which allowed them to quickly return. Although under police surveillance, the third (1925) and fourth (1928) state workers congresses were held in complete normality, being advertised and reported on in the daily newspapers, while in the rest of the country arbitrary arrests, beatings of militants, and raids on offices piled up.[26]

The reason for this difference is found in the peculiar political conjuncture of the state during this period. Ruled with an iron fist by the Republicans since the end of the armed conflicts of 1893–95, Rio Grande do Sul was always distinguished by a great political polarization between the Partido Republicano Rio Grandense and the several oppositionist organizations, which after 1923 were grouped into the Aliança Libertadora (Liberation Alliance) formed by land owners and political dissidents. Even though fraudulent elections always favored the Republicans, there was a dispute for the urban votes, among which there was a great workers' constituency. In the capital there were several attempts to aggregate leaders, whether socialist or unionist, for the government. Meanwhile, in some upstate towns, like Pelotas, opposition groups were more closely aligned to the workers' leaders due to their common opposition against the government.[27]

Following civil war in 1923, the government refrained from violent repression of the Left while the Liberation Alliance adopted a respectful attitude regarding libertarians, opening newspapers to workers' news and publishing unionist columns. This respect to the syndicalist struggle was eased by the fact that the liberators' political support base was connected to agriculture and cattle raising while workers focused their efforts on urban and industrial exploitation. Still, when it came time for election, libertarians urged workers to nullify their votes. This nonpolitical approach left workers at the mercy of the traditional parties.

Thus the polarization of the political elite meant that the opposition could appeal for support in a united front versus the government while the government refrained from violence and repression so as not to be accused by the opposition of brutality, thus losing votes among workers and other strata. This is not to say that there was no governmental repression of anarchists, though. Rather, repression was selective: some more prominent militants were preferential targets for arrests in the event of disturbances, or there were limited interventions against strikes or in factory conflicts followed by surveillance of militants.[28] Therefore, anarchists benefited from the disputes between oligarchic forces, creating a protective bubble where libertarian ideology could be sustained in better conditions than in the rest of Brazil. Both militants and associations saw the south as a refuge. In fact, the main anarchist São Paulo newspaper considered relocating to Rio Grande do Sul.

Another nationwide police action also helped maintain anarchist activities in the state. Throughout the country, state police forces commonly arrested militants in one place, ill-treated them for some time, and then released them in another Brazilian state so it would be more difficult for their reintegration into the movement. One of the favorite sites for this internal deportation was Rio Grande do Sul. With that, anarchism in the south was continuously fed with new elements, taking advantage of the connections and influences of those "exiled" who would spend some time in Rio Grande do Sul, taking part in groups and associations and giving lectures before returning to the center of the country. Taking into account the strong repression in Rio and São Paulo, some ended up settling in Rio Grande do Sul, especially in towns near the Uruguayan and Argentinean borders where they benefited from the flow of libertarian activities in those countries. In time upstate Rio Grande do Sul became these militants' favorite place to establish themselves. Some of them managed to gain respect from the local communities, for their culture and humanity if not for their quality as educators.[29]

The presence of so many northern anarchists in the south could feed the imagination of a militant who dreamed of escaping from Oiapoque. One such escapee, after returning to civilization, found a copy of *O Sindicalista* on a table at the meeting place of a northern group at the end of 1927. As he read, the situation in the south shown like a beacon shining through the darkness: "As you so nicely put it: 'the libertarians of Brazil are entrenched on Rio Grande do Sul.' You are the last haven of this ideal in Brazil; you wield liberty, while the darkness of slavery takes over the rest of the region."[30]

Another reason for the survival of anarchism in the south over the years was exactly its proximity to the Río de la Plata area, where anarchist organizations were more vigorous and enduring, lasting beyond the 1930s. We must also consider the theoretical and political qualities of those libertarians acting in Rio Grande do Sul. Its peripheral geographic position was never a reason for marginal participation in the national workers' movement. Its militants had always made themselves seen in congresses and at the COB itself, in which at least 30 percent of affiliated entities were from Rio Grande do Sul.[31] An analysis of the activities held by those militants shows their cultural and intellectual development, besides the usual exchanges, due to frequent traveling and to their militancy around the country.

As for upstate towns, Bagé and Uruguaiana were the most expressive anarchist centers in the late 1920s. In a reunion among the state's unionists in 1927, the FORGS headquarters was moved to Bagé, which at that moment became the strongest libertarian center in Brazil. In the Fourth Congress in 1928, Uruguaiana's delegate called the others' attentions to the significant part played by the UGT of that town, which according to him "is destined to influence the Argentinean town of Libres, that town's local has asked to be affiliated with the 'Uruguaiana Federacy.'" This organization helped to spread propaganda not only in northern Argentina but also in northern Uruguay and Paraguay.[32] It is no accident that, in 1933, of the five Brazilian associations affiliated with the Continental Workers Association, four of them were from Rio Grande do Sul, all from border areas or near them: Uruguaiana's União Geral de Trabalhadores, Bagé's Workers Federation, Pelotas' Workers Federation, and the Capão do Leao's Stone Mason Trade Union, besides Rio de Janeiro's Workers Federation.[33]

Nevertheless, the relation between anarchists residing in the state with their River Plate fellows is still to be uncovered, due to the lack of transnational research on the issue. Ironically, while the libertarians did not conform to nation-state boundaries, Latin American researchers who study them have only begun to trespass the same borders. Still, even studying the issue only from the "Brazilian side," we notice how vast those transnational relationships must have been. These relations appear in radicals' biographies, which frequently talk about international militancy. Transnational relations are also illustrative when examining strikes, especially in seaports where the phenomenon of workers' solidarity unfolded with the refusal of Argentinean longshoremen to unload products originally destined to Brazilian ports that were on strike, or the mobilizations to retrieve from ships that were docked on Brazilian ports Argentinean or Uruguayan militants deported to Europe. FORGS, affiliated to the Workers International Association, had delegated its representation at least once to representatives of the Federación Obrera Regional Argentina (FORA).[34]

Although in the south they had better space for the maintenance of libertarian activities, this does not mean that there were no changes in the kind of activity developed. After all, their participation and influence in syndicates was constantly and firmly decreasing throughout the decade, resulting in few anarchist-directed economic struggles, a decline in the number of labor unions, and the disappearance of most associations that had developed. However, anarchist theater clubs and libertarian study groups remained, while FORGS became much more active in solidarity defense campaigns. For instance, it held about thirty public gatherings in support of Nicola Sacco and Bartolomeo Vanzetti, Italian-born anarchists convicted (many believe wrongly) of murder in the United States.

This anarchist turn toward more cultural work actually dated to before the 1917 and 1919 general strikes, when anarchist leaders in central Brazil in 1916 issued a manifesto that offered meaningful criticisms of syndical activities. The authors argued that unions were ineffective as a means of propagating libertarian ideas.[35] Furthermore, the leaders suggested, unions corrupted the principles of worker fraternity and equality. The manifesto urged anarchists to organize affinity groups instead. However, because the manifesto was released at the same time as the labor movement's expansion, it did not have much impact on anarchist involvement with union activity.

Yet in the repressive environment of the early 1920s, several militants began to rethink their actions. Many had become disillusioned with union activities, but they were still willing to work for the cause. To this end, they shifted from union to cultural work, arguing for the necessity of a cultural revolution that would help to form a "new man." This idea first appeared in Rio Grande do Sul's Third Workers Congress in 1925 when culture and education were promoted as weapons in the work of raising awareness, linking this idea to the creation of libertarian groups acting to achieve human liberation. They would not use dynamite bombs, which their opponents denounced, but "brain dynamite."[36] In 1925 this tactic was still viewed as complementing union action, not replacing it. Yet in the Fourth Congress in 1928, cultural work took center stage—a development that owed as much to the special conditions in which the anarchist movement was at the time as well as the absence of many of the state's important revolutionary union leaders from the meeting.[37]

By this time, too, the anarchist leadership was growing older. The men who were part of the struggles over the two previous decades were now in their forties, some bearing on their bodies the marks of illnesses acquired during their militancy, like Florentino de Carvalho, who died in 1934 of an ulcer he developed in prison. Many were at the end of their productive lives, like Friedrich Kniestedt, who retired from his activities as a broom maker in 1930 and stopped agitating at FORGS.[38] Finding new members was very difficult since young militants felt more attracted to their rivals' propositions. Militancy always takes a steep toll individually, in professional life as much as in family life. Furthermore, it usually represents one stage of life. Very few militants managed to remain leaders throughout their entire lives. If for some prioritizing cultural actions was a matter of revolutionary strategy, to others it represented an option to keep propagating libertarian ideas without the dangers of union militancy or—which was decisive—demanding big individual and family sacrifices that labor militancy demanded. That way privileging discussion and study groups was a way to conciliate their ideals with a private life without drawing too much attention from the authorities and the police.

The most important means of cultural action in this decade was the release of magazines and newspapers. The most important was the *Liberal Magazine*, published from 1921 to 1923 in Porto Alegre and edited by Polidoro Santos, a former militant union activist. The magazine published the work of local and international anarchist intellectuals and sought to develop the working man, aiming to "reach the discussion and exposition of social issues, in a clarifying way. . . . The *Liberal Magazine* wants our men, and especially our workers, to echo this evolution, to be the vehicle of the ideas that agitate people all around, the word that awakes intelligence for the study of social issues and the organ that announces that workers do not have only arms with which to work but also a brain that thinks and reasons."[39] In the same vein, new publications appeared throughout Rio Grande do Sul as affinity groups discussed issues such as the propagation of Esperanto or the fight against alcoholism. In some cases, these new publications belonged to trade unions or union centers, but through the end of the decade this was increasingly rare. Rare also were newspapers that made it beyond their first year. Some of them, like *O Sindicalista*, published for a longer time, frequently due to the stubbornness of their editors. That was the case for this and other papers edited by Friedrich Kniestedt, such as *Der Freie Arbeiter*, for ethnic German anarchists, which was published for exactly ten years.[40]

There was also an attempt to develop educational projects such as Rational Schools, but budgetary frailty and the schools' continued detachment from organized movements, as in the previous decade, conspired against these projects. Still, some initiatives prospered, such as the Institute for Childhood Assistance and Protection, a communitarian entity in Porto Alegre that was founded by a libertarian couple in 1936.[41] On the other hand, theaters, *veladas*, and musical activities suffered because they were largely linked to labor associations and, as union activity was diminished, they also lost performance space and audiences that they once had, even though some still were able to maintain themselves.[42]

In the 1920s and 1930s anarchists expressed concern with attempts to enlarge the Catholic Church's role in government and civic life. Anarchists fought against the introduction of religious education in public schools and against the privileges of the Roman Church in the 1933 Constitution. Anarchists were not alone as they joined forces with other groups such as freemasons, intellectuals, and even politicians or members of other churches to form a Pro Freedom of Conscience Committee or Anti-Clerical Leagues.[43]

As in the past, anarchists continued to publish books, promote conferences, and give courses to educate workers and the public. Sometimes these actions brought controversy. In 1927, on the heels of publishing his first book, *From Slavery to Freedom*, Florentino de Carvalho launched a one-man crusade against spiritists. Wherever a caravan of spiritists and their marketers went, he soon followed. The anarchist staged public conferences where he criticized and refuted certain aspects of spiritist doctrine.[44]

But perhaps the best example of a libertarian who made the most of every space to announce his ideas and knew how to act on all fronts was Friedrich Kniestedt. Kniestedt was a militant in the German libertarian movement who immigrated to Brazil for the first time in 1909, seduced by the idea of taking part in the ensemble forming an agrarian colony; the experience did not work out. Returning to Germany, he was arrested for his antiwar ideas and forced into exile in July 1914, returning to Brazil. During the First World War he tried to launch a new agricultural collective in the state of Paraná, but he left there in 1917, settling in Rio Grande do Sul.

In his own words, he had previously lived the libertarian experience building a community of production without employers in part out of frustration with the goals of urban workers. However, he could not refrain from taking part in the workers struggles in the cities, especially after hearing about the great strikes of 1917. Settling in Porto Alegre, he soon became a vital member of union organization and union newspapers—a role he continued from 1917 to 1930.[45] After 1930 he remained politically active, dedicating himself to work among ethnic Germans, becoming active in the antifascist fight, opening a library, and editing several German-language papers. In times of governmental repression, his name always rose to the top of the target list. Local Nazi groups also targeted him in response to the public war of words he waged with them in the newspaper *Akction* and elsewhere. Even when he was a union militant, he did not abstain from other ways to propagate his ideas as, for example, during the Christmas of 1922 when he set off on a pilgrimage of sorts through several German settlements in the state, giving lectures in which, using the pretext of the Christian message "Thou shall not kill," he made a comparison between the bloody capitalist society and the peaceful future socialist community. The tour managed to raise some workers' interest and created libertarian groups in various places.[46]

The Fourth Stage: 1930–1945

Between 1930 and 1945 major political, economic, and social transformations swept Brazil. Beginning with the 1930 Revolution and lasting until a military coup that overthrew him fifteen years later, Getúlio Vargas rose to power, served as interim president, constitutional president, and ultimately dictator during the Estado Novo. In those long fifteen years, Vargas and his supporters completely transformed Brazil, redefining its economic and social evolution while placing the state firmly behind a surge in industrialization and development. The government tried to harness the power of workers by promoting abundant union legislation and placing unions under state control.[47] In addition, the government promoted a new labor ideology within this state union known as *trabalhismo*. Especially during his period of dictatorship, Vargas developed a winning propaganda strategy among workers and other popular groups, gaining fame as protector of the poor and creator of union laws. This propaganda became the base of so-called Brazilian populist politics.

During the Vargas years, libertarians practically took no part in the southern regional union movement. This was not true elsewhere. For instance, anarchists in São Paulo were still active in that city's labor movement as a force in the Workers Federation and leading several unions in the early 1930s.[48] However, such anarchist presence in Estado Novo labor politics did not exist in Rio Grande do Sul except for their May 1934 participation in the Anti-Political Nucleus Federation during the FORGS Congress.

In part this is due to an aging anarchist body and its growing shift toward cultural militancy and away from unions, which were now government controlled. Anarchists maintained a minimal trade union presence for a few years, especially in Rio Grande. In Porto Alegre they controlled very few corporate unions. Communists and *trabalhistas* created a new labor organization also called FORGS and developed union activities in line with government directives. Throughout Rio Grande do Sul in the 1930s, all union work fell under the shield of the Ministry of Work, Industry, and Commerce. Anarchists refused to swear allegiance or participate. Their propositions no longer found receptiveness, and soon anarchists found themselves practically thrown out from union participation. In Rio Grande do Sul's case, this is particularly serious because the majority part of the population supported Vargas. Therefore, any anarchist criticism was viewed, initially, as counterrevolutionary and encountered public defense of the regime. In the following years the strong reach of the *trabalhista* ideology among laborers brought extra difficulties, especially for those who wanted to work along the laboring class and other popular groups in Vargas' home state.

The case of Pelotas' Worker's League is exemplary. In this town until 1933, two libertarian-oriented unions remained active. The unions also owned the deeds to the Worker's League, a valuable building downtown and just a few blocks from City Hall. Since they were no longer legal unions, they ceased holding any more of their own union activities. The league's managers then rented the headquarters for meetings of the Frente Sindicalista (Unionist Front, FSP)—a collection of the government's official trade unions. The Frente attempted to take control of the league, trying to get the anarchists to abandon their principles and affiliate with the Frente. But they were stopped by the anarchists. For their part, the libertarians tried to interfere with and disrupt the meetings.[49]

With the impasse, the members of FSP took measures to take over the Worker's League. In April they appealed judicially, considering themselves the legitimate representatives of Pelotas organized labor and, as such, having rights over the league headquarters. There was an unsuccessful attempt to expel the anarchists by force around May Day 1933. At last the FSP came to the mayor asking for measures, claiming that the libertarians were interfering with union organization. The anarchists were arrested and sent to Porto Alegre but were imprisoned for only eight days and then released due to a lack of any evidence of conspiracy or subversive activities. They immediately returned to Pelotas. Two months later, a judge returned the league to the anarchists.[50]

Even though it all ended without damage, the occasion shows the isolation of the anarchists not only from the union movement but also from workers because the small anarchist group (eight people) had only one demonstration in their favor when the Porto Alegre Antipolitical Nucleus Federacy rallied on their behalf. It also reveals the lack of any practical libertarian activities at this time: they were released from arrest because nothing was found—besides pamphlets and newspapers—that would make them a threat to the public order or that could give the impression that they were meddling into Pelotas' union organization. There could not be a more complete failure for a group of anarchists.

As to their other activities, Edgar Rodrigues describes a Regional Anarchist Congress in Rio Grande do Sul on January 26, 1930. The congress' participants "discussed nine themes of the upmost importance to the libertarian movement, most importantly an anti-authoritarian position against the new political currents."[51] This was not a workers' congress but an ideological meeting. And it probably only happened because it took place in January of 1930 since, from March on, as a result of a pact between the old oligarchic adversaries in the state, an intense repression unfolded against all opposition groups, including the anarchists.[52]

Effectively, repression was a great reason to limit activities in those years. After 1934 the police-military dictatorship hardened its grip on Brazil. Authorities dealt harshly with most of the left-wing opposition, putting them in jail until 1945. While some anarchists were arrested, most responded to the tyranny by completely suspending their activities. After 1937 no newspapers or books were published and no cultural centers were opened as anarchists entered into long years of political darkness.

There would also be no "dawn of freedom" in 1945 with the dictatorship's demise. Instead continuity ruled as unions and other leftist groups continued to look to the state for help to solve their problems and to make social demands on the state. In that context it was difficult to spread libertarian ideas. Anarchists were relegated to small ghettos of nonconformist thinkers or to collective practices in small rural communities. Then the new military dictatorship from 1964 to 1988 destroyed any remaining seduction of leftist ideas in Rio Grande do Sul. However, with the dictatorship's demise, there would once again be room for new ideas that would again plead to each person and their freedom, both collective and individual.

Notes

1. Gaucho was the name given to the errant riders of the platinian region of the Pampas. In Brazil, it is the name of Rio Grande do Sul's inhabitants, and of the state itself.

2. Souza, *O anarquismo da colônia Cecília*.

3. *Correio Mercantil* (Pelotas), September 10 and 11, 1902; *Diário Popular* (Pelotas), September 12, 25, and 26, 1892; and *Almanaque Literário e Estatístico do Rio Grande do Sul para 1898*.

4. *Echo Operário* (Rio Grande), January 18, 1898.

5. Bak, "Class, Ethnicity and Gender in Brazil," 83–123.

6. Rodrigues, *Os libertários*.

7. Tragtenberg, "Editorial."

8. Suriano, *Anarquistas*; Abad de Santillán, *La FORA*; and D'elia e Miraldi, *Historia del movimiento obrero*.

9. Loner, *Construção de classe*; and Petersen, "Que a união operária."

10. In Pelotas, there were two central entities, the Worker's League and the Worker's Union. The latter involved anarchists and black or poor workers discriminated against by the league. After 1913, with the migration of libertarians to the league, the union repre-

sented a majority of black workers, keeping a diffuse ideological definition to socialism but without opposing the libertarian propositions.

11. Petersen, "Que a união operária."

12. Polidoro dos Santos, report in the magazine *A Vida*, December 31, 1914, 14.

13. Bartz, *O horizonte vermelho*.

14. Oliveira, *A neutralidade política*.

15. Polidoro dos Santos, report in the magazine *A Vida*, December 31, 1914, 14.

16. All data concerning the movement in Porto Alegre is from Petersen, "Que a união operária"; and Silva, *A bipolaridade política rio-grandense*.

17. Petersen, "Que a união operária."

18. Loner, *Construção de classe*, 314–20.

19. Bartz, *O horizonte vermelho*, 58.

20. Minute's Book no. 11, from 1914 to 1924; and Minute's Book no. 18, from 1924 to 1929, Labor Union Society of Rio Grande Meetings.

21. *O Syndicalista*, September 3, 1919, 2.

22. Oliveira, *Anarquismo, sindicatos e revolução no Brasil*.

23. For example, see the newspaper *O Syndicalista* from 1919.

24. Bartz, *O horizonte vermelho*.

25. From 1924 to 1926, 946 prisoners were admitted and there were 491 deaths. See Azevedo, *A resistência anarquista*, 49.

26. Loner, "O IV Congresso Operário gaúcho."

27. For reference concerning the consequences of party disputes on the movement, see Loner, "O canto da sereia."

28. Kniestedt, one of these preferential targets of Rio Grande do Sul's repression, shows the difference between the state and the center of the country: "In Sao Paulo and Rio the situation was much harder, almost every worker's organization was dissolved and their most distinguished members were sent to the penal camp of Oiapoque. Here in Rio Grande do Sul we didn't feel any of that." Gertz, *Memórias*, 41.

29. Rodrigues, *Os libertários*.

30. Rodrigues, *Alvorada operária*, 300.

31. Silva, *A bipolaridade política*.

32. Rodrigues, *Alvorada operária*, 73.

33. See *A Opinião Pública*, August 4, 1933; and *O Libertador*, August 4, 1933, both of Pelotas.

34. Rodrigues, *Alvorada operária*.

35. Rodrigues, *Nacionalismo e cultura social*, 119–26.

36. *O Sindicalista*, December 1925; and Dulles, *Anarquistas e comunistas no Brasil*, 233n80.

37. Loner, *O IV Congresso Operário gaúcho*.

38. Gertz, *Memórias*.

39. *Revista Liberal*, February 1921.

40. Gertz, *Memórias*.

41. Marçal, *Os anarquistas no Rio Grande do Sul*.

42. Rodrigues, *Os libertários*.

43. Azevedo, *A resistência anarquista*.

44. *O Rebate*, April 1927; and *Diário Popular*, April 26, 1927, both from Pelotas.

45. He edited *A Luta*, *O Syndicalista*, and *Der Freie Arbeiter*, the latter directed to the German communities, besides working in collaboration with several other newspapers.

46. All references to F. Kniestedt are from Gertz, *Memórias*.

47. French, *Drowning in Laws*.

48. Azevedo, *A resistência*.

49. *Correio do Povo* (Porto Alegre), August 9, 1933.

50. *O Libertador*, August 12, 1933; *Diário Liberal*, September 4, 1933; and *Diário Liberal*, November 3, 1933. All papers were published in Pelotas.

51. Rodrigues, *Nacionalismo e cultura social*, 317.

52. Loner, *Construção de classe*, 394.

8

Memories and Temporalities
of Anarchist Resistance

Community Traditions, Labor Insurgencies, and Argentine
Shipyard Workers, Early 1900s to Late 1950s

GEOFFROY DE LAFORCADE

In 1956 and 1957 the legendary cosmopolitan barrio of La Boca del Riachuelo, where waterfront workers had staged epic uprisings and forged
strong labor traditions since the turn of the century, witnessed a dramatic
lockout and general strike in the shipyards. The movement was led by a federation of well-established craft societies with a history of converting anarchist and syndicalist organizational forms into a vivid legacy of cultural
protagonism in the neighborhood. Working-class anarchism in Argentina
was, in its impact and longevity, second only to its counterpart in Spain,
and Buenos Aires was its main point of entry in the Americas. At the turn of
the twentieth century shipyard braziers, caulkers, riveters, and other local
crafts joined longshoremen, mariners, and related sectors of the port transportation industry in organizing resistance societies that would form the
core of the anarchist Federación Obrera Regional Argentina (FORA).[1] They
cultivated solidarity pacts with movements from the interior ports of Argentina and across the bay in Uruguay in defense of skill, craft pride, union
wages, and closed shop hiring as well as trade union autonomy, working-
class education, direct action, ethnic diversity, and antistatist, revolutionary traditions. These societies exercised a strong influence over the larger
labor movement for several decades, giving rise to traditions of federalism,
solidarity, and autonomy that were later transmitted to even more powerful syndicalist movements—with which they sometimes clashed, and often
united—after the First World War.

What follows is the story of how their epic struggles—grounded in community activism and strategies of direct action so effective as to unleash constant, brutal campaigns of state repression and capitalist counterrevolution—were invoked to bequeath historical legitimacy on a movement to revive anarchist ideals locally in the seemingly incongruous setting of Argentina in the mid-1950s, between the military-led coup that deposed President Juan Domingo Perón (1955) and the reorganization of labor under the auspices of the state that began with the presidency of Arturo Frondizi (1958). Barely noticed by historians of Argentine labor due to its occurrence well after the decline of anarcho-syndicalism nationally, the 1956–57 shipyard workers' strike was emblematic of deeper transformations in the urban and industrial contours of Buenos Aires and its southern fringes, and of the resilience of anarcho-syndicalist traditions in the community that had anchored them for decades.

Class, Memory, and Ideology

A hypothesis underlying this chapter is that formal political or revolutionary ideologies and their self-defined tenets, which are routinely inventoried in traditional approaches to the history of organized labor, cannot be abstracted from the lived experience of those who interpret and appropriate them, and from an understanding of the social and symbolic contexts and spatial localities within which they were contested. To understand class as an occurrence, and to document its tangibility as a discourse of collective belonging, is not just to placate a master narrative of group formation on diverse shades of subjectivity or ideological positioning. Rather, it is to identify the "relational spaces," as Pierre Bourdieu called them, within which social identities and representations take form, to locate the places and interpret the meanings of workers' agency in the conflictive contexts of their oppression, exclusion or marginalization from power.[2] While not all resistance against alienation, fragmentation, or rationalization takes on the form of collective action, "class"—to which anarcho-syndicalists as well as their rivals ritually referred—is, like "community," an endeavor of symbolic unification and sedimentation over time, a staged, theatrical ordering of events and interpretation of experience by its advocates, particularly in moments of crisis or rapid transformation that threaten how it is understood. Margaret Somers has suggested that as an ontological narrative, class "is structured by emplotment, relationality, connectivity and selective appropriation"; it "embeds identity in time and special relationships [place]."[3]

Anarcho-syndicalist ideology in the barrio of La Boca, which cast resistance societies and trade unions as vehicles of working-class consciousness, education, and emancipation, provided such a story, one of relentless revolutionary yearning that unfolded with dramatic theatricality in the very real chapters of local history, in tangible experiences of direct action and community solidarity. It survived constant challenges for half a century among waterfront workers and was critical in forging the contours of class identity in the Riachuelo district of Buenos Aires, the abundance of available alternatives notwithstanding. The "repertoires of performances," to paraphrase Charles Tilly, of the labor movements chronicled here ranged from everyday instances of popular sociability, staged campaigns of popular education, and cultural events to informal work practices, harangues, assemblies and strikes, ritualized demonstrations, marches and commemorations, acts of concerted solidarity by neighbors and allies, and violent, sometimes riotous confrontations with rivals and enemies.[4] This ongoing theater of resistance informed the memories and meanings of labor conflict for generations in La Boca, where local history was continuously spotlighted on the national stage.

Another hypothesis put forth here is that the traditional division of twentieth-century Argentine history into two contrasting epochs, a "before" and an "after" the presidency of Juan Domingo Perón (1946–1955), while not devoid of empirical value, is a heuristic device that would, at face value, disqualify efforts by labor organizations rooted in anarcho-syndicalist traditions from attempting to resurface once the welfare state had been established. Yet the specific urban socioeconomic contours of the port of Buenos Aires set the stage for Peronism's rivals, such as the anarchism of the FORA tradition, to endure as alternative "repertoires of performances," still capable of challenging the dominant paradigm of labor mobilization in the immediate aftermath of the regime's demise. To understand this requires that we demystify the underlying teleology of narratives that dismiss anarchism as a premodern expression of ideals diametrically opposed to the mass movement that displaced them. Daniel James argued that Peronism's social impact was "heretical" in that it "spoke to working-class claims to greater social status, dignity within the workplace and beyond, and a denial of the élite's social and cultural pretensions" while enabling the protagonism of workers as citizens without the mediation of traditional political parties. In this sense it bears striking similarities to the anarcho-syndicalist movement that preceded it. He also points out, however, the "passive and demobilizing" aspects of a doctrine that resulted in the "controlled, limited mobilization" of workers "under the aegesis of the State."[5] In this reading the "sense of predisposed continuity" conveyed by decades of popular struggles allowed a new "selective tradition," as defined by Raymond Williams, to emerge: "An intentionally selective version of the past which is intended to connect with and ratify the present, which is then powerfully operative in the process of social and cultural definitions and identification."[6] One could argue that the resurgence of anarchism on the shipyards of Buenos Aires represented an alternative selective tradition in its final throes at a time when Peronism was persecuted and its prewar antagonists struggled to preserve their historic legitimacy in the community.

If we are to understand memories as "collective" and read into the process of selection that unifies them over time, then to dismiss the traditions that were "lost" or "abandoned" in that selection as aberrations, to reduce the working class to "a cipher, almost an ideal construct at the service of different ideological paradigms," is to miss the ambivalence, multiple meanings and historical contingencies of specific situations, actions, processes, and conflicts as they unfolded simply because we know how they ended.[7] This chapter will explore the historical backdrop and dramatic staging of an anarcho-syndicalist general strike in which thousands of shipyard workers, young and old, responded to the organizational efforts and rallying cries of anarchist trade union leaders with resounding enthusiasm and unanimity decades after the swan song of the anarchist FORA in the larger labor movement and in the aftermath of the Peronist regime. The movement should not, I suggest, be dismissed as an aberrant resurgence of antiquated ideas. It was as a manifestation of deeply entrenched local memories, organizational forms and working-class dispositions that they met (and clashed) with popular Peronism in the making—that is, with the convulsions and expectations of a community in transition, and the response of that community to the erosion of its traditional social fabric, the modernization of its industries, and the stigmatization of its riotous and cosmopolitan heritage as anathema to the nation's future, which was embodied by the modern state.

La Boca, the small historic neighborhood bordering on the Vuelta de Rocha estuary of the Riachuelo River on the southern edge of Buenos Aires, played a role in Argentine history far disproportionate with its size. Between the mid-nineteenth and mid-twentieth centuries it was a crucible of class, ethnic, and urban identity formation in which multiple voices, meanings, discursive strategies, and utopias competed for historical recognition—an urban palimpsest replete with contrasting meanings and struggles over historical representation that shaped collective memories in Argentina. Local waterfront unions, representing mariners and merchant seamen, longshoremen, shipyard workers and other quayside laborers, found themselves for a half century at the center stage of the community's history. They were also critical actors in the dramatic unfolding of the labor movement and the emergence of the Argentine welfare state, of working-class citizenship and the invention of national identity. As such, they left a unique legacy of anarcho-syndicalist dreams of popular empowerment and class emancipation, dreams that were very much alive in La Boca in the 1950s.[8]

Yet this anarchist past has since succumbed to virtual erasure in the contemporary collective memory and public history of the neighborhood. The "new beginning" of Argentine working-class history proclaimed by modernist and nationalist discourses under the impulse of Peronism contributed to this process of forgetting in ways that the struggles of the shipyard workers' federation—the Federación Obrera en Construcciones Navales (FOCN)—sought to reverse in the aftermath the 1955 military coup. Militants of the prewar shipyard workers' movement strove to unmask the violence that had been done to the historical memory of La Boca and its anarcho-syndicalist traditions of popular struggle, and to rescue the part of that past which, despite efforts to completely obliterate it, had left behind tangible physical and cultural traces. To paraphrase an expression coined by David Gross, organized shipyard workers embodied the "relative non-contemporaneity" of that bygone era. "Beginning with traces that are immediately at hand," Gross writes, "individuals in the present may work their way back imaginatively to the lost wholes and former registers of meaning that such traces indirectly recall, and in this manner bring back to consciousness the otherwise absent reality of the past."[9]

The Backdrop: A Barrio on the Margins

La Boca del Riachuelo had acquired its distinct configuration as a center of immigrant sociability and waterside traditions in the mid-nineteenth century. Italians had settled the Vuelta de Rocha and traveled the Paraná River as master mariners, ship captains, and sailors since the early days of Spanish colonization. Their presence grew substantially from 1821 onward, when Ligurians and other northern Italians fleeing Sardinian domination added to an already flourishing population of Genoese mariners and crafts-people who, with the growth of coastwise shipping along the littoral in the 1830s, dominated navigation, shipbuilding, and small commerce. By 1850, 70 percent of the river trade was carried out by vessels built either in Liguria or in the Río de la Plata region by Ligurian workers and with crews of identical origin. In this age of sail and pioneering settlement, the population of La Boca largely consisted of Italian mariners, shipyard workers, carpenters, caulkers, painters, riveters, craftsmen of all sorts, tailors, shoemakers, barbers, butchers, shopkeepers, vendors, and boardinghouse and café owners and their families, many of whom spoke in Genoese dialect and preserved a strong sense of cultural distinctiveness with respect to the physically remote center of Buenos Aires.[10] Despite the presence of numerous Piedmontese, Lombard, Tuscan, and, later, Neapolitan and Sicilian immigrants throughout the broader city, where spatial segregation along the lines of ethnicity tended to be the exception rather than the rule, the Riachuelo port district was already commonly referred to by visitors and residents alike as a foreign settlement, as "la Picola Italia" (Little Italy).[11]

By 1880 the growth of a vast network of railways entirely geared toward export activity reflected the economic hegemony of the Pampa region and confirmed the strategic location of river ports in Argentine trade, foremost among them the capital city itself.[12] The preindustrial work relations of the early Italo-Argentine community on the Riachuelo banks soon gave way to a greater differentiation among crewmen on the basis of skill, to a predominance of wage-earners in the work force, and to a generalized collapse of the position of small sail ship owners displaced by ocean liners and large coastwise shipping concerns. Shipyard workers were among the many established residents of La Boca whose fortunes and social hierarchies were adversely affected by these developments. They would appeal long thereafter to the memory of a classless, idealized past, extolling the foundational role of Genoese "*gente del mar*" in the birth of the community.[13] Even before the rise of anarchism, their sense of frustrated destiny and lost opportunities was heightened by the impact on the Riachuelo district of urban and spatial configurations stemming from the modernization of the port of Buenos Aires.

The Vuelta de Rocha nonetheless remained a center of coastwise shipping and ship repair as well as a base for tugboats and lighters that were to operate on the estuary and in the basins of the modern facility to its north, Puerto Madero. Upriver and Atlantic coastal trade would continue to flow into the Riachuelo for decades to come, even as the lion's share of transoceanic shipping gradually moved northward with the development of the new docks and slow transition from sail to steam. Another trend indicated that defeat was not total: the emergence, in subsequent years, of port facilities capable of receiving transatlantic steamships on the right bank of the Riachuelo, in Barracas del Sud (present-day Avellaneda). This strengthened the potential for industrialization and urban expansion south of Buenos Aires and ensured the sustained vitality of the tightly knit local quayside community of La Boca on the opposite side. In 1913 an elevator bridge linked the two banks of the river, and in 1927 the establishment of a large meatpacking plant, the Frigorífico Anglo, stimulated the growth of Dock Sud as an important railway port of the province. At the same time, Buenos Aires modernized, with the Plaza de Mayo as its center.

The parts west and north increasingly received services, facilities, and economic opportunities at the expense of the popular barrios of the south, where the bulk of waterfront laborers lived and worked. As Argentina became increasingly dependent on foreign (mostly British) expertise, capital, markets, railways, imports, and fashions, the élite ostentatiously remodeled the capital to reflect its seemingly inexorable rise. With the completion of the modern port facility at the turn of the century, a symbolic division between two worlds crystallized. To the north were concentrated the new commercial élite, government offices and agencies, influential banking and export interests, land speculators, Haussmannian urban renewal, and expensive shopping districts. To the south one encountered small contractors and concessions, immigrant craftspeople, skilled and semiskilled workers, seasonal migrants and casual poor, crowded housing tenements, widespread urban neglect, and minimal fixed investment in construction or public works. The concentration of traffic and tonnage in Buenos Aires ultimately worked in favor of the Riachuelo district by enhancing the strategic importance of the upriver coastal shipping industry that worked out of the Vuelta de Rocha. Thus, the health of the entire export economy depended on the smoothness of shipping and cargo handling operations on the crowded quays and docks of La Boca and the southern basin of Puerto Madero.

This state of affairs had immensely important implications for the labor movement that emerged on the waterfront at the turn of century. It also rescued the Riachuelo district from its much-clamored late-century economic decline, and resurrected local pride in its seafaring traditions and immigrant heritage. It was a center of intense social and cultural interaction in which rebellious anarchist activists emerged alongside the reputable Italian immigrants who owned the boardinghouses, shops, restaurants, cafés, and dance halls. By all accounts, historical and testimonial, the riverside community of La Boca had developed into a *"ciudad aparte"*—a separate city—visited daily by ships and people from distant provinces and foreign lands.[14] The barrio had acquired its definitive urban contours by the turn of the century, when it was officially included in the administrative divisions of the capital. Twentieth-century organized labor among mariners, longshoremen, shipyard workers, and other categories of port workers was grounded in *boquense* society and would remain so for the first half of the twentieth century.

Early Labor Organization

Socialists and anarchists in Buenos Aires began to organize workers in the shipping and cargo handling trades as early as the 1890s, when the microcosm of the city's south end first became a focal point of labor unrest and oppositional politics. The Sociedad de Resistencia Obreros del Puerto de la Capital (SROPC), a longshoremen's union led by the Spanish-born anarchist Francisco Rós, drew its legitimacy from a web of informal alliances with gang foremen, cart drivers, and lighter skippers as well as the widespread social and cultural influence of anarchist orators and activists in the tenements and hiring halls of La Boca. A quintessentially *boquense* community of settled immigrant craft workers employed by the Mihánovich company on the Isla Maciel (opposite the river), whose overseers were convinced of their impermeability to "anarchist agitation," also unionized into craft societies.[15] Like the SROPC, they would continue to exert influence in the port as late as mid-century. Coal trimmers, wool and leather warehouse workers, grain threshers, port construction workers, and other local unions, including those of mariners and seamen, joined anarchist longshoremen and ship repair workers year after year in paralyzing the port. These continuous disruptions raised such high stakes for the country that the localized, semiclandestine leaderships of the anarchist resistance societies met with Chamber of Commerce officials in 1902 to hammer out the terms of a strike settlement that would establish their prominence and weigh significantly on national politics for decades to come—even after a residency law promoted that same year caused many foreign-born anarchist activists to be deported.[16] Thus, La Boca had become, by the early years of the twentieth century, a crucible of conflicts between capital and labor with tremendous nationwide visibility, home to revolutionary as well as conservative and clerical associations, and to socialist clubs, all of which enjoyed a firm anchorage in the community. The labor process in the shipping industry and the port itself, in addition to the presence of foreign-born activists, immigrant traditions, and an annual influx of native seasonal laborers from the interior, endowed the neighborhood with its colossal powers of social integration as well as economic and political subversion.

Atilio Biondi, a shipyard brazier by trade and foremost representative at the time of the anarchist Federación Obrera Local Bonaerense (FOLB) in La Boca, was identified by the police as a leading figure of the longshoremen's SROPC with ties to the shipyard workers' and sailors' unions. His residency on Olavarría 882, in the heart of La Boca, and his fluency in Italian dialects made him a key player in the relationship of the longshoremen's resistance society to the larger immigrant and working-class community.[17] Biondi would go on to become a founder and legendary leader of the FOCN and a prominent figure of Argentine revolutionary syndicalism as well as anarchism, and was still active in the shipyard workers' union during its epic showdown with capital in the 1950s. César Pagliarini was another founder of anarchism in the shipyards who would advise and inspire the young generation of strikers during the 1956–57 standoff.

Following the end of the European war, when the glowing economic prospects of reconstruction and renewed high seasonal employment restored the exceptional bargaining leverage traditionally enjoyed by waterfront unions, the craft-based anarchism of the historic FORA (renamed FORA-V) coexisted and competed with a larger breakaway syndicalist federation known as FORA-IX.[18] The shipyard workers' FOCN, founded in 1916, would alternate between anarchist, syndicalist, and autonomous platforms over the course of the next four decades, linking its fortunes to those of the powerful Federación Obrera Maritima (FOM—formed in 1910 as an alliance of historic craft societies of mariners and merchant seamen) but never surrendering the anarchist organizational principles and tactics— federalism, local autonomy, deliberative direct democracy, informal labor market control, community activism, and the dissemination of working-class education—that structured the identity of its component parts.

All of these movements—the shipyard workers' FOCN, the maritime workers' FOM, and the longshoremen's SROPC—claimed La Boca as their birthplace and bastion. All were effective, despite their legal nonexistence, intense conservative competition, and recurrent violent persecution of their leaders, in preserving traditional networks of influence and job placement in the community. During the Great Depression, with the decline of foreign immigration and of the seasonal in-and-out migration that had characterized cyclical periods of high employment, the cosmopolitan quayside district of La Boca became increasingly identified with its foundational myths: electoral socialism, Italian ethnic traditions, craft pride, and—as the ultimate symbol of cultural resistance to the industrial expansion, the bureaucratization of labor, and the corruption of workers by the politics of clientage—anarchist agitation and proselytizing.

Shipyard braziers were revered as one of the most radical and antistatist sectors of the labor movement as well as a respected unionizing force in the yards and workshops that consistently commanded the respect of employers. Their resistance society, the Sociedad de Resistencia Obreros Caldereros y Anexos, was founded in 1902 in the headquarters of the *Centro Socialista* de La Boca by mostly Italian activists—Dante Golfarini, Domingo Castelletti, Atilio Morando, Aristides Baldini, Julio Testa, Juan and Nicolás Papola, Carlos Strerini, José Filipini, Carlos Jacarini, and others.[19] In 1903 the young movement, which positioned itself as anarchist, succeeded after a protracted struggle in abolishing the intermediary role of contractors and, along with shipyard caulkers and painters, won an eight-hour workday as well as substantial wage hikes.

The ship repair industry was one strategic area where the much larger mariners' and longshoremen's resistance societies were most likely to jointly display the efficiency of direct action and "solidarity pacts." Forgers, metalworkers and caulkers frequently shared the company of mariners on board the ships while they were moored in Buenos Aires, and some shipyard owners also possessed a locally moored fleet of lighters, tugs and barges on which affiliates and inspectors of the anarchist Sociedad de Resistencia de Marineros y Foguistas, founded by Italian-born anarchist Sinforiano Corvetto and later a component of the syndicalist FOM, were present. Braziers, riveters, carpenters, painters, and occasional workhands were casually employed, and many sought hire in other quayside occupations, especially stevedoring through the anarchist SROPC when work was unavailable in the yards. When in September of 1905 the braziers' union walked out to protest violations by the Mihánovich company of a 1903 strike settlement, provoking an open-shop drive in retaliation, the longshoremen's, mariners', sawmill workers', and painters' unions called solidarity strikes in unison, a pattern that would be repeated in ensuing decades. Transnational activism was facilitated, as would become a pattern, by the existence of shipyards on both sides of the Río de la Plata owned by Argentina's largest shipping concern, the Companía Argentina de Navegación Nicolás Mihánovich. Workers in Buenos Aires boycotted the Mihánovich yards throughout the 1905 state of siege, and numerous anarchist deportees were reported to be reentering the country through Montevideo and Salto Oriental (Uruguay) with help from the shipyard braziers' resistance society.[20]

During this period, in which the original FORA adopted anarchist communism and radicalized its tactics, shipyard braziers Atilio Biondi and Julio Testa were instrumental in fomenting boycotts and economic sabotage against antiunion employers.[21] The ability of anarchist activists to work and agitate in different professions of port work and move between different branches of organized labor heightened their effectiveness as federators of protest. Biondi, for example, a jack-of-all-trades, participated in the election of native-born Francisco García to the helm of the maritime workers' FOM in 1910 following the passage of the anti-immigrant Social Defense Law. After the braziers' resistance society lost a strike in 1914 in which anarchist principles had been invoked to reject government arbitration, he went from being a historic leader of anarchist communism to an advocate of a more pragmatic syndicalism, becoming a founder of the breakaway FORA-IX. He would be instrumental in allying the shipyard workers with the FOM after the creation of the FOCN in 1916, and seven years later in rallying the shipyard workers' federation to the revolutionary syndicalist Unión Sindical Argentina (USA), of which he was treasurer.[22] By then Biondi, who had traveled to Russia, was an active member of an "anarcho-bolchevik" fraction of the labor movement led by former FORA leader Rodolfo González Pacheco, the Alianza Libertaria Argentina (ALA), which also included a future leader of the maritime workers' federation, Juan Antonio Morán.[23] This fluidity in ideology and alignments is an important and often understated caveat to the reading of organized labor as anarchist, syndicalist, socialist, or something else. While the craft societies federated in the FOCN left the FORA-V and would spend the next three decades in the orbit of the syndicalist movement, in practice they remained autonomous of one another and retained the deliberative, grassroots organization and principles, often cooperating with the anarchist resistance societies through strike and solidarity movements. The older societies, such as the braziers', caulkers', and carpenters' unions, remained strongly anarchist-oriented, as did the sailors' and firemen's sections of the nominally syndicalist maritime workers federation, whereas the more industrial metalworkers' branch advocated apolitical syndicalism, attracted voting men in the orbit of the reformist Radical Civic Union (Unión Cívica Radical, UCR), and, in the 1940s, expressed communist sympathies in its leadership and rank and file.

Anarcho-Syndicalism and the Rise of the Welfare State

After participating in all of the epic maritime workers' movements (1917–24 and 1927–30) and successfully combating nationalist and fascist movements in the port, the FOCN, which remained committed to a federalist organizational model and objected to the involvement of political parties in the workers' movement, resisted the rise of industrial unionism under socialist and communist auspices in the mid-1930s. From 1937 and until the creation of the pro-Peronist Partido Laborista in 1945, shipyard workers' unions were, along with the FOM, the backbone of a revived USA, and they cooperated locally with the longshoremen's resistance society and its autonomous allies federated in what remained of the anarchist FORA-V. Numerically, the syndicalist USA and anarchist FORA in the 1930s no longer represented but a tiny fraction of the labor movement nationwide. In La Boca, however, the disproportionate weight of prominent traditional unions (SROPC, FOM, and FOCN) in two "national" labor federations with professed revolutionary goals was a factor of local pride. The "localization" of anarcho-syndicalist traditions did not entail their disappearance. On the contrary, as the strategic location of waterfront workers made itself increasingly felt with the growth of the merchant marine, the defense of these traditions, a matter of survival for the aforementioned unions, became increasingly intertwined with the memory of the local community. Already shaken by the urban transformations induced by industrialization and internal migration, La Boca braced for a clash between tradition and modernity. The perenneality of strong riverside unions represented a shield against irreversible decline.

The advent of the Second World War, growth of the merchant marine, and succession of conservative administrations in the 1940s caused waterfront unions to step up their wage demands and establish their prerogatives over new representative institutions that were tolerated by the regime. In 1942, when the FOM won control of a new retirement pension fund for maritime workers, Atilio Biondi, by then a living anarcho-syndicalist legend in the port (who, true to anarchist principles, always worked and never accepted a functionary's pay), was elected to manage the fund alongside FOM leader Fortunato Marinelli (a full-time paid union secretary). In La Boca, this victory of workers' control over the first welfare institution ever to directly address their future was celebrated in the streets by thousands of men and women; three decades of "revolutionary syndicalist" struggle had culminated in the official recognition of workers' rights, and of the unions' right to represent them.[24] Soon thereafter, however, a succession of events caused the antistatist and antipolitical heritage of these same unions to mobilize in defense of their threatened autonomy. The general secretary of the FOCN, metalworker Luis Bergamonite, was deposed by a quintessential anarcho-syndicalist assembly vote for politicizing the federation under communist auspices.[25] Before and after the June 1943 military coup, state repression intensified, particularly against anarchists affiliated with the longshoremen's SROPC and suspected anarchists and communists in the maritime and shipyard workers' federations.[26] The headquarters of the FOCN on Pedro Mendoza 1915, a popular center of working-class sociability in La Boca, were raided and its leadership accused of being led by "foreign elements who deny jobs to workers of Argentine nationality."[27] The passage of the decree (no 2.669) on professional associations in the aftermath of the coup required unions to apply for "*personería gremial*," or the official recognition of their right to represent workers in a given trade. The decree effectively outlawed all anarchist and syndicalist organizations while communist ones were dissolved and the National Labor Department placed under the tutelage of the chief secretary to the ministry of war—and future Argentine President—Col. Juan Domingo Perón.

The most important episode of this well-known transitional period of Argentine political history, however, was the creation in late November of the Secretaría de Trabajo y Previsión, a government arbitration body that centralized all labor and welfare-related issues in the hands of a single authority. On December 1, 1943, Perón was named to the helm of the new labor secretariat, a position from which he inaugurated a policy of calculated concessions to the noncommunist trade union movement in an effort to rally working-class support for the "national revolution."[28] Anarchism on the waterfront was resurrected by these developments and would soon draw the shipyard workers back into the orbit of the nationally decimated but locally revered historic FORA. The shipyard workers' federation had been plagued by dissention since 1938, when the anarchist painters' union had broken with the syndicalist USA, and particularly since 1941 when a third of the federated rank and file had voted against the acceptance of the retirement pensions law negotiated with the conservative government of Roberto Ortiz. In November 1944 the entire FOCN withdrew its support for the law, and an internal debate on the two-decade-old alliance with the maritime workers' federation caused the anarchist braziers' union to temporarily leave the FOCN.[29] In September 1945 the FOLB, the local anarchist federation of Buenos Aires, sent veteran organizer Gregorio Maso to rally shipyard workers behind its beleaguered reorganization and by January of the following year the FOCN had reestablished its formal solidarity pact with the anarchist longshoremen's resistance society.

Thus, the return of the FOCN to the anarchist principles of its founding components was an immediate consequence of the rise of working-class Peronism. In June of 1945 anarchist legend César Pagliarini had triumphantly announced the withdrawal of the port subprefecture's attempt to impose the requirement of a state-sanctioned identity card as a condition for working in the shipyards. Six months later the braziers' resistance society denounced, in an editorial of its newspaper *El Obrero Calderero*, the "ridiculous processions" and "venomous politics" of the October 17 popular uprising against the attempted military detention of Juan Perón.[30]

Maritime Workers Confront Peronism

Expectations engendered by the mobilization of October 1945 and subsequent liberalization of the military regime, coupled with the end of the European war and the pro-labor platform of the Peronist campaign, opened a Pandora's box of class combativeness that largely outflanked pro-government unions among meatpackers and other industrial workers but especially in the port. The hostility of employers to the pro-labor government led them to prefer direct negotiations with strike commissions that were often controlled by locally entrenched craft societies. During a memorable longshoremen's strike in 1946, for example, these circumstances contributed to the effectiveness of traditional direct action strategies and to the revival of anarchist influence (still enshrined by the SROPC and the small anarchist FORA) on the docks, forcing significant concessions by contractors and more extreme measures of direct repression and intervention by the Peronist state.[31]

As for organized maritime workers, shipyard workers' allies who had embraced syndicalism for three decades after participating in Argentine anarchism's early uprisings, they entered the first Perón presidency firmly united behind the five-year economic plan but committed to the preservation of trade union independence. On August 24, 1946, thousands of workers filled the José Verdi theater in La Boca, where orators representing the full ideological spectrum of waterfront unionism invoked the need to form "one big union" to press demands before the ship owners for improved wages and working conditions. The underlying purpose of the meeting was to join forces in an effort to reassert full trade union control over the allocation of work and implementation of rules while steering clear of state agencies and consolidating traditional organizational forms. In February the seamen's and officers' unions unified all existing craft societies into the Confederación General de Gremios Marítimos y Afines (CGGMA), a federalist, decentralized body that would thereafter represent all categories of workers in negotiations with the ship owners and the state. It was the most formidable independent, nationwide organization of seafarers ever created in Argentina, and it continued to bear the standard of trade union autonomy long after the Peronist state had abandoned it.[32] Not a single of its member unions had been created or "intervened" (placed under administrative tutelage) by the authorities during the military dictatorship. All were living symbols of the epic battles of mariners and merchant seamen and well-known entities in La Boca. In March of 1949 the still-illegal CGGMA secured full control of hiring in the merchant marine through an industry-wide *acuerdo solidario* excluding all nonunion labor from the ships. The state had no alternative but to involve the technically clandestine unions of the CGGMA in the negotiation of a long-awaited labor code for the merchant marine.[33]

The ability of workplace custom and traditional organizational forms to withstand political and administrative challenges is an undeniable aspect of this story. While the postwar Peronist state drew its legitimacy from popular consent and the advocacy of workers' economic rights, history had demonstrated that nothing short of an authoritarian crackdown on organized labor and a full-fledged open-shop drive could durably undermine the time-tested legitimacy of maritime workers' unions based in the Riachuelo district. Conditions of abundant employment and unprecedented export growth worked in favor the unions and put pressure on the government, as it had under Hipólito Yrigoyen in the aftermath of the First World War, to lean on the shipping establishment when it threatened industrial peace by violating wage scales and working standards. Maritime workers held their employers to the standards set by the regime, and the language of social justice in which Peronist officials framed their arbitration in work-related conflicts seldom contradicted the mandates of democratically elected union officials, many of whom continued to proclaim their anarchist and syndicalist affiliations.

In May of 1949 a transformational event occurred that would also directly impact the shipyard workers and sow the seeds of their insurgency in the mid-1950s. The nationalization of the largest shipping concern in the country, the Dodero (ex-Mihánovich) company, brought the state's share in

the Argentine shipping industry from 40 to 70 percent.[34] The announcement that the workers' most-feared and notorious adversary since the turn
of the century would be nationalized initially provoked jubilant applause
from the ranks of maritime workers, their allies, and sympathizers. It soon
became apparent, however, that the shift of balance between public and
private ownership of the merchant marine spelled trouble for the syndicalist CGGMA. Once again, as they had been by Catholic, conservative, and
nationalist forces from the very beginning of the century, these historic
unions were vilified by the Peronist establishment as the instruments of a
foreign conspiracy against the nation. They were defeated in 1950 after a
strike that was remembered by its protagonists, until the 1956–57 shipyard
workers' strike, as the heroic "last stand" of anarcho-syndicalist tradition
in La Boca in which Radical Civic Union, communist, and socialist activists at odds with the regime took part.[35] Only after the defeat of that major
strike movement did the regime succeed in dismantling the CGGMA and
bureaucratizing maritime unionism under the authority of the mainstream
Confederación General de Trabajadores (CGT). The circumstances of this
climactic showdown illustrate the power of nationalist ideology to selectively transform the past, and of political triumphs achieved by the state in
the name of workers to silence even the most unyielding historical voices
within the labor movement. In a context of firm public control over shipping capital, militarization of the port of Buenos Aires, marginalization of
private contractors, and rationalization of labor throughout the waterfront,
the maternal heroine of the seafaring plebe delivered the final blow to her
adorers in La Boca. Eva Perón, a vocal advocate of progressive social pro-
grams for waterfront workers, and her protégé, José Espejo, of the CGT
turned their efforts to eradicating the influence of pervasive anarcho-syndicalist traditions in the merchant marine.

The community of La Boca was shaken by this war of wills between
the CGGMA and the Peronist regime. For many workers employed in the
largest ship repair concern of the Riachuelo district, for example, this was
their first exposure to the perils of nationalization and to the militancy
of the historic anarcho-syndicalist FOCN.[36] Leaders of the locally revered
union who had radicalized their struggle against the regime in coordination with anarchist resistance societies in the port suspended work in numerous smaller shipyards and workshops on both banks of the Riachuelo.
La Boca braced for yet another prolonged paralysis of commercial activity, ship movement, and job opportunities. Within maritime unionism, the
historic identification of several local craft societies with the Radical Civic

Union; the presence of anarchists, communists, and socialists in position of authority; and the internationalism of the syndicalist leadership provided nationalists with strong rhetorical claims against the legitimacy of the CGGMA. The UCR, communist party, and anarchists of the FORA threw their support behind the forty-thousand-odd striking maritime workers, who within days succeeded in paralyzing 90 percent of shipping activities in the country.[37]

The denunciation of the maritime workers' unions as "unpatriotic" took on a special meaning at this conjuncture of institutional and economic modernization in Argentina. On the one hand, the spectacular rise in the capacity of the merchant marine was singled out by the regime as its single greatest achievement.[38] Not surprisingly, when in June news reached Buenos Aires that the International Transport Workers' Federation was considering a boycott of Argentine ships in reprisal for the government's crackdown on strikers, the reaction of the Peronist establishment was indignant. "To attack the Argentine merchant fleet," wrote the newspaper *El Líder*, "is to attack one of the vital strengths of the fatherland, and the peoples served by the relentless efficiency of its work. Above all, it is to attack the Justicialist regime that Argentina has built by the sovereign will of its people."[39] CGT spokesmen lashed out against the *"canalla apátrida, sin Dios ni Patria"* (wretched traitors without God nor fatherland) who had "sold out the nation for silver coins" and betrayed Peronist ideals, deemed "the genuine expression of Argentineness" (*argentinidad*).[40] The government threatened foreign-born members of the maritime and shipyard workers' unions with expulsion from the country and ordered raids of offices and meeting halls in La Boca.

When, after three months, the strike was defeated, known activists of the CGGMA and FOCN were locked out of employment on the ships and yards for several years. A pro-government body, the Asociación Marítima Argentina (AMA) was established to replace the banned craft societies that had belonged to the syndicalist and anarchist federations. The goals of the new entity were stated as follows: "To assist work, punctuality, productivity; all in support of the National Economic Plan, which means collaborating with our Fatherland in the new Justicialist era."[41] One year later, shortly before her death, Eva Perón addressed an assembly of maritime workers to commemorate "the first year in the life of the trade union movement" in the merchant marine.[42] The verdict was in, it seemed, on a half century of virtually uninterrupted labor activism on the Buenos Aires waterfront. Yet the community of seasoned anarcho-syndicalist activists rooted in that history would continue, for the remainder of the Peronist period, to resist this state of affairs, and in 1956–57 a dramatic strike and lock-out again convulsed the neighborhood, fomented this time by the FOCN and resurgent nuclei of the anarchist FORA in La Boca.

The Final Stand of Anarchist Shipyard Workers

Time and time again over four decades, unmanageable centralization schemes and belated efforts to undermine the informal leverage of water-front unions in the labor process and their legitimacy in the local commu-nity had failed. The AMA was no exception: its records report numerous cases of insubordination, inefficiency at work, and organized rank-and-file dissidence. After the defeat of the maritime workers' strike, the clandestine FOCN exhorted its members to ignore the new entity: "Resist obedience; resist paying dues; resist all the orders and maneuvers of the delegates of the AMA and CGT, of Peronism and all its instruments."[43] In 1952 AMA officials reported the discovery of five independent labor exchanges in the streets of La Boca that provided employment to shipyard workers without official authorization.[44] The FOCN continued to claim its historic head-quarters in La Boca despite its occupation by the AMA, and rank-and-file discontent with the bureaucratic directives of the new union caused the older craft societies to recruit new members among the growing number of younger workers in the industry. The predominance of FOCN influence in small, private artisanal workshops notwithstanding, the Departamento de Construcciones Navales of the AMA was unable even to incorporate the union of the Flota Argentina de Navegación de Ultramar (FANU, ex-Dodero) shipyards, which was not affiliated with the clandestine federa-tion.[45] Its leader, Antonio Lorenzini, was a dedicated Peronist who would support, after the fall of the regime, the unification of his movement with the anarcho-syndicalist FOCN.[46] In November of 1954 FANU workers led a successful illegal strike against the layoff of fifty-five workers, which was supported by the underground FOCN, and won their reinstatement.[47]

During and after the Peronist experiment, the shipyard sector was one in which large, state-owned facilities competed with smaller, more traditional employers to rationalize, modernize, and bureaucratize the labor process at a time of rapid industrial expansion. When the state seized control of the merchant marine or decasualized employment on the docks, anarcho-syndicalist practices rooted in community networks of informality, trust, and local patronage had resisted the change and sought to preserve their influence with (and power over) small private entrepreneurs. They had, however, always encountered stiff competition from unions tied to the public sector, many of them willing to trade their independence for welfare benefits. In the shipyards, the ability of the authorities to rally even small firms to the position of state-owned companies radicalized the rank and file in both sectors against rationalization, uniting older Italian anarchists and seasoned syndicalists with a growing young generation of workers for whom regular employment was unachievable until one of the two forces in contention—the state (and, until 1955, its allies in the CGT) or the anarchist FOCN—prevailed as the main purveyor of work and arbiter of contracts.

In September of 1955 the AMA offices of Lamadrid Street in La Boca were stormed by rank-and-file workers after Perón had been deposed in a military coup. The FOCN reemerged on October 10 and claimed representation of the entire ship repair industry, which it had not relinquished in practice since 1916, despite decades of illegality and repression. In the prewar era, however, the vast majority of employers in the industry had been small- or medium-scale or private. They were as grounded in the community of the Riachuelo district as the anarchist resistance societies and syndicalist unions that organized their workers. By 1955, 80.6 percent of the activity was state-owned, with FANU (ex-Dodero, the historic Mihánovich fleet), the Flota Mercante del Estado and Yacimientos Petrolíferos Fiscales (the government-owned petroleum company) dominating all shipbuilding and ship repair activity.[48]

Almost immediately private shipyard owners and state administrators began obstructing the process of reorganization initiated by the emboldened FOCN. With the backing of the Labor Ministry, the firm of Tognetti & Co. resolved to lock out the workers rather than face the return of their representatives to the bargaining table. The conflict rapidly escalated into a standoff between activists who sought to revive the proud heritage of the anarcho-syndicalist tradition, and entrepreneurs organized in the Unión de Constructores Navales who, by refusing to recognize the FOCN, set the stage for the polarization and direct action in which those traditions had thrived. Violence broke out between strike commissions and suspected blacklegs, instances of economic sabotage were reported, and police searched the streets of La Boca for suspected "anarchist provocateurs."[49] In the provincial port city of Rosario, another historic bastion of Argentine anarchism, shipyard worker and activist Ramiro García Fernández was stabbed in the back and killed. By September 1956 seven thousand workers on both banks of the Riachuelo were idle. The industry had closed down rather than negotiate on the basis of the federation's demands, the boldest of which was an old anarchist aspiration: the establishment of a six-hour work day in order to compensate for hazardous working conditions and to free up time and distribute jobs fairly to those who needed them.[50]

The workers' initial response was to declare a general strike, which, although it became partial in January 1957, would last fourteen months, mobilizing some eighteen thousand workers nationwide and ten thousand in Buenos Aires alone.[51] The strike invited local, national, and international expressions of solidarity and resurrected the rituals, diatribes, deliberations, and fervent belief in direct democracy that had sustained anarchist and syndicalist traditions in La Boca since the turn of the century. The owners attacked the FOCN for disregarding decrees and legislation passed on from the previous (and vilified) Peronist regime, warned against the dangers of a return to recurrent conflicts of the prewar past, and deplored the illegality of anarchist direct action tactics.[52] The FOCN, in the meantime, celebrated the pre-1950 era of trade union independence. It revived the cultural, educational, vocational training, and medical activities of its heyday and activated traditional solidarity pacts with the Sindicato Obreros Marítimos Unidos (ex-FOM), anarchist SROPC, and other waterfront unions. The federation also fiercely defended wage scales and safety regulations and reinvented itself as the incarnation of the promethean aspirations of preindustrial revolutionary labor movements—especially the anarchist FORA—as well as the guardian of community traditions against rapid urbanization and faceless bureaucratization.

At the beginning of the general strike, the Labor Ministry committed to recognizing the FOCN if work were resumed. The government administrators of FANU refused, however, to implement union standards, causing workers throughout the industry to rally to the cause of the federation in defense of its historic conquests and fueling nostalgia for its influence of old.[53] Ultimately, the intransigence of both public and private employers, who were determined to reestablish their control over the labor process, forced the ministry to relent and withdraw its initial willingness to negotiate with the workers.[54] The absence of an effective state interlocutor and the success of direct action tactics reestablished anarcho-syndicalist authority among the rank and file, causing the unions to anticipate victory by voting a new *pliego de condiciones*, or basis for resolution of the conflict (establishing wages, shifts, holidays, vacations, insurance, and accident compensation standards). Employers were given twenty days to respond.[55]

The August 20 decision by a massive assembly vote in La Boca's Teatro Verdi to revive the old anarchist aspiration of a six-hour workday represented an effort by the leadership of the FOCN to launch a more positive, offensive, and ideologically inspiring campaign for workers' emancipation, in addition to the simple defense of wages and working conditions articulated in the *pliego*. With Peronist influence over the larger labor movement on the rise, the intent of the federation's ideologues was to establish the supremacy of their ideals and instill a culture of resistance to rationalization and productivity-driven measures of labor discipline and control. FANU responded by closing the yards and firing its entire workforce, including wounded and hospitalized workers as well as apprentices who were already limited to six-hour shifts.[56] Private employers organized in the Unión de Constructores Navales followed suit shortly thereafter; those who refused to disrupt their relationship with the FOCN were threatened with intervention by the Labor Ministry and ultimately relented.

That the offensive of Gen. Pedro Aramburu's government against the anarchist shipyard workers' movement coincided with his repression of Peronist organizations increased the impression of a wholesale assault on labor in general. Whereas Peronists demanded government recognition of the CGT, however, the anarchists, by insisting on direct resolutions of conflicts between capital and labor without state intervention, became the post-Peronist standard-bearers of "free trade unionism," which was also advocated by communists, socialists, radicals, and independents who rejected the legacy of collaboration between unions and the state that had characterized the previous regime. In the case of the FORA-affiliated shipyard workers and their allies, "free" trade unionism not only excluded politics from working-class activism and the state from meddling in the affairs of workers' organizations. It also meant reviving revolutionary, anticapitalist principles of grassroots, assembly-based direct democracy and community empowerment through education and struggle. As had historically been the case, at least before 1930, these principles did not exclude sympathizers of political parties from participating in trade union life; they simply prohibited them from subordinating the movement to parliamentary or electoral objectives and theorized that they would become "schooled" in a culture of radical emancipation by their participation in the defense of freedom through direct action and unmediated class conflict. In this context the survival of the FOCN and of the traditions it represented became the overarching goal of the movement. Economic demands took a back seat to direct democracy, community empowerment, organizational federalism, and revolutionary resistance to state-sponsored, capitalist modernization.

The movement's symbolic meaning took precedence over its immediate practical objectives and comforted its leaders in their posture of intransigence. For the employers, in turn, the "de-anarchization" of working-class representation was as paramount to their thinking about the showdown in the Riachuelo district as the "de-Peronization" of the Argentine labor movement writ large.[57] The stakes of the FORA-led general strike in the shipyards paralleled those of national offensive against organized workers and were widely perceived as a legitimate defense of the rights of labor to resist, which explains why the popularity of the movement largely exceeded the arena of anarchist assemblies and localized, community-based expressions of solidarity.

The impact of this localized movement on national politics did not go unnoticed. As in 1902, when anarchist and socialist workers who had paralyzed the Argentine export industry earned an audience before the Chamber of Commerce, in September of 1956 one group of striking anarchist shipyard workers' unions, dissenting from the others, accepted an invitation by Alfredo Palacios (who in 1904 had been the first elected socialist member of parliament from La Boca) to meet, alongside a delegation of Uruguayan labor leaders who supported the strikers' cause, with President Aramburu himself.[58] Considering that the unions were illegal and that their recognition by employers was their overarching demand, this incident—which was inconsequential and ignored by the anarchist newspaper *La Protesta*—illustrates how concerned the authorities were with the conflict.

The more telling story, however, is the extent of grassroots solidarity with the movement and its ability to mobilize the barrio in tangible ways—through assistance to striking workers' families, public demonstrations of support, pickets admonishing blacklegs, student rallies, emergency fundraising for prisoners and their families, and massively attended assemblies in traditional places of popular sociability, such as Italian and Yugoslav ethnic societies. On November 20 a solidarity rally in the Plaza Constitución, north of the Riachuelo district, summoned representatives of Uruguayan, Paraguayan, and Chilean labor movements. Maritime workers' unions opened their medical facilities to strikers, transport workers' and plumbers' unions petitioned the Labor Ministry on their behalf, and medical students organized a public debate on the conflict. The anarchist longshoremen's union organized temporary job placement on the docks for idle shipyard workers.[59] Women were mobilized to guard the gates of shipyards against the hiring of nonunion workers and extend food to hungry strikers.[60]

The owners, the state and the CGT (which at the time was administered by a government "*interventor*," Capt. Patrón Laplacette), established a parallel union, the Sindicato Argentino de Obreros Navales, to represent workers under the leadership of a former leader of the AMA from the metalworkers' union, Eduardo de Luca. As the sole provider of employment, the new union, which was legally recognized on June 5, gradually enabled the resumption of activity in the yards.[61] Six months later the strike ended from exhaustion: on November 13, 1957, an assembly vote of the FOCN authorized the reincorporation of workers to their posts. Thousands of FOCN activists and affiliates who had been replaced by less experienced outsiders—who had been reviled as "*carneros*," or blacklegs, during the strike— were permanently banned, and the federation never reclaimed its stature as a pivotal labor organization in the industry.

Remembrances of the Anarchist Storyline

In their vivid remembrances and personal interpretations of the drama that unfolded, many retired shipyard workers conveyed a feeling of almost mystical reverence for the old anarchists who lurked in assemblies dispensing advice, recounting their life stories and lore. Manuel Novoa, who was the young provisional secretary of the FOCN during its reorganization, was reluctant to even claim the mantle: "I'm a freethinker. To be an anarchist you have to achieve a whole different level of virtue and accomplishments in your life. . . . The police kept saying I was an anarchist," he quipped. "What did they know? If I had been, they would never have caught me." While he had long since abandoned his faith in unions and become estranged from many of his old comrades, Novoa took care to show pride in his role in the movement. When I asked him detailed questions about places, he—who had commuted to the shipyards from Sarandí in Buenos Aires province— responded as if he had lived in La Boca all his life. His knowledge of local history and of the anarchist past, acquired second-hand, seemed almost autobiographical, as if he had always been there. In reality, he had worked for only a brief period in ship repair before being banned, along with scores of other FOCN activists, from the yards. Yet the cathartic experience of the strike and what it stood for seemed to make him feel part of a much larger historic occurrence, of which he was clearly in awe.[62] Armando Freire, a veteran of the 1950 maritime workers' strike as well as the 1956–57 movement in the shipyards, expressed similar feelings: "I have always wanted to be an anarchist. It's a way a life, a form of action and ethic of dignity. Let the real anarchists decide whether I have deserved to be one."[63]

Domingo Trama, another former secretary of the FOCN, recalled that he had been fascinated by anarchism since a shipyard brazier named Juan Nabone lent him Errico Malatesta's book, *En el café*. At the age of seventeen, Trama became a union spokesman, and by his early twenties he had experienced all the indignities of every anarchist vitae—jail, intimidation, and the loss of employment. When I asked his former comrades if they regarded him as an anarchist, however, neither his friends nor detractors would agree. None more than Trama, who was eighty years old at the time, could recite with such precision the history of the organized labor movement in Argentina, and he had presided for decades over the local commemoration of the 1956 strike. He shunned discussion of Peronism altogether ("a Peronist has no ideas") and of the communists among the rank and file who had been critical of the general strike ("nonsensical political cronies who were always trying to get their foot in the door"). The "official" history he intended for my microphone meticulously recounted the achievements of the shipyard workers' unions and the names and biographies of anarchist "great men." A self-proclaimed "anarchist all my life," Trama could not bring himself to talk at length about the travails of the strike and its eventual defeat. "You keep asking why we failed," he finally said in an exasperated tone. "Why don't you ask, have we not won? What history remembers is the example." Rather than convey his personal impressions, Trama seemed intent on preserving the collective memory of the strike from extinction.[64]

When I discussed the events of 1956 and 1957 with Horacio Torrado and Juan Taborski, both rank-and-file shipyard workers who had labored in the FANU (ex-Dodero) yards, their arguments over what went wrong during the strike are very instructive. Both admired, as did many others who worked with him, the Peronist leader-turned-FOCN-sympathizer of the FANU union, Antonio Lorenzini. They even had words of praise for Eva Perón. Whenever one wanted to gain an authoritative upper hand on the other, however, he referred to something that César Pagliarini, a veteran Italian anarchist from the foundational days of the FOCN a half century earlier, had said to them during the conflict. Through Pagliarini, these comparatively young men had been versed not just in the history of the local labor movement and community but in anarchist political philosophy. Like Novoa, they venerated the wisdom of an old anarchist and blushed at the suggestion that they might be in the same league. Taborski, in particular, was disheartened by the failure of his later efforts to "transform society" by founding a shipyard workers' cooperative on the basis of equal pay for equal work. "The old ones were right. Class struggle is inevitable, and without resistance on the part of unions to protect them, workers become drifters and thieves. Liberation is a question of education." When I asked him if he held out any hope for Argentine labor, he answered, "Yes. Why not? Don't you? Anarchists are defeated but their ideas live." "Nah," Horacio scoffed, "cut the nonsense, Juan. We were fools to give up. The honor of anarchists was that they never did. Argentina needs people like the old Pagliarini. Without them we have no hope."[65]

Older anarchists whom I interviewed placed much more emphasis on the pride in work and craftsmanship, memories of fraternity and solidarity, grand hopes of social revolution, and the unrelenting turpitudes of betrayal. Rarely did I encounter in my conversations with veterans of waterfront unions tearful nostalgia for a golden age long since passed. Almost always, however, the "experiences" and "knowledge" these men volunteered transcended the immediate recollection of their personal actions. "La Boca was never subdued by the reactionaries," Humberto Correale of the painters' union marveled. "I learned what it meant to be free when I came to work there. It was an anarchist city." Born and raised in Argentina, he remarked, "The police always called me a foreign agitator. They were foreign to me. And the nationalists, well, their ideas are the most foreign there are."[66] Activists like Correale, who upheld the banner of the FORA, remembered the past not just as they lived or observed it but through the prism of traditions and meanings conveyed by a larger story, which continued to serve a purpose in their lives.

Stigmatization and Erasure

In the end, the victory of state-sponsored capitalist rationalization in the shipyards was total, and the institutionalization of collective bargaining under the auspices of the CGT "normalized" labor relations in accordance with modern industrial norms. The strike of 1956–57 indeed represented "anarchism's last stand" in a historically rebellious, tightly knit cosmopolitan community that had been in steady decline since the turn of the century, in transition from a cosmopolitan *aldea* (village) of craftspeople, sailors, and seasonal laborers to an urban-industrial complex on the outlying fringes of the modern city. The history of the conflict reveals the extraordinary resilience of anarcho-syndicalist ideals, traditions, organizational forms, cultural references, counterhegemonic resistance, and tangible expressions of leverage in the labor processes exercised by craft-based unions with proven revolutionary credentials.

The vilification by nationalists and capitalist interests of La Boca as a breeding ground for exotic revolutionary agitation and disorderly lifestyles was a representation of space and identity that stigmatized one historical enactment of class formation in order to validate another. To the standard-bearers of the new Argentina, La Boca symbolized the uncontrollable, dangerous, uncivilized, sexually promiscuous, unmarried community of traitors to the nation infected by foreign-inspired conspiracies of revolution, in direct opposition to the "national," "patriotic" Argentina in which domesticity, family-oriented freedoms, patriarchal protections, respectability, hard work, and male valor were celebrated. The incorporation of unions into the state accompanied the rise of nationalism, and the localization/stigmatization of La Boca and its labor heritage as "foreign," a place of counterintuitive disorder and defiance that enshrined a prenational history in urgent need of forgetting. The episode of the 1956–57 strike was the last stand of activists who hoped to preserve the traditions and independence of working-class organizations nurtured by decades of support in the barrio. Their spirited defense of direct democracy and anticapitalist struggle meshed with a longing, shared by many in the community, for the preservation of an idealized preindustrial past in which informal relations among neighbors took precedence over the authoritarian structures of the modern state, and workers held capitalists at bay with the threat of withdrawing their labor.

Throughout the emergence of powerful waterfront unions in the first half of the twentieth century, the stigma of foreignness in La Boca and the radicalization of the waterfront workers' unions contributed to the crystallization of class combativeness and capitalist fears of localized labor traditions. The enemies of organized labor in the early decades of the century had been accused by anarchists and syndicalists of using native Argentine workers to undermine the cosmopolitan constituencies and internationalist solidarity of revolutionary, class-based movements. By the late 1930s and 1940s, and during the epic last stand of anarchism in the shipyards, labor traditions were co-opted by more conservative, nationalist circles while the community of La Boca itself was derided as the birthplace of foreign ideologies and agitation, as a place of betrayal and antipatriotic loyalties, as the "weak sex" of the nation. Already represented in the late nineteenth and early twentieth centuries as an Italian "*barrio infestato fai mali sociali*" (neighborhood infected by social ills), a "modern Babylon of all languages," "l'inferno del Dante" (Dante's Hell), La Boca became a "representational space" (the "dominated—and, hence, passively experienced—space in which the imagination seeks to change and appropriate . . . , making symbolic use of its objects") of an Argentine historicity purged of its "anti-national" voices.[67]

Today La Boca is remembered as the birthplace of tango and hub of historic soccer clubs as well as a romanticized bastion of "foreign" or immigrant heritage; it has been thoroughly "cleansed, sanitized and rearranged for the delectation of the tourist gaze."[68] The labor history chronicled in this essay is conspicuously absent from commemorations and public history.[69] The past of the "*orillera*" or riverside culture is represented as downcast and dangerous, hybrid and volatile, a symbol of "*gringo*" or antinational sentiment, a marginal and exotic environment in which the nostalgia and sinfulness of a wild and uprooted past has become a substitute for historical reflection on the history of organized labor and revolutionary alternatives to the status quo.[70] "Italianness"—the creation of decades of ethnic mutualism, of nostalgic celebrations of craft pride, and of the representation of the barrio as a fallen bastion of cultural and moral integrity burdened by the "loose morality" and "barbarism" of "La Boca's others"[71]—is all that remains of this history in the social imaginary of the contemporary city. The defeat of organized labor on the Buenos Aires waterfront, the erasure of its epic battles for class emancipation, and the forgetting of La Boca as its dramatic stage are casualties of a complex history in which the state-sanctioned representation of social progress and conservative nationalism of postwar labor politics triumphed at the expense of the dreams and heterotopias that engendered them.

Argentine anarchism translated the practices, language, and modes of identification of a European ideology transmitted by immigrant workers and activists into a novel "autochthonous" discourse of myth and belonging, blending class and popular identities by rooting their militancy in local settings and oppositional movements.[72] In the case of the powerful waterfront unions of Buenos Aires, which built sustained relays in the interior as well as transnational networks of mutual solidarity, the decline of the Riachuelo district, from which they drew their strategic power of nuisance, spelled the erosion of the relational settings that lent effectiveness to direct action, tangibility to cultural resistance, and legitimacy to their movements. The "classical" era of anarchism rooted in labor movements ended when state-sponsored administrations, industrial rationalization, and political institutions displaced localities and traditional unions as the theater of popular resistance and working-class citizenship. Whether the ethical and philosophical underpinnings of anarchist ideas themselves, and the belief in popular empowerment outside of bureaucratic institutions that they reflected, were a definitive casualty of that transition remains to be seen.

Notes

1. The most well-documented standard accounts of the early FORA's history in relation to the labor movement remain Abad de Santillán, *La F.O.R.A., ideología y trayectoria*; Bilsky, *La FORA y el movimiento obrero(1900–1910)*; and Yoast, "The Development of Argentine Anarchism." The cultural contours of Argentine anarchism's during this initial period are discussed in Suriano, *Paradoxes of Utopia* and in a forthcoming study by Moya, "Rebels with Many Causes." Worthy background studies of anarchism in late nineteenth century are González Rivera, *Anarquismo argentino (1876–1902)*; and Oved, *El anarquismo*.
2. Bourdieu, "Espace social et genèse des classes."
3. Somers, "Deconstructing and Reconstructing Class."
4. Tilly, "Contention and the Urban Poor."
5. James, *Resistance and Integration*, 21–23, 34, and 263.
6. Williams, *Marxism and Literature*, 115.
7. James, *Resistance and Integration*, 2.
8. de Laforcade, "A Laboratory of Argentine Labor Movements"; and de Laforcade, "Straddling the Nation and the Working World."
9. Gross, *Lost Time*, 142–43.
10. Chiaramonte, *Mercaderes del litoral*, 93–94; Pugliese, *Páginas de historia*; and Silvestri, *El color del río*.
11. Gardia de D'Agostino et al., *Imágen de Buenos Aires*, 160.
12. Lazzaro, *Estado, capital extranjero y sistema portuario argentino*; Vásquez Presedo, "Navegación y puertos"; and Ortiz, *Valor económico de los puertos argentinos*.
13. Pinasco, *Biografía del Riachuelo*, 66; Scobie, *Buenos Aires*, 81, 85–86; and Pikulski and Orguiquil, *Dock Sud*, 9–19.
14. Bucich, *La Boca del Riachuelo*; Nogues, *Buenos Aires*; Pugliese, *Páginas de historia*; and Silvestri, *El color del río*.
15. *El Pueblo*, November 18–19, 1901; letter of Bartolo Mihánovich to Elias Lavarello dated November 17, 1901, assuring the director of the company that his workers were distinct from other groups and less prone to succumb to anarchist agitation. Shipyard workers ultimately were the longest-lasting bastion of anarcho-syndicalist trade union culture.
16. *La Vanguardia*, December 21, 1901; *La Prensa*, January 3, 1902, and January 5, 1902; *La Prensa*, February 21, 1902; and Policía de la Capital, Comisaria 20, *Informe sobre la pacificación de la zona portuaria*, February 25, 1902.

17. Prefectura General de Puertos, "Agitadores, vividores y violentos en la zona portuaria," mimeo taped to División de Investigaciones, *Copiador interno no. 6 (1905/1906)*.

18. In early April of 1915, the ninth congress of the anarchist FORA officially proclaimed its unification with the syndicalist Confederación Obrera Regional Argentina and adopted the fundamental precepts of syndicalist doctrine: reliance on direct action and the concerted general strike, independence from political parties and the state, and organization along the lines of industrial unionism. Those unions that rejected the departure from anarcho-communist precepts, such as the SROPC and the Federación Obrera Local Bonaerense, remained coalesced in the FORA-V, whereas the new syndicalist federation became known as the FORA-IX. Both the Federación Obrera Maritima (FOM) and the SROPC enjoyed their most successful campaigns in the years immediately following this reorganization.

19. *La Vanguardia*, August 7, 1923.

20. *La Vanguardia*, September 13, 1905; and September 15, 1905.

21. Policía Federal, Division Orden Social, *Copiador de investigaciones*, no. 25 (October 22, 1906): 378–79; *Copiador de investigaciones*, no. 26 (November 7, 8, and 26, 1906): 80–82, 96–98, and 268.

22. Prefectura General de Puertos, *Copiador interno*, no. 12 (August 25, 1910): 116–17; interview with Humberto Correale in 1991; and Cassaretto, *Historia del movimiento obrero argentino*, 2:53–58.

23. Interview with Domingo Trama, February 14, 1991. The creation of the ALA coincided with the assassination of Lt. Col. Héctor Varela, author of the Patagonia massacres in 1921 and 1922, by a young German worker named Kurt Wilckens. His murder on June 16 provoked a nationwide general strike called by the USA and FORA-V, during which the ALA lobbied intensively among waterfront unions for the adoption of revolutionary violence as a mode of action. See *La Antorcha*, February 1, 1924; May 6, 1924; September 25, 1925; September 9, 1925; and October 16, 1925.

24. *El Marino*, May 1941, May 1942, and March 1942; Federación obrera marítima, *Memoria al congreso*, 83–88; and Federación obrera marítima, *La Caja de jubilaciones marítimas*.

25. *Orientación*, September 23, 1942; October 1, 1942; and May 27, 1943; *El Marino*, November 1942; and *Boletín informativo de la FOM*, September 1942 and May 1943.

26. Policía de la Capital, División de Investigaciones, Archivo General, Sección 24, *Copiador de Notas no. 2*, 10–11 and 21–22, February 17, 1943, and March 17, 1943.

27. Policía de la Capital, *Copiador Orden Gremial 1943/1944*, September 24, 1943; 6–7.

28. *Boletín Oficial*, July 24, 1943, September 13, 1943, September 15, 1943, November 15, 1943, and December 4, 1943; República Argentina, Ministerio de Trabajo y Previsión de la Nación, *Memoria Junio 1946-Diciembre 1951*, Buenos Aires: División de Publicaciones del Ministerio de Trabajo y Previsión, 1953, 7–8; Matsushita, *Movimiento obrero argentina, 1930–1945*, 260–61; and Torre, *La vieja guardia sindical y Perón*, 60–61.

29. *Libro de Actas de Asamblea General de la Federación Obrera en Construcciones Navales (FOCN)*, 1938/1946, July 16, 1938, 16; November 21, 1941, 75; December 14, 1941, 77; November 25, 1944, 152; March 17, 1945, 166–67; September 6, 1945, 173–76; September 15, 1945, 180; and January 26, 1946, 190.

30. *El Obrero Calderero*, March 1945, June 1945, and December 1945.

31. de Laforcade, *A Laboratory of Argentine Labor Movements*, ch.6.

32. *La Unión del Marino*, February 1947–October 1947; and interviews with Regino Rodríguez, December 10, 1990; Florentino Antonio Romero, March 7, 1991; and Liberato Fernández, March 9, 1991.

33. *La Unión del Marino*, January 1949, March 1949, and May 1949; and *Marina Mercante Argentina*.

34. *Libro de Actas Dodero No. 4, Directorio (1947–1949)*, Acta no. 301, April 29, 1949; *El Marino*, July 1, 1949; *La Unión del Marino*, July 1949 and August 1949; *Marina*, no. 158, September 1949; González Climent, *Historia de la Marina Mercante Argentina*, vol. 5, 73–74; Luna, *Perón y su tiempo*, 109–11; and Archivo General de la Armada, República Argentina, Ministerio de Marina, "Nota S-4-0-252 al Ministro de Hacienda referente a la vinculación de los intereses del Estado con los de la Companía Argentina de navegación Nicolás Mihánovich," July 12, 1934. Between 1944 and 1949, the state-owned company expanded its yearly tonnage by fifty times, and by 1950 it handled nearly a quarter of the nation's coastal shipping. The nationalized Dodero fleet accounted for about one-third; *El Líder*, May 16, 1949; and Chamber of Commerce of the USA in the Argentine Republic, *Comments on Argentine Trade*, vol. 30, no. 3, October 1950, 75.

35. Contreras, "Clase obrera y peronismo"; and Di Tella, *Perón y los sindicatos*, 258–59.

36. *La Nación*, May 30, 1950; *El Líder*, May 10, 1950; Confederación general de gremios marítimos y afines, *CGGMA: Informativo* no. 2, May 31, 1950; *CGGMA: Informativo* no. 3, June 3, 1950; and interview with Orlando Torrado, September 5, 1993.

37. *El Líder*, May 20, 1950, and October 10, 1950; Rotóndaro, *Realidad y cambio en el sindicalismo*, 245–46; Luna, *Perón y su tiempo*, 398–99; and interview with Florentino Antonio Romero, January 7, 1991.

38. *Marina*, May 1950.

39. *El Líder*, June 29, 1950.

40. Ibid., July 2, 1950.

41. Asociación Marítima Argentina, Departmento de Construcciones Navales, Seccional Astilleros y Talleres Nacionales, Sub-Secretaría de la Marina Mercante, Secretaría General, *Actas 1951–1952*, February 19, 1952, 107.

42. Speech reprinted in a special issue of the monthly newspaper *AMA*, no. 17, February 1952, dedicated to the recently deceased first lady.

43. *El Constructor Naval*, March 1952.

44. Asociación Marítima Argentina, Departamento de Construcciones Navales, *Libro de Actas 1951–1952*, 36–41.

45. Calello, Marin, and Murmis, "Formas de lucha," 32–33.

46. Ministerio de Trabajo y Previsión, Dirección de Asociaciones Profesionales, *Actas del Consejo Directivo de la Asociación Marítima Argentina*, vol. 2 (1952): 138–55; and interview with Orlando Torrado, September 7, 1992.

47. *El Constructor Naval*, December 1954–January 1955.

48. González Climent, *Historia de la Marina Mercante*, 142.

49. República Argentina, Policía Federal, Sección 24, *Copiador de Notas no. 2, año 1956*, March 8, 1956; *Copiador de Notas no. 3, año 1956*, "Al señor Jefe de la Sección Orden Gremial," April 5, 1956; and *Copiador de Notas no. 11, año 1956/57*, January 11, 1957.

50. *El Constructor Naval*, October 11, 1986.

51. The figures were given by FOCN leader Manuel Novoa and published in the organ of the FORA, *La Protesta*, March 1956.

52. Unión de Constructores Navales, *La verdad sobre la situación de la industria naval* Buenos Aires: 1956; Federación Obrera en Construcciones Navales, "Respuesta a la Unión de Constructores Navales," (flyer), September 1956; and *La Unión del Marino*, November 1956.

53. *Reconstruir*, March 1956; and *La Protesta*, March 1956, contain interviews with several FOCN militants.

54. *El Constructor Naval*, May 1956; and *Reconstuir*, August 1956.

55. *La Protesta*, August 1956; and *Reconstruir*, December 1956.

56. *La Protesta*, September 1956; and *Reconstruir*, September 1956.

57. Kravetz, "Anarquistas durante la resistencia peronista."

58. *Reconstruir*, September 1956; Federación de obreros en construcciones navales, *Ocho meses de conflicto en la industria naval: Breve historia de un movimiento de gran significación social y humana* (pamphlet, 1957), 8.

59. *La Protesta*, November 1956; and *La Vanguardia*, September 1957.

60. Domingo Trama interviewed by Atán, *Cuatro historias de anarquistas*, 185.

61. *El Constructor Naval*, April 1958.

62. Interviews with Manuel Novoa, August 31, 1992, and September 3, 1992.

63. Interview with Armando Freire, September 5, 1992.

64. Interviews with Domingo Trama, February 8, 1991, February 11, 1991, and February 14, 1991.

65. Interview with Horacio Torrado and Juan Taborski, February 13, 1991.

66. Interview with Humberto Correale, March 11, 1991.

67. Barrancos, "Vita materiale e battaglia ideológica," 172; *La Nación*, September 9, 1908; *La Protesta*, October 15, 1908; and Lefebvre, *The Production of Space*, 19.

68. Wilson, "Against Utopia," 257.

69. See, for example, Clementi, *La Boca*.

70. Matamoro, *La Ciudad del tango*.

71. Guano, "A Stroll through La Boca," 365.

72. Moreno Sainz, *Anarchisme argentin, 1890–1930*.

III

THE PERSONAL TO THE POPULAR

Nation, Identity, and Gender

9

From Radicals to Heroes of the Republic

Anarchism and National Identity in Costa Rica, 1900–1977

DAVID DÍAZ-ARIAS

In the early 1900s, *nueva intelectualidad*—a group of young radical intellectuals—challenged the way Costa Rican liberal politicians had defined national identity and politics. This chapter describes and examines these radicals through the study of articles they published in their newspapers and journals between 1900 and 1914. Through this discourse we see not only how these leftists challenged liberal politicians but also the relationships they built with urban Costa Rican workers and artisans.[1]

The young intellectuals rooted their critiques of Costa Rican society in the ideas of European anarchism and socialism. But the specific Costa Rican sociocultural reality forced them to transform these conceptions and ideas—a transformation further developed by interactions with workers. Although they framed their analysis in anarchist terms and used anarchist ideas to confront Costa Rica's status quo, this group did not get to the level of other anarchist movements in Latin America or Europe. These young intellectuals basically were able to articulate a cultural defiance, but they were not large enough or influential enough to radically shape labor politics or forge a countercultural social movement. In sum, their key role in Costa Rican politics was as cultural critics, challenging society through their journals, newspapers, poetry, essays, and short stories.

The new intellectuals were most influenced by anarchist thought between 1900 and 1914. After 1914 they became part of government administrations in an attempt to construct their new social project from above. Their anarchist position became less radical at that point. After the civil war of 1948, when most of the *nueva intelectualidad*'s participants had already passed away, several governments started to integrate their intellectual legacy into the official discourse while disavowing their young radicalism. Then the Ministries of Public Education and Culture reedited books and anthologies of essays written by the *nueva intelectualidad*, recommending them as school textbooks. In that new context, several of those who had been recognized as anarchists during the twentieth century's first decade won the title of *beneméritos* (literally, meritorious ones or national heroes), which meant their total integration within official Costa Rican culture. In a certain sense, the liberal national identity that the *nueva intelectualidad* had combated finally devoured them, thus diminishing and trivializing their anarchist past.

An Era of Transition

Late-nineteenth-century Costa Rica underwent major cultural and social transformations. The coffee boom after the 1840s produced several changes in relation to the cultural patterns of consumption. During the 1850s, for the first time, newspapers advertised goods, new public services, the building of shops and workshops, and the spread of lawyers' and doctors' offices.[2] This publicity increased from 1850 to 1900, accompanied by a tremendous cultural differentiation between popular and high classes if we compare it to the previous period.[3]

The last thirty years of the nineteenth century saw the consolidation of a liberal state represented by a new political group self-identified as El Olimpo (the Olympians), which took control of the state in 1882 when Tomás Guardia's dictatorship ended. El Olimpo started a series of reforms based on a new perception about the role of the state in transforming Costa Rican society.[4] For example, in 1884 the El Olimpo–dominated government launched liberal reforms that attempted to reduce the Catholic Church's influence on the popular classes and to expand scientific and secular visions of life and nature among them.[5]

Between 1870 and 1900 Costa Rican writers composed essentially of young people born between the 1850s and 1860s emerged. Authors such as Manuel de Jesús Jiménez (1854–1916), Pío Víquez (1850–99), Jenaro Cardona (1863–1930), Manuel González Zeledón (1864–1936), Carlos Gagini (1865–1925), Aquileo Echeverría (1866–1909), and Ricardo Fernández Guardia (1867–1950) grew up within El Olimpo's framework and developed a literature deeply linked to its liberal ideas. Most of their narratives claimed that the solution to social conflicts rested in finding a balance between "tradition" and capitalist "progress."[6]

The new politicians also believed that the state should control education. Steven Palmer and Gladys Rojas have pointed out that, after 1885, Costa Rican politicians expanded the role of the central government to both control and support public schools as a way to confront the power of both municipalities and the Catholic Church. At the same time, by controlling schools, liberal politicians could "more directly oversee the 'civilizing' of the popular sectors and the forging of a homogeneous national culture."[7] One example concerns literacy. In 1864 total literacy reached 38.4 percent in urban areas while rural areas were just above 10.5 percent. In 1927 total literacy for all above nine years old reached 85.7 percent in urban areas, 66.8 percent in small cities, and 56.4 percent in the countryside.[8]

But El Olimpo had its critics, as a socially heterogeneous group emerged to oppose these liberal reforms. Within this opposition were sectors that El Olimpo had excluded from governmental positions, priests who were against social secularization, and peasants and urban artisans affected by socioeconomic and cultural differentiation as well as proletarization brought about by the growth of a rural wage labor force related to the coffee boom.[9] In response to growing electoral opposition, Costa Rican politicians increased investments in education, health, and public works as a strategy to gain votes.[10] Those investments helped to forge a national vision of Costa Rican state-building that would emphasize social equality and racial homogeneity.[11]

Beginning in the 1870s Costa Rican liberals began to create a new national identity for the country based on liberal political concepts. Fundamental ideas that related to this national discourse involved ethnicity (a country of "white" people), politics (democracy and social peace), and history. In the construction of a suitable past, Costa Rican liberal historians embraced the image of a poor country in the colonial era that progressed rapidly because of the coffee boom after the 1840s. At the same time liberal historians and politicians promoted the 1856–57 war against William Walker's filibusters as the most important part of Costa Rican history and transformed one among its participants—soldier Juan Santamaría—into Costa Rica's most important national hero. Santamaría, a mulatto who died fighting against Walker's troops in Rivas, Nicaragua, had been ignored by politicians until the 1880s. But in 1885, with the threat of war with Guatemala, liberals rescued Santamaría's memory and proposed him as a model citizen for peasants and urban workers. At the same time, the antifilibuster National War of 1856–57 was reimagined as a second independence struggle for Costa Rica. Meanwhile, September 15—when Costa Rica commemorates its independence—became the most important day each year for national festivals.

But all was not well, according to liberals. In 1894 the *Boletín de Escuelas Primarias* (BEP), a journal founded to inform Costa Rican teachers about education and discuss news related to it, published an article pointing out the danger that Costa Rican youth faced. According to this publication, Costa Rican society was experiencing the growth of an evil from within. "Nowadays, we can see the anarchist hydra raising its head in Costa Rica."[12] What was BEP talking about? Essentially its news was related to another cultural change that had been occurring in this period: the publishing of certain books.

The content of books changed considerably by the end of the nineteenth century. Contrary to books about saints' lives that ruled supply during the first years after independence (1821), new books brought to the country after the 1860s tended to be seen as profane in their content due to their strong secularist views. For example, in 1889 the library of the Sociedad de Artesanos de San José (the San Jose Artisans' Association) had pieces by Victor Hugo, Walter Scott, Honoré de Balzac, Eugenio Sue, and Alexandre Dumas. Anarchist literature also started to circulate toward the end of the 1880s. In 1887 the Librería Española sold books written by leading socialist and anarchist authors of the day. Radical books were not typical at this time, however.[13] In that sense, the BEP's alarm referred not so much to the widespread reach of anarchist publications but to their very presence among the Costa Rican working class, a danger that liberal intellectuals— scholars and teachers included—needed to face as soon as possible.

Yet it was the larger political culture of the period that provided the framework that made possible such "dangers." The Catholic and liberal press warned readers about anarchist ideas in Costa Rica. However, such warnings also exposed readers to those very anarchist ideas. As Mario Oliva Medina has argued, "these means publicized a type of anarchism focused in negative and destructive aspects, linked to events taking place in Europe by the end of the 19th century."[14] For instance, since 1877 the newspaper *El Pueblo* claimed to have been founded following this ideal: "To defend democratic institutions by resisting anarchist tendencies."[15] In 1894 the newspaper *Periódico* identified anarchists as "wrongdoers who try to disguise their assaults under a mask of social theories so senseless and so dangerous."[16] Ultimately, liberal politics that promoted the free expression of ideas facilitated the creation of a new group of radical intellectuals in Costa Rica at the beginning of the twentieth century.

Becoming Radical in Early-Twentieth-Century Costa Rica

The number and diversity of anarchist and socialist books increased significantly after 1887 in Costa Rica. Librería Española led this project; its catalogue from 1887 to 1912 shows a wide selection of radical books by Pierre-Joseph Proudhon, Alfred Sudre, Louis Blanc, Karl Marx, Mikhail Bakunin, Peter Kropotkin, and others.[17] Between 1880 and 1912 some working-class newspapers founded by workers started publishing excerpts of anarchist books in an effort to organize mutual aid societies and cooperatives. However, these workers were not alone. In 1905 the newspaper *El Noticiero* reported that some people were teaching "strange views" on love and government at a high school in San José. According to *El Noticiero*, teachers talked to workers about religion as a utopia, the government as a product of coercion, and proposed that workers practice free love. The mainstream press was shocked. In its coverage, *El Noticiero* emphasized the commanding verbal skills of one teacher: José María Zeledón.[18]

In the eyes of the Costa Rican government, Zeledón was neither an ordinary teacher nor a common person. In 1900 Zeledón participated in a contest to write new lyrics to the national anthem. The contest was organized by the newspaper *El Heraldo* and supported by the government between 1902 and 1903.[19] Zeledón won the contest against the government's wishes. The Costa Rican government rejected Zeledón's triumph not only because he had been part of the opposition during the 1901–2 national elections but also due to Zeledón's participation with a group of young intellectuals and writers who had radicalized their discourse against the liberal status quo since the beginning of the century.[20] Ironically, the writer of the national anthem was at the same time a well-known young radical intellectual, known by his peers as "the most anarchist among anarchists." Indeed, Zeledón and his friends were the most important audience for anarchist literature throughout early twentieth-century Costa Rica.

Roberto Brenes Mesén and Joaquín García Monge led this group. The way they became the leaders of the so-called second generation of Costa Rican writers is the way young people from poor backgrounds benefited from liberal education policies. In fact, the government sent Brenes Mesén and García Monge to take classes at the Pedagogical Institute of the University of Chile in 1897 and 1901, respectively. In Chile they combined their studies with an active participation at the Ateneo de Santiago. After returning to Costa Rica, Brenes and García started teaching at the Liceo de Costa Rica and at the Colegio Superior de Señoritas, the capital city's most important public high schools. At the Liceo de Costa Rica, Brenes and García imbued their students with their charismatic and critical personalities and particular conceptions of life.[21] Brenes and García discussed Latin American identity, the impact of imperialism, and the influence of modernist aesthetics brought by the transformation of this young generation that would become leftist intellectuals.[22] This leftist group included Zeledón, Carmen Lyra, Rómulo Tovar, Omar Dengo, Mario Sancho, Vicente Sáenz, Roberto Villalobos, Joaquín Barrionuevo, José Guerrero, Emel Jiménez, José Albertazzi Avendaño, Luis Castro Saborío, Solón Núñez, Rubén Coto, Juan Elías Hernández, Arturo Aguilar, Salomón Castro, José Casasola, Ricardo Falcó, Arturo Torres, José Fabio Garnier, Eduardo Calsamiglia, Víctor Fernández Güell, Agustín Luján, Camilo Cruz Santos, Víctor Manuel Salazar, Octavio Montero, and Moisés Vincenzi.

Most members belonged to what can be considered, in broad terms, middle-class households. As a result, these bourgeois youngsters conceived of themselves as part of neither the oligarchical elite nor the working class.[23] Yet, rather than embracing the liberal creed, this generation identified urban workers' struggles as their own and also portrayed themselves as the only group called to solve workers' social problems. Therefore, both their political essays and their novels presented social problems as the result of class differentiation produced by the liberal state.[24] Furthermore, they saw their mission as fighting against the liberal political beliefs that had given birth to the proletariat.

Following the example of other Latin American anarchists and socialists, Costa Rican intellectuals founded newspapers and journals to spread their message.[25] They conceived culture as the first social sphere that they had to change in order to reshape society. Between 1900 and 1914 these young anarchists published over twenty newspapers and journals. The *nueva intelectualidad* transformed these newspapers into ideological weapons to criticize politics, to communicate anarchist ideas, and to solve social problems. Costa Rican anarchist intellectuals believed they had a social duty that consisted in educating workers to challenge the social order they lived in.

Ivan Molina has argued that there was another cohesive factor that bound the group: besides ideologically radical thoughts, intellectuals shared personal concerns. In effect, they wanted to climb the Costa Rican social and cultural ladder. "Yet, they found growing but limited working positions and they realized their literary pieces were not very appreciated by the high political class and that they had to be subordinated to old, outdated intellectuals whose values they did not share."[26] Living within that environment, young intellectuals opened up cultural venues with a strong social critique that emphasized the problems they were able to solve. From this perspective, young intellectuals combined their leftist beliefs and their possibilities to construct a public space to work and carry out their cultural agenda.[27]

Unlike other Latin American experiences, Costa Rican intellectuals did not choose a particular tenet of anarchism to express their critiques. As we will see regarding their visions about Costa Rican national identity and politics, the *nueva intelectualidad* quoted and used anarchist ideas without regard to their original divisions. As a result, it is possible to find in their articles influences that come from anarcho-collectivism, mutualism, anarcho-syndicalism, and anarcho-communism. The variety of these influences is clear in the list of thirty-nine newspapers that the Costa Rican anarchist journal *Renovación* received and promoted during 1912, a list that shows how anarchists in Costa Rica interacted with a network of anarchist activism from Italy to Spain and from the United States to Argentina.[28] Anarchists in Costa Rica clearly understood the differences between strands of anarchism. It is possible that they used the different types of anarchism and socialism more as way to criticize Costa Rican politics than as a doctrine. That could explain why they did not care about the possible contradiction within their own group's interpretations and why they changed, although slowly, their vision over the years. Moreover, since their main goal was the transformation of culture, they used anarchist ideas to appear more radical. Anarchism worked for them as a way to shake Costa Rica's official and dominant culture.

Costa Rican elites had mixed reactions. The meaning of "civilization" constructed by liberal politicians involved the acceptance of social order and state police authority. In that sense authorities did not rule out coercion. In 1903 the Congress of Costa Rica ratified the Treaty for the Extradition of Criminals and for Protection against Anarchism (TECPA) as an attempt to unify forces to stop anarchism in the country.[29] The TECPA was proposed by the United States during the Second International Conference of American States held in Mexico City on July 2, 1902, and signed by delegates from seventeen countries.[30] According to the TECPA, crimes against private property or crimes of forgery, homicide, rape, bigamy, arson, piracy, unlawful entry, theft, speculation, and destruction of railroads, bridges, cars, ships, or another communication means would be considered anarchist practices.[31]

Some conservative sectors, especially the Catholic Church, also reacted immediately against the new intellectuals' ideas. Basically, the teaching of Darwin's theory at the Liceo de Heredia, where Roberto Brenes Mesén served as director, caused the Church's anger and prompted the publication of several journal articles against Brenes Mesén and his colleagues. Young leftist intellectuals confronted the priests' irritation and in turn attacked religious notions of morality.[32] This affair indicated that there was active opposition against young radicals and an institutional framework designed to limit their actions.

Anarchists, National Identity, Class, and Politics, 1900–1914

As noted, the construction of a new national identity was one of the most important achievements of Costa Rican liberal politicians. The key elements defining this nationhood were national hero Juan Santamaría, the Campaña Nacional of 1856–57, and the vision of Costa Rican society as a white and peaceful community.[33] There is evidence enough to assert that laborers and sectors within the urban popular class had received and assimilated this discourse about their national identity by the beginning of the twentieth century. For example, in a census carried out in 1904, San José residents (laborers included) answered the question of "nationality" by replying: "Costa Rican, fortunately." Moreover, in 1914 the newspaper *La Prensa Libre* asserted that there was a Costa Rican civilization already established.[34] In that context a critique against this nationalism could be considered a betrayal. As a result, elites developed a functional mechanism to confront intellectuals in the public sphere by portraying them as "*anti-patriotas*," traitors to their motherland.

As early as 1904 the Costa Rican *nueva intelectualidad* confronted the official discourse on nationhood by proposing views on its definition based on the anarchist doctrines of Proudhon and Bakunin.[35] As editor in chief of *La Prensa Libre*, Roberto Brenes Mesén published an article on September 14, 1904, criticizing the liberal political interpretation of September 15 (Costa Rica's Independence Day) and the word "*patria*" (fatherland). For Brenes Mesén neither Costa Rica nor Central America deserved to commemorate independence because there was not any real independence to celebrate.[36] Brenes Mesén argued that the young people had to fight for a different kind of independence based on individual freedom. According to him, not until youth become conscious of their individual rights would they be able truly to commemorate Independence Day.

Brenes Mesén also defined patria in a broader sense, as any place inhabited by people who he can understand and who can understand him.[37] *Patria* was one of the words that had gained a clear meaning by the end of the nineteenth century. From being defined as synonymous with Central America or with small Costa Rican towns during the 1830s–1860s, the meaning of *patria* changed until it was related solely with Costa Rica as a country and as a nation.[38] By changing the content of *patria*, Brenes Mesén was also combating the liberal notion of nationhood.

Omar Dengo and Victor Manuel Salazar explored this theme in an article they published in *Sanción* in December 1908.[39] First Dengo and Salazar summarized the way liberal politicians often defined *patria* as a "loving mother who lulls to sleep" her children and youth and to whom one must love, venerate, respect, and be loyal because she had nourished us with her blood. Then Dengo and Salazar considered this meaning to be a strategy created by liberal politicians to hide their lies and class exploitation. They claimed: "Phonies! That is not patria. Patria is a deity created since men were divided into the group which makes everything and gets nothing and the other group which gets everything making nothing. . . . Patria is a deity who inspires that feeling, covering and disguising selfishness, bastard interests, unhealthy passions, absurd concerns."[40]

Rather than considering *patria* in the liberal meaning, Dengo and Salazar tended to go deeper into the way that Brenes Mesén had pointed out in 1904. They were interested in showing the class ideology behind the concept of *patria*. For Dengo and Salazar, *patria* is a social construction that disguises class identifications by putting together everybody within a country and hiding the real social structure within it. Therefore, Dengo and Salazar understood the construction of *patriotismo* (patriotism) as a strategy to justify this political program. They considered patriotism as a tool for the upper class and politicians to suppress liberty and individual rights.[41]

Costa Rican anarchists, like their colleagues throughout Latin America, identified this patriotism as *falso patriotismo* (false patriotism),[42] which seems to be a differentiation between "nation" and "nationalism" made by some European anarchist thinkers.[43] Dengo and Salazar thought that real patriotism rested neither upon national wars nor upon the worlds of politicians. Rather, they connected real patriotism to the working class' efforts to live every day and work for the country's health. In that sense Dengo and Salazar tried to conceptualize patriotism in a new way by emphasizing that those who truly love their country work for communal interests instead of individual ones. Finally, by appropriating the term patriotism and giving it a class meaning, Dengo and Salazar concluded their article by calling for a struggle against those who did not fulfill requirements to be included within the working class *patria*.[44]

All in all, Costa Rican anarchists' language on patriotism seems abstract in the sense that it does not clearly address the particularities of the Costa Rican situation. On the one hand, the targets of the *nueva intelectualidad*'s critiques were easy to identify within the social framework of a small urban world. In 1900–1914 San José, one did not have to directly address the target of your critique for people to realize who the targets were. Thus, it was easy to read the *nueva intelectualidad*'s articles on nationalism, understanding them as a confrontation to the way in which liberal politicians defined Costa Rican national identity. On the other hand, the *nueva intelectualidad* did develop a more direct discourse through which they emphasized the Costa Rican experience. Yet that language was based on class exploitation rather than on nationalism. For example, in 1908, confronting those who denied that there was capitalist exploitation in Costa Rica, Omar Dengo affirmed that both the working class and youth were the object of a harmful action by mercantilism.[45] In 1912 Dengo insisted that the idea that there was no class exploitation in Costa Rica was a total lie.[46]

Moreover, Costa Rica's rebellious young intellectuals tended to relate patriotism and class exploitation to politics too. Their intention was to show the relationship between the bourgeoisie, *patria*, and electoral mobilization. The *nueva intelectualidad* fought against what they considered as the hypocritical way politics was understood, that is to say, as a tool to mobilize peasants and laborers in order to get political positions.[47] As Zeledón wrote in 1904, politics was a tool to acquire political rule, and rather than fulfill the popular class' needs after winning election, politicians used coercion against those groups.[48]

How did the *nueva intelectualidad* propose to stop this politics? First of all, avoid politics and government-related issues.[49] Roberto Brenes Mesén explained this in an article, describing the lives of Chilean young intellectuals who had abandoned Santiago de Chile and decided to live in the Andes Mountains, becoming vegetarians and eating what they planted. In this world, according to Brenes Mesén, those young intellectuals had divided day hours into three shifts: eight hours to work, eight hours to think, and eight hours to sleep.[50] In their first attempt to propose a way to combat politics, Costa Rican intellectuals rejected life in modern cities. Moreover, rejecting politics at the same time meant to show the popular classes a new anarchist way to live.[51] Second, for those intellectuals, rejecting politics meant not voting. Since politicians belong to a state that anarchists viewed as fraudulent, radicals considered voting to be a fraud by itself. Arturo Torres argued that "electoral struggle is synonymous with a struggle of lies. . . . The electoral struggle is the fight for the comfort of one group and the exploitation of the other."[52]

The solution was to mobilize the popular classes against elections. In 1904 Brenes Mesén asked the Costa Rican masses to not go to the polls.[53] While the intellectuals asserted an anarchist antipolitics agenda, other intellectuals did not share their comments about Costa Rican politics. For instance, Dana Gardner Munro commented that elections had been genuine and transparent, if a bit corrupt, during the period 1902–14, when practically every adult male had been able to participate in them.[54] New studies on elections support Munro's comments, finding that after 1885 Costa Rica started an impressive inclusion of adults into the national lists of voters and competition increased within the political arena.[55] Thus, during this period (1902–14) Costa Rican national discourse about its democratic system started to mature, and political parties accepted governmental power sharing.[56] By criticizing this democratic discourse, radical intellectuals also challenged the affirmation of a national identity no longer described only in cultural terms—that of whiteness, for example—but also in political terms. If Costa Ricans, especially urban workers and artisans, identified democracy with their national identity, the struggle against politics would become more difficult for young radicals. Ultimately, though, the growing recognition of this difficulty led these radicals to soften their arguments.

There is something else that can help us to understand why these young intellectuals would come to embrace a less radical agenda. During their conflict with Catholics in Heredia in 1907, the *nueva intelectualidad* began to realize that both police and governmental power might help them to combat conservatism. At that moment, when Catholics chased and almost killed Brenes Mesén and planned to burn the Liceo de Heredia's building, intellectuals like José María Zeledón applauded the police actions against conservatives.[57] On balance, radicals considered liberal authorities better than a conservative mob. Costa Rican young intellectuals were in a hard position. While a part of this group continued to strongly criticize elections, another part started to think of politics as a way to confront social problems. These considerations took place as the political campaign of 1908–10 approached.

In December 1908, Victor Manuel Salazar wrote in the pages of *Sanción* that although he rejected politics, perhaps someone from *el pueblo* could take over political power through electoral means.[58] In this way, Salazar explicitly supported the candidacy of Ricardo Jiménez Oreamuno, the most important representative of El Olimpo. Some days later *Sanción* published propaganda inviting workers to attend a Jiménez Oreamuno political meeting in which the Club de la Juventud Jimenista [Jiménez Youth Club] was to be founded.[59] Many youth believed that Jiménez Oreamuno represented a change for the Costa Rican political style. Moreover, according to the five pages of information published by *Sanción* on December 19, 1908, describing this meeting, it is easy to see that young radicals were one of the most important sectors within Jiménez Oreamuno's political coalition.

Zeledón tried to explain the contradiction between critiquing politics and the radicals' support for the election of Jiménez Oreamuno. In a speech during the meeting, he claimed the arrival of new times. According to him, earlier electoral campaigns led to the elections of the authoritarian governments of José Joaquín Rodríguez (1890–94) and Rafael Iglesias (1894–1902). Zeledón stated that the young intellectuals' rejection of politics during those years was a direct outgrowth of their disenchantment with those administrations. By contrast, the radicals believed that Jiménez Oreamuno came to reform the political system.[60]

Zeledón's speech shows the transition from radical attitudes into more moderate ones. In order to reconcile his anarchist ideas with the new political framework, he affirmed that the young radicals had to fight to simplify public administration in order to make it benevolent and to stop its oppression.[61] Moreover, his speech gives an answer to why the intellectuals decided to assume seats within the government. According to Zeledón, if Jiménez Oreamuno were to win, his supporters agreed to not accept any political appointments except in education.

Zeledón justified the new position not as an ideological change but as a pragmatic one. His vision made it possible for the intellectual to enter the contemptible world of politics as part of a bigger program of social transformation. Such a transformation, however, must depend on the quest for the realization of benefits for the popular classes. Furthermore, Zeledón linked their political struggle with the popular voice when he finished his speech by threatening Jiménez Oreamuno's party with a resurgence of the social struggle if its program was not fulfilled.[62] However, Jimenistas did not embrace the club founded by these intellectuals, seeing this political appendage as problematic given the young intellectuals' backgrounds and their radical agenda. As a consequence, intellectuals dissolved the club but still confirmed their support for Jiménez.[63]

This first attempt to enter into the political world shows how the intellectuals were willing to stretch their radicalism. In a certain sense their attitude could be explained as political opportunism. Yet we can understand it in other ways. As I have already pointed out, this generation had to fight against a historical context that made it difficult to establish productive communication between intellectuals and the working class. Laborers might not have easily accepted the language of rejecting both the elections and Costa Rican national identity. In fact, paying attention to the way urban workers celebrated September 15 during the first decades of the twentieth century, it is clear that the national discourse had reached them and that they had embraced it.[64] In this way one can affirm that the *nueva intelectualidad* had become less radical not only in the realm of electoral politics but also in their daily attempts to organize workers.

The newspaper *Cultura*, created in 1910, shows the intellectuals' change in position. Although criticisms of politics and elections continued to be important, discussions integrated a new element: the social question. In its first issue, *Cultura* cited the social question as the key element that the *nueva intelectualidad* should address. According to *Cultura*, while the working class continued living on the margins of sociocultural processes, the main social problems would remain unsolved. Rómulo Tovar asserted that the formation of an intellectual and moral citizen should be the first priority within a larger solution to social problems. An educated worker would have a better capability to hear and evaluate the politicians' statements and face them. Furthermore, intellectuals should fight for the rights of the working class to think and make decisions by themselves.[65]

Thus, intellectuals criticized the education system and the way politicians used workers while at the same time portraying laborers as "simple" and easy to manipulate.[66] The description was unfair because urban workers had organized and struggled against patrons at the turn of the century, demanding concessions like better wages. Twelve strikes organized between 1874 and 1914 show the activism among workers, especially shoemakers, bakers, telegraph workers, and typographers.[67] However, those strikes were localized and quickly resolved. Moreover, associations founded by those workers were integrated into traditional political parties.[68] Thus, the intellectuals saw the construction of schools, the organization of study circles, and the opening of spaces to debate among the artisans and urban workers as the solution to that cooptation—an initiative they had already proposed in 1904. In November 1904 Joaquín García Monge and José María Zeledón proposed a plan for intellectuals to teach workers about social topics and labor organization. In such a plan, intellectuals identified themselves to be the chosen ones to educate the workers to struggle against the state. Following this idea, in December 1904 they founded the Club de Instrucción y Recreo in Desamparados just south of San José where workers met to read anarchist literature.[69]

The anarchist newspaper *Renovación*, founded in 1911 with Zeledón and the Spaniard Anselmo Lorenzo as editors in chief, presented the teachings of sociology as the tools to reorganize Costa Rican society.[70] In its pages these intellectuals proposed the foundation of labor unions that should become the vehicles by which the popular classes could take political power. According to Mario Oliva, *Renovación* carried out an active campaign encouraging union membership among workers.[71] To that end, Joaquín García Monge, Omar Dengo, Carmen Lyra, and other workers founded the Centro de Estudios Sociales Germinal (Center Germinal for Social Studies, or CEG) in 1912. The CEG was a center where radicals taught social sciences, organized conferences, gave lectures, and proposed labor meetings. The CEG had a library for workers; in its building an anarchist flag was always hoisted, and on its classroom walls hung pictures of Émile Zola and Élisée Reclus. When classes started, intellectuals and workers sang the anarchist song "Hijos del Pueblo" (Children of Pueblo).[72] The CEG intellectuals and urban workers organized the first May Day celebration in 1913 and founded the Confederación General de Trabajadores (Workers General Confederation, or CGT) the same year.[73]

Through conferences, journals, the CEG, and the CGT, anarchist intellectuals tried to attract and organize laborers. The *nueva intelectualidad* infiltrated into the laborers' world, looking for ways to influence and perhaps control it. For example, in 1911 intellectuals like Zeledón, Lisímaco Chavarría, and Victor Manuel Salazar participated as candidates in the election of labor representatives for the First Meeting of Central American Workers even though they did not fulfill the unique requisite that allowed people to run for a seat: being an artisan. Moreover, in 1913 the intellectuals' journal *Aurora Social* became the urban laborers' official newspaper, replacing *Hoja Obrera*, which had played that role since 1909.[74] By 1914 the *nueva intelectualidad* had achieved an important social influence that the state could not ignore.

In brief, the Costa Rican anarchists in the early twentieth century criticized the official culture and politics. The young group spearheading this confrontation used newspapers, journals, magazines, poetry, and essays to express their dissatisfaction with the Costa Rican status quo. The *nueva intelectualidad* reached out to the working class to influence workers, but their approach and language often was paternalistic, seeing themselves as saviors striving to rescue workers from religion and ignorance. Lacking credibility as workers themselves, they did not try to take over labor organizations. Rather, they focused on producing a cultural transformation of some urban workers rather than organizing them to socially fight, as anarchists did in other parts of the world.

Crossing out the Past and Becoming Beneméritos: The Cases of José María Zeledón, Roberto Brenes Mesén, and Omar Dengo

In 1914 several of the intellectuals who had played an important role urging workers to accept anarchist ideas became part of the Alfredo González Flores administration (1914–17). Although it was not the first experience they had had working for the government, this time it marked them irremediably. After having a taste of power, most of them lost their radicalism. Furthermore, they declined to organize or participate in labor organizations again. For example, there is no evidence of any participation of these intellectuals in the great strikes of urban workers in February 1920.[75] Those who continued criticizing politics, like Joaquín García Monge, collaborated indirectly in promoting the international image of a liberal, national Costa Rica through their literature and essays.[76] In the following years, as ex-radical intellectuals occupied seats in the administration, their radical past tended to disappear. A new generation of leftist youth (communists, not anarchists) appeared by the early 1930s and collaborated in this cleansing of the past by appearing more radical than their ancestors because of their political participation and union activism. In 1931 this new generation founded the Communist Party of Costa Rica (PCCR).[77]

However, not until after 1948 did the early-twentieth-century intellectuals lose their radical past completely. The process seems to have been started in 1953, when historian Carlos Meléndez organized an exposition at the National Museum for celebrating the fiftieth anniversary of the national anthem lyrics. Meléndez edited a book about that exposition which included a biography of José María Zeledón written by Zeledón's son Jorge

Zeledón Venegas. The first missing element in that biography is a reference to Zeledón's young years. Zeledón Venegas started the account emphasizing Zeledón's childhood and then skipped until Zeledón's middle-aged years, saying nothing about Zeledón's active role in the organization of anarchist groups or about his youthful radicalism.[78] None of Zeledón's radical poems like "Los Elefantes" (The Elephants) or his political articles were included among his writings published in the book. Instead, most of the published poems were part of *Jardín para niños* (Kindergarten, 1916) and *Alma infantil* (Infant Soul, 1928), as well as some nonradical poems from his book *Musa Nueva* (New Muse, 1907).[79] Zeledón himself collaborated in the process of sanitizing his past in two letters he wrote discussing the writing of the national anthem. Those letters, although they discuss personal squabbles between Zeledón and some Costa Rican politicians, said nothing about Zeledón's radicalism.[80]

The construction of Zeledón as the ideal author of the national anthem lyrics contrasts with its bad reception by Costa Rican authorities in 1903. How can we explain the new interests in Zeledón and his lyrics in 1953? Jorge Zeledón Venegas gives us a clue in his account about one of Zeledón's most important political acts during his adult life:

> The civic campaign of 1947 came and so did the revolutionary deed of 1948 which destroyed the bad government. As bullets sounded in the mountains of the south, policemen insisted on controlling the popular protest in the city. One fateful day official soldiers grotesquely came to the San Juan de Dios Hospital. An old and yet strong man stayed at the door of the Hospital confronting the cowardly attack of the soldiers. This old man just wanted to secure that holy place. He was Billo [José María Zeledón], the General Secretary of the Hospital. The sacrilegious group was led by one of Zeledón's former disciples, a former shoemaker and fireman who spit in the face of his former teacher. Then, another soldier hit Zeledón with his pistol grip and all the gang passed through the door while Zeledón was on the floor.[81]

Zeledón's defense of the hospital against the soldiers is a strong image. Regardless of its accuracy, this image imminently connected Zeledón with the winners of the 1948 civil war.[82] Furthermore, the manner that Zeledón fought against the government troops made him part of the martyrs of the so-called *caldero-comunismo* (the political alliance that governed from 1942 to 1948) not only for his courage but because, according to his son, Zeledón died in 1949 because of the blow he received defending the hospital. In other words, Zeledón was transformed into a hero of the new administration and especially of the Partido Liberación Nacional (National Liberation Party, or PLN). This happened precisely when the PLN tried to create a new national pantheon and a new civic calendar based on its soldiers, heroes, and battles.[83] Zeledón fit very well in that puzzle not as a young rebel but as the author of the national anthem. After the civil war, the Junta de Gobierno (the junta that controlled the country for a year and a half) decreed in June 1949 that Zeledón's lyrics would be the official lyrics of the national anthem of Costa Rica.[84] Finally, in 1977 the canonization of Zeledón as *santo de la patria* (a national hero) was completed. In that year, after a discussion that did not consider any rebelliousness other than that of a poet, a journalist, or a national deputy, Zeledón was declared Benemérito de la Patria.[85] From then on, Zeledón's past began to lose its heterogeneity, complexity, and power.[86]

The path to Roberto Brenes Mesén's transformation into national hero in 1974 took a similar trajectory to Zeledón's. Brenes Mesén's canonization meant the forgetting of his early years too. In his case, first as ambassador in Washington and then professor at the University of Syracuse (New York) and at Northwestern University in Illinois, Brenes Mesén had the possibility of spending a fair amount of time far away from the Costa Rican public sphere before coming back as a recognized diplomat and scholar in 1939, almost twenty-one years after he left Costa Rica.[87] While in the United States, Brenes Mesén continued publishing opinions about Costa Rican politics in the journal *Repertorio Americano* (American Repertoire) edited by García Monge. At the same time, Brenes Mesén's academic appointment in the United States as professor of romance languages and the influence his books had in Costa Rica contributed to his fame as an astute Costa Rican intellectual living abroad.[88] Like the newspaper *La Tribuna* stated during Brenes Mesén's welcome, an entire generation had come of age whose only knowledge on Brenes Mesén was from his middle-aged years. For them, the sixty-five-year-old Brenes Mesén was neither a radical intellectual nor a young anarchist but simply an old *maestro*.[89]

Brenes Mesén's background allowed him to play a key role in Costa Rica as soon as he landed. The Costa Rican press constantly sought his opinions on national and international politics. Moreover, trying to organize a new generation of young intellectuals, Brenes Mesén participated in the foundation of the Centro para el Estudio de los Problemas Nacionales (Center for the Study of National Problems) in 1940, a group called to struggle against the old liberal politicians and against Costa Rican communism.[90]

Moreover, Brenes Mesén sided with the opposition against the Rafael Ángel Calderón Guardia and Teodoro Picado administrations (1940–48). His
participation in a failed coup d'état in 1946 was the most important public
manifestation of this opposition.[91] When he died in 1947, Brenes Mesén,
like Zeledón, was considered a martyr by those who opposed the caldero-
comunismo. This recognition paved the way to his transformation into
hero, which began in 1959 when the Minister of Education, María Eugenia
Dengo, and José Basileo Acuña published a book about Brenes Mesén in an
official print run for public schools.[92]

In November 1973 the Comisión de Honores (Honors Commission) of
the Costa Rican Legislative Assembly discussed the possibility of declaring
Brenes Mesén as a *benemérito*. The commission considered this intellectual
to be the best representation of twentieth-century Costa Rican thought. In
the document presented to recognize Brenes Mesén's merits, there is no
mention of his radical past. All the reasons are based on his personal qualities rather than on his biography or the different intellectual movements
to which he contributed. In the last sentence, the commission also tried to
reconcile Brenes Mesén's work abroad and his service to Costa Rica by saying that his work had served all humanity but principally his country.[93] The
largest part of these discussions was the final section when Brenes Mesén
was recalled as a Costa Rican poet, and nothing more than a poet.[94]

Omar Dengo's destiny is similar. Dengo, who had been excommunicated
from the Costa Rican Catholic Church in 1909, was rescued as the Costa
Rican educator par excellence. The association of Dengo's name with the
Escuela Normal—an institution founded in 1914 and dedicated to graduat-
ing teachers—and his works about pedagogy were the keys to affirm his
image of maestro.[95] A year after his death in 1928, the *Repertorio Americano*
published a book with some of Dengo's essays.[96] However, it was not until
the fortieth anniversary of his death that Dengo was transformed into a
national hero. Once again, a man's anarchist past was forgotten.[97]

Omar Dengo's years as a radical intellectual, like those of Zeledón and
Brenes Mesén, were simply erased in a later context. Although the organization of workers and the critique against politics had represented one of
the most important cultural movements of early-twentieth-century Costa
Rica, such a past did not conform to the characteristics of a national hero.
Embracing these intellectuals into official national history first required
erasing their early radicalism.

Conclusion

In his anthology of texts written and published in 1903, the liberal intellectual Pío Víquez summarizes very well the gospel of liberal politicians about Costa Rican national identity.[98] For him, anarchism was not a valid option in Costa Rica, where everybody was considered equal. In that sense, Víquez echoes the discourse of social demobilization that has been present in Costa Rican history ever since. According to that discourse, there is no space for a social critique in a country where democracy rules.

Ivan Molina argues that the power of official culture in Costa Rica is based on its capacity to integrate diverse ideologies and anti-establishment people into official channels, a process in which they lose their subversive and critical discourses.[99] This statement is true for those intellectuals who became leftists and radicals in Costa Rica during the early twentieth century. Besides Zeledón, Brenes Mesén, and Dengo, Joaquín García Monge and Carmen Lyra also acquired the title of *beneméritos* after their deaths. As I have tried to show, when these intellectuals were transformed into national heroes, all their rebellious pasts and their radicalism were simply forgotten. Thus, radical intellectuals who had vigorously denounced Costa Rican national identity and politics lost all possibility of being recalled as the men and women they were.

Probably during their earlier years, the intellectuals never would have imagined the possibility of becoming *beneméritos*. As anarchists, they criticized the culture that liberal politicians had created in Costa Rica. Furthermore, their articles, essays, and political poetry evaluated, criticized, and discarded every national discourse such as patriotism, dying for the *patria*, celebrating national festivals, and voting as bourgeois and inherently limited. Instead, they wanted to create a new, free world where love could be practiced in liberty and workers would be considered the most important element within society. Inspired by Proudhon, Bakunin, and several other anarchist thinkers, Brenes Mesén and Joaquín García Monge guided a young generation on paths toward free thought. Yet their radical point of view was limited by interactions with urban workers already conceiving of themselves as Costa Ricans. This situation, combined with integration of the young intellectuals into high profile government offices, caused them to lose their anarchist ideas or change them. The *nueva intelectualidad*'s conversion was also the result of the way they had understood anarchism. Anarchism was probably only a channel that people like Roberto Brenes Mesén, José María Zeledón, and Omar Dengo considered good to express their complaints of liberalism and conservatism but not as a doctrine to be embraced for the rest of their lives. Ultimately, these anarchists did not attempt a social struggle but rather a cultural war. They believed they needed to transform culture in order to change Costa Rica's urban workers. Therefore, cultural work, not anarchist union organizing, dominated their struggle.

Could those intellectuals have avoided their transformation into national heroes if they had not changed their word? Carmen Lyra's case gives us an answer. Although she did not play an important role during the early twentieth century and maintained a low profile, Lyra was very important in the organization of the Communist Party of Costa Rica in 1931 and, according to the U.S. embassy in San José, she became the leader behind the youths who founded it.[100] Unlike Brenes Mesén, Dengo, and Zeledón, Lyra never denied her past or became less radical. On the contrary, as she matured, she strengthened her leftist ideals. Due to her Marxism, Lyra was expelled from the country after the civil war in 1948, dying in Mexico because the government denied her return. Lyra's political activism, however, did not stop communist leaders Manuel Mora and Arnoldo Ferreto from proposing her transformation into a national hero in 1975. After a long discussion, the Legislative Assembly granted the title of Benemérita de la Cultura Nacional to Carmen Lyra in 1976. Her Communist past was infrequently recalled in the discussions, as deputies emphasized her writing skills, her novels, and her tales. In the public recognition of her legacy, Lyra was integrated into the registry of beneméritos as an excellent writer (especially of tales for children), silencing her political thought and criticism.[101] Even if they never gave up their radical tendencies, early-twentieth-century intellectuals were integrated in one way or another into Costa Rican national identity, which has the power of turning everyone, no matter their ideology, into a good Costa Rican citizen.

Notes

1. For somewhat romantic portrayals, see Bermejo Martínez, *Roberto Brenes Mesén*; and Quesada Soto, *La voz desgarrada*. For more insightful analysis on how these intellectuals evolved, see Molina Jiménez's *La ciudad de los monos*; Quesada Soto's *Uno y los otros*; and Llaguno Thomas' "Pensamiento anarquista."

2. Fumero, "La ciudad en la aldea," 77–107; and Vega Jiménez, "Consumo y diversiones públicas en Costa Rica," 81–109.

3. Molina Jiménez, *Costa Rica, 1800–1850*.

4. Mahoney, *Legacies of Liberalism*, 142–63.

5. Vargas Arias, *El Liberalismo*, 145; Salazar, *El Apogeo de la República Liberal*, 262; and Badilla, "Ideología y Derecho," 187–202.

6. Quesada Soto, *Uno y los otros*, 34–54.

7. Palmer and Rojas, "Educating Señorita," 58.

8. Molina Jiménez, "Explorando las bases de la cultura impresa en Costa Rica," 23–64. Also see Molina and Palmer, *Educando a Costa Rica*.

9. Molina Jiménez, "Elecciones y democracia en Costa Rica," 14.

10. Palmer, "Adiós *laissez-faire*," 99–117; Palmer, "Salud Imperial y Educación Popular"; and Marín, "De curanderos a médicos," 65–108.

11. Molina Jiménez, "Elecciones y democracia en Costa Rica." About the construction of the Costa Rican national discourse, see Acuña Ortega, "La invención de la diferencia costarricense," 191–228; and Díaz Arias, "Una fiesta del discurso," 73–104.

12. *Boletín de Escuelas Primarias: Órgano de los intereses de la educación común*, February 10, 1894, no. 88.

13. Molina, *El que quiera divertirse*, 136–38; and Oliva, "La educación," 138.

14. Oliva Medina, *Artesanos y obreros costarricenses*, 169.

15. "Prospecto," *El Pueblo*, December 13, 1877.

16. *Periódico*, October 1, 1894, 1.

17. A full list of anarchist titles sold in Librería Española between 1887 and 1912 can be found in Morales, *Cultura Oligárquica*, 131–33.

18. *El Noticiero*, June 13, 1905, quoted by Oliva Medina, *Artesanos y obreros costarricenses*, 171–72.

19. *La República* September 22, 1900, 2. For an analysis of the Costa Rica's national anthem, see Amoretti, *Debajo del canto*.

20. Molina Jiménez, *La ciudad de los monos*, 70.

21. Garrón de Doryan, *Joaquín García Monge*; and Dengo, *Roberto Brenes Mesén*.

22. Bermejo Martínez, *Roberto Brenes Mesén*, 60–61; Morales, *Cultura Oligárquica*, 109–85; and Quesada Soto, *La voz desgarrada*.

23. Barrantes Acosta, *Buscando las raíces del modernismo en Costa Rica*.

24. For a general view of this production, see Quesada Soto, *Breve historia de la literatura Costarricense*, 25–38.

25. For instance, those in Argentina considered the press to be the best tool to spread the anarchist's ideas among workers. See Suriano, *Anarquistas*, 179–215.

26. Molina Jiménez, *La ciudad de los monos*, 171.

27. Anderson, "Creating Cultural Prestige," 3–41. In the Mexican case, Miller argues that intellectuals who rejected the state's cultural project of national integration through the ideal of *mestizaje* or *mexicanidad* were marginalized. Miller, *In the Shadow of the State*, 50.

28. This list appears in Morales, *Cultura Oligárquica*, 134–35.

29. Archivo Nacional de Costa Rica [Costa Rica's National Archives, or ANCR], *Congreso*, No. 2855 (June 9–July 2, 1903).

30. *Extradition of Criminals and Protection Against*.

31. ANCR, *Congreso*, No. 2855 (June 9–July 2, 1903), 4–15.

32. Molina Jiménez, *La ciudad de los monos*.

33. Palmer, "A Liberal Discipline"; and Díaz Arias, *Historia del 11 de abril*.

34. Molina Jiménez, *Costarricense por dicha*, 7–9 and 134.

35. According to this approach, commonly called the classical anarchist doctrine on nationalism, "anarchists should renounce all national loyalties and strive for the creation of a unified, nationless universe." Grauer, "Anarcho-Nationalism," 3–4.

36. "Reflexiones," *La Prensa Libre*, September 14, 1904, No. 4463, 1–2.

37. Ibid.

38. Acuña Ortega, "Historia del vocabulario político en Costa Rica," 63–74.

39. *Sanción*, December 17, 1908, 1.

40. Ibid.

41. Ibid.

42. For the Argentine experience, see Suriano, *Anarquistas*, 264–71.

43. Grauer, "Anarcho-Nationalism," 4. Also see Bakunin's thoughts regarding patriotism in Bakunin, *Cartas contra el patriotismo*.

44. *Sanción*, December 17, 1908, 1.

45. Ibid., December 18, 1908, 3.

46. Morales, *Cultura Oligárquica*, 205–6.

47. Bermejo Martínez, *Roberto Brenes Mesén*, 90–104.

48. *La Aurora*, November 21, 1904, 1.

49. Ibid.

50. Ibid., February 18, 1905, 1.

51. Ibid., December 8, 1904, 1.

52. Ibid., December 1904, 1–2.

53. Ibid., December 1904, 1.

54. Munro, *Five Republics of Central America*.

55. Molina Jiménez, "Elecciones y democracia en Costa Rica," 9–32; Lehoucq and Molina, *Stuffing the Ballot Box*, 34–85; and Salazar, *El Apogeo de la República Liberal*, 59–67.

56. Acuña Ortega, "Historia del vocabulario político," 69.

57. Molina Jiménez, *La ciudad de los monos*, 185–86.

58. *Sanción*, December 10, 1908, 1.

59. Ibid., December 17, 1908, 2.

60. Ibid., December 19, 1908, 1–5.

61. Ibid., December 19, 1908, 2.

62. Ibid., 3–5.

63. Ibid., December 31, 1908, 2.

64. *La República* September 13, 1906, no. 6829, 2; "Información," *La Prensa Libre*, September 13, 1907, no. 5993, 3; *Hoja Obrera*, September 22, 1910, no. 49, 2; *La Prensa Libre*, September 11, 1912, no. 7491, 3; *La Prensa Libre*, September 16, 1916, no. 6656, 2; *La Prensa Libre*, September 18, 1917, no. 8680, 3; *Diario de Costa Rica*, September 11, 1920, no. 357, 3; and *La Tribuna*, September 22, 1921, no. 427, 2.

65. *Cultura*, June 6, 1910, 1.

66. Ibid., June 27, 1910, 1.

67. De la Cruz, *Las luchas sociales en Costa Rica*; Fallas Monge, *El movimiento obrero en Costa Rica, 1980-1902*; Oliva Medina, *Artesanos y obreros costarricenses*, 65–126; and Acuña Ortega, "Clases subalternas y movimientos sociales," 255–323.

68. Acuña Ortega, *Los orígenes de la clase obrera en Costa Rica*, 15–20.

69. Morales, *Cultura Oligárquica*, 157–60.

70. *Renovación*, January 15, 1911, 1.

71. Oliva Medina, *Artesanos y obreros costarricenses*, 179.

72. "Hijos del Pueblo" or "Himno Anarquista" was composed in 1885. See Palacios, *Colección de Canciones de Lucha*.

73. Oliva Medina, *Artesanos y obreros costarricenses*, 184–85; and De la Cruz, *Los Mártires de Chicago y el 1o de mayo de 1913*.

74. Oliva Medina, *Artesanos y obreros costarricenses*, 129–95; and Molina Jiménez, "Plumas y pinceles," 55–80. On how Costa Rican Catholicism included discussion of the *cuestión social*, see Soto Valverde, *La Iglesia costarricense y la cuestión social*; Molina Jiménez, "Catolicismo y comunismo en Costa Rica," 157–72; and Molina Jiménez, *Anticominismo reformista*.

75. Acuña Ortega, *Los orígenes de la clase obrera*, 37–68. The CGT played a minor role in this movement.

76. Pakkasvirta, *¿Un Continente, Una Nación?*, 139–66.

77. García Monge and, especially, Carmen Lyra participated in the organization of the PCCR. See Botey and Cisneros, *La crisis de 1929*. Also see Molina Jiménez, "Un pasado comunista por recuperar," 9–66; and Molina Jiménez, "La exclusión del Partido Comunista," 71–82.

78. Zeledón Venegas, "José María Zeledón Brenes," 13–18.

79. Zeledón, *Jardín para niños*; Zeledón, *Musa Nueva*; and Zeledón, *Alma infantil*.

80. Letters of Jorge Zeledón Venegas, in Meléndez Chaverri, *Cincuentenario de la letra del Himno Nacional de Costa Rica*, 51–57.

81. Zeledón Venegas, "José María Zeledón Brenes," 15.

82. Chase, "José María Zeledón," 25.

83. Muñoz, "1848 y 1948," 1–2; and Díaz Arias, *Historia del 11 de abril*, 25–30.

84. *La Gaceta*, June 15, 1949.

85. "Declárese benemérito de la patria al autor de la letra del Himno Nacional y relevante hombre público y de letras don José María Zeledón Brenes," in Archivos de la Asamblea Legislativa de Costa Rica (Costa Rica's Legislative Assembly Archives or AALCR), Expediente No. 1792 (1977), 1–7.

86. This is so impressive that an author even pointed it out in her thesis title: Devandas Brenes, "Billo Zeledón, ese famoso desconocido."

87. Dengo, *Roberto Brenes Mesén*.

88. Doyle, "Roberto Brenes Mesén," 392–93; Swain, "Costa Rican Mystics"; and Swain, "Some Costa Rican Writers as Topics to Research," 183–88.

89. *La Tribuna*, July 1939, 1. Cited by Bermejo Martínez, *Roberto Brenes Mesén*, 178–79.

90. Romero Pérez, *La socialdemocracia en Costa Rica*, 78–83. For a new analysis of the Centro para el Estudio de los Problemas Nacionales, see Díaz Arias, "Social Crises and Struggling Memories," 141–63.

91. Bermejo Martínez, *Roberto Brenes Mesén*, 219–21.

92. Molina Jiménez, *La ciudad de los monos*, 201–5.

93. "Declárese benemérito de la patria a Roberto Brenes Mesén," in AALCR, Expediente No. 1408 (1974), 5–7.

94. Ibid., 13.

95. See Dengo, *Escritos y discursos*.

96. Dengo, *Meditaciones*.

97. "Declárese benemérito de la patria a Omar Dengo," in AALCR, Expediente No. 973 (1969), 140.

98. Cited by Ovares, Rojas, Santander, and Carballo, *La Casa Paterna*, 115–16.

99. Molina, "Un pasado comunista por recuperar."

100. Ibid.

101. "Declárese Benemérita de la Cultura Nacional a María Isabel Carvajal ("Carmen Lyra")" in AALCR, Expediente No. 1679, 1–38.

10

Magonismo, the Revolution, and
the Anarchist Appropriation of an Imagined
Mexican Indigenous Identity

SHAWN ENGLAND

Ricardo Flores Magón was brave and tireless, but he was also remarkably unlucky. Born in 1874, he died under mysterious circumstances in Leavenworth Penitentiary in 1921, and prior to that he spent many years serving time behind bars or fleeing from police, assassins, and intelligence agents. Some have called him "the Kropotkin of Mexico" and "intellectual author of the Mexican Revolution," but others have refuted such claims and dismissed his overall importance.[1] For example, historian Alan Knight has weighed the undeniable similarities between anarchist principles espoused by Flores Magón and important radical articles of Mexico's revolutionary 1917 constitution. His confident verdict: "Causal connections cannot be inferred from a simple ideological congruence."[2]

Ricardo Flores Magón emerged as Mexico's visionary prophet of rebellion during the twilight years of the Porfiriato, an extended period (1876–1910) of authoritarian rule and capitalist development under President Porfirio Díaz. Flores Magón was the intellectual mastermind of a dissident political group called the Mexican Liberal Party (PLM). Security forces and regime enforcers cracked down on the PLM and sent numerous *magonistas* into prison and exile, including their leader. The fact that Flores Magón "was always in jail" has convinced one recent commentator that he was a "relatively ineffective revolutionary."[3] Flores Magón died at Leavenworth Penitentiary in 1921 even as a new order was being established in Mexico by the government of Gen. Alvaro Obregón. The visionary perished, but his ideological doctrine (*magonismo*) continued to influence Mexican politics well into the twentieth century, just as earlier it inspired and informed numerous Mexican revolutionaries. Strong anarchist threads were woven into the ideological fabric of Mexico's 1917 constitution by individuals who were either onetime PLM partisans, or by people affiliated with other factions strongly influenced by *magonista* thought. Further, *magonismo* was ideologically congruent with widespread popular aspirations, in particular among rural and indigenous communities demanding greater local autonomy, the restoration of communal land ownership, and self-governing institutions premised on moral sanctions and cooperation.

Over 90 percent of Mexico's population resided in rural villages at the beginning of the twentieth century.[4] *Magonismo* drew its influence in part from agrarian indigenous Mexican cultural values, and for this reason it reflected these values and flourished in the rich cultural soil of agrarian indigenous Mexico.[5] Flores Magón encouraged Mexicans to "be strong and rich, all of you, by making yourselves master of the land!"[6] "Land and liberty" (*tierra y libertad*) were the basic principles for which hundreds of thousands of Mexican people gave their lives during the revolution, and *magonismo* was the revolutionary philosophy that best articulated these goals. It was a unique synthesis of European anarchist thought (with a heavy emphasis on Kropotkin) and an idealized—or imagined—conceptualization of indigenous cultural patterns characteristic of agrarian Mexico.

The urban population of Mexico increased by half a million during the Porfiriato, from 1.2 million to 1.7 million, and in the early 1880s the Flores Magón family was among those who made the move from rural to urban living.[7] Many years later, while incarcerated at Leavenworth Penitentiary in 1918, Ricardo Flores Magón reflected on his early childhood and shared his thoughts with cellmate Ralph Chaplin, an American Industrial Workers of the World (IWW) activist jailed for sedition. Chaplin recalled Flores Magón telling him, "I am not white like you; I am a full-blooded Indian and would not have it otherwise."[8] In a 1922 prison interview, Flores Magón again made reference to his indigenous heritage, emphasizing the early impact of indigenous communalism in shaping his revolutionary world view.[9] It is very probable that Flores Magón was fluent in a dialect of Nahuatl, as PLM associate Librado Rivera would later recall.[10]

Together with his brothers Jesús and Enrique, Ricardo was born and raised in a rural household at San Antonio Eloxochitlán, in the district of Teotítlan del Camino in southern Oaxaca.[11] Their father, Teodoro Flores, served under Benito Juárez during the Wars of the Reform, and both he and his wife fought against Mexico's French invaders during the intervention of 1862–67.[12] Colonel Flores was a Zapotec and his wife, Margarita Magón, was a *mestiza* whose Spanish grandparents had immigrated to Mexico from Cartagena.[13] Margarita moved the entire family to Mexico City in 1883 to improve educational possibilities for her three sons, and Ricardo was enrolled in the Escuela Nacional Primaria in Mexico City that same year.[14]

As with many rural Mexicans of that time, this family was driven to the capital by the relentless push for economic modernization that transformed so much of agrarian Mexico during the Porfirian era. However, this age of rapid change came relatively late to most of Oaxaca, and even during the early colonial period the Oaxacan peasantry retained a high degree of independence when compared to other areas.[15] In spite of the demographic decline that reduced the number of indigenous people inhabiting the region throughout the sixteenth and seventeenth centuries, native communities in Oaxaca were remarkably resilient and successful in retaining title to their lands during the centuries following the Spanish conquest.[16] A census taken in 1810 revealed that of Oaxaca's estimated population of 600,000, almost 530,000 (or 88.3 percent) were considered to be "Indians."[17] Little had changed by 1910, when most Oaxacans were still rural, largely indigenous peasants.[18]

The promotion of commercial agriculture and urbanization was a cornerstone of the Porfirian program for modernization. Newer forms of production introduced under the regime of liberal market capitalism signaled the gradual breakdown of many traditional social relations, and this transformation was a crucial factor in increasing the receptivity of "radical" ideas in the minds of supposedly "nonideological" peasants, many of whom became Mexico's first generation of industrial workers. Porfirian development raised the standards of the average Mexican worker by 15 percent between 1877 and 1898, but the trend was reversed and wages tended to return to the level of 1877 after 1900.[19] By 1910 four-fifths of Mexico's rural communities (home to nearly half of all rural people) were relieved of their communal lands (*ejidos*), rendering their former inhabitants landless.[20]

The Porfirian state was the principal agent in promoting this transformation. Two general techniques were applied to facilitate the disintegration of Mexico's free peasantry: economic policies and legal measures. Taxation was the most favored economic weapon to disenfranchise the poor. Throughout the second half of the nineteenth century, it figured as a prominent grievance among rebellious Indian groups, and nonpayment of exorbitant and arbitrarily applied taxes provoked more than one clash between federal troops and recalcitrant indigenous peasants. Typically, any failure to pay taxes resulted in the confiscation of property.

The legal measures introduced by the Porfirian state to weaken the peasantry centered on redefining legal definitions of property. Federal legislation first introduced in 1883, and further reinforced in subsequent years, empowered the Díaz regime to grant title of land for which no title previously existed to any individual or company willing to purchase it. Thus, people suddenly became "squatters" living on land occupied for countless generations by their ancestors when they failed to produce legal title.[21] Rural Mexico was characterized by the social constructs of indigenous and, to a lesser extent, *mestizo* peasant culture prior to the Porfirian age. These structures typically featured village societies (not necessarily egalitarian) infused with a deep sense of communality combined with a commitment to maintaining local autonomy. As in precapitalist societies around the globe, the encapsulated villages of Mexico were organized in communal modes of sustainable production, meaning that property needed for subsistence was held in common by all members of that society. Differences in social status were certainly existent, but the relative wealth or status of exulted individuals (such as caciques) did not typically entail control over the entire community's ability to subsist. This all changed with the Porfirian intervention of capitalistic markets and statist forms of stratified governance.[22]

President Díaz ruled Mexico firmly—directly or through a malleable puppet—beneath a thin veneer of quasi-democratic respectability that spanned more than three decades (1876–1910). This era of rapid economic development was guided by a clique of theorists (the *científicos*) who blended tenets of French positivism, social Darwinism, and laissez-faire doctrines of unfettered capitalist development. The Díaz regime harmonized Mexico's development with the demands of a global marketplace dominated by economic powerhouses including Great Britain, France, and even Canada; however, Mexico's economy was particularly integrated with that of the United States during this period. The value of U.S. investments in Mexico totaled about $130 million by 1890, and that figure grew to exceed 1.2 billion pesos (500 million U.S. dollars) by 1910.[23] Many of these investments flowed into Mexico's productive northern mines, where the Porfirian mineral bonanza paralleled advances in other sectors of the Mexican economy dominated by foreign investors. By the outbreak of the revolution private U.S. interests had secured more of Mexico's trade than all the European nations combined.[24] A key element of Mexico's attraction to foreign investment was the Porfirian labor code: workers were forbidden to organize, and the nation's security forces—armed with the latest weaponry from more developed nations—ensured that any unrest would be crushed. With Mexico thus transformed into a virtual economic satellite of the United States, the force-propped tranquility of the one nation was linked to the economic good fortunes of the other.[25]

After crossing into the United States in January of 1904, Ricardo Flores Magón and some followers first attempted to reorganize in San Antonio, Texas. There they began to produce new issues of *Regeneración*, "an independent journal of combat" first published in Mexico between 1900 and 1902.[26] However, a man reputed to be a Mexican agent forced his way into the PLM's San Antonio headquarters and attempted to kill Flores Magón in late 1904. Ricardo's brother, Enrique, disarmed the would-be assassin and wrestled him out into the street, but San Antonio police released the shadowy assailant and instead arrested Enrique. The exiled PLM group moved northward to St. Louis, Missouri, shortly thereafter, but this did little good.[27] The *magonistas* faced repeated harassment by private detectives hired by the Díaz regime as well as by various American industrialists working with the tacit consent of the U.S. State Department.[28] These circumstances changed little by 1910, when Luther Ellsworth, the American consul at Ciudad Porfirio Díaz, wrote to the U.S. Secretary of State, "[We have the] situation on American side of border well in hand and with assistance of federal officers of Customs, Immigration, etc., United States Marshals, Bureau of Investigation agents, United States Secret Service men, and United States Cavalry will keep it so."[29]

In spite of this, the PLM junta was able to promote and organize considerable revolutionary momentum within Mexico during the late Porfiriato. Forty-four clandestine PLM guerrilla cells and "Liberal" clubs were operating by the summer of 1906, most notably in the northern states of Sonora, Baja California, Sinaloa, and Nuevo León. These cadres enjoyed significant autonomy, with predominantly urban and rural working-class members electing their own "*jefe de guerrilla*" from among their ranks, thus giving the members a sense of self determination and organizational security at the most basic levels of the PLM network.[30] The usefulness of these cadres in promoting labor unrest became readily apparent in the early summer of 1906, when Mexican workers at the Consolidated Copper Company at Cananea, Sonora, went on a wildcat strike. The strike leaders were also leaders of the local PLM club. One of these men, Esteban Baca Calderón, planned to create a powerful regional miners' union throughout northwestern Mexico and then attach it to the PLM, "providing it with mass resolute support."[31]

When the strike erupted at the Cananea Consolidated Copper Company

mine on June 1, 1906, the owner accused the PLM of distributing inflamma-
tory pamphlets in the mines only a few days prior to the strike, thereby generating "hard feelings" among otherwise happy workers.[32] While it was true
that the strike was sparked by a small faction of activists, the wider frustra-
tions of most Mexican laborers at Cananea, combined with the hysterical
overreaction of managers, served to whip the incident into a raging inferno
of violent confrontation.[33] The American consular agent in the Sonoran
capital of Hermosillo wired Washington for immediate assistance, and local Mexican officials summoned rural police units to Cananea, where they
were joined by vigilantes from Arizona drawn by exaggerated rumors of a
"race war."[34] Writing of the subsequent carnage, historian Herbert Brayer
noted, "It was generally admitted by all witnesses that there was a good
deal of uncalled-for shooting on the part of the Americans."[35] When the
dust finally settled on June 6, it was discovered that six Americans—most
were company managers—had been killed, whereas between thirty and
one hundred Mexican strikers had perished during two days of fighting.[36]
Although the strike failed to gain any improvements for the copper miners,
it proved to be of tremendous propaganda value to the PLM as well as to a
growing number of more moderate anti-Díaz political movements.

A similar situation developed a few months later at the textile mills of
Río Blanco, Veracruz, where a series of strikes and lockouts culminated in
another brutal massacre of workers on January 7, 1907. Once again Díaz
refused to acknowledge the legitimacy of worker grievances and instead
decided to blame the disturbance solely on outside agitation. As with the
Cananea uprising, the strike leadership at Río Blanco was affiliated with
the PLM.[37] Mexico's worsening economic conditions, combined with the
intransigence of the federal government, caused more and more labor leaders to find an ideological framework for their demands in the anarchist
principles of the PLM. The Porfirian governor of Vera Cruz tried to convince Díaz that workplace grievances rather than radical propaganda were
the real causes of unrest.[38]

The Díaz regime determined to suppress the potentially dangerous
rhetoric of the PLM even prior to the Cananea and Río Blanco uprisings.
Manuel Esperón y de la Flor, a Porfirian *jefe político* from Oaxaca, appeared
suddenly in St. Louis with his wife to charge the editors of *Regeneración*
with defamation and libel in October of 1905. According to Esperón y de
la Flor, the paper defamed him falsely for cruelty and for slanderously
suggesting that he owed his political position in Mexico to "favors his attractive wife bestowed on the governor of Oaxaca."[39] Local authorities in

Missouri agreed that such an insult could not go unpunished; the Flores Magón brothers were arrested and their property seized and sold—all without benefit of a trial. The main PLM leaders languished in a St. Louis jail cell for about a year before being released on bond in March of 1906. After that they fled to Canada, pursued by private detectives, to escape possible extradition to Mexico.[40] Meanwhile mayhem unfolded at Cananea and Rio Blanco without Flores Magón's direct involvement.

The PLM issued a *"Programa y Manifiesto"* in 1906 that outlined fifty-two proposals for a "radical" agenda of reform that included demands for a national minimum wage, a six-day workweek, cash wage payments rather than company script, the abolishment of company stores, the abolition of child labor, and the establishment of minimal safety standards and working conditions. The program also called for land reform and the restoration of locally autonomous municipal authority. The entire program and manifesto contained ideological elements heavily influenced by anarchist principles, and it enjoyed wide circulation throughout the northern and central states of Mexico where there was increasing unrest among urban industrial workers.[41] Thus inspired, the PLM leadership felt the time was right to plan a series of coordinated guerrilla raids with the intention of igniting a mass upheaval in Mexico. They extended an invitation even to soldiers and officers of the Porfirian army to enlist as insurgents with the PLM forces. According to the plan, PLM guerrillas would initiate the revolt by blowing up the federal garrison at Ciudad Juárez.[42] Unfortunately, the entire scheme was exposed by undercover agents, and authorities arrested most of the revolutionists.

By 1907 the Mexican government was offering a $20,000 reward for the capture of Ricardo Flores Magón. Agents in the Furlong Detective Agency tracked him down in Los Angeles. He was captured on August 23, 1907, along with other fugitive members of the PLM junta, and was charged with violating U.S. neutrality laws.[43] In May of 1909, almost two years after their arrest in Los Angeles, the *magonistas* went to trial in Tombstone, Arizona. There an all-Anglo jury listened to ten days of testimony before finding the Mexican defendants guilty of conspiring to commit an offence against the United States.[44] As a result, they spent the next eighteen months jailed in Arizona, making a total of three years spent behind bars after their capture in Los Angeles. Most PLM leaders could only watch from afar as the Porfirian edifice crumbled with astonishing speed between 1910 and 1911, yet they were still determined to influence the ideological outcome of the approaching revolutionary struggle.

Porfirio Díaz was forced to resign the presidency on May 21, 1911, and Francisco Madero assumed the role of president after an election held a few months later. With Díaz gone, the fragile new government was poised to face a number of other challenges from both the political right and left, and these included the quixotic efforts of the second division of the "Magonista Foreign Legion" ensconced at Tijuana, Baja California. At first glance this ragtag contingent of 155 activists and adventurers—mostly American activists belonging to the IWW—seemed of little enduring importance. Together with some seventy Yaqui supporters, the *magonista* insurgents took the border town on May 10, 1911.[45]

Commanding the rebel force at Tijuana was Jack Mosby, an American IWW activist turned PLM "general."[46] Dismissed as "a wretched band of outlaws" by critics on both sides of the international border, Mosby's men represented the military wing of the PLM. Although the PLM sought to bring about an anarchist revolution in Mexico, and despite the fact that the entire political leadership of the junta was comprised of Mexican nationals, opponents branded the Magonista Foreign Legion as a "filibuster" movement seeking to capture Mexican territory in the name of U.S. Manifest Destiny. The *magonistas* intended to use the border town as a beachhead to spread their radical cause southward into the rest of Mexico. The entire plan unraveled when federal troops struck on June 22, sending Mosby and other American PLM supporters fleeing to safety in San Diego under a withering crossfire as their Mexican and Yaqui allies melted into the surrounding countryside. The *magonistas* suffered heavy casualties, with some thirty dead and an unknown number of wounded.[47] So ended any hope of establishing an anarcho-syndicalist commune in Baja California—or, for that matter, in any other part of the Mexican republic. However, the PLM alliance with Yaqui insurgents in northwestern Mexico was destined to endure the Tijuana debacle.

A June 14, 1911, police raid on the PLM headquarters in Los Angeles had preceded the military catastrophe at Tijuana. Ricardo Flores Magón was arrested yet again, along with other junta members, and all were charged with conspiracy to organize an armed expedition against a friendly nation from U.S. soil.[48] The leaders of the "Desert Revolution" went on trial in June of the following year. Flores Magón was found guilty along with three accomplices. They were sentenced to twenty-three months each in the federal penitentiary at McNeil Island on Puget Sound.[49] Civil conflict engulfed Mexico as the overthrow of President Madero by Gen. Victoriano Huerta precipitated years of grinding war; the revolutionary turmoil that Flores

Magón helped to generate, however, continued with little or no direct guidance from the "intellectual author of the Mexican Revolution."[50]

Matters turned from bad to worse after the PLM junta was released from McNeil Island Penitentiary in January of 1914. Its members rented a small farm in Edendale, a rural suburb in northeast Los Angeles, where they lived communally, grew fruit and vegetables, and sporadically published issues of *Regeneración* to an ever-shrinking base of subscribers.[51] Los Angeles police arrested Ricardo and Enrique Flores Magón on February 18, 1916, this time for allegedly distributing treasonous materials through the mail.[52] With no money to post bond, the unlucky Flores Magón brothers remained imprisoned until their trial in May, when both men were found guilty of all charges. They were released on bail pending an appeal, and Ricardo continued to print his "glorious paper of rebellion" at his farm in Edendale.

On March 16, 1918, the organizing junta of the Mexican Liberal Party issued its "Manifesto to the Members of the Party, the Anarchists of the World and the Workers in General," calling for the destruction of all forms of government worldwide.[53] This would prove to be the most radical of all *magonista* documents. A few days later, the police arrested Ricardo Flores Magón and accomplice Librado Rivera and charged them with sedition under the newly passed Espionage Act. Later that summer, on August 15, both men faced the wrath of Judge Benjamin Bledsoe, who declared that "the activity of these men has been a constant violation of the law, all the laws. They have violated both the law of God and the law of man."[54] Moreover, he reminded the jury that the United States was then immersed in "the greatest war in which the world has ever been engaged," and instructed them to deliver a guilty verdict in the name of national security.[55]

The jury did as instructed, and Judge Bledsoe sentenced Ricardo and Librado to twenty years and fifteen years, respectively. They were transferred to the federal penitentiary at Leavenworth, Kansas, where Ricardo died on November 21, 1922. In the last of a series of jailhouse letters sent to a friend prior to his death, he lamented of his treatment at the hands of U.S. authorities: "I meant well, my blonde brothers, I meant well, but you could not understand me."[56]

Ricardo Flores Magón's ideas endured and influenced others in ways that were not always obvious. Even outside of Mexico the *magonistas* attracted the sympathy of international supporters, including the American Socialist Party, the Los Angeles Labor Council, the Political Refugee Defense League of Chicago, the United Mine Workers, and even the relatively conservative

American Federation of Labor.[57] As early as 1906 the PLM leadership came into direct contact with many anarchist luminaries who shared common interests with the Mexican exiles.[58] During its 1906 hiatus in St. Louis, for example, the exiled PLM junta met with Emma Goldman.[59] In addition to spending time with Spanish anarchist Florencio Bozora, Flores Magón even recruited a remarkable fellow traveler from Canada.

Honoré Jaxon, the English-speaking former secretary to Métis rebel leader Louis Riel during Canada's 1885 North-West Resistance, became secretary of the Mexican Liberal Defense Conference in 1911. Jaxon recognized the profound similarities between the failed Métis resistance against the Canadian government's liberal state-building project of the 1880s and the PLM's anarchist opposition to Porfirian liberal-capitalist modernization schemes in Mexico during the same period. In both cases the communal well-being of indigenous societies were imperiled by the fulfillment of colonization processes that began centuries earlier with the arrival of European conquerors in the western hemisphere. Jaxon perceived the PLM's struggle in Mexico as but one theater of battle in an epic hemispheric struggle by indigenous societies to resist cultural obliteration.[60] The antiracist Jaxon attended the Universal Races Congress in London, England, in 1911, and during that same journey he attended the Forty-Fourth Trade Union Congress in Newcastle, where he presented himself as a "Special Envoy to Europe on behalf of the Insurrectos in Mexico."[61] He claimed to represent "the case of the Spanish-Indian Métis of Mexico . . . [and] their noble struggle for land and liberty against the financiering scoundrels whom we French-Indian Métis of the Red River and Saskatchewan have been trying to foil."[62]

Jaxon's Mexican Liberal Defense Conference was founded by Voltairine de Cleyre, who first met Jaxon in 1893 at the World Conference of Anarchists in Chicago. She became involved with the *magonistas* while living in Los Angeles in 1910. Through conversations with these and other noted radical thinkers, Ricardo Flores Magón attested that his anarchist convictions were strengthened.[63] The PLM's "Manifesto to the Workers of the World," issued on April 8, 1911, echoed this messianic spirit of anarchist internationalism. This manifesto described the unfolding war in Mexico as "the first act [of a] great universal tragedy," one that would eventually engulf "the surface of the whole planet."[64] As for the non-Mexican anarchists who supported the PLM cause, the "communistic customs" of indigenous rural Mexico were both "interesting and instructive."[65] Here we see revealed the broad outlines of Alan Knight's observed "simple ideological congruence," noted at the beginning of this article.

The continued existence of communal lands in Mexico, even after de-cades of erosion by Porfirian modernization schemes, appeared to vindi-cate the anarchist faith in the viability of mutualism and communalism. The attraction of supporting Flores Magón with moral, legal, and financial assistance was not lost on the internationalist minded anarchist commu-nity. "Our cause is your cause," stated Flores Magón in a letter to Emma Goldman.[66] In response, she consistently devoted space in her journal to issues directly dealing with Mexico. The English anarchist William Owen wrote a number of articles for *Mother Earth* that reiterated the interna-tional appeal and universal principles of the Mexican struggle as depicted by anarchists.[67]

The resilience of indigenous cultures throughout Mexico has been more than adequately explored by modern scholars. The speed and thoroughness of post-Conquest acculturation differed from region to region. Many Eu-ropean settlers actually chose to reverse course and "go native" during the early periods of intercultural contact.[68] Even in New Spain, where the new Hapsburg hegemony assumed direct control over the distribution of Indian labor earlier than anywhere else in the Americas, many areas of dense na-tive habitation in Mexico were able to resist being drawn into the orbit of a powerful central government until the Porfiriato.[69] This included southern Oaxaca, the birthplace of Ricardo Flores Magón.

A number of factors contributed to the enduring indigenous identity of the Oaxacan peasantry. Spanish authorities later reinforced a strong tradition of localized loyalty among pre-Conquest Zapotec communities throughout Oaxaca in the 1530s, when native communities were organized in accordance with the *cabildo* model of municipal governance. The *cabildo* system was the basic institution of Spanish town government. This system allowed for a high degree of political independence at the village or town level, and the election of alcaldes and *regidores* by the villagers themselves reinforced the self-governing and economically self-supporting nature of the system. The Crown permitted Zapotec caciques in the Valley of Oaxaca to retain much of their traditional authority, and outlying indigenous com-munities were granted legal title to their original lands.[70] Even the evolu-tion of hacienda agriculture in Oaxaca was minimal when compared to other parts of Mexico.[71] In the state's central valley, one of the few regions in Oaxaca conducive to hacienda development, this form of agriculture was largely unsuccessful.

After independence, the economic stagnation that plagued the new na-tion-state country was exacerbated in Oaxaca by geographical remoteness from the rest of Mexico.[72] The state was connected to the national center only by a single highway in very poor condition and by a series of horse trails and wagon roads. Although Oaxacan villages maintained ties with the larger society through regional markets or intervillage marriages, peasants identified primarily—if not exclusively—with their own villages.[73] This parochial tendency was essentially shared by most rural Mexican societies, and this closed corporate mentality typically resulted in a natural rejection of national political centralization and the metropolitan culture of the capital.

In time, however, the growing power of the Porfirian state evolved along with globalized capitalist economic penetration into Mexico. The central state manifested itself in the unsavory form of tax collectors, press gangs, mounted police, and federally appointed political bosses, causing the national government to be perceived, with much justification, as mostly intrusive and destructive.[74] In Oaxaca this led to a clash with traditional rural culture, and vestiges—imaginary and nostalgic perhaps—of this rural culture were mirrored in the philosophy espoused by Ricardo Flores Magón. As one observer has noted, the specific nature of actual indigenous life in diverse rural communities did not matter as much to Flores Magón as did the very fact that they endured in face of overwhelming change, and served as a model of "constructive potential for the future."[75] This imagined model was more fully articulated when he blended it with the anarchist doctrines of Peter Kropotkin and Mikhail Bakunin. Like Pierre-Joseph Proudhon, "the connoisseur of paradox and aficionado of antinomial thinking" who became the most famous French anarchist philosopher of the nineteenth century, Flores Magón promoted an idealized nostalgia for a "free peasant life," but with a Mexican twist.[76]

The intellectual life of Ricardo Flores Magón reflected an effort to "reverse dependency and fragmentation, to search for an alternative path in the encounter between memory and the imaginary."[77] These powerful sentiments formed the foundations of *magonismo* as it developed during Flores Magón's many years of bitterness and exile, first as a student reading Kropotkin in the capital and later after being jailed in a foreign land.[78]

Anarchism in Mexico emphasized local autonomy over other social goals; it was a communitarian vision. In the same vein, *Magonismo* was primarily a cultural orientation rather than a dogmatic set of fixed doctrines, hence its continued relevance after the marginalization and ultimate defeat of the PLM as a political organization.

Onetime PLM activist Primo Tapia led a six-year agrarian revolt in Naranja, a Tarascan village in central Michoacán, between 1920 and 1926. Local lands and water sources, communally accessible until the Porfiriato, were privatized in the name of progress. Tapia's anarchist philosophy was learned during the years he spent with the Flores Magón brothers in the United States. According to Paul Friedrich, "Primo's anarchist and socialist ideas were a legitimizing rationalization. Far deeper than either of these types of knowledge was [a] basic outlook stemming from his village boyhood and the discussion with his uncle: the villagers of Naranja should win back the traditional and familiar lands of which they had been unjustly deprived."[79] Once again, *magonismo* was but a reflection of more deeply held cultural values—"a legitimizing rationalization"—and "anarchist theory partly meshes with the vigorous local autonomy for which the Tarascans are renowned."[80]

The connection between the PLM and their northwestern indigenous allies survived the disaster at Tijuana, in particular with the emergence of Fernando Palomares, an associate of Flores Magón with strong connections to the Mayo and Yaqui people of Sonora and Sinaloa.[81] He was present during the uprising at Cananea and played a key role in building a strong relationship between the PLM and the Yaqui insurgents fighting against the Díaz regime on the eve of the revolution in 1908. PLM activist Manuel Sarabia wrote of this connection in the Tucson *Herald* (April 7, 1908), noting that "the Yaquis are struggling for a common cause with the revolutionists." Even in 1913, after the PLM junta was sidelined in the United States, PLM activists such as the Yaqui Juan Montero were busy fighting for Yaqui autonomy and using *magonista* doctrines to add legitimacy to their cause. As for Ricardo Flores Magón, in 1914 he called on Mexican anarchists to forget about the nostrums of European anarchist theorists and take note of the fine example set by Yaqui insurgents—natural born anarchists—who did not need formal education to understand the importance of living free and defying abusive authority.[82]

When the PLM junta was shattered in the aftermath of the failed campaign in Baja California, several of its members went on to join other revolutionary factions, thus lending elements of their philosophy to more moderate and radical factions alike. Flores Magón noted: "Many of them enter the ranks of the Carranzistas, Villistas, and Huertistas to propagate among the soldiers," and he boasted of "phalanxes of [PLM] combatants" operating as guerillas throughout Mexico.[83] In Morelos, "Zapata gives every class of guarantees to the members of the Mexican Liberal Party who are operating in the territory he controls."[84] Other states of Mexico represented by PLM guerrilla cells included San Luis Potosí, Jalisco, Colima, and Puebla.[85] PLM "alumni" Juan Sarabia and Antonio Villarreal went on to help found the syndicalist Casa del Obrero in 1912, as did Antonio Díaz Soto y Gama, once the vice president of the PLM. Díaz Soto y Gama ultimately became an advisor to Emiliano Zapata, representing the radical wing of the Zapatista contingent at the Aguascalientes Convention of 1914.[86]

Finally, and perhaps most importantly, PLM aspirations voiced in the St. Louis Manifesto were later echoed in the 1917 Constitution. In particular, Articles 27 and 123, the two articles guaranteeing land reform and labor rights, were first articulated in the PLM's radical platform of 1906.[87] These articles represented a substantial socioeconomic victory for the more radical delegates to the Querétaro Constitutional Convention. Among these delegates was none other than Esteban Baca Calderón, former labor agitator at Cananea in 1906 and later a revolutionary governor of Nayarit (1928–29).

Flores Magón also left a lasting impact on the social and legal history of the United States. The story of his political trials in exile offers a grim chronicle of injustice during the Progressive Era and the first Red Scare, when official violations of civil liberty became national virtues in the fevered imagination of a hysterical society. His ideas even inspired the Nicaraguan revolutionary leader Augusto Sandino, who had worked in Mexico in the foreign-owned oil fields near Tampico, in his struggle against the United States Marine Corps between 1927 and 1933.[88] First and foremost, however, Ricardo Flores Magón left an enduring legacy of radicalism in Mexico. Surviving elements of the PLM formed part of the Casa del Obrero Mundial during the revolution, and later many of them went on to found the Confederación General de Trabajadores.[89] In 1968 the name of Ricardo Flores Magón became a rallying cry during the bloody student uprising that occurred on the eve of the Mexico City Olympics.[90] Alan Knight suggests that the *magonistas* represented the broad "middle-class demand for reform" in a very "indifferent" manner.[91] As this study has demonstrated, "middle-class reformism" was the last thing on their minds. However, more than ample evidence exists to show an ideological congruence between PLM doctrine and the long-neglected aspirations of Mexico's rural indigenous peoples.

Notes

1. Alexander Berkman writing in *The Blast* (San Francisco), January 15, 1917; and Aguirre Beltrán, *Ricardo Flores Magón*, 78–79.

2. Knight, *Mexican Revolution*, 46.

3. Arizona Territorial Justice Program, "Forum in the Above Matter," 43.

4. Friedrich, *Agrarian Revolt in a Mexican Village*, 1.

5. Matos Moctezuma, *Mask of Death*, 11.

6. Flores Magón, *Land and Liberty*, 46.

7. Gonzalez Navarro, *Historia Moderna de México*, 20.

8. Chaplin, *Wobbly*, 278. See also Hernández Padilla, *El magonismo*, 12.

9. MacLachlan, *Anarchism and the Mexican Revolution*, 139.

10. Rivera, "Prologo," 12.

11. Carrillo Azpéitia, *Ricardo Flores Magón*, 8.

12. Cockcroft, *Intellectual Precursors*, 86.

13. She served as a *soldadera* in the armed resistance against the French invasion. See Cano Ruiz, "Ricardo Flores Magón," 27–28.

14. MacLachlan, *Anarchism and the Mexican Revolution*, 1.

15. Waterbury, "Non-Revolutionary Peasants," 419.

16. Ibid., 423.

17. Figures given in Taylor, *Drinking, Homicide and Rebellion*, 26.

18. Waterbury, "Non-Revolutionary Peasants," 424.

19. Rosenzweig, "El desarrollo económico de Mexico de 1877–1911," 405–54.

20. Knight, *Mexican Revolution*, 96.

21. Ibid., 95.

22. Patterson, "State Formation and Uneven Development," 77–87; Knight, *Mexican Revolution*, 150–55; Gledhill, "Comparative Analysis," 5–21; and Clastres, *Society against the State*, 170–81.

23. See Raat, *Revoltosos*, 13; Bernstein, *Mexican Mining Industry*, 49–77; and Pletcher, *Rails, Mines, and Progress*, 219–59.

24. Pletcher, *Rails, Mines and Progress*, 3–4.

25. Hansen, *Border Economy*, 77–81.

26. The original *Regeneración* was established as an "independent judicial periodical" in which corrupt judges and other judicial officials were exposed and lampooned on a weekly basis. This mandate was rapidly expanded to include all corrupt public officials. Within two years, the newspaper was suppressed. Ricardo Flores Magón was fined and arrested three times between 1901 and 1903.

27. Albro, "Ricardo Flores Magón and the Liberal Party" 38–39.

28. MacLachlan, *Anarchism and the Mexican Revolution*, 9.

29. Raat, "Diplomacy of Suppression," 532. The complex machinery of the Mexican and U.S. security forces are also detailed in MacLachlan, *Anarchism and the Mexican Revolution*, 15–22.

30. Hart, *Anarchism and the Mexican Working Class*, 90.

31. Letter, Esteban Baca Calderón, Cananea, Sonora, to Antonio I. Villarreal. In Calderón, *Juicio Sobre la Guerra*, 41.

32. *Bisbee Daily Review* (Bisbee, Arizona), June 10, 1906. This interview with Antonio I. Villareal, then the secretary of the PLM, was entitled "Junta Admits Interest in Revolt" and printed nine days after the strike broke out. It informed the people of Bisbee that the disturbance just across the border was incited by the PLM, and "revealed" the revolutionary character of the "St. Louis group" apparently responsible for spreading discontent. See also Brayer, "Cananea Incident," 388.

33. The story was told in vivid detail in the *Douglas Daily Dispatch* (Douglas, Arizona), June 10, 1906. Philo Freudenthal, an American trader from Solomonville, Arizona, and an employee of the Cananea Copper Co, described the events.

34. Albro, "Ricardo Flores Magón and the Liberal Party," 57; and Brayer, "Cananea Incident," 399. This was according to Tom Rynning, who wrote Brayer a letter in 1938 describing events as he remembered them.

35. Brayer, "Cananea Incident," 408.

36. *Bisbee Daily Review*, June 8, 1906.

37. Raat, *Revoltosos*, 34.

38. Koth, "'Not A Mutiny But A Revolution,'" 45.

39. Albro, "Ricardo Flores Magón and the Liberal Party," 46.

40. Brown, "Mexican Liberals," 325. Brown suggests that it was largely through the efforts of two local St. Louis newspapers, the *Post Dispatch* and the *Globe Democrat*, that the Flores Magón brothers and Juan Sarabia were released from prison. Brown also notes that the Pinkerton Agency was able to discover the whereabouts of the three fugitives in Canada through the seduction of Manuel Sarabia, Juan Sarabia's younger brother, by an attractive female agent.

41. Albro, "Ricardo Flores Magón and the Liberal Party," 76.

42. Brown, "Mexican Liberals and Their Struggle," 347.

43. Flores Magón, *Land and Liberty*, 130.

44. Account of trial given in Raat, *Revoltosos*, 149–61.

45. For details, see Gerhard, "Socialist Invasion of Baja California, 1911." See also Chaplin, *Wobbly*, 148–49. Like the PLM, the IWW was an anarchist movement that sought to "do away with capitalism."

46. Taylor, *La campana de 1911 en Baja California*, 96.

47. Casualty figures given by Gerhard, "Socialist Invasion of Baja California," 304.

48. Gómez-Quiñones, *Sembradores*, 52.

49. For details of this trial, see Turner, *Revolution in Baja California*, 70–71. See also Gómez-Quiñones, *Sembradores*, 52–54.

50. An honorable title bequeathed to the memory of Flores Magón by PLM associate Antonio Díaz Soto y Gama, "A Manera de Progo," in Aguirre Beltrán, *Ricardo Flores Magón*, 78–79.

51. An excellent online collection of this and other titles edited and written by Ricardo Flores Magón has been assembled by Jacinto Bassols Barrera and can be found at http://archivomagon.net/periodicos/.

52. The brutal arrest is described in a letter, Maria Magón (Brousse) to Alexander Berkman, February 20, 1916, printed in *The Blast* 1, no. 7 (February 26, 1916), 6.

53. Flores Magón and Rivera, "Manifesto of the PLM to Party Members," 104–5.

54. Judge Bledsoe quoted in Flores Magón, *Land and Liberty*, 142.

55. MacLachlan, *Anarchism and the Mexican Revolution*, 87.

56. Avrich, "Prison Letters," 421–22.

57. MacLachlan, *Anarchism and the Mexican Revolution*, 22–23.

58. Preston, *Aliens and Dissenters*, 46–50. The radicalization of the PLM junta between 1908 and 1912 corresponded with the growing extremism of the IWW during the same period.

59. Woodcock, *Anarchist Reader*, 374.

60. Smith, *Honoré Jaxon*, 143–45.

61. Eastman, *From the Deep Woods to Civilization*, 189.

62. Smith, *Honoré Jaxon*, 146.

63. Hart, *Anarchism and the Mexican Working Class*, 89.

64. Flores Magón et al., "Manifesto to the Workers of the World," 93–96.

65. Voltairine de Cleyre, "The Mexican Revolution," 304.

66. Letter, Ricardo Flores Magón to Emma Goldman, in "The Appeal of Mexico to American Labor," *Mother Earth* 4, no. 2 (April 1911), 48.

67. *Mother Earth* 4, no. 2 (April 1911), 42–46; and *Mother Earth* 4, no. 7 (September 1911), 199–202.

68. Wilson, "Caliban's Masque," 111. See also Axtell, *European and the Indian*, 168–206.

69. Hapsburg hegemony assumed direct control in 1542, with the enactment of the New Laws.

70. Whitecotton, *Zapotecs*, 188.

71. Taylor, *Drinking, Homicide and Rebellion*, 18.

72. Berry, *Reform in Oaxaca*, 25. See also Starr, *In Indian Mexico*, 128–29.

73. Taylor, *Drinking, Homicide and Rebellion*, 27.

74. For a more general synthesis of how this conflict between central authority and local peasants came to plague Oaxaca, see Knight, *Mexican Revolution*, 3–7. Remarkably, the few historians who have studied Ricardo Flores Magón have neglected to sufficiently document either his early life or the traditional social patterns that he later claimed had shaped his "world view."

75. Maldonado, "El indio y lo indio," 5.

76. Woodcock, *Anarchism*, 93.

77. Flores Galindo, *In Search of an Inca*, 5.

78. Hart, *Anarchism and the Mexican Working Class*, 88. Ricardo Flores Magón first read Kropotkin at an early age and testified to the strong impression that he received from having read it. In fact, it became his "bible" of sorts, giving him lots of good ideas about the ideal society.

79. Friedrich, *Agrarian Revolt in a Mexican Village*, 74.

80. Ibid., 75.

81. Gámez Chávez, "Yaquis y Magonistas." On the importance of transnationalism, internationalist revolutionaries, and indigenous peoples in revolutionary Mexico, see Weber, "Historical Perspectives on Mexican Transnationalism"; and Weber, "Keeping Community, Challenging Boundaries."

82. Flores Magón, "La revolución social en Sonora," *Regeneración* 177 (February 21, 1914).

83. Flores Magón, "The Land Question South of the Border," *The Rebel*, December 26,

1914. Flores Magón specifically mentions: "In the Yaqui district, State of Chihuahua; in the central region of the State of Durango and in various portions of Michoacán, Mexico, Guanajuato, Guerrero, Oaxaca and other States, apart from guerrillas scattered throughout the remainder of the country."

84. Ibid.

85. Ricardo Flores Magón, "El deber del Revolucionario," *Regeneración*, June 13, 1914.

86. Cockcroft, *Intellectual Precursors*, 194.

87. Ibid., 130.

88. Hodges, *Intellectual Foundations*, 24–29. See also Crawley, *Nicaragua in Perspective*, 73–74; and Navarro-Génie, *Augusto "César" Sandino*, 16–18.

89. Alba, *Politics and the Labor Movement*, 54–55.

90. MacLachlan, *Anarchism and the Mexican Revolution*, xiv.

91. Knight, *Mexican Revolution*, 47.

11

Anarchist Visions of Race and Space
in Northern Perú, 1898–1922

STEVEN J. HIRSCH

On November 30, 1899, Julio Reynaga Matute, an Afro-Peruvian anarchist, addressed the general assembly of the Liga Progresista de Artesanos y Obreros (LPAO) in Trujillo, the capital of the Department of La Libertad. He recommended the creation of a commission to visit delegates and rural workers in the Chicama Valley, roughly sixty kilometers northeast of the city. The assembly promptly approved the proposal and named three members, including Reynaga, the LPAO's founder, to the commission. Shortly thereafter, per the assembly's instructions, the small delegation traveled to the valley by horseback rather than by train to conserve the LPAO's funds.[1] Between 1899 and 1902 Reynaga repeatedly infiltrated the large sugar haciendas of the Peruvian, German, and Irish-U.S. agrarian capitalists that dominated the Chicama Valley. Bearing a message of working-class solidarity, he delivered a series of propaganda lectures to the "braceros de Chicama" who were predominantly indigenous laborers from the northern sierra.[2] As a result of Reynaga's tireless efforts the LPAO registered its first bracero members. More significantly, by October 1902, the newly renamed Liga de Artesanos y Obreros del Perú (LAOP) had established a network of affiliates on various haciendas throughout the Chicama and Moche Valleys.[3]

Reynaga's anarchist project, which centered on forging an urban-rural worker alliance capable of combating capitalist exploitation, state oppression, and the depredation of indigenous braceros, had a profound influence on the LAOP. On April 18, 1903, Reynaga persuaded the LAOP to found *La Antorcha* (1903–1907), an anarchist-inspired working-class newspaper. *La Antorcha* defined itself as "a newspaper defending the working class and the worker victims of abuses and ridicule from capitalists, authorities, and especially the new plague with the name of contractors [*enganchdores*] that have appeared in our valleys and haciendas."[4] In keeping with this mission, *La Antorcha* would assiduously promote urban and rural working-class solidarity and highlight the plight of indigenous hacienda laborers. Articles denouncing the underlying racism of hacienda labor recruitment practices and the brutal treatment of indigenous braceros appeared regularly in its pages. In an article entitled, "The Modern Slavery on the Haciendas of the Valley of Chicama," *La Antorcha* decried the abusive and dehumanizing exploitation of "beings of our species" and "men of our same form."[5] And it called on "workers and artisans . . . to gaze on those [haciendas] and contemplate the heartbreaking scene" and to recognize "that the vision that must be seen is of the braceros and their rights."[6] *El Jornalero* (1906–15), the successor organ to *La Antorcha*, stressed similar themes. Founded and edited by Reynaga, *El Jornalero* championed urban workers' solidarity with indigenous braceros and peasants. In a regularly featured column called "Echos of the Haciendas," *El Jornalero* studiously reported on the deplorable work conditions and struggles of braceros.[7] Under Reynaga's guidance, LAOP, *La Antorcha*, and *El Jornalero* would engage in a concerted effort to construct a radical workers' movement that cut across urban and rural spaces and ethnic and racial lines.

Up the coast 175 kilometers from Trujillo, in Chiclayo, the capital of the Department of Lambayeque, Manuel Uchofen Patasca formulated an anarchist project that closely paralleled Reynaga's. Like Reynaga, Uchofen was an anarchist worker-intellectual dedicated to fostering worker solidarity and class struggle against capitalist exploitation, oligarchic domination, and state oppression.[8] Gazing from Chiclayo to the eastern valleys of La Leche, Lambayeque, and Saña, Uchofen witnessed the proletarianization of rural peasants and the dispossession of indigenous communities resulting from the expansion of sugar plantations. He also observed the formation of an incipient working class linked to consumer goods production in Chiclayo and to railway and port facilities servicing the sugar export economy. With the foundation of *La Protesta Libre*, an anarchist weekly, on December 23, 1906, Uchofen articulated a vision of a radical urban and rural worker alliance. A self-proclaimed "Anarcho-Socialist Organ and Defender of the Working Class," *La Protesta Libre* urged urban and rural workers to form "unions of resistance" and a department-wide labor confederation.[9] Uchofen's second anarchist paper, *La Abeja* (1910–21), as will be seen, promoted both urban and rural worker solidarity, and the defense of indigenous and multiracial peasant communities.[10]

For anarchists in Trujillo and Chiclayo, the formation of sugar export enclaves in the late nineteenth and early twentieth centuries violated their most cherished ideals.[11] As heirs of Mikhail Bakunin and Peter (Piotr) Kropotkin, they bristled at the increasing centralization of planter power both regionally and nationally, and at the imposition of super-exploitative labor practices and restrictions on workers and peasants' movements and freedoms. Anarchists in the northern coastal departments of La Libertad and Lambayeque combated these developments in word and deed. This chapter examines anarchist attempts to promote decentralized spatial power, mutual aid between workers and peasants, and spaces of liberty and equality in northern Perú. The first section examines the communications network and discourse of the anarchist press. It highlights the ways the anarchist press contested the dominant sociospatial and racial order. The second section highlights the formation of anarchist "counterspaces" dedicated to working-class organization, education, and culture, and how these in turn challenged the hegemony of the planter class.[12] The third section discusses how anarchist visions of race and space were implicated in the movement's solidarity with multiracial subaltern insurgencies in Lambayeque and La Libertad.

Contesting the Dominant Sociospatial and Racial Order

The emergence of an anarchist press in Trujillo and Chiclayo coincided with the formation and consolidation of sugar export enclaves in La Libertad and Lambayeque. From the early 1890s until the early 1920s, a small group of sugar planters with access to foreign capital and markets increasingly gained control over and reorganized the land, water, and labor resources within these northern coastal departments. As their plantations and fortunes grew, the sugar planters, composed of unassimilated foreign immigrants (Italian, German, Spanish, Irish American) and Peruvian creoles, also acquired preeminent political influence.[13] State authorities aided and abetted the sugar planters' economic interests by granting concessions for railway and port infrastructure projects and by insuring a steady supply of cheap labor for the plantations. Not only did the state facilitate the importation of Japanese workers, it condoned *enganche* contracts that effectively indebted and exploited highland indigenous peasant laborers.[14] To prevent disruptions in sugar export production and to maintain social control in the sugar enclave, the state also intervened and applied repression when necessary. It was in this context that anarchist worker-intellectuals founded anarchist papers like *La Antorcha* and *El Jornalero* in Trujillo and *La Protesta Libre* and *La Abeja* in Chiclayo.[15] These anarchist papers penetrated the expanding enclave space and contested sugar planters' pretensions to exclusive control over social relations and resources within that space. In so doing, they provided a trenchant critique of the sugar export enclave as a constellation of spaces where despotism, exploitation, inequality, and racism reigned.

From its inception, the anarchist press in Trujillo and Chiclayo sought to establish a distribution and communications network that linked the sugar haciendas and rural towns with the coastal urban centers. In the first year of its publication, in 1903, *La Antorcha* reached rural workers on the large sugar plantations in the Chicama and Moche Valleys. Despite what it characterized as a "silent, surreptitious, and active war" against it by "bigwigs and *hacendados*," *La Antorcha* succeeded in placing distribution agents in the Chicama Valley, Ascope, and other points within the sugar enclave.[16] Similarly, *El Jornalero* developed a wide distribution network of agents and subscribers, though not without difficulty. It acknowledged as much in a 1907 editorial complaining about "the impossibility of its free introduction on the haciendas" owing to hacendado intimidation and the cowardice of some of its agents.[17] Nevertheless, it took advantage of the railway lines that linked Trujillo to the port of Salaverry, Ascope, and hacienda Laredo to disseminate its publications.[18] *La Protesta Libre*'s and *La Abeja*'s distribution network mirrored *La Antorcha*'s and *El Jornalero*'s. Radiating from Chiclayo, their networks entered rural communities like Zaña, Monsefú, and Ferreñafe; had agents on the Tumán and Pucalá sugar haciendas; and had contacts in the port of Eten and its attendant railway line, which serviced the Cayaltí sugar plantation.[19]

The Trujillo- and Chiclayo-centered anarchist press circuits functioned as a regional network.[20] Both sets of anarchist papers routinely exchanged information and reports on social conditions and worker struggles in the urban and rural areas affected by the sugar export enclaves. *El Jornalero* and *La Abeja*, in particular, shared information and provided mutual support. The information and communication in this regional anarchist press network flowed in multiple directions: between Trujillo and Chiclayo, outward from the coastal cities to the rural areas, and from rural correspondents back to Trujillo and Chiclayo. In this way the anarchist press could provide intelligence on the planter class and state authorities and coordinate solidarity actions. For example, during a strike at the Pomalca hacienda in 1917, correspondents based in the railway station in Eten immediately sent reports to *La Abeja* to warn the strikers of the impending arrival of government troops.[21]

What made the anarchist press the bane of the sugar planters' existence was not merely that it violated their proprietary sense of boundaries but that its depiction of the regional sugar enclave was so damning. A constant theme of the anarchist press was the planters' complete disregard for the human dignity of their workers. *La Antorcha*, for example, denounced the Larco Herrera family because on their estates "peons are treated with disdain" and subject to physical abuse. The whipping of an Afro-Peruvian laborer, "el negrito Marcos," on the Huabal hacienda drew strong condemnation from *El Jornalero*, which characterized it as an example of the criminal behavior of the hacendado class.[22] Reports of workers injured or killed as a result of job-related accidents on the sugar plantations were routinely published in the anarchist press. They were usually accompanied by charges that planters were indifferent to workers' suffering and were unwilling to indemnify their families.[23] Another recurring theme of the anarchist press was that sugar planters and state authorities had a penchant for perpetrating acts of violence, including massacres, against workers seeking to defend their rights. Denunciations of hacendado and state violence and the arbitrary arrests of workers appeared with deliberate regularity in the anarchist press.[24] A steady stream of articles decrying restrictions on the free circulation of foodstuffs and consumer goods on the plantations and the prevalence of exploitative company stores also reinforced the general image of the sugar export enclave as a constellation of spaces devoid of freedom, equality, and justice.[25]

For the anarchist press, the iniquitous character of the sugar export enclave was also unequivocally reflected in the abusive treatment of its highland indigenous labor force. The anarchist press attributed the harsh treatment of indigenous braceros to a system of domination predicated on the presumptive cultural and racial superiority of the hacendado and *gamonal* class.[26] Although anarchists tended to stress class identity and struggle, this did not preclude their recognition of race as a social fact in early-twentieth-century Perú. Nor did it prevent their deployment of a transgressive discourse that challenged the immorality and oppressive social and cultural practices that formed part of the dominant racial order.

Articles detailing the daily abuses of indigenous braceros at the hands of *enganchadores* and hacendados were commonplace in the anarchist press. Indigenous laborers on the sugar haciendas were reported to routinely suffer from miserable wages, excessively long work days, wretched living conditions, corporal punishment, arbitrary imprisonment, and alcohol abuse.[27] According to *El Jornalero*, the haciendas were not really "centers of work" but "prisons of torment, where the workers, principally the Indians . . . are exploited in a thousand ways."[28] Tellingly, the anarchist press analogized this exploitation to the extermination of indigenous peoples in North America: "Here as well the inhuman capitalist owners of the haciendas in the full twentieth century have manifested the purpose of completely annihilating the strong and robust race of the Incas."[29] Other comparisons were made to the brutalization and enslavement of indigenous peoples in the northwest Peruvian Amazon region by unscrupulous rubber producers who operated with impunity. Between 1904 and 1912 the Casa Arana, a Peruvian rubber export concern, had become the subject of a national and international scandal for its barbaric labor practices that included forced labor, whippings, and torture.[30] Anarchists protested these crimes and viewed the sugar barons' harsh treatment of braceros in a similar light.[31] Indigenous laborers on Lambayeque's plantations and haciendas fared no better than those in La Libertad. In describing the conditions of "the indigenous of the Department of Lambayeque," José Mercedes Cachay, the mixed-race leader of the rural community of Zaña, recounted how indigenous peons on haciendas were often bound in chains, subject to whippings and torture, and fed rotten, worm-infested rations.[32] This degrading and inhuman treatment drew the attention of anarchists in Chiclayo, who roundly denounced it in *La Protesta Libre* and *La Abeja*.[33]

The anarchist press also expressed concern for indigenous communities and peasant smallholders threatened by expansionist sugar plantations. "The large property owners shamelessly and cynically steal the water for their sugar cane," *El Jornalero* opined, leaving smallholders without the means of subsistence, such as "the indigenous of Mansiche, Manpuesto and others."[34] Years later it continued to rail against monopolistic sugar planters, like Señor Chopitea, who it accused of thinking he was the exclusive owner of the Santa Catalina Valley and who threatened the indigenous farmers of Moche by stealing their water.[35] Sugar planters and their government allies in Lambayeque incurred the wrath of *La Abeja* for similar reasons. Manuel Bancayán, an agriculturist and member of the directorate of *La Abeja*, accused the Regional Administration of Water in Chiclayo of creating conditions under which indigenous communities lived under "Modern Feudalism." "It causes me great indignation when I see in every part of this department an outcry," he opined in *La Abeja*, "and I see the indigenous race exploited and without guarantees, by this damned Regional

Administration of Water." He compared the water administrators to wolves and alligators who designed water studies to benefit the planters and to rob the indigenous communities.[36]

Anarchists in northern Perú, like their counterparts in Lima, not only sympathized with the plight of the indigenous people, they actively collaborated with the fledgling pro-indigenous rights movement. Two years after the establishment of the Asociación Pro-Indígena (API) in Lima, *El Jornalero* reprinted a manifesto from its founder, Pedro Zulén, urging that action be taken to combat the practice of *enganche*.[37] Similarly, *La Abeja* availed its pages for API communiqués and articles.[38] The LAOP went a step further. In March 1912, by unanimous vote, LAOP entered into a formal collaboration with the API. In doing so, it agreed to form a commission in charge of formulating "preliminary studies in favor of our aboriginal race."[39] In effect, the LAOP-API alliance allowed for the coordination and circulation of pro-indigenous rights propaganda.[40] Unlike the API, however, most Trujillo anarchist workers were not content to accept a strictly legalist approach to defending indigenous rights. In accordance with anarchist doctrine, they preferred direct action and supported indigenous braceros uprisings in 1912 and 1921.

Although it is beyond the scope of this chapter to give a full account of how anarchists addressed the "Indian Question" in northern Perú, it is necessary to briefly examine their defense of the indigenous worker in response to the planter class's employment of Japanese contract laborers. Between 1898 and 1923 the Peruvian state facilitated the importation of 17,764 Japanese laborers to work on coastal estates. On the sugar plantations in La Libertad and Lambayeque, the presence of Japanese workers was relatively insignificant and declined rapidly.[41] By 1920 only twenty or so Japanese peons remained on the haciendas in Lambayeque.[42] Nevertheless, initially the introduction of imported Japanese workers on the sugar haciendas in northern Perú presented anarchists with a vexing issue. The essential problem, according to the anarchist press, was the "irritating inequality" of the contracts granted to the Japanese workers.[43] The contracts guaranteed Japanese workers double the daily pay rate of indigenous braceros, a shorter working day, medical assistance, and superior food rations. For anarchists this was an affront to indigenous laborers.[44] *El Jornalero* pointedly asked, "Why aren't national farm hands treated with the same consideration as the Asians, who are inferior in physical potential and will produce less with the sum of their labor?" In another front-page editorial *El Jornalero* pondered "Why this hatred toward the strong national worker? And, why so much adulation for the sickly Japanese?"[45] The use of a nationalist and racialized rhetoric to refer to indigenous and Japanese workers, respectively, illustrates the tensions in anarchist discourse as it relates to race. At turns, anarchists could and did invoke nationality, strength of character, and physical prowess as well as weakness and vulnerability to defend the indigenous worker. Derisive comments against the Japanese laborers were often inadvertent and opportunistic. On the whole, anarchists were more interested in empowering indigenous workers. Indeed, *El Jornalero* called on indigenous workers to "unite and demand justice" and to strike across all the estates for equal pay and work conditions.[46] It made clear it did not begrudge the Japanese the terms of their contract: "We're not against the improved conditions of the Sons of the Sun. . . . What we want is equal conditions, when they're worse for *braceros*."[47]

Anarchist Counterspaces of Resistance

"All liberationist movements," Tom Goyens has astutely noted, "face the problem of finding a place to meet, to nurture solidarity, reciprocity, and community."[48] For anarchists in Trujillo, this place was LAOP's headquarters, established in 1898 at 59 Independence Street. Centrally located in the popular neighborhood of La Unión, the LAOP opened its doors to artisans and workers of all nationalities, races, and vocations in 1902.[49] Workers of diverse ideological leanings were also welcome, although anarchist workers were the driving force behind the league.[50] Under the leadership of Julio Reynaga, Pascual Meza Veliz, Francisco Figueroa, and Teodosio Moreno Machado, LAOP's union hall became the locus of working-class solidarity and anarchist-inflected propaganda, education, and cultural activities. Initially the LAOP served as a meeting place for local mechanics, bakers, carpenters, printers, braceros, and textiles workers who comprised its membership. However, it soon became a center for coordinating labor solidarity and organizing efforts with workers and labor representatives from the entire Department of La Libertad. May Day commemorations organized by the LAOP, for example, invariably involved the participation of railway and construction workers, artisans, and braceros linked to the sugar export enclave. Beginning in 1904 the LAOP sponsored elaborate annual May Day events that included public processions, performances by the musical group "The Free Ones of Trujillo," the singing of "La Marsellesa," and speeches extolling working-class unity under a red banner.[51] *La Antorcha* was published directly on site. In addition, on November 4, 1905,

LAOP established a popular library, which it made available to members and popular sectors in Trujillo. Stocked with anarchist texts, which it received from supporters all over the world, the library—dubbed "Liberty and Progress"—provided a relatively secure setting for an alternative education.[52] It also contributed to anarchist sociability by sponsoring artistic events and conferences. LAOP's library, with its accent on workers' libertarian education and cultural expression, would serve as a model for popular libraries in La Libertad's provincial towns and communities.

With the establishment of a workers' study center by Julio Reynaga in 1906, a second venue for anarchist education and sociability appeared in Trujillo.[53] The Centro de Estudios Sociales "Unión y Energia" (Center for Social Studies "Union and Energy," CESUE) had no set location, but all of its educational and propaganda activities took place in the workers' neighborhood of La Unión, where Reynaga resided and gave lectures and dance lessons at the local Union Theater, and where he began publishing *El Jornalero* in 1907.[54] Although the explicit aim of the CESUE was to make workers "aware of their duties and to be trustworthy in the defense of their inalienable rights," it also organized seminars on anarchist thought and coordinated workers' solidarity actions.[55] Like the LAOP's popular library, the CESUE would serve as a model for provincial study centers. On the hacienda Pomalca, a Center for Studies Pomalca was established in 1908, and two years later Moche founded a Center for Social Studies "Labor and Light" "to disseminate libertarian ideas."[56] The LAOP also seems to have been inspired by the CESUE. In April 1912 it organized night schools that instructed workers on economic demands, indigenous rights, and the nature of rural landlord oppression.[57]

In addition to the counterspaces of the LAOP and CESUE, artisan and workers' neighborhoods in Trujillo provided the setting for more ephemeral anarchist organizations. The organization Hacia la Humanidad Libre (Toward Free Humanity, HHL), for example, was situated in a workers' barrio, though it doesn't appear to have existed for any length of time. Nevertheless, it apparently contributed to developing an anarchist sensibility and solidarity among workers. Addressing itself to the pressing problem of the rising cost of essential commodities, the HHL organized the Committee to Reduce the Cost of Subsistence in 1916, three years before an analogous movement emerged in Lima.[58] Drawing support from a wide range of labor organizations in Trujillo, the port of Salaverry, and workers in Chicama, Ascope, and Huanchaco, the committee set out to coordinate a mass work stoppage to protest the high price of food staples.[59]

In Chiclayo the principal site of anarchist sociability and resistance was the center of the Grupo de La Abeja (Group of the Bee, GLA). Located on 87 San Marcos Street, the GLA's center housed a printing press and a libertarian popular library. From there Chiclayo's artisans and workers could pick up a copy of *La Abeja* every Saturday for five centavos. They could also hold meetings and coordinate labor organizing activities. On and off between 1907 and 1913 the center functioned as a union hall for the Confederación de Obreros Primer de Mayo (Confederation of Workers First of May, COPM), with masons, bakers, leather workers, mechanics, shoe and hat makers, and agricultural laborers among its initial 460 affiliates.[60] This is not surprising, as Manuel Uchofen, the leader of GLA and chief editor of *La Abeja*, was the prime mover behind COPM and in 1913 would be named its vice president.[61] In general, the GLA had little success in constructing a libertarian workers' community, though not for lack of effort. The GLA organized libertarian theater performances and conferences.[62] It also served as staging ground for annual May Day marches and for the dissemination of propaganda urging workers to organize "unions of anarchist socialist resistance" and to affiliate with the COPM.[63] To its credit, the GLA provided a space for COPM's union affiliates to coordinate solidarity with rug weavers in Monsefú, and protest movements against Lambayeque's Water Administration and sugar hacienda company stores.[64] For these actions and *La Abeja*'s anarchist propaganda, state authorities would repeatedly shutter the GLA center and as a result limit its effectiveness.[65]

Anarchist Solidarity with Multiracial Subaltern Insurgencies

To appreciate the geographical range and subversive nature of anarchist influence in La Libertad and Lambayeque requires an examination of four multiracial subaltern insurgencies. The first two to be discussed, the Chumán uprising (1910) and the Zaña revolt (1913), occurred in the interior rural areas of Lambayeque. The second two took place in the Chicama Valley (1912, 1921–22) in La Libertad. Together these insurgent movements reflect a new counterpower geography that emerged due partly to anarchist efforts to unify, organize, and radicalize racially diverse urban and rural workers.

Traces of anarchist influence on the indigenous peasant rebellion in Ferreñafe in November 1910 are readily discernible. The leader of the rebellion, Manuel Casimiro Chumán Velásquez, a mestizo priest and fierce critic of *latifundismo*, promulgated a revolutionary program that earned the admiration and support of anarchists. It called for the restitution of usurped Indian lands and water, "the redemption of the Lambayecano Indian," and the replacement of oligarchic rule with a "true democracy." Chumán also articulated a vision of land, liberty, and education for his indigenous peasant supporters.[66] Given the wide distribution of Chiclayo's anarchist papers and their explicit support for the Mexican Revolution and the goals of "land and liberty," and given Chumán's frequent contacts with local activist workers and intellectuals, it's reasonable to assume they informed his revolutionary program.[67] What is known for certain is that Uchofen and *La Abeja* expressed admiration for Chumán's insurgency and sacrifices in defense of Ferreñafe's indigenous community. After the rebellion had been suppressed and Chumán had been granted political amnesty in September 1911, Uchofen affirmed in *La Abeja* Chumán's radical bona fides and endorsed his candidacy for the Senate.[68]

At the same time that *La Abeja* voiced support for Chumán and the Ferreñafe uprising, it sanctioned land seizures by the peasant community of Zaña in its conflict with Cayaltí, a sugar plantation owned by the powerful Aspíllaga family. On January 1, 1913, Zañeros of indigenous, African, Chinese, and mixed-race descent destroyed the barriers that Cayaltí had erected to enclose its lands and water and the reclaimed lands they asserted rightfully belonged to the community.[69] Four days later *La Abeja* opined that Zañeros "should be left in peace on the lands that they had worked for so long."[70] As the conflict dragged on into March and April, *La Abeja* repeatedly published open letters from Zañeros as well as sympathetic interviews with José Mercedes Cachay, their mixed-race leader.[71] One letter pointedly protested the contemptuous attitude of Cayaltí's landowners for Zaña and its inhabitants, and defiantly asserted Zañeros' rights. It stated, "Zaña has no autonomous existence, its sons are day laborers that imitate parasites, but, on the other hand, they already know that THEY'RE NOT SLAVES."[72] After soldiers attacked Zañero protesters and squatters, on May 4, leaving four dead and twelve wounded, the anarchist movements in Lambayeque and La Libertad roundly condemned the "massacre." *La Abeja* and *El Jornalero* circulated a special bulletin with the victims' names and demanded punishment for the military authorities and *hacendados* responsible for the bloodshed.[73] Echoing this sentiment, the Workers Confederation First of May in Chiclayo sent a letter of protest with two hundred signatures, including Uchofen's, to the president of the republic. It also collected and sent funds to aid the victims and their families.[74]

No official action was taken to restore Zaña's lands or to punish the perpetrators. To the contrary, the prefecture of Lambayeque ordered the arrest of Mercedes Cachay and the continuation of repression as long as the Zañeros maintained "their rebellious attitude."[75] *El Jornalero* expressed outrage at the absence of liberty and rights for the poor in Perú. "To remedy all of these wrongs," *El Jornalero* editorialized, "the Peruvian proletariat only needs [to apply] large doses of blood."[76] Aimed at northern Perú's racially and ethnically diverse urban and rural working class, this anarchist clarion call for proletarian self-emancipation would ultimately reverberate in a region-wide wave of strikes in the early 1920s.

In the Chicama Valley anarchists intensified their promotion of working-class solidarity in response to the mass bracero uprising of April 1912. The conflict began on April 8 when upward of five thousand rural workers armed with hatchets and machetes converged on hacienda Casa Grande and demanded an increase in wages and a reduction in work loads. Guards stationed on the hacienda clashed with the strikers after the braceros occupied the sugar mill and assaulted a company store.[77] Fifteen workers were killed. Protests and work stoppages soon spread to the other sugar haciendas in the Chicama and Moche Valleys. To prevent further destruction to hacienda installations and the burning of cane fields in the sugar enclave, Lima sent three hundred troops to bolster the rural police and the military prefect of La Libertad declared a state of siege.[78] Anarchist propaganda in support of the braceros prompted the prefect to imprison Reynaga and block the publication of *El Jornalero*.[79] By mid-May the uprising was suppressed, but not before it had claimed the lives of 150 workers. After his release from prison in June, Reynaga continued to defend the braceros and to vent his ire on the planter class. *El Jornalero* harshly criticized the owners of Casa Grande, the German-descended Gildemeister family. It depicted Enrique Gildemeister as a cruel landowner who had fired "countless employees and braceros without any justification" and evicted them from their hacienda quarters without notice. In solidarity with the bracero strikers, *El Jornalero* also denounced the Gildemeisters for replacing Peruvians with German employees. "Peru is not a colony of Germany," it editorialized, "and we're not disposed to tolerate its whims and barbarisms. Enough already!"[80] In addition to propaganda, anarchists intervened with the authorities on behalf of the braceros. On June 13, 1913, the CESUE in Trujillo convened delegates from anarchist groups and worker organizations in La Libertad to form a commission to secure the release of jailed braceros. The next day the commission persuaded the prefect and the presiding criminal judge to free the prisoners.[81]

The spontaneous explosion of labor militancy in the Chicama Valley in 1912 set the stage for a more concerted and extensive assault on oligarchic rule and capitalist exploitation in the sugar export enclave. Between 1912 and 1921 anarchist-oriented workers circulated widely throughout the enclave promoting syndicalist organization and a counterhegemonic perspective. Driven by the desire for better job prospects or compelled to move by employers' hostility, they migrated frequently from rural to urban and urban to rural settings. In the process they laid the groundwork for an anarchist-inflected workers' insurgency that swept up much of the Department of La Libertad in 1921.

The prime movers behind the formation of "a subversive geography of mobility and solidarity" in La Libertad were a number of young radical mestizo workers.[82] Manuel Arévalo Cáceres, Eduardo Chávez Terrazas, Artemio Zavala Paredes, and Leopoldo Pita Verde, for example, were instrumental in spreading anarcho-syndicalist ideas and organization in La Libertad. Arévalo migrated from his native province of Ascope to the Chicama Valley to work as a rural laborer and a mechanic on various sugar plantations. At the age of fourteen he worked alongside Chávez Terrazas as a mechanic's assistant on the hacienda Cartavio. Both had contact with Julio Reynaga and were exposed to anarcho-syndicalist ideas promulgated in El Jornalero.[83] In 1917 Chávez founded the first workers' resistance society at Cartavio called Sociedad Obrera de Auxilios Mutuos y Caja de Ahorros. Subsequently, Arévalo went to work at Casa Grande and formed a Workers' Committee to press for the eight-hour day. For his temerity, Arévalo would be arrested and transported to Lima in August 1920. Before returning to Trujillo and the sugar enclave in 1921, he formed relationships with anarcho-syndicalists in Lima-Callao.[84] On the eve of the 1921 labor insurgency, he promoted trade-union organization and workers' cultural associations named for Manuel González Prada, the Limeño anarchist thinker, on the haciendas Chiclín, Chiquitoy, and Casa Grande.[85]

Zavala Paredes became an influential proponent of syndicalism after migrating from the sierra town of Santiago de Chuco to work as a mechanic at hacienda Roma. There he befriended Joaquín Díaz Ahumada, another worker autodidact, and together they read publications by Errico Malatesta, Peter Kropotkin, and other libertarian socialists.[86] He also had contact with Chávez Terrazas and drew on his advice to found Roma's first union organization, the Sociedad Obrera de Auxilios de Caja de Ahorros de Roma, in March 1921.[87] Shortly thereafter, as the union's leader, he drafted a list of demands that challenged the system of domination on the hacienda. Among other demands, it called for the abolition of *enganche* contracts and corporal punishment, removal of the civil guard, and the implementation of an eight-hour workday and minimum wages. Amid the ensuing strike action in April, Zavala teamed with Leopoldo Pita, a worker on hacienda Chiclín, to colligate worker organizations in La Libertad into a single, departmental labor federation.[88] In August 1921 they founded the Regional Labor Union (Sindicato Regional del Trabajo, SRT), which claimed to represent twenty-eight thousand sugar, railway, port, and urban workers and two thousand employees.[89]

The anarcho-syndicalist propaganda and organizing activities of itinerant workers and anarchists in Trujillo profoundly influenced the mass mobilization and struggle of workers in Chicama in 1921. This can be seen in the use of solidarity and general strikes that converted what was originally a local conflict over wages at hacienda Roma into a broad working-class struggle against the dominant order in the sugar enclave. On April 6 and September 13, 1921, for example, workers in Trujillo engaged in general strikes with support from enclave transport and port workers. In addition, one can discern in this labor insurgency the realization, albeit temporary, of longstanding anarchist objectives, such as the formation of an urban and rural worker alliance, the organization of bracero unions, and the establishment of a powerful departmental labor federation. The SRT's strike demands also reflected anarcho-syndicalist formulations. Among its eighteen-point list of demands, the SRT insisted on the recognition of all workers' organizations, the abolition of *enganche* labor, and the adoption of the eight-hour workday.[90]

For the planter class, there was little doubt that the escalation of worker militancy in the enclave was attributable to anarchist agitation. Rafael Larco Herrera, owner of hacienda Chiclín put it bluntly: "The recent workers' movements of this valley have been controlled by known elements of anarchist affiliation that are easily identified in Trujillo at any time."[91] In Lima the business and mainstream press shared this view. *Variedades* editorialized, for example, that provocateurs "have undermined the spirit of the workers of the valley with a bolshevist virus and with outdated Proudhonian theories and other nonsense" and "implanted in the heart of the laboring masses the most rebellious anarchist ideas."[92] The striking workers "were not strikers seeking redress for a violated right, but revolutionaries unfurling a banner of the destruction of property."[93] Sugar planters, likewise, considered SRT leaders to be recalcitrant revolutionaries and refused to recognize the legitimacy of the SRT or its affiliated worker organizations. To thwart initial government attempts to seek a negotiated solution, Rafael Larco sent a memo to the Ministry of Development, characterizing the SRT as a sinister, confrontational organization with an unstable rotating leadership bent on the creation of "soviets" in the Chicama and Santa Catalina valleys.[94] Fearing that the SRT posed a real threat to the sugar industry and Perú's national economic interests, the Leguía government, acting at the behest of the planter class, forcibly dismantled the movement in 1922. Pita, Zavala, and other SRT leaders were arrested and transported to Lima aboard a naval warship while army troops suppressed the strikes at the cost of one hundred workers killed and two hundred wounded. José Ignacio Chopitea, owner of hacienda Laredo, summed up the gratitude and relief of the sugar planters in a note to the military prefect of La Libertad. Comparing the SRT to France's anarcho-syndicalist General Confederation of Workers, he exclaimed, "you have saved Trujillo and the nation drowning in its cradle this poor imitation of that confederation, which here calls itself the Regional Labor Union."[95]

Conclusion

The formation of the anarchist movement in northern Perú coincided with the expansion of the sugar export enclave from the 1890s to the early 1920s. Anarchist worker-intellectuals and activists in Trujillo and Chiclayo founded presses, study centers, cultural associations, and labor organizations to contest the reorganization of internal space, land concentration, and water usurpation, and the imposition of coercive and exploitative labor practices by agrarian capitalists in La Libertad and Lambayeque. To counter the designs and pretensions of the sugar planters, anarchists formulated an emancipatory project predicated on worker solidarity and a racially inclusive urban-rural worker alliance. Acutely aware of the entrenched racism that permeated Perú's structures of domination, anarchists appealed to and opened spaces in their movement for the region's Afro-Peruvians, mestizos, *zambos*, Asians, and indigenous inhabitants.[96] This was reflected in their denunciation of elite racial oppression and dehumanization of subaltern groups, open membership policy in labor organizations, and solidarity with multiracial resistance movements. It also was evinced in their principled defense of indigenous rights and stance against the dispossession of indigenous and mixed-race smallholders.

Despite intense repression by landowners and the state, anarchists in northern Perú succeeded in establishing an archipelago of resistance that linked urban and rural workers' organizations and struggles. Within the lived space of this archipelago, anarchists fostered an anticapitalist, anti-authoritarian, and antiracist working-class identity and ethos. This radical outlook would continue to inform new anarchist groups and workers' movements in the 1920s and early 1930s. In Chiclayo during the 1920s, an-archist-inspired propaganda was disseminated by groups like "Chiclayanos Conscientes" and students associated with magazines such as *Germinal* and *Colónida*.[97] The foundation and strike actions of the Land and Maritime Workers' Federation of the Port of Eten in early 1926 bore the imprint of anarcho-syndicalist influence. Braceros on hacienda Cartavio in the Moche Valley staged a mass protest in 1922 demanding the right to syndical orga-nization and liberty.[98] In 1928 the Syndicalist Solidarity Group in Trujillo published *La Protesta*, a local paper established to spread anarcho-syndi-calist ideas. Urban workers, stevedores, and hacienda braceros in La Liber-tad, many of whom were former anarcho-syndicalists, eagerly participated in the mass-based Trujillo rebellion led by the American Popular Revo-lutionary Alliance in July 1932. Prominent among them were Juan Delfín Montoya, a veteran peasant leader, and Manuel Barreto Risco, who learned the tenets of anarcho-syndicalism at the side of Leopoldo Pita Verde.[99] Although the insurrection was crushed by the dictatorship of Col. Luis Miguel Sánchez Cerro, anarchist revolutionary élan, its ideals of liberty, equality, social justice, and worker solidarity, and experience of multiracial class struggle would remain a vital legacy for future workers' movements.

Notes

Field research for this chapter was funded by a generous grant from the Center for Latin American Studies at the University of Pittsburgh. I also want to thank Wilson Sagá-stegui Lozada for his research assistance.

1. By 1896 a railway line began operations linking Trujillo with Laredo and Galindo-Menocucho. Libro de Actas de la Liga de Artesanos y Obreros del Perú (hereafter LALAOP), vol. 1, November 30, 1899.

2. LALAOP, vol. 1, February 23, 1900; June 12, 1902; September 19, 1902; and October 15, 1902. "Braceros" refers to rural laborers who worked either on a temporary or permanent basis on sugar haciendas and plantations.

3. Ibid., vol. 1, June 12, 1902; and October 15, 1902.

4. Ibid., vol. 1, April 18, 1903, Private Collection of Demetrio Ramos Raú. Labor con-tractors (*enganchadores*) penetrated the highland regions of La Libertad and Cajamarca to recruit indigenous peasants for work in the coastal valleys of La Libertad and Lam-bayeque. See Bazán Alfaro and Gómez Cumpa, "Enganche y formacion," 249–67.

5. *La Antorcha*, May 20, 1905, 1–2.

6. Ibid., May 1, 1907, 3.

7. See, for example, *El Jornalero*, November 17, 1906, 2–3.

8. Before settling in Trujillo, Reynaga had been a port worker in Callao. Uchofen was a carpenter and a print worker. In all likelihood he was of a mixed racial background. Both were autodidacts.

9. *La Abeja*, February 1909, no. 3:2, First Week October 1909, no. 1:3.

10. Publication of *La Abeja* continued into the early 1930s. However, after 1921 it abandoned an anarchist orientation.

11. On the formation and dynamics of northern Perú's sugar enclaves, see Cotler, "State and Regime," 274–75.

12. Drawing on the work of Henri Lefebvre, Deborah G. Martin, and Byron Miller, I define "counterspaces" as the lived space where "alternative orders of material and symbolic space are imagined and struggled over." See Martin and Miller, "Space and Contentious Politics," 146.

13. During the so-called Aristocratic Republic in Perú, between 1900 and 1919, sugar planters controlled the presidency for twelve years and held important ministerial and other government posts. On the political power of the sugar export industrialists, see Klarén, "Sugar Industry in Peru," 39; and Burga and Flores Galindo, *Apogeo y crisis*, 84–90.

14. For an examination of the *enganche* contract labor system, see Blanchard, "Recruitment of Workers," 65–66; and Klarén, *Modernization, Dislocation, and Aprismo*, 26–31.

15. Other anarchist papers like *Justicia*, *El Rebelde*, and *El Libertario* circulated throughout the region, but they were largely ephemeral.

16. Ramos Rau, *Mensaje de Trujillo*, 65–66. See also M. Vargas Morales to Y. Y. Lombardzi [sic], January 3, 1905; Julio Rodriguez to Teodoro Moreno Machado, January 13, 1905. Liga de Artesanos y Obreros del Perú Correspondence Collection, Trujillo, La Libertad, Perú.

17. *El Jornalero*, January 26, 1907.

18. Ibid., May 9, 1913.

19. *La Protesta Libre*, March (n.d.), 1909; *La Abeja*, March 2, 1913; and June 29, 1913.

20. This regional network encompassed the departments of Ancash, Cajamarca, and Piura, which also contained anarchist groups and publications. In addition, the anarchist press in Trujillo and Chiclayo formed part of a transnational anarchist network that included reciprocal exchanges with anarchist papers in Buenos Aires, Santiago de Chile, Barcelona, Havana, Guayaquil, Mexico City, and Amsterdam.

21. *La Abeja*, July 9, 1917.

22. *El Jornalero*, December 8, 1906.

23. Ibid., November 24, 1906.

24. See, for example, *La Abeja* September 15, 1912; and July 10, 1917; and *El Jornalero*, October 10, 1914.

25. *El Jornalero*, November 17, 1906; and *La Abeja* July 11, 1917.

26. The export-oriented planter class, according to Gonzalo Portocarrero, had a "racist aristocratic ethos" that was also reflected in the implicit racist ideology of Perú's oligarchic state. See Portocarrero, *Racismo y mestizaje*, chap. 10, esp. 346–47.

27. See, for example, *La Antorcha*, May 20, 1905; and *El Jornalero*, December 20, 1906.

28. *El Jornalero*, November 17, 1906.

29. Ibid., November 24, 1906.

30. See Stanfield, *Red Rubber, Bleeding Trees*, esp. chap. 7–8.

31. See, for example, *Los Parias* (Lima), November 1905.

32. See Mercedes Cachay's letter to Dora Mayer de Zulen, reprinted in Mayer de Zulen, *El Indígena Peruano*, 117–22.

33. *La Protesta Libre*, first week February 1909; second week of November 1909; and *La Abeja*, October 3, 1911.

34. *El Jornalero*, January 26, 1907.

35. Ibid., July 25, 1912.

36. *La Abeja*, September 3, 1920.

37. *El Jornalero*, June 15, 1911.

38. *La Abeja*, May 25, 1913.

39. LALOAP, Vol. 1, March 14, 1912.

40. The worker and anarchist Herminio Cisneros, who became a formal member of the LAOP in 1914, served as an important go-between for the two organizations.

41. Gonzales, *Plantation Agriculture and Social Control*, 119–23.

42. Chinese workers, though also small in number, had a larger presence on the haciendas in 1920. See Bachman, *Departamento de Lambayeque*, 102.

43. *El Jornalero*, December 1, 1906.

44. Ibid.

45. *El Jornalero*, December 1, 1906; and December 20, 1906.

46. Ibid.

47. *El Jornalero*, December 8, 1906.

48. Goyens, "Social Space," 442.

49. In an extraordinary session, the LAOP voted to change its founding bylaws to admit "foreign workers" as members. Reynaga was the prime mover behind this change. LALAOP, vol. 1, April 24, 1902.

50. Mutualist, syndicalist, and socialist currents influenced LAOP members. See Ramos Rau, *Mensaje de Trujillo*, 69–70.

51. LALAOP, Vol. 1, April 21, 1905. The use and meaning of the symbol of a triangle is open to conjecture. Ytalo Martín Chihuala Peche, acting president of LAOP, believes the three sides of the triangle stood for liberty, equality, and fraternity. Personal communication, February 9, 2012.

52. The library remains in existence with over two thousand volumes. It contains works by Errico Malatesta, Mikhail Bakunin, Peter Kropotkin, Sébastien Faure, and Manuel González Prada that were published during the period under study.

53. Reynaga was expelled from LAOP on July 27, 1905, after having been accused of financial malfeasance. His expulsion was more likely a result of personal and ideological conflicts and his defiant radicalism, which made him a lightning rod for state repression (he was arrested in December 1904 and held until late February 1904). See Ramos Rau, *Mensaje de Trujillo*, 61.

54. The CESUE functioned in the main salon of the Worker Social Center on 59 Independence Street in 1912. *El Jornalero*, June 11, 1912. On Reynaga's political and cultural activities, see Llanos-Horna, *Los periodistas de La Libertad*, 161–63.

55. *La Antorcha*, September 20, 1906; and *El Jornalero*, June 11, 1912.

56. *El Oprimido*, April 1908; and *El Jornalero*, June 15, 1911. See also Delgado Benites, *Artemio Zavala*, 63. In 1913 the League of Artisans and Workers for Mutual Protection in Ascope founded a Popular Library.

57. LALOP, Vol. 1, April 13, 1912; and Liga de Artesanos y Obreros del Perú, "*Cien Años de Dignidad*," 13.

58. *La Industria*, June 13, 1916.

59. Police Security to Director of Government and Police, June 14, 1916, Archivo General de la Nación (AGN), Prefectura de La Libertad, folder 184; *La Industria*, June 15, 1916.

60. Castillo Rivadeneira, *Movimiento obrero en Lambayeque*, 27.

61. *La Abeja*, May 11, 1913.

62. The GLA sponsored a performance of the libertarian play "¡Mártir!" by Uruguayan playwright A. Mario Lazzoni, at the 2 of May Theatre in 1911. *La Abeja*, second week of November 1911.

63. *La Protesta Libre*, February (n.d.), 1909; and *La Abeja*, second week of October, 1911.

64. Delgado Rosado, "Movimiento intellectual en Lambayeque," 90.

65. For nearly a year between 1910 and 1911, the GLA local was closed and *La Abeja* was prevented from publishing. In August 1913 the center was again the target of repression, and Uchofen was arrested.

66. Sevilla Exebio, "La Montonera del Cura Chuman," 148 and 150.

67. See, for example, *El Jornalero*, June 1, 1911, 1–2; and *La Abeja*, second week of November 1911, 1.

68. *La Abeja*, November 2, 1911; October 27, 1912; and November 17, 1912.

69. For a discussion of the racial and ethnic composition of Zaña in the early twentieth century, see Rocca Torres, *De la multitud a la soledad*, 32–34.

70. *La Abeja*, January 5, 1913, 3.

71. José Mercedes Cachay is described by his biographer as having the features of a "mestizo-yuna-hispano." See Rocca Torres, *De la multitud a la soledad*.

72. *La Abeja*, March 9, 1913, 1.

73. Ibid., May 11, 1913, 2–3; and *El Jornalero*, May 16, 1913, 1.

74. *La Abeja*, May 8, 1913; and June 29, 1913.

75. Prefect of Lambayeque to Director of Government, January 15, 1914, AGN, folder 164.

76. *El Jornalero*, July 15, 1924, 1–2.

77. *La Industria*, April 9, 1912, 2.

78. Ramos Rau, *Mensaje de Trujillo*, 53.

79. *La Industria*, April 16, 1912.

80. *El Jornalero*, June 11, 1912, 2.

81. Ibid., June 13, 1913, 2.

82. Andrew Herod points out that labor organizing and building solidarity are geographically and spatially constituted and can produce a radical geography. Herod, *Organizing the Landscape*, 123.

83. Arévalo gave a eulogy at Reynaga's funeral in July 1923. Hidalgo Gamarra, *Arévalo*, 28 and 41; and Ñique Ríos, *Manuel Arévalo Cáceres*, 138 and 141.

84. Ñique Ríos, *Manuel Arévalo Cáceres*, 148.

85. On the influence of González Prada on Arévalo, see ibid., 158–59, 181–86.

86. Díaz Ahumada, *Luchas sindicales*, 52–53.

87. See Delgado Benites, *Artemio Zavala*, 45; and Ramos Rau, *Mensaje de Trujillo*, 137.

88. *La Industria,* August 11, 1921; and Delgado Benites, *Artemio Zavala*, 62–63.

89. *La Industria*, August 15, 1921, 2.

90. Ibid., December 12, 1921, 2. Defense of the workers' press was also another key demand. Workers at Casa Grande insisted on noninterference with the publication of their paper *El Germinal*. See *La Industria*, September 14, 1921.

91. *La Industria*, August 23, 1921, 2–3; and October 20, 1921, 3.

92. *Variedades*, October 15, 1921, 1597–98; and October 22, 1921, 1669–70.

93. Ibid., October 15, 1921, 1597–98.

94. Reprinted in Larco Herrera, *Memorias*, 66.

95. *La Industria*, January 14, 1922.

96. Writers and correspondents with Asian surnames like Lon and K. Tón worked for *La Abeja* and *El Hambriento*, the Lima-based anarchist paper in Trujillo. See, for example, *La Abeja*, July 12, 1917; and *El Hambriento*, January 1909.

97. Prefecture of Lambayeque to Minister of Government and Police, March 28, 1923, AGN, folder 249; and Gómez Cumpa, "Aprismo y comunismo," 29.

98. *La Protesta* (Lima), December 1922.

99. Margarita Giesecke characterizes the Trujillo rebellion as a "social revolution" based on the massive participation of urban, port, and bracero workers and notes the leadership role of former anarcho-syndicalist activists. See Giesecke, "Trujillo Insurrection."

12

Anarchists and Alterity

The Expulsion of Casimiro Barrios from Chile, 1920

RAYMOND CRAIB

In early twentieth century Chile, state authorities—prefects, intendents, police agents, spies, and congressmen—hassled, harangued, persecuted, prosecuted, framed, caricatured, criticized, categorized, arrested, and expelled individuals they perceived to be challenging the social and political order. One of those individuals was Casimiro Barrios Fernández. Accused of being a subversive and an anarchist, Chilean security personnel escorted Barrios out of the country on July 19, 1920. In ordering his expulsion, the administration relied on multiple notions of alterity: not only was Barrios purportedly foreign, so too were the ideas he supposedly espoused. This chapter takes up the question of anarchism as alterity by following the activities and eventual expulsion of Barrios. It is in many ways and despite Barrios' Spanish origins a very local story, rooted in Santiago, Chile.

I stress this in part for a simple reason: the politicians and critics of labor and its allies at the time were all too keen to emphasize the foreign origins of political opposition and, in particular, anarchism and anarcho-syndicalism. They leapt at every opportunity to suggest such "agitation from without." My aim in part is to emphasize how organizers and militants were often quite rooted: they were long-term residents of a place, with families and communities and political projects to whom and to which they were intensely committed. The myth of the placeless radical was oftentimes precisely that: a myth. Moreover, as will become evident in this chapter, Chilean militants and organizers bristled at the repeated and patronizing suggestions that the ideals they held dear were somehow foreign or imported, just one more finished product from the metropole shipped off for consumption in the periphery.[1] This is in some ways, then, an exploratory exercise in (forgive the anachronism) import substitution radicalization.

Errant Swallows

Casimiro Barrios Fernández arrived in Chile in 1904 at the age of fourteen. He was one of a wave of young immigrants from the sierra of Cameros in La Rioja, Spain, to set his sights on South America. His hometown of Nieva de Cameros was characteristic of many of the small villages that clung to the mountainsides of the sierra, where the population had traditionally devoted itself to sheep herding. Transhumant paths coursed across old Castile to the edges of Extremadura while the wool cloth from the sierra made its way to many of the commercial centers of the plateau and as far south as Andalucía in the eighteenth century.[2] The sierra had increasingly seen an outmigration of its young population in the late nineteenth century, prior to a larger outflux from the Ebro Valley regions of La Rioja, as the herding and wool industry declined in the nineteenth century, combined with the phylloxera plague that devastated La Rioja and a more general crisis in agricultural production.[3] Initially many of these adolescents migrated south, either to Extremadura or to Andalucía, many perhaps following centuries-old pathways.[4] But gradually, and especially by the late nineteenth century, the migration shifted toward South America, with young migrants leaving directly from their villages and towns in the sierra.[5]

Transportation changes facilitated this shift toward trans-Atlantic migration, as did the increased existence of agents actively recruiting migrants. Indeed, throughout La Rioja agents of colonization companies sought to tempt potential emigrants to make the move with offers of free travel to Chile. After Argentina, Chile was the destination of choice, and the Chilean Colonization Agency had a representative in Arnedo and branches in Logroño, Calahorra, Cervera, and Haro.[6] Although migrants had to be wary—stories circulated of phony agents and fake companies, such as the Spanish American Iron Company, whose agents promised passage to Cuba on a ship that in reality sailed for the Transvaal—many found their way to Buenos Aires, Santiago, and Valparaíso after departing from Barcelona, Santander, and Galicia.[7]

The Barrios family was no exception. Four of the five Barrios brothers left the slowly contracting village of Nieva de Cameros around the turn of the century, a decade before an even larger boom in outmigration from La Rioja.[8] While Eleuterio Barrios, like most of his fellow *neveros*, headed for Buenos Aires, the eldest brother, Ciriaco, traveled to Taltal, in northern Chile, followed shortly thereafter by his brothers Rogelio and, in 1904, Casimiro.[9] Taltal was a dusty port town of fifteen thousand souls but growing quickly as the demand for saltpeter, copper, and nitrates, all mined from the surrounding Atacama desert, expanded rapidly for export to North America and Europe. The Barrios brothers were drawn there for other reasons: their uncle, Julián Barrios, needed help in his two small shops, El Sol and Las Novedades.[10]

Barrios would not remain long in Taltal. With the deaths of his brothers Rogelio (1905) and Ciriaco (1908), he may have had little reason to remain.[11] By 1911 he had apparently relocated to the capital city of Santiago. One of the first tasks he set himself on arriving was to have Ciriaco's poetry published. It took some time, but he eventually succeeded, the volume appearing with a small eulogy from Casimiro in the prologue.[12] Ciriaco was six years Casimiro's senior. In Taltal, as well as working in his uncle's shop, Ciriaco had established a reputation for himself, under the pen name Gil Güero, as a poet and a correspondent with Santiago's El Heraldo de España.[13] His poems revealed an attention to social inequalities and seemed to evoke the plight of La Rioja's peasants; others, such as "Nostalgia," reflected the difficulties of migration: "Pobre golondrina errante! / no bien ensayado el vuelo / con rumbo a remoto suelo / mi tibio nido dejé," [Poor errant swallow! / not well tested in flight / for a land remote / I left my warm nest].[14] Just how well he had established himself as an ally of working people is suggested by the editorial that appeared in La Voz del Obrero upon notification of his death: "The cause of social justice has suffered an irreplaceable loss: with the death of señor Barrios it has lost one of its next apostles."[15]

How much of an ideological influence Ciriaco had on his younger brother is unclear, but Casimiro clearly shared his brother's sympathies for the plight of workers in Chile's burgeoning industries. This perhaps is not surprising: as well as the influence of his brother, Barrios must also have been impacted by the massacre of workers, along with their wives and children, at the nearby Escuela Santa María de Iquique in 1907.

At some point after arriving in Santiago, Barrios married a chilena with whom he raised a number of children. He had saved enough money to establish his wife with a cigarrería, with sales of nearly two hundred pesos a day, while he worked as a clerk in a garment shop on San Diego Street just south of the city center.[16] But the Great War (or, as Barrios put it, "the goddamn war") quickly put an end to his wife's business, although he later was able to set her up with a small milk stand. By the second half of the decade,

Barrios had become, with his energy and eloquence, a fairly prominent figure in the political Left of Santiago.[17] From his counter, Barrios would watch the happenings on the busy street outside. When a demonstration arose in the streets nearby, Barrios would leave his post for an hour to unleash "a torrent of fiery words and then return to selling cloth."[18] He acquired a reputation for being particularly outspoken regarding the lack of enforcement of existing labor laws, such as the 1914 "*ley de la silla,*" which required employers to provide a chair for each of their clerical workers, and the 1907 "*ley dominical,*" which provided for a day of rest each week.[19] In other instances he spoke openly and frequently about the need for a minimum wage, a limit to the number of hours one could work, and a reduction in the interest that lending houses could charge.[20] Eloquent and well informed, living and working in the heart of one of Santiago's busiest commercial districts, Casimiro Barrios would eventually feel the wrath of the business owners who feared the enforcement of such measures.

The Residency Law

On November 22, 1918, upward of one hundred thousand people took to the streets of Santiago. The demonstration was organized by the Asamblea Obrera de Alimentación Nacional (Workers' Assembly on National Nutrition, or AOAN), created in 1917 by the labor movement in conjunction with university students from the Chilean Student Federation (FECh) to address the scarcity and rapidly escalating costs of basic foodstuffs and staples at a time when the major growers were increasing their exports. A remarkably inclusive organization, the AOAN was composed of workers from various industries, *empleados* of both sexes, university students, and middle-class professionals.[21] The key issues were a demand that the government reduce or stop exports of cereals and that farmers be permitted to sell directly to consumers.[22] Among those in the leadership of the AOAN was Casimiro Barrios, who by this point had also joined the Santiago branch of the Partido Obrera Socialista (Socialist Workers Party, or POS) and spoke at meetings and demonstrations protesting the cost of food and basic necessities.[23]

The November protest clearly captured the government's attention. In the wake of the demonstrations, Juan Luis Sanfuentes' administration issued an order suspending the exportation of foodstuffs for the remainder of 1918 and for all of 1919 in order to ensure the provisioning of the country.[24] But the regime responded in other ways as well: it organized patriotic rallies in Santiago, ratcheted up repression against labor and its allies, and circulated alarmist claims of Peruvian plots to take back the northern districts of Tacna and Arica, captured by Chile in the War of the Pacific (1879–83). Such claims were largely hyperbolic responses to Peruvian attacks on a number of Chilean consulates in Peru earlier in the month, but, combined with the powerful appearance of the AOAN, they provided a strategic opportunity for the regime to push again for the enactment of a residency law.[25] Calls for the enactment of such a law were not entirely new and had increased in recent years as officials battled strikers who threatened to cripple the ports of Valparaíso and Iquique.[26] They also battled Australian officials who had seemingly adopted Chile as their first choice of destination for agitators subject to deportation in their own country: three times over the course of 1918, Australian authorities marched their unwanted Wobblies—English, Irish, Danish, American, and Spanish—on to ships bound for Valparaíso.[27] Such deportations led to moments of diplomatic strife and eventually, according to British ambassador Francis Stronge, a "hope that the incident would serve as a lever for bringing about prohibitive or restrictive legislation" within Chile.[28]

And it did. While the imagined plots brewing in Peru were the stuff of fantasy, the Residency Law soon became reality. Enacted in December 1918, the law prohibited entrance into, or residency in, Chile by "undesireable elements."[29] Like other exclusionary laws, this one also noted that entrance would be prohibited for foreigners condemned or currently under prosecution for common crimes, those without employment, individuals engaged in illicit activities, and those with certain illnesses.[30] The law also gave power to intendents to force foreigners to register with local officials and to obtain personal identity *cédulas* (documents). But the impetus for the law was to prohibit immigration to Chile by people with political ideals that challenged the status quo and, just as crucially, to allow for the expulsion of non-Chileans who were perceived to be creating problems for the administration and its allies. The first to feel its wrath was Barrios, who was ordered, on December 18, 1920, expelled from the country for "preaching the violent overthrow of the social and political order and provoking protests against the existing order."[31] Fourteen years after immigrating to Chile, Barrios now found himself the first person to be ordered expelled under the new law.

A Constant Sentinel

In early January 1919, the authorities stayed Barrios' expulsion order.[32] In part, this resulted from an intense campaign on the part of some POS members in Santiago and of organizers in the AOAN.[33] Barrios had established himself as a powerful and admired presence among Santiago's working sectors. *La Aurora* and *La Bandera Roja* published editorials condemning the Residency Law and the order for Barrios' expulsion.[34] But Barrios also had defenders in other quarters. Only two days after the issuance of the initial expulsion decree, deputies and senators from the Alianza Liberal in Chile's Parliament voiced concerns on the floor of their respective chambers.[35]

For its supporters, the law was meant to be "preventive" (perhaps preemptive?) against men such as Barrios who led others into the "thicket of social disorganization, of disorder, and in the end, the utopia of men without country and without possessions."[36] The strongest arguments made repeatedly in defense of Barrios were that he was not an individual to whom such a law ought to be applied. The reasons offered were numerous: he worked hard; he had lived in Chile for much of his adult life (an implicit questioning of what constituted a "foreigner"); he had married a Chilean woman and had children of Chilean nationality; and he was not a subversive but in fact simply worked to ensure existing laws were upheld.[37] Take, for example, the long disquisition of Sen. Zenón Torrealba, someone who had worked with Barrios while president of a Santiago artisan society and who spoke at great length in his defense of Barrios, even while emphasizing that Barrios was a member of a party "that calls itself the Socialist Worker" and not Torrealba's own Democratic Party.[38] Barrios, he noted, had joined the Sociedad de Empleados de Comercio (Business Employees' Society) and had begun to campaign hard for the enforcement of the Sunday Rest Law. To ensure compliance with, and enforcement of, this law and others that had been passed for the benefit of working people, Barrios had organized demonstrations and meetings. He had also begun to preach among workers of the need for abstention from alcohol.

> For these reasons, I imagine that this man has attracted persecution from the business owners [*comerciantes*] and distributors [*espendedores*] of alcoholic beverages, above all those who have their businesses in the barrio of San Diego, who do not want to see him continue his campaign. He has been, in effect, a constant sentinel who has forced them to close their shops on the days required by law. I

imagine that these businessmen, tired of putting up with the continuous vigilance of this citizen, would have denounced him to the Santiago intendent, accusing him of being an anarchist and a dangerous man. I believe this to be the real motive behind the accusation that, without a doubt, they have made against him.[39]

Had perhaps the intendent been swayed by such commercial interests, Torrealba suggested, particularly given that the government had nothing more than a report from a Security Section agent upon which to base their decree of expulsion? Regardless of how outspoken (*mui hablador*) Barrios might be, that did not make him a threat to the internal security of the nation, he argued.[40]

On the floor of the deputies' chamber similar defenses unfolded. Deputy Pinto Durán referred to Barrios as a "man of good" and a "modest worker," one concerned with those who were less well-off (to which a conservative deputy responded: "Then let him go preach in his own land! There is a lot more misery there than in Chile").[41] The well-off, Pinto Durán noted, see the principles that structure society as naturally indisputable, but if one were to see through the eyes of those who work ten or twelve hours per day and still cannot earn enough to feed themselves and their children, the world would look quite different. The comment provoked a heated and revealing response from a conservative deputy: there was plenty of work in the countryside at good pay, he claimed, but workers in the city did not want it and instead chose to pass their time in the taverns.[42] He and other *agricultores* offered four or five pesos a day for work in the fields, plus room and board, but still could not find workers. The root cause of the high prices of foodstuffs, he argued, was the fact that the labor force was poorly distributed.[43]

All of these comments—whether from defenders or accusers of Barrios—point to the heart of why a significant group of parliamentarians spoke in favor of a residency law and the expulsion of Barrios: large landowners and growers had just watched, in Sanfuentes' response to the AOAN demonstrations, their export possibilities and profit margins radically curtailed while businessmen in the central commercial district of Santiago had to suffer Barrios' constant efforts to get labor laws enforced. They clearly would have preferred not to admit that such was the case. Instead, they embraced the canard of the foreign agitator. Yet in Barrios the authorities had someone who hardly fit such an image. As he himself noted in an interview with *Zig-Zag*, having arrived in Chile at the age of fourteen, he had lived there for half of his life.[44] He clearly was not *so* foreign. Moreover, he had over the course of the previous decade become a prominent and important figure in Santiago's labor movement and had developed close relationships with members of Chile's political class. It seemed unlikely he could so easily be conflated with bomb-throwing fictions of the kind circulating at the time. In other words, the assertions of alterity hardly fooled many, even in the centers of government.

Misplaced Ideas?

Nor did they fool working people. Shortly after Barrios' expulsion order was stayed, tram operators in Santiago went on strike. Meanwhile, the AOAN pushed to capitalize on the momentum by calling for nationwide demonstrations in early February 1919. Having been caught off guard by the size of the demonstrations the previous November and reeling from both the tram strike and congressional criticism of cancelling Barrios' expulsion order, Sanfuentes' ministers and party stalwarts saw such mobilizations as an opportunity to regain ground and to move against the labor movement under the pretense of a subversive threat.[45] Despite the peaceful nature of the demonstrations, authorities increasingly responded with repression and threats of extensive violence. Presses were shut down, union leaders were arbitrarily detained, workers were beaten, a multitude of others were arrested under false pretenses, and claims of maximalist conspiracies were circulated.[46] One paper reported that the military presence sent to the northern pampas to suppress the AOAN organizers was of a magnitude not seen since the civil war of 1891.[47] In the midst of this crackdown, Deputy Urrutia Ibáñez took to the floor of the Parliament:

> This past week has been one of apprehension and anxious concern; one could not foresee the characteristics the strike would take; it was known that there were reckless agitators preaching sedition among the workers, and it was feared that foreign anarchists could be hatching sinister plans against the social order; and it was even feared that the "red flu," as maximalism is called, might have spread among our popular classes. . . . These events . . . should serve to teach us and serve as an example. They show us that international anarchism takes on a very dangerous form in countries of incipient organization: it does not now throw bombs [*prepara ya atentados*] at the heads of

government; it provokes the rebellious mass to rise up against work, discipline, and the social morality that exists, has existed, and always will exist in all States.[48]

Urrutia again returned to the argument that the strikes and conflicts erupting in Santiago and elsewhere were the work of foreign agitators, particularly anarchists. He could hardly have been unaware of the existence of domestic anarchists: after all, they had been organizing and agitating for some two decades in Chile.[49] But the possibility of both negating that such strikes and conflicts may have stemmed from legal and domestic organizations with legitimate grievances, and equating anarchism with foreignness was too much to pass up. Indeed, such perspectives had become commonplace in the press. Editorialists and politicians repeatedly blamed the foreign—persons and ideas—for the supposed agitation of the otherwise content Chilean worker. In his interview with Barrios, the reporter from *Zig-Zag* concluded with a predictable insult: "he is a victim of the criminal propaganda that circulates among workers in old Europe who, through the university or through books, are imbued with utopian theories which, if they don't fit there, are even less appropriate here in Chile where currently our greatest evil is an excess of liberties."[50]

These efforts to assert the presence of "misplaced ideas" and placeless agitators were obvious to many at the time. Juan Gandulfo, a medical student and prominent member of the FECh, seemed to have Barrios in mind when he scathingly remarked that "Chilean journalists, among whom there are two or three who really understand the social question, have chileanized the 'professional agitator,' in order to satisfy their bosses and the commercial businesses which advertise in this country's newspapers."[51] Barrios' own colleagues understood as much. In a revealing exchange during a meeting of the central committee of the AOAN immediately following the expulsion decree, Enrique Huerta noted: "It is not possible that they can claim that Barrios came to Chile as a foreigner to preach subversive ideas: I have known this man for nine years and his principles *were taught to him by Chileans*. First he was an anarchist and then a socialist." Evaristo Ríos agreed, remarking that Barrios had learned his ideas in Chile and that his only "crime" was to have been born abroad.[52] In other words, neither anarchism nor socialism were somehow "alien" or "misplaced" ideas, and immigrants could discover them in the societies in which they landed rather than necessarily importing them from whence they came: no idea that resonates in a given context can be said to be out of place.[53]

A Capacious Left

Even so, the stigma of being accused as an anarchist could be hard to shake and a worrisome accusation for some. An incident at a POS meeting in March of 1919 is revealing. Victor Roa Medina, long-time POS militant and the Party secretary, hosted a gathering at his home at which he suggested that the name of a weekly publication, *La Bandera Roja* (most likely modeled after the publication of the same name in Buenos Aires) be changed. Barrios seemed to take offense at the suggestion, observing that changing the name of the paper would be a problem because it was by that title that the paper was known both in Chile and Argentina, but perhaps also in part because *La Bandera Roja* had been organized in response to the expulsion order directed at him. Regardless, he responded to Medina's suggestion with sharp words, calling Roa Medina a coward and ridiculing his knowledge of socialist doctrine.[54] But what is especially striking is the response by Roa Medina and his allies, who argued that Barrios was in fact not a socialist but an anarchist, that his subversive ideas were going to get him expelled from the country, and that his continued participation in the party would ruin it.[55] A vote was taken on whether or not to expel Barrios: he survived the vote and Roa Medina stepped down while Barrios took over the publication of *La Bandera Roja*.

This dispute between Roa Medina and Barrios occurred at a particular juncture: in the wake of the tram workers' strike, Sanfuentes was granted powers of martial law and, under the threat of violence, the leadership of the AOAN cancelled a set of demonstrations, an act that angered many, particularly workers' organizations that were largely anarchist in orientation, including shoemakers, tailors, and typesetters.[56] New confederations appeared, including a Gran Confederación de Trabajo that began to meet regularly on Wednesdays at the offices of the Chilean Student Federation.[57] It was in this context of heightened repression combined with internal divisions over strategy that the dispute between Roa Medina and Barrios unfolded. While on the one hand it seems to suggest a kind of sectarianism, it also points toward the various ideological threads that made up the POS.

Clearly, ideas are important, and I have no desire to dismiss the ascriptions that people appropriated for themselves, or to disparage the communities they formed and the ideological glue that held those communities together. But I also do not wish to mimic the language of the police, or reinforce the inclinations to sectarianism that occasionally hold sway and that insist on dogmatic coherence rather than lived experience. Barrios was someone hard to "pin down," and in this I do not believe he was exceptional for the time. As one colleague noted, Barrios began as an anarchist and became a socialist, and yet we have a POS militant accusing Barrios of being an anarchist, and yet other POS militants defending Barrios and noting that he served as the secretary of the Santiago branch of the POS. (A similar ambivalence appears in the historiography in which Barrios appears.) Such efforts to rigidly situate Barrios are revealing on two fronts: First, they unsurprisingly indicate that there were differences of opinion regarding strategy, tactics and so forth. And second, they suggest that there was a capaciousness to the Left after the Great War; anarchists and socialists, if not indistinguishable from each other, certainly overlapped strongly. Was Barrios an anarchist? A socialist? Both? Or something else entirely? Barrios himself avoided too rigid a label: at various points in an interview with *Zig-Zag* he referred to himself as a socialist, a radical, a free-thinker, and a "militant in the most advanced parties" while also noting that he had mellowed over the years![58]

In fact, as was the case in many parts of the globe prior to 1920 or so, in Chile the line between anarchists and socialists could be relatively fluid.[59] University students espoused anarchist ideas as they sold copies of Trotsky's writings recently translated in to Spanish; others sustained a relationship with the Radical Party yet similarly embraced anarchist ideas and writings; meanwhile, contributors to *Verba Roja*, who self-identified strongly as anarchists, warmly embraced Lenin and the Bolshevik Revolution as a welcome "prologue" to a communo-anarchist future.[60] These should not be taken as evidence of incoherence or, conversely, of sectarianism but perhaps instead of the capaciousness of the Left in a specific place at a specific time: a city experiencing dramatic labor unrest and social change, in the wake of the Great War, and in the midst of an unfolding and inspiring revolution in Russia.

Expulsion

Despite the intendent's admonition that he steer clear of politics, over the course of 1919 Barrios continued to organize and agitate with the POS and the AOAN and was identified by authorities as one of the main instigators of a September 1919 general strike. In response to a police assault on the local office of the Federación Obrera de Chile in Limache, beer workers struck in Santiago, followed immediately by tram workers, chauffeurs, and shoe workers. This soon led authorities to order Barrios to appear yet again in the intendent's office.[61] "With his characteristic mode of innocence," reported the intendent, Barrios denied the accusations and assured the intendent that, "as a foreigner, he would not intervene in workers' movements nor preach his ideas in public."[62] Barrios clearly had cheek. A short time after this appearance, he evidently returned to demand that the police be more proactive in enforcing the law requiring Sunday as a day of rest, concluding his piece of unsolicited advice with a warning to the intendent that if this did not happen he would "raise the issue with workers' societies."[63] Shortly thereafter Barrios was accused of issuing public threats against officials who had drawn up the Residency Law.

The authorities were losing patience with Barrios. But just as crucially, as the year ended and the June elections approached, they were losing patience with the labor movement and its allies as a whole. As the presidential election scheduled for June 1920 approached, and as the candidacy of opposition candidate Arturo Alessandri garnered momentum among labor, those in power sought to find ways to control the circumstances surrounding the election and the political demography of the country. They did so through a number of mechanisms. For example, the Chilean state successfully forged agreements on immigration with some of its neighbors—Brazil, Argentina, and Uruguay—in order to "defend workers" from "undesireable elements," including persons who sought the "violent or revolutionary transformation of society."[64] The government also attempted to enforce more strictly the order that all foreigners resident in Chile register with the intendent in their zone of residence. Barrios received such an order in March.[65]

Identification itself could be a tricky business but also a profitable one. For example, seeing the possibilities, Roberto Matus and Humberto Ducci approached the intendent's chief of the Office on Identification at the end of 1919 to offer their services: a recently patented procedure for preparing personal identity cards, one which "absolutely impedes any substitution of the original picture."[66] Their letter hinted at the concerns with which any registration program would have to contend: "We have seen that with a simple change in the picture of an identity card, which has been stolen from its rightful owner, thieves can pass for capitalists or businessmen [or . . .] public employees; for diplomats; and even for Agents in the Security Section." They concluded ominously that this "could happen any day, if it hasn't already."[67] In a suggestive analogy, they noted that during the war in Europe officials would falsify identity cards of prisoners simply by changing pictures and thus giving easy access to enemy territory. Thus, Matus and Ducci developed a process that used a paper with a particular sheen that would disappear if tampered with.[68] Their work dovetailed with long-standing efforts by the police to improve identification techniques, in particular through training in dactyloscopy (fingerprinting and fingerprint identification and classification), anthropometry (the physical measurement of bodies—especially the head and face—to create a detailed description), and photography. These techniques were adopted and used as a means not only to identify individuals but also to track them, which explains why labor and anarchist leaders, such as Onofre Chamorro of the Industrial Workers of the World, intensely resisted efforts to make photographs mandatory for work permits and sought to avoid having their faces photographed.[69]

The registration and identification systems advanced in lockstep with the increased surveillance apparatus deployed by the Chilean state in 1920. In early July 1920 the Santiago intendent was asking that it be better financed and restructured.[70] His request came in part as a result of increased efforts to register, identify, and track foreign nationals living in Chile. He issued an order, simultaneous with his request for increased funding, that all foreigners resident in Santiago register in a special registry overseen by Santiago's police prefect and to also obtain a government-issued identity card.[71] In subsequent days he designed a system to facilitate the process of registration at the Identification Office, organized according to country of origin. Included near the top of the list were Russian nationals, beginning with men ages fourteen to twenty-five, to be followed by Spanish nationals. Given the fears of revolutionary and anarchist activity that seemed to drive the registration process in the first place, this is not surprising. But neither of these categories topped the list. That sad privilege went to Peruvian nationals.[72]

The government also increasingly turned to the Residency Law and applied it with full force. It had not been uncommon for the occasional ruffian or pimp to be expelled under the law, but by March of 1920 the law began to be applied to individuals perceived to be propagating doctrines incompatible with the established order.[73] Such was the case, in March, for Ecuadorian-born Lisandro Paladines and Peruvian-born Nicolás Gutarra Ramos.[74] And such was the case for Casimiro Barrios: in early July 1920, after months of being superintended, surveilled, spied on, and registered, Barrios was summoned to the offices of Santiago's police commissioner of investigations and fiscal, Fidel Araneda Luco, and accused of distributing subversive propaganda.[75] It did not help that Barrios purportedly had been "insolent" toward the Santiago intendent, who then reported that he "had to force him to leave the room."[76] Such things made it evident, the intendent reported, that Barrios was "a dangerous foreigner . . . who did not respect the authorities, and a danger to public tranquility."[77] Briefed on the case, Araneda rescinded Barrios' stay of expulsion and had Barrios sent to Valparaíso for deportation. Escorted by a senior police official from Santiago, he arrived in Valparaíso where the government's efforts soon ran into problems. The steamship company refused to take Barrios because he had no passport; Chilean authorities could not grant him one as he maintained his Spanish citizenship. The paradox of documentary regimes is precisely that they cannot be controlled solely for repressive means: it is fitting that an individual accused of being an anarchist reveals the paradoxes to be found in systems of nationalist identification.

The Valparaíso intendent had a solution: he suggested having Barrios taken as far as the port city of Arica, where he would then disembark and be transported overland to either the Peruvian frontier or Bolivian border.[78] By July 9 Barrios was on board the steamship *Palena*, bound for Arica where he would disembark, accompanied by a Santiago Security Section agent.[79] After being granted permission to withdraw funds from the Caja Nacional de Ahorros for his family, Barrios was transferred to the custody of the police in Tacna.[80] On July 19 he was taken to the border with Peru, at the Sama River, and expelled.[81]

His expulsion carried multiple meanings. For one, and perhaps most obviously, it represented the state's efforts to assert control over the social order: to expel individuals perceived as threatening to the political and social stability of the state. It carried a second meaning: a reassertion of spatial order. The choice of the Sama River, rather than, say, the border with Bolivia, was a strategic choice in that Chilean officials had long held the Sama River to constitute the northern boundary of the provinces of Tacna and Arica, against the protestations of Peru.[82] Escorting subversives to the banks of the Sama for expulsion constituted a symbolic affirmation of that claim. What better way to reaffirm the social and spatial order of the state than by expelling "foreign agitators" across a contested boundary, a simultaneous policing of national and ideological borders?

The expulsion of Barrios was followed shortly thereafter by a series of other deportations. People who hailed originally from countries as diverse as Russia, Spain, Italy, Argentina, and Cuba were given expulsion orders over the course of some four days in late July, and more deportations followed in August, all for "propagating doctrines incompatible with the unity and individuality of the nation and with public order," or, as the press was eager to note, for being "anarchists."[83] These expulsion orders came in part at the behest of José Astorquiza, a specially appointed minister to oversee the prosecution of subversives who himself had been born aboard a ship at sea, sailing under the Peruvian flag.

Coda

Upon being expelled, Barrios made his way to Lima where he continued his efforts to organize workers.[84] By January of 1921 the intendent was apprised of the fact that Barrios was back in Santiago.[85] Like many immigrants to Chile—whether from Spain, Russia, Italy, or Peru—Barrios had made a life for himself there. He had labored and loved in Santiago for his entire adult life. Santiago was home. He would remain there another six years. In 1927, under the government of Carlos Ibáñez, he would be expelled again, this time not for being an anarchist but a communist (a label that presumably Barrios would not have contested; he named his son, born in 1925, Santiago Lenin Barrios[86]). He was not alone. A number of members of Parliament as well as a number of well-known intellectuals would also be expelled. Some would end up on Chilean islands in the Pacific—the outposts of Más Atierra and Más Afuera, made famous by the story of Robinson Crusoe, or Isla Pascua (Easter Island).[87] Others would voyage to Europe. Barrios would end up in La Paz, Bolivia, where he would organize with the Bolivian labor movement under the leadership of the radical tailor and attorney Luis Salvatierra.[88]

At some point in 1930 he attempted to reenter Chile, as he had done at least once before.[89] Barrios' picture had been circulated among the police agents for fear that he might try to reenter, particularly given that Barrios had purportedly publicly "declared war without quarter against Ibáñez and all those who keep him in power."[90] He was soon recognized, stopped by two or three agents out patrolling the remote border. This time they wasted no time on passports or transit papers: in the Valley of Azapa they executed Casimiro Barrios.[91]

Notes

Previous versions of this essay were presented at the Cornell Department of History Americas colloquium and at the Trans-Americas colloquium at the University of Buffalo. I thank participants in those colloquiua as well as Barry Carr, Susana Romero, Dalia Muller, Camilo Trumper, Hal Langfur, Victor Muñoz, Mario Araya, Sergio Grez, and Alberto Harambour. Special thanks to Jorge Barrios Pulgar and his family. Research for this article was funded by a Franklin Grant from the American Philosophical Society and by the

Deans' Research Fund, College of Arts & Sciences at Cornell University. Many thanks to Geoffroy de Laforcade and Kirwin Shaffer for the invitation to contribute to this volume. This essay also appears in Barry Maxwell and Raymond Craib, eds., *No Gods No Masters No Peripheries: Global Anarchisms* (Oakland, Calif.: PM Press, 2015).

1. James Morris long ago pointed out trenchantly the degree to which intellectuals continued to reproduce this kind of importation narrative, a discourse of docility. See Morris, *Elites, Intellectuals and Consensus*, 112–14.

2. Ringrose, *Spain, Europe and the Spanish Miracle*, 273.

3. Gurría García and Lázaro Ruiz, *Tener un Tío*, 26–29.

4. García-Cuerdas, "Los almacenes Giménez," 65–68.

5. Gurría García and Lázaro Ruiz, *Tener un Tío*, 27, 31.

6. Ibid., 86.

7. On the Spanish American Iron Company, see ibid., 86n113.

8. On statistics for migration from La Rioja, see ibid., chap. 2.

9. According to an interview with Barrios, in late 1918 or early 1919, he had been in Santiago for fourteen years and he was twenty-eight years old. See "Un extremo de la ley de residencia: Dura lex, sed lex," clipping from the weekly *Zig-Zag*, International Institute for Social History, M. Segall Rosenmann Collection f. 14 (1919) [hereafter MSR]. On emigration to Chile, see Fernández Pesquero, "España en Chile," 5. For data on the destinations of inhabitants of Nieva de Cameros, see Arrellano, "Aquellos emigrantes," 58–59.

10. García-Cuerdas, "Los almacenes Giménez," 66; and Arrellano, "Aquellos emigrantes," 58–59.

11. García-Cuerdas, "Las desventuras de dos anarquistas cameranos."

12. Casimiro Barrios, "A mis padres," in Barrios, *Recuerdos*.

13. Barrutieta, "Ciriaco Barrios," 78–79.

14. Ibid., 80–81.

15. This excerpt from *La Voz del Obrero* appears in the prologue to Barrios' posthumously published drama *La Patria del Pobre*, 6–8, and reproduced in Barrutieta, "Ciriaco Barrios," 69–70.

16. "Un extremo de la ley de residencia: Dura lex, sed lex," clipping from the weekly *Zig-Zag*, MSR f. 14 (1919).

17. His "elocuencia indiscutible" comes from Vicuña Fuentes, *La tiranía en Chile*, 111.

18. González Vera, *Cuando Era Muchacho*, 136. See also González Vera, "Los anarquistas," reprinted in Soria, *Letras Anarquistas*.

19. On these and other labor laws, see DeShazo, *Urban Workers and Labor Unions*, 40.

20. Vicuña Fuentes, *La tiranía en Chile*, 111; unsigned report entitled "Asamblea Obrera de Alimentación Nacional" and dated November 11, 1919, Intendencia de Santiago [hereafter IS], v. 496, Archivo Nacional de Chile [hereafter AN]. On the passage, and nonenforcement, of the *ley de la silla* and the *ley domenical*, see DeShazo, *Urban Workers and Labor Unions*, 39–40. There is more than a little irony in the fact that the article on Barrios was entitled "Dura lex sed lex," (which roughly translates as "the law is harsh but it is the law"), given that Barrios was fighting to in fact have labor laws enforced.

21. On the AOAN, see Rodríguez Terrazas, "Protesta y soberanía popular"; DeShazo, *Urban Workers and Labor Unions*, 159–60; and Grez Toso, *Historia del comunismo en Chile*, chap. 6.

22. DeShazo, *Urban Workers and Labor Unions*, 160.

23. "De Hace Medio Siglo," *El Mercurio*, September 30, 1968, MSR f. 13. For his leadership role in the Santiago branch of the POS, see Rodríguez Terrazas, "Protesta y soberanía popular," 47.

24. 29th session, November 26, 1918, in *Cámara de Diputados*, 684.

25. DeShazo, *Urban Workers and Labor Unions*, 160–61. On the attacks on the consulates, see Skuban, *Lines in the Sand*, 172.

26. On previous calls for the creation of a residency law, see Pinto V. and Valdívio O., *Revolución proletaria o querida chusma?*, 54; and Ignotus, *Los anarquistas*, 151n9.

27. Cain, "Industrial Workers of the World, 54–62.

28. Quoted in ibid., 60.

29. Ley No. 3446: Impide la entrada al país o la residencia en él de elementos indeseables. Published in the Diario Oficial No. 12,243, December 12, 1918 (reproduced in Loveman and Lira, *Arquitectura política*, 82–83).

30. In Chile it also included pimps and "ruffians": thus, anarchists were lumped together with the idle, the ill, and the illicit.

31. The circumstances of Barrios' arrest and order of expulsion are reviewed in Intendencia de Santiago to Sr. Ministro del Interior, June 19, 1920, AN/IS v. 497; the initial expulsion decree is Decreto 760 de Intendencia de Santiago, dated December 18, 1918. For the administration's explanation for the suspension of the expulsion decree, see the remarks of Quezada in 71st session, January 7, 1919, *Cámara de Diputados*, 1840.

32. Decreto 2, Intendente de Santiago, January 4, 1919, referenced in Intendencia de Santiago a Sr. Ministro del Interior, June 19, 1920, AN/IS v. 497.

33. Rodríguez Terrazas, "Protesta y soberanía popular," 82.

34. *La Aurora: Organo del Partido Obrero Socialista*, January 10, 1919, 2; on *La Bandera Roja*, see Rodríguez Terrazas, "Protesta y soberanía popular," 82.

35. 61st session, December 20, 1918, in *Cámara de Diputados*, 1413.

36. On Barrios' writ, the quote is from Minister of the Interior Quezada explaining Barrios' petition in 71st session, January 7, 1919, *Cámara de Diputados*, 1845. On "preventive" applications of the law and "thickets," see Sánchez Gárcia de la Huerta, 71st session, January 7, 1919, *Cámara de Diputados*, 1839.

37. 69th session, January 3, 1919, in *Cámara de Diputados*, 1718. Even the Minister of Interior, who was asked to visit the Parliament to explain the suspension of Barrios' expulsion order, made note of Barrios' long-term residency in Chile and of his domestic situation. 71st session, January 7, 1919, *Cámara de Diputados*, 1844; see also the summation in Intendencia de Santiago a Sr. Ministro del Interior, June 19, 1920, AN/IS v. 497.

38. Session of December 24, 1918, in *Cámara de Senadores*, 907.

39. Session of December 24, 1918, in *Cámara de Senadores*, 906–7. Note the interesting fact that Torrealba refers to Barrios as a "citizen."

40. Session of December 24, 1918, in *Cámara de Senadores*, 907.

41. 69th session, January 3, 1919, in *Cámara de Diputados*, 1717–18.

42. I say "heated" because Pinto Duran calls him out for "arranques un poco violentos." 69th session, January 3, 1919, in *Cámara de Diputados*, 1718.

43. 69th session, January 3, 1919, in *Cámara de Diputados*, 1719.

44. "Un extremo de la ley de residencia: Dura lex, sed lex," MSR f. 14 (1919).

45. That such was the case was all too clear to Luis Emilio Recabarren, who noted that the repression had little to do with fear and everything to do with weakening the labor movement. See Rodríguez Terrazas, "Protesta y soberanía popular," 92.

46. Ibid., 89–92.

47. *La Opinión*, cited in ibid., 91.

48. The speech was given on January 16, 1919. Cited in ibid., 87.

49. For excellent studies, see Grez Toso, *Los anarquistas*; Muñoz Cortés, *Armando Triviño*; Muñoz Cortés, *Cuando la Patria Mata*; and Araya Saavedra, "Los Wobblies Criollos."

50. "Un extremo de la ley de residencia: Dura lex, sed lex," MSR f. 14 (1919).

51. Cited in Ignotus, *Los anarquistas*, 5–6. The "importation" paradigm persisted: James Morris would lament in the 1960s that Chile's Marxist historians continued to understand historical radicalization as merely ideational and a result of the increased circulation of texts, from Europe to the "periphery." That said, the diffusionist paradigm—whether in the history of science, of ideas, or of politics—has been subject to repeated and withering critique over the years. See, for example, the varying critiques in Raj, *Relocating Modern Science*; Pratt, *Imperial Eyes*, in particular the elaboration on Fernando Ortiz's concept of transculturation; Coronil, "Beyond Occidentalism"; and, more broadly, Latour, *We Have Never Been Modern*. Particularly useful in understanding the context within which such ideas are generated is Schwarz, *Misplaced Ideas*; and the recent engagement with that work by Palti, "The Problem of 'Misplaced Ideas' Revisited." For works that challenge productively Schwarz's assertions, and with which I tend to align the argument in this essay, see Viotti da Costa, "Liberalism"; and de Carvalho Franco, "As idéias estão no lugar."

52. Unsigned report by Sección de Seguridad on the AOAN, dated December 21, 1918, of a meeting held on December 20, in AN/IS, v. 470. My emphasis.

53. There may indeed have been a nationalistic sentiment at work here, certainly for those militants in the POS who identified clearly with socialism, but it is worth at least proffering a complementary possibility: that such arguments were in effect kinds of early postcolonial critiques of Eurocentrism, and ones that anarchists particularly were well-positioned to offer.

54. Unsigned report date March 16, 1919, Sección de Seguridad, AN/IS v. 476 (Comunicaciones 1919); and unsigned report dated March 17, 1919, Sección de Seguridad, AN/IS v. 476 (Comunicaciones, 1919).

55. Unsigned report dated March 17, 1919, Sección de Seguridad, AN/IS v. 476 (Comunicaciones, 1919).

56. For an excellent discussion, see Rodríguez Terrazas, "Protesta y soberanía popular," 84–92; see also "El comité de Alimentación Nacional," *Verba Roja*, February 1919, 2.

57. Rodríguez Terrazas, "Protesta y soberanía popular," 101. The importance of the FECh to anarchist and labor politics at the time is worth emphasizing. For more on the linkages between students, workers, and worker-intellectuals, see Craib, "Students, Anarchists and Categories of Persecution"; and DeShazo, *Urban Workers and Labor Unions*.

58. "Un extremo de la ley de residencia," MSR f. 14 (1919).

59. See, for example, Anderson, *Under Three Flags*; and Khuri-Makdisi, *Eastern Mediterranean*.

60. For the selling of Trotsky's writings, see the July 1920 interrogation of university stu-

dent Rigoberto Soto Rengifo in "Proceso contra Pedro Gandulfo Guerra, et al.," Segundo Juzgado del Crimen de Santiago, AN, Judicial de Santiago/Criminales, legajo 1658 (f. 50). For the comments on the Russian revolution, see "El maximalismo," in *Verba Roja*, August 29, 1919, 3; "Lenin," *Verba Roja*, July 1919, 2; and "La dictadura del proletariado: El el Prologo del comunismo anárquico: Lenin, Trotsky y los maximalistas rusos van hacia él," *Verba Roja*, July 1919, 1. As much as this reveals that divisions were not necessarily strong, it also reveals the degree to which, as it unfolded, the Russian revolution had a number of possible paths, some of which appeared agreeable to those with more anarchistic persuasions. It was with the massacre of the Ukrainian anarchists that the split began to widen. Even then the divide between communists and anarchists was not all-encompassing. As late as the early 1940s Manuel Rojas, a lifelong anarchist, would pen a beautiful obituary of Trotsky in the intellectual journal *Babel*.

61. On the general strike, see Rodríguez Terrazas, "Protesta y soberanía popular," 134–35. The strike in September had again raised the specter of expulsions as an editorial in the leading daily *El Mercurio* pointed to the United States as an exemplar of how to handle undesirables: "El noble gesto con que la Federación Obrera de los Estados Unidos señaló la puerta de la expulsión a los elementos maximalistas, es la mejor demonstración de que la educación política del pueblo norteamericano le permite distinguir con claridad la verdadera democracia de la demogagia anarquista." From "De hace medio siglo (el Mercurio del 17 de septiembre de 1919)" MSR f. 14.

62. Intendente de Santiago al Sr. Fiscal en Comisión don Fidel Araneda Luco, July 7, 1920, AN/IS v. 505 (Gobernadores, Prefectos y Varias Autoridades, 1920). These are the intendent's words, not Barrios.'

63. Intendente de Santiago al Sr. Fiscal en Comisión don Fidel Araneda Luco, July 7, 1920, AN/IS, v. 505 (Gobernadores, Prefectos y Varias Autoridades, 1920).

64. See the *convenio* outlined in Enrique Cuevas [head of the Chilean Legation in Uruguay] al Ministro de Relaciones Exteriores, March 16, 1920, vol. 801b, Archivo General Histórico, Ministerio de Relaciones Exteriores de Chile.

65. Decreto of March 5, 1920 (f. 60), AN/IS, v. 504, Decretos, 1920.

66. Matus and Ducci al Señor Jefe del Gabinete de Identificación, December 30, 1919, included in Coronel-Prefecto al Intendente de la Provincia, January 24, 1920, AN/IS v. 504 (Decretos), 1920. On the creation of the Office of Identification, see Decreto 715 of the Ministry of the Interior.

67. Matus and Ducci al Señor Jefe del Gabinete de Identificación, December 30, 1919, included in Coronel-Prefecto al Intendente de la Provincia, January 24, 1920, AN/IS v. 504 (Decretos), 1920. Such passing, of course, had already happened, just not as Matus and Ducci imagined it: agents in Santiago's Security Section were passing themselves off as organizers and agitators.

68. Matus and Ducci al Señor Jefe del Gabinete de Identificación, December 30, 1919, included in Coronel-Prefecto al Intendente de la Provincia, January 24, 1920, AN/IS v. 504 (Decretos), 1920.

69. For a detailed discussion of the possibilities, limits, and applications of identification techniques at the time, see Prieto Lemm, *Identificación de las personas*; on Chonofre and photography, see Pinto V. and Valdívio O., *Revolución proletaria o querida chusma?*

70. Intendente de la Provincia al Sr. Ministro de Interior, July 5, 1920, AN/IS, v. 506;

Coronel-Prefecto al Intendente de la Provincia, December 21, 1920, AN/IS, v. 500 (December 1920).

71. Decreto of July 7, 1920 (f. 290), AN/IS, v. 504 (Decretos 1920).

72. *El Mercurio*, Saturday, July 17, 1920, p. 1. Space limitations prevent me from discussing this issue further. I discuss the manner in which the government would conflate anarchists and Peruvians, as diseases of the social body, in the forthcoming book *Cry of the Renegade*.

73. For examples of foreigners expelled "por ser rufianos conocidos i dedicarse a esplotar la prostitución," see the cases discussed in Coronel-Prefecto al Intendente de Santiago, January 20, 1919; and Sub-prefecto al Coronel-Prefecto, January 18, 1919, both in AN/IS v. 496.

74. For Paladines, see Decreto of March 11, 1920 (f. 72), AN/IS, v. 504, (Decretos 1920); Nicolás Gutarra of Peru was ordered expelled on May 18 and placed on a steamship for Arica and expelled from the country on June 5, 1920. Gutarra had initially been expelled from his native Peru for the same reason, "por propagar ideas contrarias al orden establecido." For Gutarra, the original order is in Decreto of May 18, 1920 (f. 178), AN/IS, v. 504, (Decretos 1920); the actual date of expulsion is given in Coronel-Prefecto al Intendente de la Provincia, June 14, 1920, AN/IS, v. 496.

75. Fidel Araneda Luco, Comisario de Investigaciones, al Señor Intendente de la Provincia, July 7, 1920, AN/IS, v.497.

76. Intendencia de Santiago a Sr. Ministro del Interior, June 19, 1920, AN/IS, v. 497. Such "insolence" should not be underestimated: the writer and anarchist José Santos González Vera would remark that it was the perception of insolence and breach of social protocols that led to the brutal detention and death of the poet José Domingo Gómez Rojas. See González Vera, *Cuando Era Muchacho*. On the death of Gómez Rojas, see Moraga Valle and Vega Delgado, *José Domingo Gómez Rojas*; Craib, "Students, Anarchists and Categories of Persecution"; and Craib, "Firecracker Poet."

77. Intendencia de Santiago a Sr. Ministro del Interior, June 19, 1920, AN/IS, v. 497. The Minister of the Interior confirmed the expulsion on June 28. See Ministerio del Interior al Intendente de Santiago, June 28, 1920, AN/IS, v. 496.

78. Intendente de Valparaíso al Señor Intendente, don Francisco Subercaseaux, July 7, 1920, AN/IS, v. 497; and Telegram de García de la Huerta al Gobernador de Arica, July 9, 1920, Archivo del Siglo XX de Chile [hereafter ARNAD], Fondo Ministerio del Interior [hereafter MI], v. 5427.

79. Telegram de García de la Huerta al Gobernador de Arica, July 9 1920, ARNAD/MI, v. 5427; and Telegram de García de la Huerta al Gobernador de Arica, July 10, 1920, ARNAD/MI, v. 5426.

80. Telegram de García de la Huerta al Gobernador de Arica, July 9 1920, ARNAD/MI, v. 5427; and Certificate, Policia Fiscal, Tacna, July 16, 1920, AN/IS v. 498.

81. Telegram de Fernando Edwards al Prefecto de Policia, Santiago, July 28, 1920, AN/IS v. 498. On the idea of expelling him to Bolivia, see telegram from Fernando Edwards, Intendente de Tacna, al Intendente de Santiago, August 1, 1920, AN/IS v. 498. See also Sub-Prefecto Jefe al Coronel-Prefecto, July 30, 1920; and Casimiro Barrios, "Desde Lima," *Claridad* 1:9 (December 11, 1920), 9.

82. Skuban, *Lines in the Sand*, 185.

83. See Decreto 2900, July 24, 1920, ARNAD/MI, v. 5393; Decreto of July 26, 1920 (f. 314); Decreto of July 26, 1920 (f. 317); Decreto of July 28, 1920 (f. 324); Decreto of July 28, 1920 (f. 325), Decreto of August 18, 1920 (f. 388), Decreto of August 19, 1920 (f. 390), all in AN/IS, v. 504 (Decretos 1920); and Coronel-Prefecto al Intendente de la Provincia, September 9, 1920, AN/IS, v. 502.

84. Telegram from Fernando Edwards to Prefecto de Policia, Santiago, July 28, 1920, AN/IS v. 498; Sub-Prefecto Jefe al Coronel-Prefecto, July 30, 1920; and Casimiro Barrios, "Desde Lima," *Claridad*, December 11, 1920, 9.

85. Coronel-Prefecto to Intendente de la Provincia, 6 de enero de 1921, AN/IS, v. 506.

86. I am indebted to Casimiro Barrios' grandson, Jorge Barrios Pulgar, for a copy of his father's birth certificate and for the numerous conversations he had with me about his grandfather and his family.

87. For a remarkable account of his exile on the Juan Fernández island of Más Afuera, see Meza Fuentes, *Los trágicos días de Más Afuera*, originally published as a series of articles in the daily *Las Ultimas Noticias*, from August 1 to September 23, 1931.

88. Lora, *Historia del movimiento obrero boliviano*, 3:63.

89. Marcos Burich Parra, Carabrineros de Chile, Prefectura de Tarapacá, a la Sub-Prefectura de Carabineros "Arica" Guarnación, September 24, 1930, in Loveman and Lira, *Los actos de la dictadura*, 290–91.

90. Marcos Burich Parra, Carabrineros de Chile, Prefectura de Tarapacá, a la Sub-Prefectura de Carabineros 'Arica' Guarnación, September 24, 1930 in Loveman and Lira, *Los actos de la dictadura*, 290.

91. González Vera, *Cuando Era Muchacho*, 136. His family, including his widow, Rosario Riveros Martínez, were paid reparations by the government in 1931 as part of the political investigations and reparations regarding the Ibañez dictatorship. Lira and Loveman, *Políticas de reparación*, 25. At the time of Barrios' execution, in his hometown of Nieva de Cameros, his father was finishing a term as mayor and his brother Juan was assuming a role on the municipal board. Both would be murdered by Franco's forces in 1936. Aguirre González, "Nieva," 38–42.

13

The Anarchist Wager of Sexual Emancipation in Argentina, 1900–1930

LAURA FERNÁNDEZ CORDERO

TRANSLATED BY GEOFFROY DE LAFORCADE

Anyone who has approached the history of anarchism in Argentina knows that both militant and academic historiography have privileged the analysis of its relationship with organized labor. Diego Abad de Santillán, a prominent activist and one of the first historians to recount the cycle of Argentine anarchism's "golden age" through 1910, mentions the particular intersection of anarchism with bohemian local history, theater, and poetry during this period. These aspects of the libertarian legacy would only be recovered years later, however, as new trends in the historiography focused interest on such dimensions of dominated space as culture, everyday life, aesthetics, and the private sphere, all which have recently achieved the status of legitimate objects of inquiry. During the last decade the number of researchers working on Argentine anarchism increased substantially, analyzing a broad range of issues and encompassing periods that had until then received scant attention. Until recently, however, questions pertaining to the emancipation of women, personal relationships, and sexuality tended to be ignored or dismissed. Both militants and professional historians acknowledged calls for women's participation and activism as remarkable, but their approaches still focused heavily on other aspects, most notably the role of anarchism in the unions and organized labor.

The purpose of this chapter is to assess significant milestones in the historiography of anarchism in Argentina with respect to its treatment of the sexual question, which, while often overlooked, was a cornerstone of its ideology. Anarchism is approached as a discourse in support of the sexual emancipation of women. One of the main singularities of Argentine anarchism is the participation of women through two newspapers that were written and directed exclusively by them, one in the late nineteenth century (*Voz de la Mujer*, 1896–97) and another in the 1920s (*Nuestra Tribuna: Quincenario femenino de ideas, arte, crítica y literatura*, 1922–25). However, it is not the singularity of women per se that this chapter will underscore.

While a few decades ago it was of utmost importance to recover the involvement of women in various historical moments and rescue their work from a male-generated canon that rendered them invisible, it has become increasingly evident that highlighting women's leadership roles, or employing the concept of gender as synonymous with the term "woman," will not suffice. Hence, the second objective of this work will be to reorient the discussion toward a gendered relational perspective, underscoring dialogues and controversies between anarchist men and women on the question of sex through a cross-reading and comparison of newspapers and pamphlets of the time. I will pay particular attention to how women approach the practice of reciting the doctrine in the first person, and the ways they respond to criticism in their texts. Finally, this chapter attempts to propose a rereading of local anarchism as it relates to sexual questions.

Women's Emancipation and Sexuality in the Historiography of Anarchism in Argentina

The autobiographical story of Edward Gilimón, a militant and early historian of the movement, narrating the first steps of anarchism in Argentina did not discuss libertarian interventions on the subject of free love or on the emancipation of male and female partners.[1] Abad de Santillán said nothing about anarchist feminism either, even in his section on "other forms of action and propaganda" in which he discussed cooperatives, free schools, antimilitarism, and anticlerical propaganda. He did mention the newspaper *La Voz de la Mujer* and named Virginia Bolten as a prominent orator as well as one of the first victims of deportation.[2]

The first extensive academic work devoted to Argentine anarchism, Yaacov Oved's dissertation, noted that "the anarchist movement attributed a special meaning" to the "issue of the moralization and emancipation of women."[3] His study only devoted a few paragraphs, however, to such matters as the participation of Pepita Gherra or the existence of *La Voz de la Mujer* as the "mouthpiece of a group of women in Buenos Aires who was very active in disseminating feminist propaganda in Argentina."[4] Oved did not fail to mention that "feminist concepts" were deployed to criticize the domestic lives of anarchists themselves, and he also briefly characterized the role of women in labor unions as highly problematic, citing the conclusions of the fifth congress of the Federación Obrera Regional Argentina (FORA) in 1905: "The Fifth Congress invites resistance societies to actively pursue propaganda to teach women to fight, so that they may increase their range of knowledge and second men in the struggle for emancipation."[5]

Another standard history of anarchism appeared in 1996 with the publication of Gonzalo Zaragoza Rivera's dissertation in the form of a book. While he maintained the focus on the labor movement, Zaragoza, taking note of changes that had occurred in the historiographical field, was more attentive to other dimensions of the libertarian world, particularly those of politics and culture. He even reproduced this auspicious quote: "The struggle for the defense of women is in theory as important to anarchists as the workers' struggle, because it reflects another oppressed group; anarchist discourse is not first and foremost meant to construct the working class, but addresses the oppressed in general."[6] While this was a promising point of departure, the author devoted very little space to it: a subsection on "Sexual Liberation, the Liberation of Women" in the chapter entitled "Cultural Manifestations and Ideology." While Zaragoza did refer to columns signed by Andorinha, described the activism of Pepita Gherra, and characterized *La Voz de la Mujer* as "a distinctive anarchist effort," the struggle referred to in the aforementioned passage was not central to his narrative and was ultimately buried in a brief but well-documented description.[7]

Similarly, the Argentine historian Juan Suriano advocated addressing anarchism in Buenos Aires as a political, ideological, and cultural phenomenon of major importance. This approach allowed him to wade into the foray of power and politics, the press, the use of leisure time, and the rites and symbols employed by the movement—areas that had not been sufficiently highlighted, as his own rich description of the libertarian cultural universe demonstrated.[8] However, the author explained in a footnote that "issues of marriage, free love and sexuality do not fall under the scope of this study." Thus these questions were confined to barely two pages of his chapter "Leisure time, Holidays and Theater," under the subheading "Women and the Family."[9] Suriano based his decision on the assumption that "women's rights" and "the sexual question" were not exclusively the purview of anarchism but rather part of a "thematic fringe" that anarchist discourse shared with socialism, Catholicism, freethinkers and others."[10]

In other words, while the leading historians of the movement were not unaware of such questions, their interest in exploring them remained rather marginal. Yet there is clear evidence of the decisive participation of women in Argentine anarchism and the centrality that emotional and sexual issues held in the eyes of a majority of militants. In an overview of anarchist writing published in 1927 by Max Nettlau—who is sometimes called the Herodotus of anarchy—*La Voz de la Mujer* was mentioned among the most significant publications. According to Nettlau, one of the first known anarchist pamphlets to appear in Argentina was published by the newspaper *La Lucha Obrera* (1884) and was entitled *La Mujer* (Woman). The second locally issued publication addressed the same theme; immediately after issuing *La sociedad. Su presente. Su pasado y su porvenir* in 1896, the anarchist Dr. Emilio Z. Araña published *La mujer y la familia* (1897) in the city of Rosario. The pamphlet was not only circulated widely by the city's newspapers, it was also enthusiastically received by *La Protesta Humana.*[11] Moreover, each new propaganda campaign began with a statement of principles in which the anarchist commitment to the emancipation of women was always prominently featured. The same is true of associations involved in organizational efforts. The founding program of the Círculo Internacional de Estudios Sociales (1897), in its first declaration, proposed the dissemination of the following: "May all beings be equal to each other, regardless of the gender and nationality to which they belong, so that the superiority of men over women and the rivalry between nationalities may be extinguished."[12]

As for the manifesto of the Federación Libertaria de los Grupos Socialistas-Anarquistas de Buenos Aires (1899), its third point denounced the "the matrimonial lie," advocated the "complete equality of interests between the sexes," and demanded a restoration "of love, free from impediments, interests and prejudices, the exclusive sovereignty in sexual union, from which, purified and established on the basis of indissoluble affection, the family of the future will emerge."[13] Successive resolutions of the labor union federation, FORA, also contained statements about the emancipation of women, their trade organization, and their contribution to overall progress.[14] Finally, it is worth recalling that women's emancipation was among the inevitable issues raised by the lectures delivered in Argentina by the Italian anarchist Pietro Gori, who is widely believed to have exercised great influence on the local movement.[15]

This brief review shows that there is substantial documentary evidence of the centrality of the sexual question in anarchism as it developed in Argentina. The movement's earliest editorials called for the participation of women and spread ideas about free love. Moreover, the first anarchist or-

ganizations addressed the sexual question when they set out to organize
workers or to trigger general strikes. Statements on the issue in the press
and the debates they provoked show that far from being a marginal question, sexual emancipation—understood as the questioning of traditional
marriage and the invention of new types of relationships—was more force-
fully addressed by anarchists than it was by other movements on the Left,
and was regarded as a nonnegotiable aspect of liberation.

In the absence of a general work dedicated to this aspect of the history
of Argentine anarchism, several partial efforts have been made to expand
our understanding of the movement in this regard.[16] For example, in 1982
María del Carmen Feijóo cited some old anarchist propaganda leaflets for
women (1895) and argued that "it was the anarchists who took the lead in
systematically discussing the problem."[17] Maxine Molyneux described *La
Voz de la Mujer*, the anarchist newspaper of the late nineteenth century, in
the overall context and framework of anarcho-communism within which
it was specifically addressed.[18] Pioneering work by Mabel Cristina Bellucci
and Cristina Camusso emphasized the role of anarchists in the rent strike
of 1907.[19] These early efforts culminated in a book by Dora Barrancos in
1990 in which the author not only opened new directions for the study
of anarchism but also in two chapters set the basic parameters through
which to interpret anarchist discourse on sexuality and the emancipation
of women in the early twentieth century.[20] A few years later, María del
Carmen Feijóo and Marcela Nari concluded that there seems to have been
a problematic chasm between the claims put forth by *La Voz de la Mujer*'s
editors and their ineffectual reception by the readership.[21]

It would take too long to mention all of the tributes issued by activist
groups, blogs, and other web-based publications that have sought to recover "the voices of anarchist women" either to commemorate or identify
with them. In such forums, as in academia, the general tendency has been
to demonstrate the contribution of women and highlight their uniqueness—not only with respect to competing discourses of the time but also
in relation to the anarchist movement itself. These authors attribute to
anarchists a militant embrace of feminism and an intuitive penchant for
"gender issues," some of which caused tensions within the movement itself.
Indeed, many anarchist men seem to have been more convinced of theoretical proclamations than willing to accept the emancipation of women in
practice.

Anarchism was not just a movement that incidentally drew attention to
matters of sexuality, nor was it simply more attentive to women's participa-

tion than other competing movements on the Left. It was, I argue, a novel form of political expression that tackled the challenge of struggling to end labor exploitation while simultaneously proposing new forms of emotional and sexual relationships. While this was an issue that remained central for decades, the debate became intensified and gained in nuance and complexity at two specific conjunctures: the last years of the nineteenth century and the beginning of the 1920s.

The Early Stages: Anarchist Propaganda among Women

In the late nineteenth century, when local medical studies began to observe and classify the sexual realm, anarchists had already begun, without euphemisms, to edit brochures, to lecture, and to publish debates in the press on the vicissitudes of sexual relations. In spite of the movement's criticism of traditional marriage, Barrancos demonstrated that the representations of sexuality articulated by anarchists were not far removed from statements circulated at the time by moralists, sociologists, and physicians.[22] In that sense the anarchists can be said to have been responding to a "moral imperative" that established their framework of possibility. Indeed, the contribution of anarchists was not distinctive because of the content of their arguments per se, as it was often shared by other political and ideological strands; rather, what made their contribution unique was the manner in which they discussed the issue of sex. Convinced as they were that oppression extended to love and eroticism, they understood sexual emancipation as an indispensable dimension of human emancipation. To that premise, which was at the core of their doctrine, anarchists added the imperative of subjective revolution; that is, they understood that the criticism of the bourgeois forms of love, and the innovations proposed by the libertarian framework, must have an impact on their everyday lives.

One of the first calls came from a group of men who edited the magazine *La Questione Sociale*, which was almost entirely in Italian.[23] The publication's foremost writer, Fortunato Serantoni, lived in Argentina between 1892 and 1902 and, along with other members of his group, belonged to the anarcho-communist tendency championed by the newspaper of the same name, published by Errico Malatesta during his stay in Buenos Aires. In general, references to women's issues in the anarchist movement were voiced by all anarchist currents in Argentina, which shared and articulated such objectives as promoting awareness among women in relationships, encouraging the participation of their husbands, drawing them away from religious influences, guaranteeing the libertarian education of children, and so on. The series published by *La Questione Sociale*—composed of pamphlets entitled *A las hijas del Pueblo* (To the daughters of the people), *A las muchachas que estudian* (To girls who study), *A las proletarias* (To proletarian women), and *Un episodio de amor en la Colonia Socialista Cecilia* (An episode of love in the Socialist Cecilia Colony)[24]—synthesized these objectives, and their remarkable continuity was evidenced by citations and reissues over the course of the following three decades.[25]

The manner in which this series was presented seems, at first sight, to constitute a clear call to women that was somewhat paternalistic in its tone. The way that anarchists in Argentina imagined the oppression of women and their eventual liberation was reflected in a variety of strategies. The most common was to simply add the issue to the equation by incorporating it into larger social question, to exhort readers by mentioning it specifically, to call for the burden to be shared, and so on. As the militants writing in *La Questione Sociale* put it: "Come with us, fight within our ranks, be our companions of struggle and love." At the same time, it was suggested that women bore the brunt of a kind of multiplier effect as a result of the dual exploitation (economic and religious) that they endured. To this the anarchists added another form of oppression related to sexuality as it was present in the home, in the reign of husbands, in prerogatives exercised by bosses over female workers' bodies, and so on. This cumulative effect of oppression made women "slaves among slaves," a characterization that was never called into question. While certain aspects of the discourse emanating from both genders described women somewhat harshly, sometimes accusing them of being fickle, flirtatious, ignorant, or unconscious, women themselves were always, by virtue of their status as "victims of all injustices," excused. One of the most often cited and transcribed texts in the newspapers of the time, *La mujer esclava* (The woman slave) by René Chaughi, provides a clear example of this:

> Women, over the centuries, have retained habits of slavery; even the most honorable among them will demonstrate traces of venality, including in their dealings with their husbands. The minute the man promises his wife new clothing, or a gift of any sort, she will become more caring, more loving. . . . She suffers from an unhealthy need to show off, to draw attention to herself; she has a wicked desire to dominate, to humiliate. Like savages, women love gilding, useless and

uncomfortable trappings; they spend entire hours in front of the windows of jewelry shops, transfixed by ugly but shiny things.[26]

Besides adding women to the concerns of the movement and underscoring the multiplier effects of different forms of oppression to which they were subjected, the strategy of choice employed by anarchists was to highlight their difference. They were viewed not only as "the fair sex" but also as "the other sex." A delicate balance was maintained by the coexistence of these three discourses so that "the emancipation of women" could stand as an undisputed formula that would complete human emancipation. However, this "difference" became voiced in the first person and destabilized the discursive field when a group of anarchist propagandists undertook the project of founding their own newspaper. While *La Voz de la Mujer* was not the first publication issued by women in Argentina, it was the first in Argentina that was exclusively written by women and directed to a female readership.[27]

> Hence: fed up as we are with tear and misery, weary of the eternal and dismal picture painted by our unfortunate children, those tender pieces of our heart, weary of begging and pleading, of being toys, objects of our hated exploiters or of vile husbands, we have decided to raise our voice in the social arena and to demand, demand we say, our share of the pleasure in the banquet of life.[28]

The first paragraph of this exposé—entitled "Our Purpose"—contains an entire program that is not reducible to its content but is announced as the form of expression itself: "We have set out to fight . . . without God and without a leader." The authors demand their fair share as mothers from the frontlines and, in a disturbing distinction, view themselves as objects of pleasure subjected to the domination of both spouses and employers. As is customary, the new publication announces that women may "appear when possible and opt-in," that is, raise money through other publications, rendering their task somewhat vulnerable and dependent. The biographies of the women who undertook this new venture are difficult to reconstruct. Almost nothing is known of Josefa Martínez or Josepha Calvo, the two signatures that appear in presentations and advertisements in other newspapers requesting funds. Martínez authored some poems and columns throughout the nine issues of the journal, but Calvo does not appear at all and may have used a pseudonym.[29] Most of the columns were written by editors, but some articles were signed by Louisa Violeta, Carmen Lareva, Milna Nohemi, and María Muñoz.

The name of Virginia Bolten has been linked by several authors to the newspaper, but nothing indicates that she participated in the venture in Buenos Aires. However, along with the group "Las Proletarias," she is undoubtedly responsible for the version of *La Voz de la Mujer* that was published in Rosario, which has unfortunately been lost.[30] In a description of the anarchist movement published by the weekly magazine *Caras y Caretas*, certain activists are named: Ana López is described as a "propagandist"; Olga S. Bianchi, as a "contributor to *L'Avvenire*"; Mary Calvia as "an initiator of the group "Las Proletarias" and contributor to *La Voz de la Mujer*"; and Virginia Bolten and Teresa Marchisio, as "director and member of the editorial board, respectively, of the same newspaper."[31] These names evidently belong to the Rosario experience, and no data is offered on the main protagonist of the Buenos Aires edition of the newspaper, Pepita Gherra. Although she was the most active writer in the group of women anarchists, not many clues regarding her life can be gleaned from other sources than her writings.[32] She was the author of several poems as well as of the dialogue entitled "Ante el Cadalso," (Before the gallows), and her signature appeared in several major newspapers of the period: *La Protesta Humana*, *La Anarquía*, *El Rebelde*, and *La Revolución Social*. In a column published in *La Anarquía*, "A las mujeres" (To women), Gherra launches a strong attack on men in general, an indication that such virulent discourse sometimes appeared in the anarchist media run by men. In the same issue another piece by Gherra contains various allusions to the ways in which men responded specifically to the participation of women in the movement.[33]

The news of the publication of *La Voz de la Mujer* was favorably received in anarchist circles. Greetings and congratulations were common whenever a new "champion of propaganda" appeared, but in this specific case, newspapers representing the broad ideological spectrum of the time announced the venture with remarkable enthusiasm. The first issue had a print run of a thousand copies and began with an editorial addressed to "compañeros y compañeras" (male and female comrades). It told of how, seeing the struggle waged by men, women decided to lift "a wisp of red banner." Toward the end of the issue, in a column entitled "Notes," the authors introduce themselves as "one more voice" and ask "that we receive us into your ranks."[34]

While it was not unusual for newspapers to salute the field of propaganda into which they inserted themselves, this request takes on new meaning in the second issue, in which the tone changes dramatically. The women writing do allude to the barrage of criticism they claim to have encountered; however, their complaints are not recorded in the press, as usually occurred when internal debates, however virulent, broke out.[35] The editors of anarchist newspapers seldom had any problem taking a stance against a given group or publication, and often advertised these dissentions in their editorials or invited public debate. In the case of La Voz de la Mujer, however, opposition voices can only be detected through the manner in which the newspaper's contributors articulated their comments when it came to defending themselves: "We're not worthy of that much, oh, no sir!," "women, emancipate themselves?," "why?," "what female emancipation, eight radishes or what?," "ours," "let us get ours first and then, when we 'men' are emancipated and free, then we shall see."[36]

The severity of the confrontation is further emphasized in the newspaper's third issue. The editorial is entitled "Firmes en la brecha" (Steadfast in the gap) and is directed not only at critics but also at "a nuestros enemigos" (to our enemies).[37] Moreover, the women use their own words as an epigraph: the "sin Dios ni jefe" (without God or leader) for their first editorial. Here the defense clearly distinguishes between two very different targets: on the one hand, "enemies/false anarchists" and on the other, offended peers. Before making that distinction, the editors offer a bit of a complaint: "What did they expect?" they ask of all men; "how could you believe that being determined as we are, we would determine our course of action according to the views of Juan, Pedro or Pelayo?" The biggest problem occurred when these women activists began to face criticism from the same peers who had once been supporters. They then offered a clarification in order to "iron out the scowls" and apologize for having spoken out in general terms without making a necessary distinction between themselves and "the beetles of the idea." This clarification suffered from a tension, however, insofar as the women sought to differentiate between men who were enemies and men who were friends, and attempted to resolve it by concluding that what brought them together, in the last instance, was "the common enemy, the bourgeoisie."[38]

If the appearance of a women's newspaper could be met with such enthusiasm, and its first issue generate so much resistance, clearly the debate was not over the participation of women per se but the manner in which they did so. The series of pamphlets entitled "Propaganda entre las mujeres" (Propaganda among women) and various columns signed by men transmitted the slogan of women's emancipation, but they also contained detailed instructions on how this emancipation should occur. Equality was generally described as "within reason," and women expected to "second" men or intervene in "a loving manner" so as to bring a touch of (feminine) virtue to the world of propaganda. What the men couldn't have foreseen was that the manner in which women sought to incorporate themselves into the movement exceeded such guidelines. That their style came as a surprise is evidenced by another common criticism directed at the women: that theirs was "no way to write." There is also the nickname with which they claimed to have been saddled: the "fierce ones of tongue and pen."[39]

Rather than in the content or originality of the ideas that they added to the anarchist repertoire, I believe that the importance of women's "true voice" lay in the availability of newspapers in which they could cite and re-cite the terms of the doctrine. In other words, such platforms offered them the possibility of appropriating, paraphrasing, enunciating in first person, and articulating discourses of which they were the object. While they also gained access to the "mainstream" anarchist press and continuously inter-vened in it, the ability to edit their own newspaper allowed women to sum-mon a greater number of contributors and to establish a distinctive voice by making editorial decisions, such as which authors to disseminate, which fragments to transcribe, which arguments to dismiss, and which texts to comment upon.

The information gleaned from detailed administrative summaries indi-cates that after the publication of its most aggressive issue, the third, *La Voz de la Mujer* almost doubled the amount of its original fundraising.[40] By the time of its fifth issue, the paper had managed to double its production and roll out two thousand copies. What I am arguing is that the originality of *La Voz de la Mujer* was not its feminine identity per se, because such an in-terpretation renders invisible the women activists who actively participated in the enterprise by limiting their identity to their membership in a gender. These women upheld a diversity of ideological opinions with which they contributed to the larger field of discourse. Male activists did the same, but they are seldom referred to as "men in the anarchist media," simply (and in equally problematic fashion) as individuals who expressed themselves from the perspective of an identity without gender. In this sense it is clear that use of the concept of gender must be articulated analytically with other dimensions rather than simply replace them.

The 1920s: A Platform Specifically for Women

While the early years of Argentine anarchism have their "classic" historians (Abad de Santillán, Oved, Zaragoza), the 1920s lack a similar coverage that would aid us in identifying the most active groups and militants.[41] This section addresses the main groups of that period and is centered on three newspapers: *La Protesta* and *La Antorcha* from Buenos Aires and *Ideas* from the city of La Plata.[42] Alongside these, a new newspaper, *Nuestra Tribuna*, written and edited exclusively by women, took the position that a publication was necessary to educate female anarchists and serve as their central mouthpiece.

Very few columns of *La Protesta* in the 1920s were signed by women, although the female figure was prominently displayed in writings about women and work, emancipation, or prostitution. The editors denounced violence against women, generally amplifying police reports published in the mainstream press of the period. *La Antorcha*, on the other hand, gave considerable space to well-known foreign woman authors such as Angelina Arratia, Leda Rafanelli, Emma Goldman, and Federica Montseny. The young Uruguayan anarchist María Álvarez's female militancy was of special interest to the paper's editors. Before her untimely death, she had written widely about a pantheon of female libertarians, including Louise Michel, Germana Berton, Gabriela Mistral, Carolina Muzzili, and Raquel Camaña. *La Antorcha* offered concrete support for women's ventures by collecting money for *Nuestra Tribuna* and regularly quoted from the newspaper during its existence. Meanwhile, in spite of a growing conflict with *La Protesta*, *La Antorcha* continued to list *Nuestra Tribuna* in its list of publications with which it continued to interact. For its part, *Ideas* praised the female anarchist venture, and its pages verify an active relationship with the *compañeras*. Under the title "Colaboración Femenina," *Ideas* included a dozen regular writers who also dominated the pages of *Nuestra Tribuna*. Furthermore, *Ideas* disseminated Émile Armand's proposal for plural love and continued to focus on the sexual question toward the end of the decade when other publications gave less space to such gendered issues.[43]

Compared to other materials, these newspapers offer useful information about the rich editorial activity of anarchism in a period that also saw the growth of the publishing trade and the consolidation of low-cost literature oriented toward the new urban sectors.[44] In contrast to the reliance on voluntary subscriptions in earlier decades, various anarchist groups in the 1920s organized "libraries" to sell cheaply produced books that included not only imported material but also their own publications. These lists included various pamphlets and books dedicated to the sexual question. Editor Ángel Zucarelli donated material to *Nuestra Tribuna* that was relevant to constructing a female ideology, including *Mujer esclava* by René Chaughi and Paul Robin, *La mujer* by Teresa Claramunt, *La Mujer pública* and *La Inmoralidad del Matrimonio* by René Chaughi, *Degeneración de la especie humana* by Paul Robin, and *A las mujeres* by José Prat. The editors noted that "every *compañera* who wants to elevate herself culturally and mentally should read these pamphlets."[45] To add to these works, all four newspapers offered for sale two recently republished pamphlets: "Generación consciente: Anatomía, fisiología, preservación científica y racional de la fecundación no deseada" by Franck Sutor, and "Huelga de vientres" by Luis Bulffi. These two pamphlets, widely circulated among anarchists in Latin America and Europe, were disseminated in Argentina by Bautista Fueyo, the local representative of the Biblioteca y Editorial "Salud y Fuerza" of Barcelona.[46]

For its part, the editorial board of *La Protesta* obtained permission from Luigi Fabbri to republish *Cartas a una mujer sobre la anarquía.* Beyond the ventures led by the larger anarchist groups, the Centro de Canillitas de Avellaneda brought out *La mujer en la lucha social* by Galo Díez, a prominent Basque anarchist militant. As one can see, the authors were mainly European men; however, local production was not absent as witnessed in the 1920s by two pamphlets written by Argentine women. In 1924 the group Vida y Luz in Buenos Aires published *El canto de la juventud en marcha* by Teresa Maccheroni, a regular contributor to *Nuestra Tribuna.* Meanwhile, the publishing firm Lux from Chile published *Mis proclamas* by Juana Rouco. Thus, the existence of a library for women, coupled with the press regularly publishing themes important to women's issues—some of which were written by women—illustrates the indisputable presence of women in the libertarian camp at this moment. However, some local militants insisted on the necessity of publishing their own newspaper. By undertaking such a project, anarchist women inserted themselves directly into the controversial realm of anarchist propaganda in the 1920s.

In dramatic style, *La Voz de la Mujer* in a previous era had proclaimed that its mission was for women to claim "our share of pleasures from the banquet of life."[47] Twenty-six years later, and without recognizing that precursor, the editors of *Nuestra Tribuna* called for "those left out of the banquet of life" to accompany them on their own venture.[48] While the newspaper included the work of Fidela Cuñado, Terencia Fernández, and

María Fernández, the editorial offices were always under the leadership of Juana Rouco. For twenty years she had been a well-known militant who had taken part in national speaking tours organized by FORA. Before that she had arrived from Spain as Juana Buela—a woman who had worked for the libertarian cause from a young age, had known the inside of a jail cell, and, due to deportations, had traveled the unexpected journeys one was obliged to make as an exile.[49] Thanks to her autobiography published in the 1970s, we can follow her steps first to Montevideo, where she worked with Virginia Bolten on *La Nueva Senda* (1909). With that experience and after discovering a very active group of women in Necochea—a port and seaside resort five hundred kilometers southeast of the capital—she set out to fulfill an old dream: to publish an anarchist newspaper for women.[50]

The semimonthly paper first appeared in August 1922 with 2,500 copies. It offered an unsurpassed opportunity for women to introduce topics that they considered priorities, or to convert questions that concerned them into anarchist themes. As such, they dedicated fourteen editorials to women's emancipation as well as to sexual and affective relations with a special emphasis on maternity and children's education. The rest of the paper covered themes generally found in anarchist newspapers, such as anti-militarism, religion, war, the celebration of some martyrs to the movement, commemoration of a particular date, and so on. However, after repeating conventional anarchist arguments and points of view, the newspaper almost always brought a woman's perspective to the issue at hand.

Nuestra Tribuna published the work of dozens of women from around the country and the world who sent their small notices and commentaries to the paper. A few of these included Irma Penovi from Buenos Aires, Mercedes Vázquez from Balcarce, Ceferina Sánchez from Pergamino, and Teresa Maccheroni from Buenos Aires. The newspaper also included a space for children in the column "Colaboración Infantil." Because they were dedicated to publishing a women's newspaper, the editors were inflexible when it came to male collaboration. They rejected, for instance, the help of Eusebio Souza, explaining that "our little paper is written by women."[51] Furthermore, they refused to use pseudonyms or identify authors by their initials, which might otherwise obscure the author's gender, always asking that authors send "their clear and correct name."[52] While women ran the newspaper, however, some male involvement did occur. Many men were *paqueteros*; that is, they received and distributed copies of the newspaper while other men subscribed and regularly sent money to support the paper's operation.

Despite including works by renowned women anarchist intellectuals like Soledad Gustavo, Willy Witkop Rocker, Federica Montseny, Angelina Arratia, and Teresa Claramunt, the editors could at times—as did other anarchist sectors—betray a certain degree of anti-intellectualism: "The 'intellectual anarchist' women, in spite of being informed of our previous propositions, could not remember us, the anonymous female *journalists*."[53] Or, "And our contributors? Also like us—exploited female workers. But we promise that it is our intention to be more 'literate' without ceasing to be workers, anarchists."[54] The editors also criticized feminists who were often intellectuals and university students, and therefore far removed from the world of the woman worker. Female anarchists rejected the bourgeois nuance, the suffragette force, and the measured intervention of Argentine feminism in a position that Dora Barrancos has labeled the "counter-feminism of anarchist feminism."[55]

Prior to the first issue of *Nuestra Tribuna*, there were echoes of its forthcoming appearance in the pages of *Ideas*, a newspaper in which women played a larger role than in other anarchist publications of the period. From Necochea in January 1922, a writer posing as "Flor de Ideal" proposed creating a newspaper "for women and written by women."[56] Two months later the need for a specifically female newspaper was reinforced from Avellaneda, a community bordering Buenos Aires, when Esther Rivarola wrote that "the newspaper ought to have as its mission (making it the organ of the female anarchist movement in the country) working for women's libertarian organization, with views toward the next congress, studying problems that if not solely anarchic, still are of particular value to us, such as maternity."[57] Five months later the first edition of *Nuestra Tribuna* appeared on the streets, and in a notice titled "Plasmando una iniciativa" (Shaping an initiative) Rouco claimed maternity of the idea of creating a newspaper "written solely by women writers."[58]

The need to establish the newspaper at the request of various *compañeras*, and in such a concerted operation, encountered some reticence toward a venture that would exist parallel to the daily print run of *La Protesta*, in which some militants preferred to concentrate their efforts. However, the project took the form of a standard newspaper of four pages (except for an extraordinary issue of eight pages on September 1, 1923) that maintained a stable format with an editorial boxed in the middle of page one, surrounded by columns, a few regular sections ("Our Mail" and "Administration"), and various sections such as "International Collaboration," "Our Notes of Criticism," and "Discussed Readings." It remained financially solvent through subscriptions and donations, which were always vulnerable to the vagaries of external support. The paper was distributed to numerous cities and towns around the country and abroad; the editors even boasted in their final issues about having a "World Subscription." Ultimately, dwindling funds and the flare up of police persecution in Necochea hampered the newspaper until it ceased publication. By then Rouco was the only person in charge and, although she tried to publish three more issues in Buenos Aires, she ultimately had to close the newspaper.

When it came to the sexual question, the women of *Nuestra Tribuna* did not offer an alternative version to what was then circulating in the press, nor did they propose radical innovations with respect to sexual freedom. In editorials they defined free love as a union that gave primacy to affection, affinity, and free consent. There were no traces of support for, or commentaries about, plural love or polygamy, which some male comrades advocated.[59] They described instead the numerous dangers inherent in the exercise of sexuality. This tendency was particularly discernible among writers such as Mercedes Vázquez de Balcarce who, intending to distinguish love from desire, recommended that "we should not listen to men."[60] Vázquez's comment referred to discourses that insisted on the uncontrollable "lewdness" of men and women's own naïveté. In an even more moralistic tone, Carmen Gutiérrez criticized men who pursued "vulgar love" and did nothing more than "feed vice."[61] Celia Lazcano, from the small Pampa town of Ingeniero Luiggi, sent a warning to young women that they should dignify themselves through reflection and study.[62] For her part, Florinda Mondini from Olavarría urged women to warn their daughters about the dangers of love: "Explain to them the dangerous slope that awaits them from succumbing to just one second of pleasure, disgraced then for the rest of their lives!"[63] Thus, in the opinions of the editors and contributors, as in the writings of recognized female authors, women found little space to express their desires. Instead, they filled their writings with warnings, lists of consequences that could derive from sexual freedom, and surmised the necessity of a profound and shared revolution in customs.

With respect to maternity, the editors were in complete harmony with the rest of the libertarian camp as they assumed that motherhood was a woman's natural mission. They considered themselves to be mothers of the children of the revolution, felt that the state had robbed mothers of their children by sending them to war, were concerned with related themes of childhood and education, and usually identified melodramatically with the selfless mother, sacrificing for her offspring, governed by instinct, and

destined for procreation. At the same time and in line with the other newspapers analyzed here, they distributed birth control literature, or, as the editors put it, the proposition of a "conscious motherhood" in which children
brought into the world could receive the necessary care and education. In
an editorial titled "La Maternidad," one author wrote in favor of her ability
to control her reproduction by means of a "rationalist education."[64] Yet the
newspaper did not publish information on strategies or methods to plan
conception, nor did it run stories about the experience. It simply stressed
the need for them and recommended neo-Malthusian pamphlets "to all
women and men of free conscience" ("Huelga de vientres," "Generación
consciente," and "La educación sexual").[65] Likewise, authors published by
the paper agreed with the rest of the movement regarding masturbation
and abortion; both were rarely discussed and always in a condemnatory
tone.[66]

If their approach to affective and sexual relations did not take a position that was too controversial or broke from the standard anarchist line,
then what was the motive for saying that they had declared war? One way
to answer this question is to examine the other issue that runs through
this chapter: women's emancipation. The title and first epigraph of *Nuestra
Tribuna* contained the signs of a dialogue that carried through for several
decades. To begin, the title itself maintains a clear position relative to a
discussion that had not been settled: should diverse anarchist groups concentrate their scarce resources on just one publication? Or, in keeping with
their ideological, cultural, and idiomatic heterogeneity, could these groups
produce multiple newspapers? "*Nuestra Tribuna*" embodied in two words
the notion that the difference between men and women required that they
have separate forums for expression. Indeed, while these anarchists were
"struggling for a community of equals," they had something particular to
say as "revolutionary and insurgent" women.[67]

To read the paper's epigraph with no contextual reference is to expose
oneself to surprise: "There is no female emancipation. The emancipation
that we free women favor is social, completely social." But if we frame this
assertion within the libertarian field, the discursive context of which it was
a part clearly shows that the women anticipated the accusation that they
would be weakening the movement by being seen as favoring division, in
this case by sex. On the other hand, they spoke to the libertarian legacy
for which women's emancipation is not an accessory of social emancipation but rather unfailingly contained within it. No one could object to the

newspaper's second epigraph: "Women's mental inferiority is a teleological lie, repeated and propagated by every religious and legal congregation."

In a sign that women were generally accepted—as dictated by anarchist doctrine—male-led newspapers did not issue explicit attacks against *Nuestra Tribuna*. Instead, as in the case of *La Voz de la Mujer*, one perceives a more subtle opposition in the manner in which *Nuestra Tribuna*'s editors quoted passages from these male-led newspapers. The editors of *Nuestra Tribuna* used subtle choices of words to frame the insult, the criticism, and the scathing commentary. Judging by the objections that they received, their most radical proposition was to have their own newspaper, with all of the issues that arise from such an undertaking. Their exercise of economic independence and making decisions about each edition was an inversion of roles that were traditionally held by men, even when the latter professed to adhere to the doctrine of female emancipation.

The newspaper's autonomy allowed women to make decisions about which texts to publish. Some of the most widely distributed pamphlets and books were recommended and distributed without commentary. Oddly, they contained arguments that one would assume were opposed to the opinions of the majority of the female editors. Surely they rejected the paternalistic call of the letters of Fabbri written in 1905, and republished by *La Protesta* without explanation, as though women had not actively participated for decades.[68] However, the practice of editing allowed them to exercise in the newspaper other uses of someone else's word, ranging from critical commentaries and transcriptions to newspaper clippings. More than just reprinting these words for simple distribution purposes, these selectively edited pieces authored by female writers were very significant. For example, the editors recovered a forgotten pamphlet by Paola Cleolleo that had been published at the end of the nineteenth century, and that reproduced the most high-sounding fragments with respect to women's sexual freedom. They also selected various paragraphs from a recently published book by Julio Barcos. While the newspaper rejected submissions from men, one cannot say that men were absent. The editors transcribed excerpts of the works of Victor Hugo, J. Novicow, and Rabindranath Tagore as if these men's voices were authorized by the women and constrained by the passages themselves.

By evaluating the position of columns and the layout of others' voices, one can observe the tensions that were roused by the call for female emancipation. For example, in one of her last columns for *Nuestra Tribuna*,

Rouco noted, without mentioning the author, "a sensationalist and swollen hyperbole of praise" directed at María Álvarez, a young Uruguayan anarchist who had recently died: "Never before had such a great female life illuminated America."[69] A cross-reading of other newspapers reveals that a notice signed by "HGB" in *La Antorcha* lamented the loss of the young militant.[70] However, Rouco's words suggested a different interpretation: for many *compañeros* it seemed to be easier to accept two or three recognized authors writing from time to time than to bridge the gap with mothers, sisters, or emancipated lovers on a daily basis. Men could praise a single anarchist woman but had trouble working together in true solidarity with many (or all) women.

On another occasion, and with even greater subtlety, Rouco engaged in a polemic with *La Protesta*'s editors, who supposedly had insulted her by employing the word "prostitute." Why do that if respecting opinions is one of the most constant positions held by the anarchist camp? In general, all anarchists maintained a common discourse with respect to prostitutes: they were indisputably martyrs, victims among victims, deserving of understanding and pity. In every case, they were alleged to have been "thrown" into their situation by the same society that took advantage of them; among the leading causes that resulted in a woman prostituting herself was the young gentleman who "dishonored" her and caused her "to fall" into poverty. Women from *Nuestra Tribuna* shared that interpretation as evidenced by an editorial dedicated to the issue in March 1923.[71] Thus, when *La Protesta* referred to Rouco in these terms, just what kind of prostitution was this that had to be bracketed in quotations? The male author's use of the word suggested that the appearance of women in the public sphere as editors or militants was no different than the condemnable presence of women in public as prostitutes and libertines. One notice remembering the anniversary of María Álvarez's death appeared to strengthen the complaint against Rouco. Extending praise to Álvarez, Eugenio Almada summarized: "She was talented and had a great soul. She was different from other women! She spoke little."[72] Clearly, while certain forms of participation were encouraged and accepted, others generated considerable resistance.[73] We can see why women anarchists insisted on having their own newspaper—not only for the sake of publishing it but also to embrace a distinct form of inclusion. In this new way they autonomously expressed and realized their doctrine as anarchist women.

At the same time, as was the case of *La Voz de la Mujer*, their behavior should not be interpreted only through the lens of their condition as women but also as evidence that the editors of *Nuestra Tribuna* were political actors whose opinions and actions generated support and rejection in a manner no different than the other newspapers. The early 1920s constituted a moment of intense conflict within the Argentine anarchist movement that included everything from simple insults to murder.[74] Rouco was a very active militant with strong opinions regarding these events and the vicissitudes of propaganda. Clearly, she did not restrain herself from expressing her opinions, as evidenced in her August 1922 talk entitled "La misión del periodismo revolucionario" (The mission of the revolutionary press).[75] Meanwhile, in an editorial under her name ("Un llamado a la concordia anarquista"—A call for anarchist harmony), she rejected violence, slander, and the personal attacks that filled the pages of many newspapers and undermined the anarchist cause in Argentina.[76] The editors of *Nuestra Tribuna* tried to distance the newspaper from factions dominated by *"protestismo"* and *"antorchismo"* and denounced pressures placed upon groups that, like they did, understood that it was unnecessary to join in this division. As a result of the accusatory and injurious columns published in *La Protesta* and because the women of Necochea were closer ideologically to the groups publishing *Ideas* and *La Antorcha*, *Nuestra Tribuna* tended to align more closely with the latter. Amid this battle the paper's editors took their own stance and refused to publish contradictory statements or rebuttals because they considered such actions divisive and injurious to the libertarian press.

The Sexual Question in Argentine Anarchism

It has been pointed out that the anarchist appeal to humanity—as a subject of oppression and therefore also of emancipation—was countered by appeals to class, the dominant focus in Marxist socialism, revolutionary syndicalism, as well as most anarchists. Anarchist discourse wavered back and forth between a plea to all oppressed people and a more specific appeal directed at workers.[77] What this chapter has demonstrated is that class was not the only dimension upon which anarchist emancipation was based. The call to women, the responses to this call, and the general treatment of the sexual question brought gender to a discussion of the larger concept of humanity. Gender expanded the vague concept of humanity not just in theoretical discussions but also as expressed in the first person in the women's newspapers. Sexual difference provoked new challenges and opened the discussion about concrete ways in which women and relationships would be emancipated.

In tracing the way in which they recited doctrine, one finds resistance to more active modes of women's participation and the material changes needed to free *compañeras*. Their status simply as women appeared to be the main source of resistance or rejection on the part of male militants. However, such an interpretation, completely coincident with the editors' assertions, can only come from a selective reading of the publication. As we have seen, upon entering the heterogeneous world of propaganda, the women's newspaper faced resistance not only due to the editors' gender but also for its political opinions on the world in which they lived. If one does not recognize this important difference between groups and reads resistance to *La Voz de la Mujer* and *Nuestra Tribuna* only as a problem of "women in the press," then one runs the risk of not perceiving these women as political subjects who formed an active part of a specific camp pursuing power and legitimacy.

To conclude, I have proposed in this chapter to critically evaluate the way in which the historiography has understood the relationship between anarchism and discourses relating to the emancipation of women. In addition, I have explored how affective and sexual relations—or what can be synthesized as the sexual question—were debated within Argentine anarchism. In spite of efforts by feminists, the history of women and the study of gender have failed to produce a rereading of anarchism from that perspective. Instead, these women's actions tend to be interpreted in aggregate as an exception or in a manner that isolates them from the rest of the movement. Building from the most basic steps undertaken by these historians, I proposed in this chapter to identify the sexual question as a central, constitutive dimension of anarchist ideology and a concrete activity of diverse groups working in the last decade of the nineteenth and first decades of the twentieth century. From a perspective that envisions gender as "relational" as opposed to "attributive," and seeking to articulate that dimension with other aspects of political intervention by propaganda activists, this chapter has proposed a rereading of Argentine anarchism in which the sexual question acquires the centrality that other ideas generally attributed to the movement—antistatism, antimilitarism, and more—had for the militants themselves. The early debate on the intrinsic politicization of the sexual (both as difference and as exercising sexuality) continues to make anarchism eerily relevant today.

Notes

1. Gilimón, *Un anarquista en Buenos Aires.*
2. Abad de Santillán, *El movimiento anarquista*, 77.
3. Oved, *El anarquismo*, 360.
4. Ibid., 70.
5. Ibid., 421.
6. Zaragoza, *Anarquismo argentino*, 438.
7. Ibid., 165.
8. See Suriano, *Anarquistas.*
9. Ibid., 174n20.
10. Ibid., 119.
11. *La Protesta Humana*, September 15, 1897.
12. Ibid., August 1, 1897.
13. Oved, *El anarquismo*, 100.
14. Bilsky, *La FORA*, 193.
15. "La familia," Luján, July 31, 1898; "La mujer y la familia en el presente y en el porvenir," Mar del Plata, January 1899; and "La mujer y la familia," Teatro Iris, Buenos Aires, November 25, 1900. See Zaragoza, *Anarquismo argentino*, 237.
16. In this essay I address Argentina only, but several historians in other countries have produced valuable works along these lines: Nash, *Mujeres Libres* (1975); Nash, "La reforma sexual" (1995); and Ackelsberg, *Mujeres libres* (1999) for Spain; Sapriza, *Memorias de rebeldía* (1988), for Uruguay; Rago, *Anarquismo e feminismo no Brasil* (1998) for Brasil; Palomera and Pinto, *Mujeres y Prensa Anarquista* (2006); and Hutchinson, "From 'la mujer esclava' to 'la mujer Limón'" (2001) for Chile, and so on.
17. Feijóo, *Las feministas*, 7.
18. Molyneux, "No God, No Boss, No Husband."
19. Bellucci and Camusso, "La huelga de inquilinos de 1907." The project that this work was part of was entitled "Articulación de clase y género en las luchas de las mujeres anarquistas," CONICET, 1987–1989, and was directed by Dora Barrancos. Mabel Bellucci continued to compile biographies of women anarchists and of their press.
20. Barrancos, *Anarquismo, educación y costumbres.*
21. Scholars continue to be interested not only in analyzing the anarcho-feminist press but also in recovering and publishing the newspapers. See, for instance, Masiello, *La mujer y el espacio público*; Ansolabehere, "La voz de la mujer anarquista"; Ardanaz, "Mujeres que levantan sus voces"; Rodríguez, "El feminismo anarquista en Argentina"; Finet, "Anarchisme et sociabilités au féminin"; Calzetta, "Estudio preliminary"; and Vassallo, "'Sin Dios y sin jefe.'"
22. See Fernández Cordero, "Amor y sexualidad."
23. *La Questione Sociale: Rivista mensile di studi sociali*, Buenos Aires (1894–1896); publication in Italian that was preceded by a newspaper of the same name edited by Errico Malatesta during his stay in Argentina.
24. Pamphlet No. 3, *La Religión y la Cuestión Social* by Juan Montseny, not, as the editors note, oriented to propaganda for women.
25. See Fernández Cordero, "Queremos emanciparos."

26. *El Rebelde*, July 30, 1899. Anarchist newspaper in Buenos Aires edited by M. Reguera (who, in its initial issues, signed J. Mayorka).

27. See Masiello, *La mujer y el espacio público*; and Auza, *Periodismo y feminism en la argentina*.

28. *La Voz de la Mujer*, January 8, 1896.

29. There are traces of a number ten. Only eight issues have been preserved, with the sixth having been lost.

30. See *La Protesta Humana*, April 29, 1900. The anarchist press abundantly documents the existence of the paper in Rosario and Virginia Bolten's role in it. Her initials follow the announcement of its appearance in *El Rebelde*, September 3, 1899. A second issue is listed among newspapers received by *La Protesta Humana*, December 10, 1899. In *La Nueva Humanidad*, October 1899, the newspaper is announced with the following comment: "Although it is small in format, it is big, very big in ideals." *El Rebelde* also acknowledges receipt of the paper: "We are satisfied to have read the following colleagues: . . . *La Voz de la Mujer*." April 1900. In *La Protesta Humana* a meeting is mentioned in which *La Voz de la Mujer* was represented by Virginia Bolten, January 21, 1900. I thank Agustina Prieto for the opportunity to communicate with Delia Bolten.

31. *La Voz de la Mujer*, November 4, 1900.

32. Tarcus, *Diccionario biográfico de la izquiedra argentina*, 425.

33. *La Anarquía*, August 8, 1897.

34. *La Voz de la Mujer*, August 1, 1896.

35. See Anapios, "Del debate al atentado."

36. *La Voz de la Mujer*, January 31, 1896.

37. Ibid., February 20, 1896.

38. Ibid.

39. Ibid.

40. For a detailed analysis of the economic situation of the paper, see Vassallo, "'Sin Dios y sin jefe,'" 82.

41. An earlier version of this section was presented at the conference "Anarchism and Sexuality in Spanish- and Portuguese-speaking Countries" in Leeds, UK, February 2010.

42. I have selected the newspapers with the largest circulation of the period, but in the 1920s many other publications emerged: *Pampa Libre*, Gral. Pico (1922–30); *La Voz del Paria*, Balcarce (1923–25); *El libertario: Decenario anarquista*, Buenos Aires (1923–32); *Via libre: Publicación mensual de crítica social* (1919–22); *Adelante*, Tucumán (1922–27); *Brazo y cerebro: Sociología e información gremial*, Pergamino (1922–30); *Idea libre, Periódico mensual de ideas y crítica*, Buenos Aires (1926); *La palestra*, Buenos Aires (1924–29); *Renovación: Publicación quincenal de ideas*, Avellaneda (1924–28); *La social: Órgano de la Agrupación Anarquista "Aurora Libertaria,"* Buenos Aires (1923); and *Voluntad*, Mar del Plata (1924).

43. Fernández Cordero, "Amor y sexualidad."

44. Gutiérrez and Romero, *Sectores populares, cultura y política*.

45. *Nuestra Tribuna*, November 15, 1922.

46. Masjuan, "El pensamiento demográfico"; and Cleminson, *Anarquismo y sexualidad en España*.

47. *La Voz de la Mujer*, January 8, 1896.

48. *Nuestra Tribuna*, August 15, 1922.
49. Tarcus, *Diccionario biográfico de la izquierda argentina*.
50. Rouco, *Historia de un ideal vivido por una mujer*.
51. *Nuestra Tribuna*, February 28, 1923.
52. Ibid., April 16, 1923.
53. Ibid., September 1, 1923.
54. Ibid., August 15, 1922.
55. Barrancos, *Anarquismo, educación y costumbres*.
56. *Ideas*, January 1922.
57. Ibid., March 1922.
58. *Nuestra Tribuna*, August 15, 1922.
59. Fernández Cordero, "Amor y sexualidad."
60. *Nuestra Tribuna*, February 15, 1923.
61. Ibid., March 15, 1923.
62. Ibid., July 15, 1923.
63. Ibid., April 1, 1925.
64. Ibid., April 15, 1923.
65. Ibid., April 1, 1925.
66. Ibid., September 1, 1923; and August 1, 1924.
67. Ibid., August 15, 1922.
68. Fernández Cordero, "Amor y sexualidad."
69. *Nuestra Tribuna*, August 1, 1925.
70. *La Antorcha*, May 1, 1925.
71. *Nuestra Tribuna*, March 31, 1923.
72. *La Antorcha*, April 2, 1926.
73. Fernández Cordero, "¡Apareció aquello!"
74. Anapios, "Del debate al atentado."
75. *Nuestra Tribuna*, August 15, 1922.
76. Ibid., September 1, 1924.
77. Suriano, *Anarquistas*.

Epilogue

Transference, Culture, and Critique

The Circulation of Anarchist Ideas and Practices

JOSÉ C. MOYA

Anarchism is neither the first nor the most successful mix of ideology and cultural practices to have spread transnationally and reached quasi-global dimensions. From the seventh to the fourteenth centuries, Islam expanded over a territory that extended from Mali to Mindanao, and today there are 1.6 billion Muslims in the world. Christianity's diffusion, particularly after the fifteenth century, is even more global, stretching over northern Eurasia from Portugal to South Korea and including the Philippines, Australasia, Sub-Saharan Africa, and the Western Hemisphere. Since the early twentieth century its adherents have accounted for about one-third of humanity and number 2.2 billion today. More secular mixtures of ideologies and praxis also dwarf anarchism. Nonlibertarian socialism began its diffusion earlier, spread wider, and attracted many more followers.[1] After 1917 the international reach of Soviet Communism would surpass by far that of anarchism, with the Comintern counting 913,000 members outside Russia by 1932.[2] By 1970, 36 percent of the world's population lived under communist regimes.

Anarchism, however, was arguably the world's first and most widespread transnational movement organized from below and without the backing of state and formal institutional power. Unlike Islam, Christianity, and Communism, it never spread through military conquest or imposition, or through political or economic power and pressure. Unlike most other political movements, from socialism to the Tea Party and al-Qaeda, it never had the backing—overt or covert—of nation-states, organized religion, theocracies, business interests, rich patrons, or political parties. And more than most other movements, with the exception of al-Qaeda, it was often denounced as terrorist and persecuted by governments ranging from communist regimes to liberal democracies.

Yet by its belle époque heyday (1890–1914) anarchism had spread throughout Europe; the European diaspora in the Americas, Northern Africa, and Australasia; much of Latin America; and parts of India, China, and Japan. It was then one of the two most important working-class ideologies, along with socialism. Even without the density and mass appeal of its halcyon days, anarchism continued to spread geographically after the 1920s and has proven to be remarkably durable, or as a *New York Times* headline once put it, "the creed that won't stay dead." It has greatly influenced movements as diverse as the beatniks in the 1950s, the student movements of the 1960s, Christian liberation theology and punk rock in the 1970s, and the Zapatistas in the 1990s; it continues to be one of the most important epistemological and ethical sources for radical feminism and environmentalism, the so-called antiglobalization movement, and various forms of poststructuralist arts and cultural studies.

Such resilience and diffusion is not easy to explain. Anarchism's principal positions and practices seemed tailor-made to generate a geographically small and ephemeral movement at best. It questioned most received wisdom and denounced as mechanisms of domination the most revered trilogy of both traditional and modern societies (god, family, and country). It demanded, often with a sense of exasperating moral purity, the apparently contradictory goals of libertarianism (unfettered individual freedom) and communism (comprehensive social equality based on the principle of to each according to their needs). Swimming against the historical current, it proposed decentralization and small, grassroots organization at a time when political, bureaucratic, and economic power was becoming more concentrated and centralized just about everywhere. Its distaste for hierarchies of any sort, and even elections, seemed to undermine organization and institutional development.

Yet, as the chapters in this volume show, some of the very qualities that may have prevented anarchism from becoming a political success also explain its appeal and spread. The iconoclasm and irreverence that could alienate older persons often attracted the young. That was clearly the case for the young intellectuals in early-twentieth-century Costa Rica whose careers are traced by David Díaz-Arias, who shows also how this cohort became less radical with age. That is also true of the young women who founded what seems to be the first anarchist-feminist newspaper in the New World, *La Voz de la Mujer*, in Buenos Aires in 1896. Laura Fernández

Cordero could not trace the evolution of these young women's ideology, so we do not know if their revolutionary ardor diminished with time. But they clearly reveled in anarchism's assault on bourgeois morality and its emancipatory vision of affective and sexual relations. The presence of the young also surfaces conspicuously in Raymond Craib's chapter on foreign anarchists in Chile and in Geoffroy de Laforcade's essay on shipyard strikes in 1950s Argentina.

This highlights one of the elemental driving forces in the growth of an-archism: youthful energy and passion. Today that is obvious, given the as-sociation of anarchism with punk rock, squatter movements, cyber rebels, and other forms of youth subculture. On the other hand, we tend to as-sociate classical anarchism with the working class. The association is not inaccurate. Anarchism had a mass labor foundation that it does not have today. But the movement did not attract all workers equally, even within labor unions that were nominally anarchist. My own research indicates that those more active in the movement were generally younger than their coworkers, and that the average age of anarchist workers (mid-twenties) was lower than that of workers involved in socialist or syndicalist activism. Anarchism may have been a workers' movement, but it was also a youth movement, and this is critical for its understanding. It is not a coincidence that the movement tended to flourish in cities, and even neighborhoods, with proportionally high numbers of young people.

Youth, however, cannot fully explain why anarchism flourished in some places and not others. A particular type and level of socioeconomic devel-opment, political space, and labor market seem to characterize the places where it did thrive. Despite the movement's self-definition as a reaction against misery and oppression, and despite historians' tendency to take this rhetoric at face value, anarchism did not emerge where the laboring classes were the most miserable and oppressed. On the contrary, it thrived in places where wages and opportunity for upward mobility were relatively high, public education and literacy were common, working-class culture and institutions were robust, and proletarianization, Fordism, and deskill-ing were low, particularly relative to the level of socioeconomic and indus-trial development of the place.

This characterized the cradle of the movement in the 1850s, the Jura region of France and francophone Switzerland, with its large numbers of independent artisans and watchmakers who nevertheless feared that the state and capitalism were encroaching on their independence. The suspicion of state socialism in the region and its organic egalitarianism had a transformative impact on Kropotkin, who wrote in his memoir: "The egalitarian relations which I found in the Jura Mountains, the independence of thought and expression which I saw developing in the workers, and their unlimited devotion to the cause appealed far more strongly to my feelings; and when I came away from the mountains, after a week's stay with the watchmakers, my views upon socialism were settled. I was an anarchist."[3]

In less bucolic settings, and with greater inroads of the factory system in some cases, the other loci of anarchist militancy also shared the combination of relatively high levels of socioeconomic development and relatively low levels of concentration and automatization of industrial production. This combination produced a labor market characterized by employment in small and mid-size workshops and factories; a large number of independent or semi-independent artisans and skilled workers (bakers, printers, mechanics, tailors, shoemakers, etc.); and workers in the service sector (carters, sailors, stevedores). Anarchism, an ideology that stressed personal autonomy and group solidarity as well as idealized smallness, decentering, localism, horizontal organization, and federalism, had a special appeal to workers that still retained and prized a level of skill and independence. It was precisely this class of literate typographers, carpenters, bakers, garment workers, and so on, laboring independently or in small and medium shops, that made up the bulk of the anarchist movement just about everywhere.[4]

Anarchism's emphasis on small, grassroots, decentralized, horizontal, and federalized organizations not only appealed to the ethos of artisans working semi-independently or in smaller enterprises but it also fit quite well the structural traits of the cities and regions where they lived. Small, nonhierarchical organizations perform well in work sites with a limited number of employees. Indeed, they may be the most suited and effective type in this milieu. Egalitarianism does not detract from efficiency and may actually promote it so that ideal and practice act symbiotically. This is not likely the case in situations where gargantuan factories employ thousands, or even tens of thousands of highly proletarianized workers with scaled pay, skill, and authority levels; at times ethnic or racial hierarchies; and no obvious common interest. Labor organizations in these types of settings tended to be large, centralized, vertical trade union structures dominated not by anarchists but by socialists, syndicalists, communists, or "bread and butter" unionists. This explains why anarchism flourished in the Jura valleys but not in the Ruhr valley (the massive core of Germany's heavy industry); in Buenos Aires and Barcelona but not in Birmingham; in Montevideo and Milan but not in Manchester and Pittsburgh; and in Chicago in the 1880s but not in the 1920s.

Contemporary sources regularly described these divisions in broad terms: Latin Europe and Latin America, anarchist; Northern Europe and the United States, socialist.[5] Others perceived the division as reflections of ethnonational cultural character with the putatively passionate southern Europeans drawn temperamentally by the Dionysian nature of anarchism and the supposedly cerebral northerners by the Apollonian spirit of social-ism.[6] The British philosopher Bertrand Russell claimed in 1919 that anar-chism had "remained confined almost exclusively to the Latin countries," where it had taken an intemperate character based more on "envy of the fortunate than pity for the unfortunate" that seemed "scarcely sane," and where "it was associated with the hatred of Germany."[7]

These presumed ethnocultural spatial divisions reflected temporal tele-ologies that depicted anarchism as a utopian, infantile, and primitive pre-political movement that had been, or should be, replaced by the scientific, mature, modern, and fully political form of socialism of the advanced in-dustrial proletariat. That discourse surfaces in the titles of publications by Marxists, from Engel's *Socialism: Utopian and Scientific* (1880) to Lenin's *Leftwing Communism: An Infantile Disorder* (1920) to Eric Hobsbawm's *Primitive Rebels: Studies in Archaic Forms of Social Movement in the 19th and 20th Centuries* (1959).

The Marxist critics did have a point below the dismissive rhetoric. Anar-chism *was* utopian. It did have primitivist elements. It did commune with all sorts of "unscientific" transcendental trends from Tolstoy's Christian anarchism and Madame Blavatsky's Theosophy to Kardecian spiritism and philosophical naturism. Its critique was more culturalist than materialist, and it opposed the material basis of modernization (capitalism—whether private or state-controlled—and the factory system), proposing instead a preindustrial order based on independent artisans. Although anarchists did not abandon the Enlightenment's faith in science, they often used the term "scientific" ironically in order to question the positivist presumptions of their "scientific socialist" opponents. They treated technology with more suspicion than respect, fearing its use as a mechanism of domination and its capacity to produce human alienation. And they were more likely to express their ideas in the neo-Romantic language of analogic symbolism than in Marxist economicism.

Yet at the turn of the twentieth century, all of this made anarchism post-rather than prepolitical, fashionably primitivist rather than primitive, the edge of modernity rather than premodern. By 1900 modernity's most emblematic creed was not liberalism, which had already come to represent the past among the avant-garde, but anarchism. For foes and friends alike, the term "advanced ideas" had become almost synonymous with anarchism. The phrase "modern schools" came to be automatically identified in the first decade of the twentieth century with the anarchist pedagogy associated with Francisco Ferrer. At the time of the French Revolution, the term "avant-garde" was used only in military strategy. By the late nineteenth century it was used almost exclusively for political radicalism, principally anarcho-communism, and in the following decades it came to include the artistic vanguard, which often overlapped these political, or "antipolitical," movements. Anarchism had become then almost de rigueur among Western literary writers, artists, and musicians.[8]

Anarchism was intimately linked not only to the ethos of belle époque modernity but also to the socioeconomic process of modernization. And it was particularly dependent on this process precisely because of its lack of military, economic, and political power. Without steamers, railroads, and mass migration, neither the ideology nor the ideologues could have disseminated as broadly as they did during the late nineteenth and early twentieth centuries. Without the spread of schooling and mass literacy, an institutionally weak movement so dependent on written propaganda could not have diffused as massively as it did. Cheap paper and the linotype made it possible for folks of modest means to publish, for the first time in history, thousands of books and millions of pamphlets and newspaper pages. Photoengraving allowed the massive reproduction of revolutionary iconography. These technological innovations of the nineteenth century allowed subalterns to become producers, not only consumers, of mass culture and knowledge—a phenomenon often associated with the twenty-first century and the Internet.

These technologies facilitated the circulation of people, ideas, and cultural practices that made anarchism a paradigmatic type of transnational political activism. The pioneer activism in the Jura region attracted foreign exiles and militants who later spread the movement elsewhere in Europe. By the 1860s it had taken root in the rest of France, Italy, Spain (particularly in Catalonia and Andalusia), Belgium, and, to a lesser extent, Central Europe. It later spread to the rest of the Continent and the British Isles, developing particularly strong roots among Ashkenazi Jews, who made up less than 5 percent of the Russian Empire's population but more than half of its anarchist activists. French, Italian, and Spanish migrants took it to Algeria and other areas of European settlement in North Africa. German and Bohemian immigrants played a leading role in its introduction to the United States in the 1870s, but by the early twentieth century they were outnumbered by Italian and Jewish newcomers. Spanish and Italian militants disseminated it throughout Latin America. Upper-class students returning from European sojourns introduced it to Japan and China in the early twentieth century, and returning immigrants from the Americas helped to spread it to the working classes. After World War I, anarchist activism surfaced in much of the rest of Asia and sub-Saharan Africa.[9]

The local intensity of the movement, however, varied much and depended on the density of its external connections. In places where the ideology entered only through commerce in printed material like books and magazines, the diffusion was limited to ideas (with the individualist strains of the ideology predominating) and circumscribed to literary or artistic circles. The addition to these channels of returning students or workers could, as in Japan and China, spread the ideas beyond the literati and forge a social movement.[10] Peripatetic militants added another proselytizing element in many places.[11] But only mass migration and a dense circulation of working-class people could diffuse anarchism not just as a set of ideas but also as a mass social movement with dedicated structures. And although immigrants from all over Europe participated in this spread, by the early twentieth century three specific groups had become the most notorious disseminators of this diasporic anarchism: Italians, Spaniards, and Jews.

The predominance of these three groups, particularly the first two, in southern transatlantic crossings partially explains the importance of anarchism in Latin America.[12] Spaniards are omnipresent in this volume. In Díaz-Arias' chapter, a Spanish bookstore and newspaper acted as the pioneer disseminators of anarchist ideas in Costa Rica. Craib's chapter focuses on the expulsion from Chile of a Spanish anarchist, and Baer's chapter, on the connections between Argentine and Spanish anarchism during the Civil War. Spaniards are at the core of Shaffer's chapters on Cuba and Panama and are an important presence in Daniel's chapter on cigar workers in Havana and Florida. Italians abound in the chapters on Buenos Aires by Fernández Cordero and de Laforcade, in Loner's chapter on Southern Brazil, and appear in the chapters on Chile and the Caribbean.

Latin America, however, also offers an illustrative example of the varying intensities of this transnational movement. Anarchist ideas and even labor organizations could be found in every country of the region. But the movement only engaged a large proportion of the population in regions of heavy European immigration: Cuba, Southern Brazil, Uruguay, and eastern Argentina. And within these regions, it was, as elsewhere, basically an urban phenomenon. By the outbreak of World War I, Buenos Aires had become one of the largest foci of anarchist militancy in the world, along with Paris and Barcelona; Santos, the port of São Paulo, and Rosario (another port city in Argentina) became widely known as the "Barcelonas" of their respective countries.

In these areas of Latin America, anarchism developed its fullest manifestation in both ideology and praxis. Ideologically, it included both the individualist and Tolstoyan strains favored by bohemians and the anarcho-communism and syndicalism of the toiling classes. The large size of the movement also allowed it to retain its distinctive character without dissolving into a generic "socialist" Left, as it happened in places where organized labor and radical groups were smaller. In terms of practice, it promoted and was an important presence in extensive webs of labor unions and federations. And it transcended organized labor to create a veritable subculture marked by meeting places, public celebrations, institutions, theater, education, bookstores, a large and varied alternative press, its own music and songs, a visual iconography, and even its own lingo.

This volume admirably captures both the fullness of anarchism in its primary foci in Latin America and its vitality in places where it may not have reached the level of a mass movement. It also demonstrates—in some cases, like in de Laforcade's suggestive exploration of anarchist memory, explicitly, in others indirectly—the continuing, if often undetected, legacy of anarchism in Latin America's social movements and general culture of collective action.

Notes

1. The first anarchist international congress of 1907 in Amsterdam attracted 80 delegates from 14 countries, compared to the socialist Second International of 1889 in Paris, which attracted 404 delegates from 24 countries. *The International Anarchist Congress Held in Amsterdam, 1907*, 1–4; and van der Esch, *La Deuxième Internationale*, 21–28. Maxwell Adereth shows that in France, one of the cradles of the anarchist movement, the socialist party had a membership of 91,000 by 1914 and an electorate of 1.4 million. See Adereth, *French Communist Party*, 15.

2. Worley, *In Search of Revolution*, 35.

3. Kropotkin, *Memoirs of a Revolutionist*, 287.

4. For the proportion of skilled workers among anarchists in several countries, drawn from archival sources, see Moya, "What's in a Stereotype?," 77–78, 88.

5. *The New International Encyclopedia*, 589.

6. Eltzbacher, *Anarchism*, 153–54.

7. Russell, *Proposed Roads to Freedom*, 45–46, 52.

8. For the anarchist influence among writers, see Redding, *Raids on Human Consciousness*; Saulquin, *L'anarchisme littéraire de Octave Mirbeau*; Williams, "Politics without Love"; and Casey, "Naked Liberty and the World of Desire." For the fascination with anarchist violence in two trilogies of novels by the Spaniard Pio Baroja and the Argentine Roberto Arlt, see Close, *La imprenta enterrada*. For Baudelaire, Mallarmé, and the French symbolists in general, see Nematollahy, "Anarchism and Literature in France, 1870–1900." For anarchism's connection to the plastic arts, see Hutton, *Neo-Impressionism and the Search for Solid Ground*; Gourianova, "The Early Russian Avant-Garde, 1908–1918"; Leighten, *Re-Ordering the Universe*; Papanikolas, *Anarchism and the Advent of Paris Dada*; Antliff, *Anarchist Modernism*; and Honeywell, *A British Anarchist Tradition*, 42–45. Hamilton, "Wagner as Anarchist, Anarchists as Wagnerians"; Huebner, "Between Anarchism and the Box-Office"; and Garcia, "Alexander Skryabin and Russian Symbolism" for the "mystical anarchism" of this Russian composer.

9. Moya, "Anarchism."

10. Dirlik, *Anarchism in the Chinese Revolution*.

11. Deportations normally did not spread anarchism because most of the expelled militants came from regions where the movement was already strong. But I have found several cases in which immigrants who had converted to anarchism in Argentina and France were deported to Italy and Spain and ended up in hometowns where they introduced radical ideas and practices.

12. Moya, "El anarquismo argentino y el liderazgo español"; and Moya, "Italians in Buenos Aires' Anarchist Movement."

Bibliography

Abad de Santillán, Diego. *La F.O.R.A., ideología y trayectoria*. Buenos Aires: Editorial Proyección, 1971.

———. *LA FORA: Ideología y trayectoría del movimiento obrero revolucionario de la Argentina*. Buenos Aires: Libros de Anarres, 2005.

———. *Memorias, 1897–1936*. Barcelona: Planeta (Coll. Espejo De España num. 39), 1977.

———. *El movimiento anarquista en la Argentina desde sus comienzos hasta 1910*. Buenos Aires: Argonauta, 1930.

———. "*La Protesta*: Su historia, sus distintas fases y su significación en el movimiento anarquista de la América del Sur." *Certamen Internacional de La Protesta*, Buenos Aires, Ed. La Protesta. Edición digital, CeDInCI-Biblioteca Popular José Ingenieros, 1927.

Ackelsberg, Martha. *Free Women of Spain: Anarchism and the Struggle for the Emancipation of Women*. Oakland: AK Press, 2004.

———. *Mujeres libres: El anarquismo y la lucha por la emancipación de las mujeres*. Barcelona: Virus, 1999.

Acuña Ortega, Víctor Hugo. "Clases subalternas y movimientos sociales en Centroamérica, 1870–1930." In *Historia general de centroamérica: Las repúblicas agroexportadoras (1870–1945)*, edited by Víctor Hugo Acuña Ortega, 255–323. España: FLACSO-Ediciones Siruela S. A., 1993.

———. "Historia del vocabulario político en Costa Rica: Estado república, nación y democracia (1821–1949)." In *Identidades nacionales y Estado moderno en Centroamérica*, edited by Arturo Taracena and Jean Piel, 63–74. San José: Editorial de la Universidad de Costa Rica, 1995.

———. "La invención de la diferencia costarricense, 1810–1870." *Revista de Historia* (San José-Heredia) 45 (January–June 2002): 191–228.

———. *Los orígenes de la clase obrera en Costa Rica: Las huelgas de 1920 por la jornada de ocho horas*. San José: CENAP-CEPAS, 1986.

Adereth, Maxwell. *The French Communist Party: A Critical History, 1920–1984*. Manchester, U.K.: Manchester University Press, 1984.

Aguirre Beltrán, Gonzalo, ed. *Ricardo Flores Magón, Antología*. Mexico: UNAM, 1972.

Aguirre González, Jesús Vicente. "Nieva: El largo verano del 36." *Boletín Informativo de la Asociación Benéfico-Cultural Nieva de Cameros* Año 2006, 22 (2007): 38–42.

Alba, Victor. *Politics and the Labor Movement in Latin America*. Stanford, Calif.: Stanford University Press, 1968.

Albornoz, M. "Anarquismo y extranjería: Notas en torno a la vida y la obra de Rafael Barrett." *Entrepasados: Revista de Historia* 32 (2007): 11–26.

Albro, Ward. *Always a Rebel: Ricardo Flores Magón and the Mexican Revolution.* Fort Worth: Texas Christian University Press, 1992.

———. "Ricardo Flores Magón and the Liberal Party: An Inquiry into the Origins of the Mexican Revolution of 1910." PhD diss., University of Arizona, 1967.

———. *To Die on Your Feet: The Life, Times, and Writings of Práxedis Guerrero.* Fort Worth: Texas Christian University Press, 1996.

Alexander, Robert. *The Anarchists in the Spanish Civil War.* 3 vols. London: Janus Publishing Company, 1999.

Alexander, Robert J. *A History of Organized Labor in Cuba.* Westport, Conn.: Praeger, 2002.

Almanaque Literário e Estatístico do Rio Grande do Sul para 1898. Edited by Carlos Pinto e Sucessores. Rio Grande, chronicle the year 1894. n.p., n.d.

Almeyra, Guillermo. *La protesta social en la Argentina, 1900–2004.* Buenos Aires: Peña Lillo/Cotinente, 2004.

Álvarez Junco, José. *La ideología política del anarquismo español.* Madrid: Siglo XXI de España Editores, 1976.

Alves de Seixas, Jacy. *Memoire et oubli: Anarchisme et Syndicalisme Revolutionnaire au Brésil, Mythe et Histoire.* Paris: Editions de la Maison des sciences de l'homme, 1992.

Amoretti, María. *Debajo del canto.* San José: Editorial de la Universidad de Costa Rica, 1987.

Anapios, L. "Del debate al atentado: La lucha por el control de los recursos en el movimiento anarquista, 1915–1924." In *Miradas sobre la Historia Social en la Argentina en los comienzos del siglo XXI,* edited by Silvia C. Mallo y Beatriz E. Moreira, 607–26. Córdoba: Centro de Estudios Históricos Profesor Carlos S. A. Segreti y Centro de Estudios de Historia Americana Colonial, Universidad Nacional de La Plata, 2008.

Anarchopedia. "Types of Anarchism," online article: http://eng.anarchopedia.org/index.php/types_of_anarchism.

Anderson, Benedict. *Under Three Flags: Anarchism and the Anti-Colonial Imagination.* London: Verso, 2005.

Anderson, Danny. "Creating Cultural Prestige: Editorial Joaquín Mortiz." *Latin American Research Review* 31, no. 2 (1996): 3–41.

Anderson, Rodney D. *Outcasts in Their Own Land: Mexican Industrial Workers, 1906–1911.* Dekalb: Northern Illinois University Press, 1976.

Andreu, Jean, Maurice Fraysse, and Eva Golluscio de Montoya. *Anarkos: Literaturas libertarias de América del Sur, 1900.* Buenos Aires: Editorial Corregidor, 1999.

Ansolabehere, P. *Literatura y anarquismo en Argentina (1879–1919).* Rosario: Beatriz Viterbo, 2011.

———. "La voz de la mujer anarquista." *Mora* no. 6. Instituto Interdisciplinario de Estudios de Género (IIEGE), Facultad de Filosofía y Letras, Universidad de Buenos Aires (2000): 109–19.

Antliff, Allan. *Anarchist Modernism: Art, Politics, and the First American Avant-Garde.* Chicago: University of Chicago Press, 2001.

Araya Saavedra, Mario. "Los Wobblies Criollos: Fundación e ideología en la región chilena de la Industrial Workers of the World (1919–1927)." BA thesis, Universidad ARCIS, Santiago, 2008.

Archer, Julian P. W. *The First International in France, 1864–1872: Its Origins, Theories and Impact*. Lanham, Md.: University Press of America, 1997.

Ardanaz, E. "Mujeres que levantan sus voces: Aportes para el análisis de un discurso con-trahegemónico." Actas del III Coloquio Nacional de Investigaciones en Estudios del Discurso, Universidad del Sur, 2005.

Arias Escobedo, Osvaldo. *La Prensa Obrera en Chile*. Chillan, Chile: Universidad de Chile-Chillan, 1970.

Aricó, José. "Para un análisis del socialismo y del anarquismo latinoamericanos." In *La hipótesis de Justo: Escritos sobre el socialismo en América*, edited by José Aricó, 13–30. Latina Buenos Aires: Editorial Sudamericana, 1999.

Arizona Territorial Justice Program. "Forum in the Above Matter." Tombstone Court-house State Historic Park, Tombstone, Arizona, 1999.

Arrellano, Ramón. "Aquellos emigrantes." *Boletín 2008 Asociación Benéfico-Cultural Nieva de Cameros* Año 2007, no. 23 (2008): 58–65.

Atán, Adriela. *Cuatro historias de anarquistas: Testimonio orales de militantes del anarco-sindicalismo argentine*. Buenos Aires: Ediciones del Signo, 2002.

Auza, N. *Periodismo y feminismo en la argentina: 1830–1930*. Buenos Aires: Emecé, 1988.

Avrich, Paul. *Anarchist Portraits*. Princeton, N.J.: Princeton University Press, 1988.

———, ed. "Prison Letters of Ricardo Flores Magón to Lilly Sarnoff." *International Review of Social History* 22, no. 3 (December 1977): 379–422.

———. *Sacco and Vanzetti: The Anarchist Background*. Princeton, N.J.: Princeton Univer-sity Press, 1991.

Axtell, James. *The European and the Indian: Essays in the Ethnohistory of Colonial North America*. Oxford: Oxford University Press, 1981.

Azevedo, Raquel de. *A resistência anarquista: Uma questão de Identidade (1927–1937)*. São Paulo: Arquivo do Estado/Imprensa Oficial, 2002.

Bachman, Carlos J. *Departamento de Lambayeque: Monografia Historico-Geografica*. Lima: Imprenta Torres Aguirre, 1921.

Badilla, Patricia. "Ideología y Derecho: el espíritu mesiánico e la reforma jurídica costar-ricense (1882–1888)." *Revista de Historia* (Heredia-San José) No. 18 (1989): 187–202.

Bak, Joan. "Class, Ethnicity and Gender in Brazil: the Negotiation of Workers' Identities in Porto Alegre's 1906 Strike." *Latin American Research Review* 35, no.3 (August 2000): 83–123.

Bakunin, Mikhail. "Appeal to the Slavs" (1848); "Circular Letter to Friends in Italy" (1871); "Federalism, Socialism, Anti-Theologism" (1867). In *Bakunin on Anarchy*. Sam Dol-goff, ed. London, 1973.

———. *Cartas contra el patriotismo de los burgueses*. Mexico City: Premia Editora, 1977.

Baliño, Carlos. "This Is the Road to Take." In *Carlos Baliño: Documentos y Artículos*. Ha-vana: Departamento de Orientación Revolucionaria del Comité Central del Partido Comunista de Cuba, 1976.

Bantman, Constance. "Internationalism without an International? Cross-Channel An-archist Networks, 1880–1914." *Revue belge de philologie et d'histoire* 84, no. 4 (2006): 961–81.

———. "The Militant Go-Between: Émile Pouget's Transnational Propaganda (1880–1914)." *Labour History Review* 74, no. 3 (December 2009): 274–87.

Barclay, Harold. *People without Government: An Anthropology of Anarchism*. London: Kahn & Averill, 1982.

Barrán, José Pedro. *Los conservadores uruguayos (1870–1933)*. Montevideo: Banda Oriental, 2004.

Barrancos, Dora. *Anarquismo, educación y costumbres en la Argentina de principios de siglo*. Buenos Aires: Contrapunto, 1990.

———. "Mujeres de *Nuestra Tribuna*: El difícil oficio de la Diferencia," *Mora* 2 (1996): 273–92.

———. "Vita materiale e battaglia ideológica nel quartiere della Boca (1880–1930)." In *Identità degli Italiani in Argentina: Reti Sociali/Famiglia/Lavoro*, edited by Gianfausto Rosoli. Rome: Edizioni Studium, 1993.

Barrantes Acosta, Ana C. *Buscando las raíces del modernismo en Costa Rica*. Heredia: EUNA, 1995.

Barrera Bassols, Jacinto. *Los rebeldes de la bandera roja: Textos del periódico ¡Tierra!, de La Habana, sobre la Revolución Mexicana*. Mexico City: Instituto Nacional de Antropología e Histtoria, 2011.

Barrios, Ciriaco. *La Patria del Pobre*. Santiago: Imprenta I Encuadranación Galvez, 1911.

———. *Recuerdos: Poesías*. Santiago: Imprenta Franklin, 1912.

Barrutieta, José Ángel. "Ciriaco Barrios: Un poeta nevero en ultramar." *Boletín 2008 Asociación Benéfico-Cultural Nieva de Cameros* Año 2007, no. 23 (2008): 66–75.

Barton, Josef. "Borderland Discontents: Mexican Migration in Regional Contexts, 1880–1930." In *Repositioning North American Migration History*, edited by Marc S. Rodriguez, 141–205. Rochester, N.Y.: University of Rochester Press, 2004.

Bartz, Frederico. *O horizonte vermelho: O impacto da revolução russa no movimento operário do Rio Grande do Sul: 1917–1920*. Master's diss., UFRGS, Porto Alegre, 2008.

Batalha, Claudio H. de M. *Dicionário do movimento operário: Rio de Janeiro do século XIX aos 1920, militantes e organizações*. São Paulo: Editora Fundação Perseu Abramo, 2009.

Bayer, Osvaldo. "The Influence of Italian Immigration on the Argentine Anarchist Movement." https://libcom.org/library/influence-italian-immigration-argentine-anarchist-movement-osvaldo-bayer.

Bazán Alfaro, Inés, and José Gómez Cumpa. "Enganche y formacion de espacios regionales en el peru: Lambayeque 1860–1930." In *Congreso Nacional de Investigación Histórica*, vol. 1, edited by Humberto Rodríguez Pastor, 248–67. Lima: Concytec, 1991.

Bekken, Jon. "Marine Transport Workers IU 510 (IWW): Direct Action Unionism." *Libertarian Labor Review* 18 (Summer 1995): 12–25.

Bellucci, M. "Anarquismo, sexualidad y emancipación femenina: Argentina alrededor del 1900." *Nueva Sociedad* 109 (1990): 148–57.

———. "Anarquismo y feminismo: El movimiento de mujeres anarquistas con sus logros y desafíos hacia principios de siglo." *Todo es Historia*. No. 321 (1994).

———. "De la Pluma a la Imprenta: Voces contestatarias femeninas en el periodismo argentino (1830–1930)." In *Mujeres y cultura en la Argentina del siglo XIX*, edited by L. Fletcher. Buenos Aires: Feminaria, 1994.

Bellucci, M., and C. Camusso. "La huelga de inquilinos de 1907. El papel de las mujeres anarquistas." *Cuadernos CICSO* 58 (1987).

Bergquist, Charles. *Labor in Latin America*. Stanford, Calif.: Stanford University Press, 1986.

Bermejo Martínez, Carlos. *Roberto Brenes Mesén: Conductor e ideólogo de la Costa Rica de 1900 a 1947*. Heredia: EUNA, 2002.

Bernstein, Marvin D. *The Mexican Mining Industry, 1890–1950: A Study of the Interaction of Politics, Economics, and Technology*. New York: State University of New York, 1964.

Berry, Charles R. *The Reform in Oaxaca, 1856–76: A Microhistory of the Liberal Revolution*. Lincoln: University of Nebraska Press, 1981.

Berry, David, and Constance Bantman, eds. *New Perspectives on Anarchism, Labour and Syndicalism: The Individual, the National and the Transnational*. Cambridge: Cambridge University Scholars, 2010.

Bezza, Bruno, ed. *Gli Italiani Fuori d'Italia*. Milano, Italy: Angeli Franco Editore, 1983.

Bilhão, Isabel. "Família e Movimento Operário: A anarquia dentro de casa." *Estudos Ibero-Americanos*. Porto Alegre, PUCRS, 22, no. 2 (December 1996): 195–210.

———. *Rivalidades e solidariedades no movimento operário (Porto Alegre 1906–1911)*. Porto Alegre: EDIPUCRS, 1999.

Bilsky, E. *La FORA y el movimiento obrero 1900–1910*. Tomos 1 y 2. Buenos Aires: Centro Editor de América Latina, 1986.

Biondi, Luigi. "Na Construção de uma Biografia Anarquista: os Últimos Anos de Gigi Damiani no Brasil." In *Historia do Anarquismo no Brasil*, Vol. 1, edited by Rafael Borges Deminicis e Daniel Aarão Reis Filho, 251–78. Rio de Janeiro: EdUFF; Mauad, 2006.

Bird, Stewart, Dan Georgakas, and Deborah Shaffer, eds. *Solidarity Forever: An Oral History of the IWW*. Chicago: Lake View Press, 1985.

Black, Bob. *The Abolition of Work and Other Essays*. Port Townsend, Wash.: Loompanics Unlimited, 1986.

Blaisdell, Lowell. *The Desert Revolution: Baja California*. Madison: University of Wisconsin Press, 1962.

Blanchard, Peter. "The Recruitment of Workers in the Peruvian Sierra at the Turn of the Century: The Enganche System." *Inter-American Economic Affairs* 33, no. (1980): 63–83.

Bonomo, Alex Buzeli. "O anarquismo em São Paulo: as rezões do declínio (1920–1935)." MA thesis, PUC/São Paulo, 2007.

Borges Deminicis, Rafael, and Daniel Aarão Filho, eds. *História do anarquismo no Brasil*. Rio de Janeiro: Mauad X; Niterói, RJ: EdUFF, 2006.

Botey, Ana María, and Rodolfo Cisneros. *La crisis de 1929 y la fundación del Partido Comunista*. San José: Editorial de la Universidad de Costa Rica, 1984.

Bourdieu, Pierre. "Espace social et genèse des classes." *Actes de la recherché en sciences sociales* 52–53 (June 1984): 3–14.

Bouvard, Marguerite Guzman. *Revolutionizing Motherhood: The Mothers of the Plaza de Mayo*. Wilmington, DE: SR Books, 1994.

Braunthal, Julius. *History of the International, 1864–1914*, Vol. 1. New York: Frederick Praeger, 1967.

Brayer, Herbert O. "The Cananea Incident." *New Mexico Historical Review* 13, no. 3 (October 1938): 387–415.

Brenan, Gerald. *The Spanish Labyrinth*. Cambridge: Cambridge University Press, 1950.

Brignardello Valdivia, Andrés. *Valparaíso Anarquista*. Valparaíso: Puerto de Escape, 2006.

Brown, Lyle C. *The Mexican Liberals and Their Struggle Against the Díaz Dictatorship; 1900–1906*. Mexico: Mexico City College Press, 1956.

Browne, Jefferson B. *Key West: The Old and the New*. Gainesville: University Presses of Florida, 1973.

Bucich, Antonio. *La Boca del Riachuelo en la historia*. Buenos Aires: n.p., 1965.

Bufe, Chaz, and Mitchell Cowen Verter, eds. *Dreams of Freedom: A Ricardo Flores Magón Reader*. Oakland, Calif.: AK Press, 2005.

Buhle, Paul. "The Legacy of the IWW." *Monthly Review* 57, no. 2 (June 2005): 13–27.

Buhle, Paul, and Nicole Schulman, eds. *Wobblies!: A Graphic History of the Industrial Workers of the World*. London: Verso, 2005.

Burga, Manuel, and Alberto Flores-Galindo. *Apogeo y crisis de la republica aristocratica*. Lima: Ediciones Rikchay Perú No. 8, 1984.

Cabrera, Olga. *Alfredo López: Maestro del proletariado*. Havana: Editorial de Ciencias Sociales, 1985.

———. "Enrique Creci un patriota cubano." *Santiago* 36 (December 1979): 121–50.

———. *Los que viven por sus manos*. Havana: Editorial de Ciencias Sociales, 1985.

Cain, Frank. "The Industrial Workers of the World: Aspects of its Suppression in Australia, 1916–1919." *Labour History* 42:54–62.

———. *The Wobblies at War: A History of the IWW and the Great War in Australia*. Melbourne: Spectrum, 1993.

Calderón, Esteban Baca. *Juicio Sobre la Guerra del Yaqui y Genesis de la Huelga de Cananea*. Mexico: Centro de Estudios Históricos del Movimiento Obrero Mexicano, 1975.

Calello, E., J. C. Marin, and M. Murmis. "Formas de lucha e ideología del sindicato y el medio social e industrial." Trabajos e Investigaciones del Instituto de Sociología, no. 10, Universidad de Buenos Aires (mimeo), 1962.

Calzetta, E. *Estudio preliminar a la edición facsimilar de Nuestra Tibuna: Hojita del sentir anárquico femenino (1922–1925)*. Bahía Blanca: Editorial de la Universidad del Sur, 2005.

Cámara de Diputados: Boletin de las Sesiones Estraordinarias en 1918–1919. Santiago de Chile: Imprenta Nacional: 1918.

Cámara de Senadores: Boletín de las Sesiones Estraordinarias en 1918. Santiago de Chile: Imprenta Nacional, 1918.

Cano Ruiz, B. "Ricardo Flores Magón: Su Vida." In *Ricardo Flores Magón: Su vida, su obra y 42 cartas en facsímil*, edited by B. Cano Ruiz. México: Editores Mexicanos Unidos, 1976.

Cantón Navarro, José. *Algunas ideas de José Martí en relación con la clase obrera y el socialismo*. Havana: Instituto Cubano del Libro, 1970.

Cappelletti, Ángel. *Hechos y figuras del anarquismo hispanoamericano*. Madrid: Ediciones Madre Tierra, 1990.

Carbonell y Rivero, Nestor. *Tampa, cuna del Partido Revolucionario Cubano*. La Habana: Academia de la Historia de Cuba, 1957.

Carrillo Azpéitia, Rafael. *Ricardo Flores Magón: Esbozo Biográfico*. México: Centro de Estudios Históricos del Movimiento Obrero Mexicano, 1976.

Casanovas, Joan. *Bread, or Bullets!: Urban Labor and Spanish Colonialism in Cuba, 1850–1898*. Pittsburgh: University of Pittsburgh Press, 1998.

———. "Pedro Esteve: A Catalan Anarchist in the United States." *Catalan Review* 5, no. 1 (July 1991): 57–77.

Casey, Simon D. "Naked Liberty and the World of Desire: Elements of Anarchism in the Work of D. H. Lawrence." PhD diss., University of Toronto, 2000.

Cassaretto, Martín S. *Historia del movimiento obrero argentino*, 2 vols. Buenos Aires: Imprenta Lorenzo, 1947.

Castellanos, Gerardo. *Motivos De Cayo Hueso: Contribución a la historia de las emigraciones revolucionarias cubanas en los Estados Unidos*. Habana: UCAR, 1935.

Castillo Rivadeneira, Oscar. *Movimiento obrero en Lambayeque, 1900–1930*. Chiclayo, Perú: UNPRG Taller de Investigaciones de Ciencias Sociales, 1977.

Catriel, Etcheverri. *Rafael Barrett*. Buenos Aires: Capital Intelectual, 2007.

Caulfield, Norman. "Wobblies and Mexican Workers in Mining and Petroleum, 1905–1924." *International Review of Social History* 40, no. 1 (April 1995).

Censo de la República de Cuba. Año de 1919. Havana: Maza, Arroyo y Caso, S. en C., 1919.

Chaplin, Ralph. *Wobbly: The Rough-and-Tumble Story of an American Radical*. Chicago: Chicago University Press, 1948.

Chase, Alfonso. "José María Zeledón: La inmensa patria humana" (prologue). In *Poesía y prosa escogida*, by José María Zeledón, 11–29. San José, Editorial Costa Rica, 1979.

Chiariamonte, Juan Carlos. *Mercaderes del litoral: Economía y sociedad en la provincia de Corrientes, primera mitad del siglo XIX*. Buenos Aires: Fondo de Cultura Económica, 1991.

Cimazo, Jacinto (psued. Jacobo Maguid). *Recuerdos de un libertario*. Buenos Aires: Editorial Reconstruir, 1995.

———. *La Revolución Libertaria Española (1936–1939)*. Buenos Aires: Editorial Reconstruir, 1994.

Civil Report of Brigadier General Leonard Wood, Military Governor of Cuba, 1901. Vol. 7. Washington, D.C.: War Department, 1902.

Clark, Samuel. *Living without Domination: The Possibility of an Anarchist Utopia*. Aldershot, U.K.: Ashgate, 2007.

Clark, Victor S. "Labor Conditions in Cuba." *Bulletin of the Department of Labor* (July 1902): 663–793.

Clastres, Pierre. *Society against the State: The Leader as Servant and the Humane Uses of Power among the Indians of the Americas*. New York: Urizen Books, 1974.

Clementi, Hebe. *La Boca: Un Pueblo*. Buenos Aires: Instituto Histórico de la Ciudad de Buenos Aires, 2000.

Cleminson, R. *Anarquismo y sexualidad en España (1900–1939)*. Cádiz: Universidad de Cádiz, 2008.

Close, Glen S. *La imprenta enterrada: Baroja, Arlt y el imaginario anarquista*. Rosario, Argentina: Beatriz Viterbo, 2000.

Cleyre, Voltairine de. "The Mexican Revolution." *Mother Earth*. December 1911: 301–6; January 1912: 335–41; and February 1912: 374–80.

Cockcroft, James. *Intellectual Precursors of the Mexican Revolution, 1900–1913*. Austin: University of Texas Press, 1968.

Cohn, Deborah. "The Mexican Intelligentsia, 1950–1958: Cosmopolitanism, National Identity, and the State." *Mexican Studies/Estudios Mexicanos* 21, no. 1 (Winter 2005): 141–82.

Cohn, Jesse. *Anarchism and the Crisis of Representation: Hermeneutics, Aesthetics, Politics*. Selinsgrove, Pa.: Susquehanna University Press, 2006.

Cole, Peter. *Wobblies on the Waterfront*. Urbana: University of Illinois Press, 2007.

Collier, Ruth Berins, and David Collier. *Shaping the Political Arena: Critical Junctures, the Labor Movement, and Regime Dynamics in Latin America*. Notre Dame: University of Notre Dame Press, 2002.

Condron, Rebecca. "The Sindicato General de Obreros de la Industria Fabril: A Study of Anarcho-Syndicalism in Urban Cuba, 1917–1925." PhD diss., University of Wolverhampton, 2006.

Conlin, Joseph R., ed. *At the Point of Production: The Local History of the I.W.W.* Westport, Conn.: Greenwood Press, 1981.

Conniff, Michael. *Black Labor on a White Canal: Panama, 1904–1981*. Pittsburgh: University of Pittsburgh Press, 1985.

Contreras, Gustavo Nicolás. "Clase obrera y peronismo: La 'gran' huelga marítima de 1950." *XXI Jornadas de História económica, Asociación Argentina de História Económica*, Universidad Nacional Tres de Febrero, Caseros (Buenos Aires) 9, no. 23 (2008). http://xxijhe.fahce.unlp.edu.ar.

Coronil, Fernándo. "Beyond Occidentalism: Toward Non-Imperial Geo-Historical Categories." *Cultural Anthropology* 11, no. 1 (February 1996): 51–87.

Corral, Francisco. *Vida y pensamiento de Rafael Barrett*. Madrid: Universidad Complutense, 2002.

Costanzo, Gabriela Anahí. "The Inadmissible Turned History: The 1902 Law of Residence and the 1910 Law of Social Defense." Translated by Marta Inés Merajver. *Sociedad* (Publicación de Universidad de Buenos Aires. Facultad de Ciencias Sociales) 26 (2007).

Cotler, Julio. "State and Regime: Comparative Notes on the Southern Cone and the 'Enclave' Societies." In *The New Authoritarianism in Latin America*, edited by David Collier, 255–82. Princeton, N.J.: Princeton University Press, 1980.

Craib, Raymond B. "The Firecracker Poet: Three Poems of José Domingo Gómez Rojas." *New Letters: A Magazine of Writing & Art* 78, no. 1 (Fall 2011): 71–79.

———. "Students, Anarchists and Categories of Persecution, Chile, 1920." *A Contracorriente* 8, no. 1 (Fall 2010): 22–60.

Crawley, Eduardo. *Nicaragua in Perspective*. New York: St. Martin's Press, 1979.

Daniel, Evan. "Rolling for the Revolution: A Transnational History of Cuban Cigar Makers in Havana, South Florida and New York City, 1853–1895." PhD diss., New School for Social Research, 2011.

Dávila Santiago, Rubén. *Teatro obrero en Puerto Rico (1900–1920), Antología*. Río Piedras, PR: Editorial EDIL, 1985.

Day, Richard J. F. *Gramsci Is Dead: Anarchist Currents in the Newest Social Movements*. London: Pluto Press, 2005.

De Carvalho Franco, Maria Sylvia. "As idéias estão no lugar." *Cadernos de Debate* 1 (1976): 61–64.

De la Cruz, Vladimir. *Las luchas sociales en Costa Rica, 1870–1930.* San José: Editorial Costa Rica/Editorial de la Universidad de Costa Rica, 1980.

———. *Los Mártires de Chicago y el 1o de mayo de 1913.* San José: Editorial Costa Rica, 1985.

de Laforcade, Geoffroy. "Dissonant Preludes to Latin American Socialism: Territory, Identity, and Authority in the 1929 Latin American and Communist Conferences in Buenos Aires." Paper presented at the European Social Science History Conference, Glasgow, Scotland, April 12, 2012.

———. "Federative Futures: Waterways, Resistance Societies, and the Subversion of Nationalism in the Early 20th Century Anarchism of the Río de la Plata Region." *Estudios Interdisciplinarios de América Latina y el Caribe* 22, no. 2 (2011): 71–96.

———. "A Laboratory of Argentine Labor Movements: Men's Work, Trade Unions and Social Identities on the Buenos Aires Waterfront, 1900–1950." PhD diss., Yale University, 2001.

———. "Straddling the Nation and the Working World: Anarchism and Syndicalism on the Docks and Rivers of Argentina, 1900–1930." In *Anarchism and Syndicalism in the Colonial and Post-Colonial World, 1870–1940: The Praxis of National Liberation, Internationalism, and Social Revolution,* edited by Steven Hirsch and Lucien van der Walt, 321–62. Leiden: Brill, 2010.

de la Fuente, Alejandro. *A Nation for All: Race, Inequality and Politics in Twentieth-Century Cuba.* Chapel Hill: University of North Carolina Press, 2001.

de la Rosa, F. "Diego Abad de Santillán y el anarquismo argentino. 1897–1930." MA thesis, Universidad Torcuato Di Tella, Buenos Aires, 2004.

Delgado Benites, Javier. *Artemio Zavala: Paladín del Sindicalismo Liberteño.* Trujillo: Perú: Impresos Gráficos Gutemberg, 2011.

Delgado Rosado, Pedro. "Movimiento intelectual en Lambayeque 1920–1930, José Carlos Mariátegui y el 'Grupo de Chiclayo.'" *Utopia Norteña* 1 (1995): 89–108.

Delhom, Joël. "Le mouvement ouvrier anarchiste au Pérou (1890–1930).Essai de synthèse et d'analyse historiographique." In *¡Viva la Social! Anarchistes et anarcho-syndicalistes en Amérique latine (1860–1930),* edited by Joël Delhom, David Doillon, Hélène Finet, Guillaume de Gracia, and Pierre-Henri Zaidman. Paris: Saint-Georges d'Oléron, Nada Éditions/Éd. Noir et Rouge/Les Éditions libertaires, 2013.

———, ed. *¡Viva la Social! Anarchistes et anarcho-syndicalistes en Amérique Latine (1860–1930).* Paris: America Libertaria, 2013.

D'elia e Miraldi, Armando. *Historia del movimiento obrero em el Uruguay.* Montevideo: Ediciones de La Banda Oriental, 1984.

de Lidia, Palmiro (a.k.a. Adrián del Valle). *Fin de fiesta: Cuadro dramático.* New York: n.p., 1898.

del Valle, Adrián. "Amor de padre," in *Por el camino.* Barcelona: F. Granada, 1907.

———. "Cero." Barcelona: La Revista Blanca, n.d.

———. "En el mar: Narración de un viaje trágico." In *Cuentos inverosímiles.* Havana: Nuevo Ideal (1903): 127–65.

———. "El fin de un marinero," in *Por el camino.* Barcelona: F. Granada, 1907.

———. *La mulata Soledad.* Barcelona: Impresos Costa, 1929.

———. *El tesoro escondido.* Barcelona: La Revista Blanca, n.d.

———. *Tiberianos.* Barcelona: La Revista Blanca, n.d.

Dengo, María Eugenia. *Roberto Brenes Mesén*. San José: Ministerio de Cultura, Juventud y Deportes, 1974.

Dengo, Omar. *Escritos y discursos*. San José: Editorial del Ministerio de Educación Pública, 1961.

———. *Meditaciones*. San José: Ediciones Repertorio Americano, 1929.

DeShazo, Peter. "The Industrial Workers of the World in Chile: 1917–1927." MA thesis, University of Wisconsin, 1973.

———. *Urban Workers and Labor Unions in Chile, 1902–1927*. Madison: University of Wisconsin Press, 1983.

DeShazo, Peter, and Robert J. Halstead. "Los Wobblies del Sur: The Industrial Workers of the World in Chile and Mexico." Unpublished article manuscript, October 1974, Archives of Labor and Urban Affairs, Walter P. Reuther Library, Wayne State University.

Devandas Brenes, Vinyela. "Billo Zeledón, ese famoso desconocido." San José: MA thesis, Universidad de Costa Rica, 1994.

Dias, Everardo. *História das lutas sociais no Brasil*. São Paulo: Alfa-Omega, 1977.

Díaz Ahumada, Joaquín. *Luchas sindicales en el valle de chicama*, 2nd ed. Trujillo, Perú: Libreria Star, n.d.

Díaz Arias, David. *La fiesta de la independencia en Costa Rica, 1821–1921*. San José: EUCR, 2007.

———. "Una fiesta del discurso: Vocabulario político e identidad nacional en el discurso de las celebraciones de la independencia en Costa Rica, 1848–1921." *Revista Estudios* 17 (2003): 73–104.

———. *Historia del 11 de abril: Juan Santamaría entre el pasado y el presente (1915–2006)*. San José: EUCR, 2006.

———. "Social Crises and Struggling Memories: Populism, Popular Mobilization, Violence, and Memories of Civil War in Costa Rica, 1940–1948." PhD diss., Indiana University, 2009.

Dirlik, Arif. *Anarchism in the Chinese Revolution*. Berkeley: University of California Press, 1993.

Di Stefano, M. "Esperanto y anarquismo en la Argentina de principios del siglo XX." *Spanish in Context*, Vol. 7, 100–119. Amsterdam: John Benjamins, 2010.

Di Tella, Torcuato. *Perón y los sindicatos: El inicio de una revolución conflictiva*. Buenos Aires: Ariel, 2003.

Documentos para servir a la historia de la Guerra Chiquita Havana: Archivo Nacional de Cuba, 1949–50.

Doeswijk, A. "Entre camaleones y cristalizados: Los anarco-bolcheviques rioplatenses, 1917–1930." PhD diss., Instituto de Ciencias Humanas, Campinas, Brasil, 1998.

Dolgoff, Sam, ed. *Bakunin on Anarchism*. Montreal: Black Rose Books, 1990.

Dorado Romo, David. *Ringside Seat to a Revolution: An Underground Cultural History of El Paso and Juárez: 1893–1923*. El Paso: Cinco Punto Press, 2005.

Doremus, Anne. "Indigenism, Mestizaje, and National Identity in Mexico during the 1940s and the 1950s." *Mexican Studies/Estudios Mexicanos* 17, no. 1 (Summer 2001): 375–402.

Doyle, Henry Grattan. "Roberto Brenes Mesén." *Hispania* 30, no. 3 (August 1947): 392–93.

Drachkovitch, Milorad M., ed. *The Revolutionary Internationals, 1864–1943*. Stanford, Calif.: Stanford University Press, 1966.

Drinot, Paul. *The Allure of Labor: Workers, Race, and the Making of the Peruvian State.* Durham, N.C.: Duke University Press, 2011.

Dubofsky, Melvyn. *We Shall Be All.* Chicago: Quadrangle Books, 1969.

Dulles, Jonh F. *Anarquistas e comunistas no Brasil (1900–1935).* Rio de Janeiro: Nova Fronteira, 1977.

Eastman, Charles. *From the Deep Woods to Civilization.* 1916. Reprint, Lincoln: University of Nebraska Press, 1977.

Eltzbacher, Paul. *Anarchism.* New York: Benjamin R. Tucker, 1907.

Esenwein, George. *Anarchist Ideology and the Working-Class Movement in Spain, 1868–1898.* Berkeley: University of California Press, 1989.

Esparza Valdivia, Ricardo Cuauhtémoc. *El fenómeno magonista en México y en Estados Unidos, 1905–08.* Zacatecas: Universidad Autónoma de Zacatecas, 2000.

Estrade, Paul. *La colonia cubana de París, 1895–1898: El combate patriótico de betances y la solidaridad de los revolucionarios franceses.* Havana: Editorial de Ciencias Sociales, 1984.

Etchenique, Jorge. *Pampa libre: Anarquistas en la Pampa argentina.* Santa Rosa, Argentina: Ediciones Amerindia, 2000.

Extradition of Criminals and Protection Against: Message from the President of the United States, Transmitting a Treaty for the Extradition of Criminals and for Protection against Anarchism, Signed at the City of Mexico on January 28, 1902, by the Delegates of the American Republics to the Second International Conference of American States. Washington, D.C.: GPO, 1902.

Falk, Candace, Barry Pateman, and Jessica Moran, eds. *Emma Goldman: A Documentary History of the American Years,* Volume 1, *Made for America, 1890–1901.* Berkeley: University of California Press, 2003.

Fallas Monge, Carlos Luis. *El movimiento obrero en Costa Rica, 1980–1902.* San José: Editorial de la Universidad Estatal a Distancia, 1983.

Federación obrera maritima. *La Caja de jubilaciones marítimas y el control obrero.* Buenos Aires: n.p., 1942.

———. *Memoria al congreso a realizarse de septiembre de 1942 en adelante.* Buenos Aires: Imprenta Minerva, 1942.

Feijóo, M. *Las feministas.* Buenos Aires: CEAL, 1982.

Feijóo, M., and M. Nari. "Imaginando las/los lectores de *La Voz de la Mujer.*" In *Cultura y mujeres en el siglo XIX,* edited by Lea Fletcher. Buenos Aires: Feminaria, 1994.

Fernández, Frank. *El anarquismo en Cuba.* Madrid: Fundación Anselmo Lorenzo, 2000.

———. *Cuban Anarchism: The History of a Movement.* Translated By Charles Bufe. Tucson: See Sharp Press, 2005.

Fernández Cordero, L. "Amor y sexualidad en las publicaciones anarquistas (Argentina, 1890–1930)." *Entrepasados: Revista de Historia* 32 (2007): 59–75.

———. "¡Apareció aquello! Sobre Nuestra Tribuna. Hojita del sentir anárquico femenino (1922–1925)." *Políticas de la Memoria, Anuario de investigación e información del CeDInCI* no. 5 (2004): 182–83.

———. "Queremos emanciparos: Propaganda anarquista entre las mujeres. (Buenos Aires, 1895)." *Izquierdas* (Instituto de Estudios Avanzados de la Universidad de Santiago de Chile, USACH) no. 6, 2010.

Fernández Pesquero, Javier. "España en Chile: Preliminar." In *Monografía Estadística de la Colonia Española de Chile en el año 1909*, edited by Javier Fernández Pesquero, Cádiz: Manuel Álvarez, 1914.

Fernández Riera, M. *Rosario de Acuña y Villanueva: Una heterodoxa en la España del Concordato*. Madrid: Zahorí, 2009.

Fine, Sidney. "Anarchism and the Assassination of McKinley." *American Historical Review* 60, no. 4 (July 1955): 777–99.

Finet, H. "Anarchisme et sociabilités au féminin dans le monde ouvrier de Buenos Aires (1890–1920)." *Ecritures latino-américaines* (2006): 123–38.

Flores Galindo, Alberto. *In Search of an Inca: Identity and Utopia in the Andes*. Cambridge: Cambridge University Press, 2010.

Flores Magón, Ricardo. "A Los Patriota." *Regeneración, 1900–1918*. México: Ediciones Era, 1977.

———. *Land and Liberty: Anarchist Influences in the Mexican Revolution: Ricardo Flores Magón*. Edited by David Poole. Montreal: Black Rose Books, 1977.

Flores Magón, Ricardo, Antonio de P. Araujo, Anselmo L. Figueroa, Librado Rivera, and Enrique Flores Magón, "Manifesto to the Workers of the World." In *Land and Liberty: Anarchist Influences in the Mexican Revolution*, edited by David Poole, 93–96. Montreal: Black Rose Books, 1977.

Flores Magón, Ricardo, and Librado Rivera. "Manifesto of the PLM to Party Members, the Anarchist of the World and the Workers in General." In *Land and Liberty: Anarchist Influences in the Mexican Revolution*, edited by David Poole, 104–5. Montreal: Black Rose Books, 1977.

Fos, C. *En las tablas libertarias: Experiencias de teatro anarquista en Argentina a lo largo del siglo XX*. Buenos Aires: Atuel, 2011.

Franco Muñoz, Hernándo. *Blázquez de Pedro y los orígenes del sindicalismo panameño*. Panama City: Movimiento Editores, 1986.

French, John D. *Drowning in Laws: Labor Law and Brazilian Political Culture*. Chapel Hill: University of North Carolina Press, 2004.

Friedrich, Paul. *Agrarian Revolt in a Mexican Village*. Chicago: University of Chicago Press, 1977.

Fumero, Patricia. "La ciudad en la aldea: Actividades y diversiones urbanas en San José a mediados del siglo XIX." In *Héroes al Gusto y Libros de Moda: Sociedad y cambio cultural en Costa Rica (1750–1900)*, edited by Iván Molina and Steven Palmer, 77–107. San José, Costa Rica: Editorial Porvenir, Plumsock Mesoamerican Studies, 1992.

Gambs, John S. *The Decline of the I.W.W.* New York: Columbia University Press, 1932.

Gámez Chávez, Javier. "Yaquis y Magonistas: Una alianza indígena Y popular en la Revolución Mexicana." *Pacarina del Sur: Revista de Pensamiento Crítico Latinoamericano*. http://www.pacarinadelsur.com/home/oleajes/88-yaquis-y-magonistas-una-alianza-indigena-y-popular-en-la-revolucion-mexicana.

Gandásequi, Marco. *Las luchas obreras en Panamá, 1850–1978*. Panama City: CELA, 1990.

García, Marina Serra. *La Aurora y El Productor*. La Habana: Editora Política, 1978.

Garcia, Susie P. "Alexander Skryabin and Russian Symbolism: Plot and Symbols in the Late Piano Sonatas." DMA diss., University of Texas at Austin, 1993.

García, Vivien. *L'Anarchisme aujourd'hui*. Paris: L'Harmattan, 2008.

García Álvarez, Alejandro, and Consuelo Naranjo Orovio. "Cubanos y españoles después del 98: de la confrontación a la convivencia pacífica." *Revista de Indias* 58, no. 212 (1998): 101–29.

García-Cuerdas, Juan Antonio. "Los almacenes Giménez." *Boletín Informativo de la Asociación Benéfico Cultural Nieva de Cameros y Montemediano* Año 2008, 24 (2009): 65–69.

———. "Las desventuras de dos anarquistas cameranos en el norte de Chile." *Análisis* dialnet.unirioja.es/servlet/fichero_articulo?codigo=2954359&orden=0.

Gardia de D'Agostino, Olga M., Elena Rabok, Norma Asato, and Juan Severina López. *Imágen de Buenos Aires a través de los viajeros, 1870–1910*. Buenos Aires: EUDEBA, 1981.

Garrón de Doryan, Victoria. "Los almacenes Giménez." *Boletín Informativo de la Asociación Benéfico Cultural Nieva de Cameros y Montemediano* Año 2008, no. 24 (2009): 65–69.

———. *Joaquín García Monge*. San José: Ministerio de Cultura, Juventud y Deportes, 1971.

Geraldo, Endrica. "Práticas libertárias do Centro de Cultura Social Anarquista de São Paulo (1933–1935 e 1947–1951)." *Cadernos AEL [Arquivo Edgard Leuenroth]* 8–9 (1998): 165–92.

Gerhard, Peter. "The Socialist Invasion of Baja California, 1911." *Pacific Historical Review* 15, no. 3 (September 1946): 295–304.

Gertz, René, ed. *Memórias de um imigrante anarquista (Friedrich Kniestedt)*. Porto Alegre: EST, 1989.

Geth, Hans. *The First International: Minutes of the Hague Congress of 1872 with Related Documents*. Madison: University of Wisconsin Press, 1958.

Giesecke, Margarita. "The Trujillo Insurrection, the APRA Party, and the Making of Modern Peruvian Politics." PhD diss., University of London-Birkbeck College, 1993.

Gilimón, E. *Un anarquista en Buenos Aires, 1890–1910*. Buenos Aires: CEAL, 1971.

Gledhill, John. "The Comparative Analysis of Social and Political Transitions." In *State and Society: The Emergence and Development of Social Hierarchy and Political Centralization*, edited by J. Gledhill, B. Bender, and M. T. Larsen, 1–27. London: Unwin Hyman, 1988.

———. "Legacies of Empire: Political Centralization and Class Formation in the Hispanic-American World." In *State and Society: The Emergence and Development of Social Hierarchy and Political Centralization*, edited by J. Gledhill, B. Bender, and M. T. Larsen, 302–19. London: Unwin Hyman, 1988.

Godio, Julio. *Historia del movimiento obrero latinoamericano*, vol. 2. San José, Costa Rica: Editorial Nueva Sociedad, 1983.

Goldar, Ernesto. *Los argentinos y la guerra civil española*. Contrapunto: Buenos Aires, 1986.

Gómez Cumpa, José. "Aprismo y comunismo en Lambayeque: (1900–1931)," *Alternativa* 5 (1987): 23–37.

Gómez Cumpa, José, and Inés Bazán Alfaro. *Capitalismo y formación regional: Chiclayo entre los siglos xix y xx*. Chiclayo, Perú: Población y Desarrollo Instituto de Investigación y Capacitación, 1989.

Gómez Luaces, Eduardo. "Monografía histórica del movimiento obrero en Regla (1833–1958)." Unpublished manuscript, n.d.

Gómez-Quiñones, Juan. *Sembradores Ricardo Flores Magón y el Partido Liberal Mexicano: A Eulogy and Critique*. Monograph No. 5. Los Angeles: Aztlan Publications, Chicano Studies Center, UCLA, 1973.

González, Manolo. "The Politics of Betrayal: Part Two of Life in Revolutionary Barcelona." *Anarchy; A Journal of Desire Armed* 36 (Spring 1993).

Gonzales, Michael J. *Plantation Agriculture and Social Control in Northern Peru, 1875–1933*. Austin: University of Texas Press, 1985.

González Casanova, Pablo. *Historia del movimiento obrero en américa latina*, vol. 4. Mexico City: Siglo Veintiuno Editores, 1984.

González Climent, Aurelio, and Anselmo González Climent. *Historia de la Marina Mercante Argentina*, 5 vols. Buenos Aires: n.p., 1973.

González Navarro, Moisés. *Historia Moderna de México. El Porfiriato. La Vida Social*. México: Editorial Hermes, 1957.

González Prada, Manuel. "Nuestros Indios." In *Horas de lucha* Lima: Tipografía Lux, 1924; pp.311–38; translated as "Our Indians," in *Free Pages and Other Essays: Anarchist Musings*, by González Prada. New York: Oxford University Press, 2003.

González Rivera, Gonzalo. *Anarquismo argentina (1876–1902)*. Madrid: Ediciones de la Torre, 1996.

González Vera, José Santos. "Los anarquistas." *Babel* 49 (1949).

———. *Cuando Era Muchacho*. 1951. Reprint, Santiago: Editorial Universitaria, 1996.

Gori, Pietro. "La questione sociale e gli anarchici." In *Scritti Scelti*, vol. 1. Imola: Edizioni l'Antistato, 1968.

Gourianova, Nina. "The Early Russian Avant-Garde, 1908–1918: The Aesthetics of Anarchy." PhD diss., Columbia University, 2001.

Goyens, Tom. "Social Space and the Practice of Anarchist History." *Rethinking History* 13, no. 4 (December 2009): 439–57.

Granberry, Julian. *The Americas That Might Have Been: Native American Social Systems through Time*. Tuscaloosa: University of Alabama Press, 2005.

Grauer, Mina. "Anarcho-Nationalism: Anarchist Attitudes towards Jewish Nationalism and Zionism." *Modern Judaism* 14, no. 1 (February 1994): 1–19.

Greene, Julie. *The Canal Builders: Making America's Empire at the Panama Canal*. New York: Penguin Press, 2009.

———. "Spaniards on the Silver Roll: Labor Troubles and Liminality in the Panama Canal Zone, 1904–1914." *International Labor and Working Class History* 66 (Fall 2004): 78–98.

Grez Toso, Sergio. *Los anarquistas y el movimiento obrero*. Santiago: LOM Ediciones, 2007.

———. *Historia del comunismo en Chile: La era de Recabarren (1912–1924)*. Santiago: LOM Ediciones, 2011.

Gross, David. *Lost Time: On Remembering and Forgetting in Late Modern Culture*. Amherst: University of Massachusetts Press, 2000.

Grunfeld, José. *Memorias de un anarquista*. Buenos Aires: Nuevohacer, Grupo Editorial Latinoamericano, 2000.

Guano, Emanuela. "A Stroll through La Boca: The Politics and Poetics of Spatial Experience in a Buenos Aires Neighborhood." *Space & Culture* 6, no.4 (November 2003).

Gurría García, Pedro A., and Mercedes Lázaro Ruiz. *Tener un Tío en América: La emigración riojana a ultramar (1880–1936)*. Logroño: Instituto de Estudios Riojanos, 2002.

Gutiérrez, L., and Romero, L. A. *Sectores populares, cultura y política: Buenos Aires en la entreguerra*. Buenos Aires: Siglo XXI, 2007.

Guzzo, C. *Las anarquistas rioplatenses 1890-1990*. Phoenix: Editorial Orbis Press, 2003.

Hall, Michael B., and Hobart A. Spalding Jr. "Urban Labor Movements." In *Latin America: Economy and Society, 1870-1930*, edited by Leslie Bethell. Cambridge: Cambridge University Press, 1989.

Hamilton, Carol V. "Wagner as Anarchist, Anarchists as Wagnerians." *Oxford German Studies* 22 (1993): 168-93.

Hansen, Niles. *The Border Economy: Regional Development in the Southwest*. Austin: University of Texas Press, 1981.

Hart, John M. *Anarchism and the Mexican Working Class, 1860-1931*. Austin: University of Texas Press, 1978.

Henderson, Paul. "The Rise and Fall of Anarcho-Syndicalism in South America, 1880-1930." In *Ideologues and Ideologies in Latin America*, edited by Will Fowler, 11-26. Westport, Conn.: Greenwood Press, 1997.

Hernández Padilla, Salvador. *El magonismo: Historia de una pasión libertaria, 1900-1922*. Mexico: Ediciones Era, 1984/1988.

Herod, Andrew, ed. *Organizing the Landscape: Geographical Perspectives on Unionism*. Minneapolis: University of Minnesota Press, 1998.

Hewitt, Nancy. *Southern Discomfort: Women's Activism in Tampa, Florida, 1880s-1920s*. Champaign: University of Illinois Press, 2001.

Heyward, Jack. *After the Revolution: Six Critics of Democracy and Nationalism*. New York: New York University Press, 1991.

Hidalgo Gamarra, José Daniel. *Arévalo: Hombre Completo*. Trujillo, Perú: Servicios Gráficos Litton's EIRL, 2004.

Hirsch, Steven. "The Anarcho-Syndicalist Roots of a Multi-Class Alliance: Organized Labor and the Peruvian Aprista Party, 1900-1933." PhD diss., George Washington University, 1997.

———. "Peruvian Anarcho-Syndicalism: Adapting Transnational Influences and Forging Counterhegemonic Practices, 1905-1930." In *Anarchism and Syndicalism in the Colonial and Post-Colonial World, 1870-1940: The Praxis of National Liberation, Interntionalism, and Social Revolution*, edited by Steven Hirsch and Lucien van der Walt, 227-71. Leiden: Brill, 2010.

Hirsch, Steven, and Lucien van der Walt, eds. *Anarchism and Syndicalism in the Colonial and Post-Colonial World, 1870-1940: The Praxis of National Liberation, Interntionalism, and Social Revolution* Leiden: Brill, 2010.

———. "Rethinking Anarchism and Syndicalism: The Colonial and Postcolonial Experience, 1870-1940." In *Anarchism and Syndicalism in the Colonial and Post-Colonial World, 1870-1940: The Praxis of National Liberation, Interntionalism, and Social Revolution*, edited by Steven Hirsch and Lucien van der Walt, xxxi-lxxiii. Leiden: Brill, 2010.

Hodges, Donald C. *Intellectual Foundations of the Nicaraguan Revolution*. Austin: University of Texas Press, 1986.

Holloway, John. *Changing the World without Taking Power: The Meaning of Revolution Today*. London: Pluto Press, 2002.

Honeywell, Carissa. *A British Anarchist Tradition*. London: Continuum, 2011.

Horowitz, Joel. "Argentina's Failed General Strike of 1921: A Critical Moment in the Radicals' Relations with Unions." *Hispanic American Historical Review* 75, no. 1 (February 1995): 57–79.

———. *Argentina's Radical Party and Popular Mobilization, 1916 1930*. University Park: Pennsylvania State University Press, 2008.

Horrox, James. *A Living Revolution: Anarchism and the Kibbutz Movement*. Edinburgh, U.K.: AK Press, 2009.

Huebner, S. "Between Anarchism and the Box-Office: Gustave Charpentier's Louise." *Nineteenth Century Music* 19, no. 2 (1995): 136–60.

Hutchison, Elizabeth Quay. "From 'la mujer esclava' to 'la mujer Limón': Anarchism and the Politics of Sexuality in Early Twentieth-Century Chile." *Hispanic American Historical Review* 81, nos. 3–4 (2001): 519–53.

Hutton, John G. *Neo-Impressionism and the Search for Solid Ground: Art, Science, and Anarchism in fin-de-siècle France*. Baton Rouge: Louisiana State University Press, 1994.

Ignotus. *Los anarquistas: Vidas que se autoconstruyen*. Santiago: Ediciones Spartacus, 2011.

Ingalls, Robert P. *Urban Vigilantes in the New South: Tampa, 1882–1936*. Knoxville: University of Tennessee Press, 1988.

The International Anarchist Congress Held in Amsterdam, 1907. London: Freedom, 1907.

James, Daniel. *Resistance and Integration: Peronism and the Argentine Working Class, 1946–1973*. Cambridge: Cambridge University Press, 1988.

James, Winston. *Holding Aloft the Banner of Ethiopia: Caribbean Radicalism in Early Twentieth Century America*. New York: Verso, 1998.

Jensen, Richard Bach. *The Battle against Anarchist Terrorism: An International History, 1878–1934*. Cambridge: Cambridge University Press, 2014.

Johnston, Laurie. "Cuban Nationalism and Responses to Private Education in Cuba, 1902–1958." In *Ideologues and Ideologies in Latin America*, edited by Will Fowler, 27–43. Westport, Conn.: Greenwood Publishing, 1997.

Kaplan, Temma. *Anarchists of Andalusia, 1868–1903*. Princeton, N.J.: Princeton University Press, 1977.

Katz, Friedrich. *The Secret War in Mexico: Europe, the United States and the Mexican Revolution*. Chicago: University of Chicago Press, 1981.

Khuri-Makdisi, Ilham. *The Eastern Mediterranean and the Making of Global Radicalism, 1860–1914*. Berkeley: University of California Press, 2010.

Kirk, Neville, Donald M. MacRaild, and Melanie Nolan. "Introduction: Transnational Ideas, Activities, and Organizations in Labour History 1860s to 1920s." *Labour History Review* 74, no. 3 (December 2009): 221–32.

Klarén, Peter F. *Modernization, Dislocation, and Aprismo: The Origins of the Peruvian Aprista Party, 1870–1932*. Austin: University of Texas Press, 1973.

———. "The Sugar Industry in Peru." *Revista de Indias*, 65, no. 233 (2005): 33–48.

Knight, Alan. *The Mexican Revolution*. Vol. 1, *Porfirians, Liberals, and Peasants*. Cambridge: Cambridge University Press, 1986.

Koth, Karl B. "'Not a Mutiny but a Revolution': The Río Blanco Labour Dispute, 1906–1907." *Canadian Journal of Latin American and Caribbean Studies* 18, no. 35 (1993): 39–65.

Kravetz, Dalmiro. "Anarquistas durante la Resistencia peronista: La huelga de los constructores navales (1956–57)." Unpublished paper, n.d.

Kropotkin, Peter. *Act for Yourselves: Articles from Freedom 1886–1907*, edited by Nicolas Walter and Heiner Becker. London: Freedom Press, 1998.

———. *Fugitive Writings*, edited by George Woodcock. Montreal: Black Rose Books, 1993.

———. *Memoirs of a Revolutionist*. 1899. Reprint, Mineola, N.Y.: Dover, 2010.

La Botz, Dan. "American 'Slackers' in the Mexican Revolution: International Proletarian Politics in the Midst of a National Revolution." *Americas* 62, no. 4 (2006): 263–90.

Lagos Valenzuela, Tulio. *Bosquejo histórico del movimiento obrero en Chile*. Santiago: Imprenta El Esfuerzo, 1941.

Larco Herrera, Rafael. *Memorias*. Lima: Editorial Rimac, 1947.

Lasso de la Vega, Leoncio. *¡Yo acuso!* Montevideo: Sala Uruguay, 1907.

Latour, Bruno. *We Have Never Been Modern*. Translated by Catherine Porter. Cambridge, Mass.: Harvard University Press, 2003.

Lazarte, Juan. *Federalismo y decentralización en la cultura argentina*. Buenos Aires: Editorial Cátedra Lisandro de la Torre, 1957.

Lazzaro, Silvia B. *Estado, capital extranjero y sistema portuario argentino*, 2 vols. Buenos Aires: Centro Editor de América Latina, 1992.

Lear, John. *Workers, Neighbors, and Citizens: The Revolution in Mexico City*. Lincoln: University of Nebraska Press, 2001.

Lefebvre, Henri. *The Production of Space*. Translated by Donald Nicholson-Smith. Oxford: Basil Blackwell, 1991.

Lehning, Arthur. "Bakunin's Conceptions of Revolutionary Organizations and Their Role: A Study of His 'Secret Societies.'" In *Essays in Honour of E. H. Carr*, edited by Chimen Abramsky and Beryl J. Williams. London: Shoe String Press, 1974.

Lehoucq, Fabrice, and Iván Molina. *Stuffing the Ballot Box: Fraud, Electoral Reform, and Democratization in Costa Rica*. New York: Cambridge University Press, 2002.

Leighten, Patricia D. *Re-Ordering the Universe: Picasso and Anarchism, 1897–1914*. Princeton, N.J.: Princeton University Press, 1989.

Leuenroth, Egar. *Anarquismo: roteiro da libertacão social*. Rio de Janeiro: Editorial Mundo Livre, 1964.

Levine, Daniel. "Constructing Culture and Power." In *Constructing Culture and Power in Latin America*, edited by Daniel H. Levine, 1–40. Ann Arbor: University of Michigan Press, 1993.

Levy, Carl. *Gramsci and the Anarchists*. Oxford: Berg, 1999.

Lida, Clara, and Pablo Yankelevich, eds. *Cultura y política del anarquismo en España e Iberoamérica*. Mexico City: COLMEX, 2012.

Liga de Artesanos y Obreros del Perú. *Cien años de dignidad*. Trujillo, Perú: Liga de Artesanos y Obreros del Peru, 1998.

Lira, Elizabeth, and Brian Loveman. *Políticas de reparación: Chile 1990–2004*. Santiago: LOM Ediciones, 2005.

Litvak, Lily. *Musa libertaria: Artes, literatura y vida cultural del anarquismo español (1880–1913)*. Barcelona: Antoni Bosch, 1981.

Llaguno Thomas, José Julián. "Pensamiento anarquista, cultura política y nueva intelectualidad en Costa Rica, 1900–1914." Licenciatura thesis, University of Costa Rica, 2010.

Llanos-Horna, Segundo J. *Los periodistas de La Libertad: Historia y paradigmas.* Lima: Universidad de Alas Peruanas, 2010.

Lomnitz, Claudio. *The Return of Comrade Ricardo Flores Magón.* New York: Zone Books, 2014

Loner, Beatriz. *Construção de classe: Operários de Pelotas e Rio Grande (1888–1930).* Pelotas: Ed.UFPel, 2001.

———. "O canto da sereia: Os operários gaúchos e a oposição na República Velha." *História Unisinos* 6, no.6 (2002): 97–126.

———. "O IV Congresso Operário gaucho." *Patrimônio e Memória* 7, no. 2 (December 2011): 176–203.

Loner, Beatriz, and V. Menezes. "Entrevista com Otávio Brandão." *História em Revista* (UFPel) 2 (1996): 209–54.

López, Antonio. *La FORA en el movimiento obrero.* Buenos Aires: Ediciones Tupac, 1998.

López, Rick A. "The India Bonita Contest of 1921 and the Ethnicization of Mexican National Culture." *Hispanic American Historical Review* 82, no. 2: 291–328.

López D'Alesandro, Fernándo. *Historia de la izquierda uruguay.* Tomo II, *1911–1918: La izquierda durante el batllismo [Segunda Parte].* Montevideo: Ediciones del Nuevo Mundo, 1988.

López Trujillo, F. *Vidas en rojo y negro: Una historia del Anarquismo en la "Década Infame."* La Plata: Letra Libre, 2005.

Lopreato, Christina da Silva Roquette. *O Espirito da Revolta: A greve geral anarquista de 1917.* FAPESP, 2000.

Lora, Guillermo. *Historia del movimiento obrero boliviano (1923–1933)* 3 vols. La Paz: Editorial Los Amigos del Libro, 1967–1970.

Loveman, Brian, and Elizabeth Lira. *Arquitectura política y seguridad interior del Estado: Chile 1811–1990.* Santiago: LOM, 2002.

———. *Los actos de la dictadura.* Santiago: LOM, 2006.

Luna, Félix. *Perón y su tiempo.* Buenos Aires: Sudamericana, 1992.

MacLachlan, Colin M. *Anarchism and the Mexican Revolution: The Political Trials of Ricardo Flores Magón in the United States.* Berkeley: University of California Press, 1991.

Mahoney, James. *The Legacies of Liberalism: Path Dependence and Political Regimes in Central America.* Baltimore: Johns Hopkins University Press, 2001.

Maitron, Jean, ed. *Dictionnaire Biographique du movement ouvrier français.* 1887. Reprint, Paris: Éd. Ouvriéres, 1964.

———. *Histoire du Mouvement Anarchiste en France (1880–1914).* Paris: Société Universitaire d'Éditions et de librairie, 1951.

Maldonado, Benjamin. "El indio y lo indio en el anarquismo Magonista." *Cuadernos del Sur* 6, no. 15, 2000: 115–37.

"Manifiesto-programa del Círculo de Trabajadores." In *El movimiento obrero cubano: documetos y articulos.* 2 vols. Havana: Instituto de Historia de Cuba Havana, 1975–1976.

Marçal, J. Batista. *Os anarquistas no Rio Grande do Sul.* Porto Alegre: Unidade Editorial, 1995.

Marcela de Vito, Lina. "Siguiendo las huellas literarias de una periodista colombiana, anarquista, y feminist: Blanca de Moncaleano, y la producción de su obra en Colombia,

Cuba, México y en Los Ángeles, California en el siglo XX." Paper presented at XVI Colombianists Congress, 2009.

Marco Serra, Yolanda. *Los obreros españoles en la construcción del canal de Panamá: La emigración española hacia Panamá vista a través de la prensa española*. Panama: Editorial Portobelo, 1997.

Marín, Juan José. "De curanderos a médicos: Una aproximación a la historia social de la medicina en Costa Rica: 1800–1949." *Revista de Historia* (Heredia-San José) 32 (July–December 1995): 65–108.

Marina Mercante Argentina: Reglamentación del Trabajo a Bordo para Puertos Argentinos. Buenos Aires: n.p., 1949.

Marshall, Peter. *Demanding the Impossible: A History of Anarchism*. London: Fontana Press, 1993.

Martí, José. *Obras Completas* 2 vols. Editorial Trópico: Havana, 1930–1946.

Martin, Deborah G., and Byron Miller. "Space and Contentious Politics." *Mobilization: An International Journal* 8, no. 2 (June 2003): 143–56.

Martínez Núñez, Eugenio. *La vida heróica de Práxedis G. Guerrero*. Mexico: BIEHRM, 1960.

Marx, Karl. "Les prétendues scissions de l'internationale" (1872).

Marx, Karl, and Friedrich Engels. *The Communist Manifesto*. New York: Washington Square Press, 1964.

Masiello, F., ed. *La mujer y el espacio público: El periodismo femenino en la Argentina del siglo XIX*. Buenos Aires: Feminaria, 1994.

Masjuan, Eduard. "El pensamiento demográfico anarquista: Fecundidad y emigración a América Latina (1900–1914)." *Revista de Demografía Histórica* 20, no. 2 (2004): 153–80.

Matamoro, Blás. *La Ciudad del tango (Tango histórico y sociedad)*. Buenos Aires: Editorial Galerna, 1969.

Matos Moctezuma, Eduardo. *The Mask of Death*. México: García Valadés Editores, 1988.

Matsushita, Hisroshi. *Movimiento obrero argentina, 1930–1945: Sus proyecciones en los orígenes del peronismo*. Buenos Aires: Siglo Veinte, 1983.

Maximoff, G. P., ed. *The Political Philosophy of Bakunin: Scientific Anarchism*. Glencoe: Free Press, 1953.

Mayer de Zulen, Dora. *El Indígena Peruana: A los cien años de república libre e independiente*, Lima: n.p., 1921.

McAdam, Doug, John McCarthy, and Mayer N. Zald, eds. *Comparative Perspectives on Social Movements: Political Opportunities, Mobilizing Structures, and Cultural Framings*. London: Cambridge University Press, 1996.

McLaurin, Melton Alonza. *The Knights of Labor in the South*, Westport, Conn.: Greenwood Press, 1978.

Meléndez Badillo, Jorell. *Voces libertarias: Los origines del anarquismo en Puerto Rico*. Bloomington, IN: Secret Sailor Books, 2013.

Meléndez Badillo, Jorell, and Nathan J. Jun, eds. *Without Borders or Limits: An Interdisciplinary Approach to Anarchist Studies*. Newcastle upon Thyne: Cambridge Scholars, 2013.

Meléndez Chaverri, Carlos, ed. *Cincuentenario de la letra del Himno Nacional de Costa Rica, 15 de setiembre 1903–1953*. San José: Imprenta Nacional, 1954.

Melgar Bao, Ricardo. *Sindicalismo y milenarismo en la region andina del Perú (1920–1931)*. Mexico: Instituto Nacional de Antropología, 1988.

Meza Fuentes, Roberto. *Los trágicos días de Más Afuera*. Santiago: LOM Ediciones, 2006.

Migueláñez Martínez, María. "Anarquismo argentino transnacional: cooperación y conflicto (1917–1940)." Paper presented at the Semenario de Investigación, Departmento de Historia Contemporanea, Universidad Complutense de Madrid, March 27, 2012. http://www.ucm.es/data/cont/media/www/pag-13888/MariaMiguelanez.pdf.

———. "Anarquistas en red: Una historia social y cultural del movimiento libertario continental (1920–1930)." Paper presented at the Encontro Internacional da ANPHLAC, Goiás, Brazil, July 2010.

———. "Atlantic Circulation of Italian Anarchist Exiles: Militants and Propaganda between Europe and Río de la Plata (1922–1939). *Zapruder World: An International Journal for the Study of Social Conflict* 1 (June 2014). http://www.zapruderworld.org/content/mar%C3%ADa-miguel%C3%A1%C3%B1ez-mart%C3%ADnez-atlantic-circulation-italian-anarchist-exiles-militants-and.

———. "1910 y el declive del anarquismo argentino. ¿Hito histórico o hito historiográfico?" XIV Encuentro de Latinoamericanistas Españoles. Congreso internacional, Santiago de Compostela, España, 2010. http://halshs.archives-ouvertes.fr/halshs-00529699/en/.

Miller, David. *Anarchism*. London: J. M. Dent and Sons, 1984.

Miller, Grace. "The I.W.W. Free Speech Fight: San Diego, 1912." *Southern California Quarterly* 54, no. 3 (Fall 1972): 211–38.

Miller, Nicola. *In the Shadow of the State: Intellectuals and the Quest for National Identity in Twentieth-Century Spanish America*. London: Verso, 1999.

Minguizzi, A. "Españoles y argentinos en la literatura anarquista de Buenos Aires, 1895–1920: Sugjetividad y estética." PhD diss., Universidad Autónoma de Madrid, 2009.

Mintz, Jerome R. *The Anarchists of Casas Viejas*. Chicago: University of Chicago Press, 1982.

Molina, Iván, and Steven Palmer. *Educando a Costa Rica: Alfabetización Popular, Formación Docente y Género (1880–1950)*. San José: Editorial Porvenir; Guatemala: Plumsock Mesoamerican Studies, 2000.

Molina Jiménez, Iván. *Anticomunismo reformista: Competencia electoral y cuestión social en Costa Rica (1931–1948)*. San José, Costa Rica: Editorial Costa Rica, 2007.

———. "Catolicismo y comunismo en Costa Rica (1931–1940)." *Desacatos* (September–December 2006): 157–72.

———. *La ciudad de los monos: Roberto Brenes Mesén, los católicos heredianos y el conflicto cultural de 1907 en Costa Rica*. San José: EUCR; Heredia: Editorial EUNA, 2002.

———. *Costa Rica, 1800–1850: El legado colonial y la génesis del capitalismo agrario*. San José: Editorial de la Universidad de Costa Rica, 1991.

———. *Costarricense por dicha: Identidad nacional y cambio cultural en Costa Rica durante los siglos XIX y XX*. San José: Editorial de la Universidad de Costa Rica, 2002.

———. "Elecciones y democracia en Costa Rica (1885–1913)." In *Democracia y elecciones en Costa Rica: Dos contribuciones*. Cuaderno de Ciencias Sociales, no. 120. San José: FLACSO, 2001, 9–32.

———. "La exclusión del Partido Comunista de Costa Rica en 1931: una interpretación institucional." *Cuadernos Americanos* (Mexico City) 6, no. 108: 71–82.

———. "Explorando las bases de la cultura impresa en Costa Rica: La alfabetización popular (1821–1950)." In *Comunicación y construcción de lo Cotidiano*, edited by Patricia Vega, 23–64. San José: DEI, 1999.

———. "El 89 de Costa Rica: Otra interpretación del levantamiento del 7 de noviembre." *Revista de Historia* (Heredia-San José) 20 (July–December 1989): 175–92.

———. "Un pasado comunista por recuperar: Carmen Lyra y Carlos Luis Fallas en la década de 1930." In *Ensayos Políticos*, edited by Carmen Lyra and Carlos Luis Fallas, 9–66. San José: Editorial de la Universidad de Costa Rica, 2000.

———. "Plumas y pinceles: Los escritores y los pintores costarricenses: entre la identidad nacional y la cuestión social (1880–1950)." *Revista de Historia de América* (Mexico) 24 (January–June 1999): 55–80.

———. *El que quiera divertirse: Libros y Sociedad en Costa Rica (1750–1914)*. San José: EUCR; Heredia: EUNA, 1995.

Molyneux, Maxine. "No God, No Boss, No Husband: Anarchist Feminism in Nineteenth-Century Argentina." *Latin American Perspectives* 13, no. 1 (September–December 1986): 119–45.

Moraga Valle, Fabio, and Carlos Vega Delgado. *José Domingo Gómez Rojas: Vida y Obra*. Punta Arenas: Editorial Atelí, 1997.

Morales, Gerardo. *Cultura Oligárquica y Nueva Intelectualidad en Costa Rica: 1880–1914*. Heredia, Costa Rica: Editorial de la Universidad Nacional, 1995.

Moreno Sainz, María. *Anarchisme argentin, 1890–1930: Contribution à une mythanalyse*. Lille: Atelier national de reproduction des theses, 2004.

Mormino, Gary R. "The Reader and the Worker: 'Los Lectores' and the Culture of Cigar making in Cuba and Florida." *International Labor and Working-Class History* 54 (Fall 1998): 1–18.

Mormino, Gary R., and George E. Pozzetta. *The Immigrant World of Ybor City: Italians and Their Latin Neighbors, 1885–1985*. Chicago: University of Illinois Press, 1990.

Morris, James. *Elites, Intellectuals and Consensus: A Study of the Social Question and Industrial Relations in Chile*. Ithaca, N.Y.: Cornell University Press, 1966.

El movimiento obrero cubano: Documentos y artículos. Vol. 1. *1865–1925*. Havana: Editorial de Ciencias Sociales, 1975.

Moya, José. "Anarchism." *The Palgrave Dictionary of Transnational History*. New York: Palgrave Macmillan, 2008.

———. *Cousins and Strangers: Spanish Immigrants in Buenos Aires, 1850–1930*. Berkeley: University of California Press, 1998.

———. "El anarquismo argentino y el liderazgo español." In *Patriotas entre naciones: Elites emigrantes españolas en Argentina*, edited by Marcela García Sebastiani, 361–73. Madrid: Editorial Complutense, 2010.

———. "Italians in Buenos Aires' Anarchist Movement: Gender Ideology and Women's Participation." In *Women, Gender, and Transnational Lives: Italian Women around the World*, edited by Donna Gabaccia and Franca Iacovetta, 33332–67. Toronto: University of Toronto Press, 2002.

———. "The Positive Side of Stereotypes: Jewish Anarchists in Early-Twentieth-Century Buenos Aires." *Jewish History* 18 (2004): 19–48.

———. "Rebels with Many Causes: Anarchists in Belle Époque Buenos Aires." Unpublished manuscript. http://www.rci.rutgers.edu/~triner/20CColloq/MoyaAnarchistsIntro.pdf.

———. "What's in a Stereotype? The Case of Jewish Anarchists in Argentina." In *Rethinking Jewish-Latin Americans*, edited by Jeffrey Lesser and Raanan Rein, 55–88. Albuquerque: University of New Mexico Press, 2008.

Muñoz, Mercedes. "1848 y 1948: Dos repúblicas y dos identidades." *Actualidades del CIHAC* Año. 1, no. 7 (March 1995): 1–2.

Muñoz, Vladimiro. *Barrett*. Asunción-Montevideo: Ediciones Germinal, 1994.

Muñoz Cortés, Victor. *Armando Triviño, Wobblie: Hombres, ideas y problemas del anarquismo en los años'20. Vida y escritos de un libertario criollo*. Santiago: Editorial Quimantú, 2007.

———. *Cuando la patria mata: La historia del anarquista Julio Rebosio*. Santiago: Editorial USACH, 2011.

———. *Sin dios ni patrones: Historia, diversidad y conflictos del anarquismo en la región chilena (1890–1990)*. Valparaíso, Chile: Mar y Tierre Ediciones, 2013. http://argentina.indymedia.org/uploads/2014/09/sin_dios_ni_patrones__historia__diversidad_y_conflictos_del_anarquismo_en_la_regi_n_chilena__1890-1990_.pdf.

Munro, Dana Gardner. *The Five Republics of Central America: Their Political and Economic Development and Their Relation with the United States*. New York: Oxford University Press, 1918.

Nahmad Molinari, Daniel. *Teatro anarquista: La obra dramática de Ricardo Flores Magón y los sindicatos veracruzanos*. Oaxaca, Mexico: Secretaría de Cultura del Gobierno del Estado de Oaxaca, 2009.

Naranjo Orovio, Consuelo. "Trabajo libre e inmigración española en Cuba, 1880–1930." *Revista de Indias* 52, no. 195–196 (May–December 1992): 749–94.

Nari, M. "Las prácticas anticonceptivas, la disminución de la natalidad y el debate médico, 1890–1940." In *Política, médicos y enfermedades: Lecturas de historia de la salud en la Argentina*, edited by Mirta Lobato, 152–89. Buenos Aires: Biblos, 1996.

Nascimento, Rogério Humberto Zeferino. *Florentino de Carvalho: Pensmento social de um anarquista*. Achiamé, 2000.

Nash, June. *Mayan Visions: The Quest for Autonomy in an Age of Globalization*. New York: Routledge, 2001.

Nash, M. *Mujeres Libres, España 1936–1939*. Barcelona: Tusquets, 1975.

———. "La reforma sexual en el anarquismo español." In *El anarquismo español: Sus tradiciones culturales*, edited by Bert Hofmann, Pere Joan I. Tours, and Manfred Tietz, 281–96. Frankfurt/Madrid: Vervuert Iberoamericana, 1995.

Nataf, André. *Des Anarchistes en France, 1880–1910*. Paris: Éditions Hachette, 1986.

Navarro-Génie, Marco. *Augusto "César" Sandino: Messiah of Light and Truth*. Syracuse, N.Y.: Syracuse University Press, 2002.

Nematollahy, Ali. "Anarchism and Literature in France, 1870 1900." PhD diss., City University of New York, 2001.

Nettlau, Max. *Actividad anarquista en México. Rhodakanaty y Zalacosta: Ricardo Flores Magón, Regeneración y last insurrecciones por "tierra y libertad." Apuntes sobre la propaganda anarquista y sindical tardía*. Mexico: Instituto Nacional de Antropolgía e História, 2009.

———. "Contribución a la bibliografía anarquista de la América Latina hasta 1914." In *Certamen Internacional de La Protesta*. Buenos Aires: Ed. La Protesta, 1927. Edición digital, CeDInCI-Biblioteca Popular José Ingenieros.

———. *A Short History of Anarchism*. London: Freedom Press, 1996.

The New International Encyclopedia. New York: Dodd, Mead & Co., 1918.

Nido, Enrique (a.k.a. Amadeo Luan). *Informe general del movimiento anarquista de la Argentina*. Buenos Aires: Ediciones FORA, 1991.

Nieto, A. "Notas críticas en torno al sentido común historiográfico sobre 'el anarquismo argentino.'" *A Contracorriente: Revista de Historia Social y Literatura en América Latina* 3 (2010): 219–48.

Ñique Ríos, Juvenal. *Manuel Arévalo Cáceres: Apuntes Históricos*. Lima, Perú: Universidad de San Martín de Porres, Escuela Profesional de Ciencias de la Comunicación, 2007.

Nogues, Germinal. *Buenos Aires, ciudad secreta*. Buenos Aires: Ruy Diaz/Sudamericana, 1993.

Oliva Medina, Mario. *Artesanos y obreros costarricenses, 1880–1914*. San José: EUNED, 2006.

———. "La educación y el movimiento artesano obrero costarricense en el siglo XIX." *Revista de Historia* (Costa Rica) nos. 12–13 (July 1985–June 1986): 129–49.

Oliveira, Tiago Bernardon. "Anarquismo, sindicatos e revolução no Brasil (1906–1936). PhD diss., Universidade Federal Fluminense, 2009.http://www.historia.uff.br/stricto/td/1142.pdf.

———. "Mobilização operária na república excludente." MA thesis, Universidade Federal do Rio Grande do Sul, 2003.

———. "A neutralidade política no sindicalismo anarquista brasileiro (1906–1913)." In *Cultura Operária: Trabalho e resistências*, edited by Evangelia Cesar Queiros e Aravanis, 177–92. Brasília: Ex Libris, 2010.

O'Neill Cuesta, Fernando. *Anarquistas de acción en Montevideo, 1927–1937*. Montevideo: Editorial Recortes, 1993.

Ortiz, Ricardo. *Valor económico de los puertos argentinos*. Buenos Aires: Editorial Losada, 1943.

Ovares, Flora, Margarita Rojas, Carlos Santander, and María Elena Carballo. *La Casa Paterna: Escritura y nación en Costa Rica*. San José: Editorial de la Universidad de Costa Rica, 1993.

Oved, Yaccov. *El anarquismo y el movimiento obrero en Argentina*. México: Siglo XXI, 1978.

———. "Influencia del anarquismo español sobre la formación del anarquismo argentino." *Estudios Interdisciplinarios de América Latina y el Caribe* 2, no. 1 (January–June 1991). http://www1.tau.ac.il/eial/index.php?option=com_content&task=view&id=800&Itemid=264.

———. "The Uniqueness of Anarchism in Argentina." *Estudios Interdisciplinarios de América Latina y el Caribe* 8, no. 1 (1997).

Páez, Alexei. *El anarquismo en el Ecuador*. Quito: INFOC, 1986.

Pakkasvirta, Jussi. *¿Un Continente, Una Nación? Intelectuales latinoamericanos, comunidad política y las revistas culturales en Costa Rica y en el Perú (1919–1930)*. Finland: Academia Scientiarum Fennica, Sarja-ser. HUMANIORA nide-tom, 1997.

Palacios, Carlos. *Colección de Canciones de Lucha*. Madrid: Ediciones Pacific, 1939.

Palmer, Steven. "Adiós *laissez-faire*: La política social en Costa Rica (1880–1940)." *Revista de Historia de América* (México) No. 124 (January–June, 1999): 99–117.

———. "Getting to Know the Unknown Soldier: Official Nationalism in Liberal Costa Rica, 1880–1900." *Journal of Latin American Studies* 25, no. 1 (February 1993): 45–72.

———. "A Liberal Discipline: Inventing Nations in Guatemala and Costa Rica." PhD diss., Columbia University, 1990.

———. "Salud Imperial y Educación Popular: La Fundación Rockefeller en Costa Rica desde una perspectiva centroamericana (1914–1921)." In *Educando a Costa Rica: Alfabetización popular, formación docente y género (1880–1950,* edited by Iván Molina and Steven Palmer, 201–58. San José, Costa Rica: Editorial Porvenir, Plumsock Mesoamerican Studies, 2000.

Palmer, Steven, and Iván Molina. "Popular Literacy in a Tropical Democracy: Costa Rica 1850–1950." *Past & Present* 184 (August 2004): 169–207.

Palmer, Steven, and Gladys Rojas. "Educating Señorita: Teacher Training, Social Mobility, and the Birth of Costa Rican Feminism, 1885–1925." *Hispanic American Historical Review* 78, no. 1 (February 1998): 45–82.

Palomera, A., and A. Pinto. *Mujeres y Prensa Anarquista en Chile, 1897–1931.* Santiago de Chile: Ediciones Espíritu Libertario, 2006.

Palti, Elías José. "The Problem of 'Misplaced Ideas' Revisited: Beyond the 'History of Ideas' in Latin America." *Journal of the History of Ideas* 67, no. 1 (January 2006): 149–79.

Papanikolas, Theresa. *Anarchism and the Advent of Paris Dada: Art and Criticism, 1914–1924.* London: Ashgate, 2010.

Pareja Pflucker, Piedad. *Anarquismo y sindicalismo en el Perú (1904–1929).* Lima: Ediciones Rikchay, 1978.

Parker, David. "Peruvian Politics and the Eight-Hour Day: Rethinking the 1919 General Strike. *Canadian Journal of History* (1995): 417–38.

Parlee, Lorena M. "The Impact of United States Railroad Unions on Organized Labor and Government Policy in Mexico (1880–1911)." *Hispanic American Historical Review* 64, no. 3 (August 1984): 443–75.

Parra, Lucia Silva. *Combates pela liberdade: O movimento anarquista sob a vigilância do DEOPS/SP (1924–1945).* São Paulo: Arquivo do Estado e Imprensa Oficial, 2003.

Parra V., Pedro. *Bautismo de fuego del proletariado peruano.* Lima: Linotipo Los Rotaries, 1969.

Patterson, Christine, and Thomas C. "State Formation and Uneven Development." In *State and Society: The Emergence and Development of Social Hierarchy and Political Centralization,* edited by J. Gledhill, B. Bender, and M. T. Larsen, 77–90. London: Unwin Hyman, 1988.

Peirats, José. *Appendix to Anarchists in the Spanish Revolution.* Detroit: Black and Red, 1993.

———. *La CNT en la revolución española,* 3 Vols. Paris: Ruedo Ibérico, 1971.

Penelas, Carlos. *Los gallegos anarquistas en la Argentina,* Segundo edición aumentaqda. Buenos Aires: Ediciones del valle, 1999.

Penichet, Antonio. *¡Alma Rebelde!, novela histórica.* Havana: El Ideal, 1921.

———. "Salvemos el hogar." *Nueva Luz,* August 10, 1922.

———. *Tácticas en uso y tácticas a seguir.* Havana: El Ideal, 1922.

———. "La venta de una virgen." In *La vida de un pernicioso*. Havana: Avisador Comercial, 1919, 193–210.

———. *La vida de un pernicioso*. Havana: Avisador Comercial, 1919.

Pérez, Pablo M. "The Anarchist Movement and the Origins of the Argentinian Libertarian Federation." *International of Anarchist Federations* online archive (nd). http://i-f-a.org/index.php/the-archive.

Pesquero, Javier Fernández. "España en Chile: Preliminar." In *Monografía Estadística de la Colonia Española de Chile en el año 1909*, edited by Fernández Pesquero. Cádiz: Talleres Tipográficos de Manuel Alvarez, 1909.

Petersen, Silvia. *A circulação da imprensa operária brasileira no final do século XIX e primeiras décadas do XX*.

———. *"Que a união operária seja nossa patria": História das lutas dos operários gaúchos para construir suas organizações*. Santa Maria: Editora da UFSM, 2001.

Petra, A. "¿Sueñan los anarquistas con mansiones eléctricas? Ciencia y utopía en las ciudades ideales de Pierre Quiroule." In *El hilo rojo: Palabras y prácticas de la utopía en América Latina*, edited by Marisa González de Oleaga y Ernesto Bohoslavsky, 55–70. Buenos Aires: Paidós, 2009.

Pikulski, María Teresa, and Oscar Félix Orguiquil. *Dock Sud: Un sentimiento*. Avellaneda: n.p., 1990.

Pinasco, Eduardo H. *Biografía del Riachuelo*. Buenos Aires: EUDEBA, 1968.

Pinto V., Julio, and Verónica Valdívio O. *Revolución proletaria o querida chusma? Socialism y Alessandrismo en la pugna por la politización pampina (1911-1932)*. Santiago: LOM, 2001.

Pittaluga, R. "Lecturas anarquistas de la revolución rusa." *Prismas: Revista de Historia Intelectual* 6 (2002): 179–88.

———. "La recepción de la revolución rusa en el anarquismo argentino (1917–1924)." Tesis de Licenciatura, Universidad de Buenos Aires, 2000.

Pizarro, Crisostomo. *La Huelga Obrera en Chile, 1890-1970*. Santiago de Chile: Ediciones Sur, 1986.

Pletcher, David. *Rails, Mines, and Progress: Seven American Promoters in Mexico, 1867–1911*. Ithaca, N.Y.: Cornell University Press, 1958.

Poblete Troncoso, Moisés, and Ben G. Burnett. *The Rise of the Latin American Labor Movement*. New Haven, Conn.: College and University Press, 1960.

Porrini, Rodolfo. "Izquierda uruguaya y culturas obreras en el tiempo libre (1919–1950)." PhD diss., Universidad de Buenos Aires, 2005.

Portocarrero, Gonzalo. *Racismo y mestizaje y otros ensayos*. Lima: Fondo Editorial del Congreso del Perú, 2007.

Poyo, Gerald. "The Anarchist Challenge to the Cuban Independence Movement, 1885–1890." *Cuban Studies* 15, no. 1 (1985): 29–42.

———. "Cuban Émigré Communities in the United States and the Independence of Their Homeland, 1852–1895." PhD diss., University of Florida, 1983.

———. "Cuban Patriots in Key West, 1878–1886: Guardians at the Separatist Ideal." *Florida Historical Quarterly* 6, no. 1 (July 1982): 20–36.

———. "The Impact of Cuban and Spanish Workers on Labor Organizing in Florida, 1870–1900." *Journal of American Ethnic History* 5, no. 2 (Spring 1986): 46–63.

————. "Key West and the Cuban Ten Years War." *Florida Historical Quarterly* 57, no. 3 (January 1979): 289–307.

————. "Tampa's Cigarworkers and the Struggle for Cuban Independence." *Tampa Bay History* 7, no. 2 (Fall/Winter 1985): 94–105.

————. *"With All for the Good of All": The Emergence of Popular Nationalism in the Cuban Communities of the United States, 1848–1898*. Durham, N.C.: Duke University Press, 1989.

Pratt, Mary Louise. *Imperial Eyes: Travel Writing and Transculturation*. London: Routledge, 1993.

Preston, William. *Aliens and Dissenters: Federal Suppression of Radicals, 1903–1933*. Chicago: University of Illinois Press, 1995.

Prieto, Agustina. "Notas sobre la militancia anarquista. Rosario, 1890–1903." *Entrepasados: Revista de Historia* 32 (2007): 77–88.

————. "Rosario, 1904. Cuestión social, política y multitudes obreras." *Estudios Sociales* (Santa Fe, Argentina) (segunda semester 2000): 105–19.

Prieto Lemm, Enrique. *Identificación de las personas*. Santiago: Imprenta de la Bolsa, 1923.

Proceedings of the First Canal Commission: March 22, 1904 to March 29, 1905. Washington, D.C.: Isthmian Canal Commission, 1905.

Proudhon, Pierre-Joseph. "Idée générale de la Révolution au dix neuvième siècle" (1851). In *Marx et l'anarchisme, essai sur les sociologies de Saint-Simon, Proudhon et Marx*, edited by Pierre Ansart. Paris: Presses Universitaires de France, 1969.

————. "Du principe fédératif et de la nécessité de reconstituer le parti de la révolution"(1863). In *Marx et l'anarchisme, essai sur les sociologies de Saint-Simon, Proudhon et Marx*, edited by Pierre Ansart. Paris: Presses Universitaires de France, 1969.

Pugliese, José. *Páginas de historia de la Boca del Riachuelo*. Buenos Aires: Editorial de la Agrupación de Gente de Letras "Impulso," 1981.

Queiros, Cesar, and Evangelia Aravanis. *Cultura Operária: trabalho e resistências*. Brasília: Ex Libris, 2010.

Quesada, F. "*La Protesta*: Una longeva voz libertarian." Parts 1 and 2. *Todo es Historia* 82 (1974): 74–96; 83: 68–93.

Quesada Soto, Álvaro. *Breve historia de la literatura Costarricense*. San José: Editorial Porvenir, 2000.

————. *La voz desgarrada: La crisis del discurso oligárquico y la narrativa costarricense, 1917–1919*. San José: Editorial de la Universidad de Costa Rica, 1988.

————. *Uno y los otros: Identidad y literatura en Costa Rica 1890–1940*. San José: EUCR, 2002.

Quiroule, Pierre. *La ciudad anarquista Americana*. Reproduced in *Utopías libertárias latinoamericanas*, Vol. 1, *La ciudad anarquista Americana de Pierre Quiroule*, edited by Luis Gómez Tovar, Ramón Gutierez, and Silvia A. Vásquez. Madrid: Ediciones Tuero, 1991.

Raat, William Dirk. "The Diplomacy of Suppression: Los Revoltosos, Mexico, and the United States, 1906-1911." *Hispanic American Historical Review* 56, no. 4 (November 1976): 529–50.

————. *Revoltosos: Mexico's Rebels in the United States, 1903–1923*. College Station: Texas A&M University Press, 1981.

Rago, Margareth. *Anarquismo e feminismo no Brasil.* Río de Janeiro, Achiamé, 1998.

———. *Entre a história e a liberdade: Luce Fabbri e o anarquismo contemporâneo.* Editora UNESP, 2001.

Raj, Kapil. *Relocating Modern Science: Circulation and the Construction of Knowledge in South Asia and Europe, 1650–1900.* Basingstoke, U.K.: Palgrave McMillan, 2006.

Rama, Carlos. *Utopismo socialista (1830–1893).* Caracas: Biblioteca Ayacucho, 1977.

Rama, Carlos, and Ángel Cappelletti. *El anarquismo en América Latina.* Caracas, Venezuela, 1990.

Ramos Rau, Demetrio. *Mensaje de Trujillo: Del anarquismo al aprismo.* Trujillo, Perú: Instituto Nor Peruano de Desarrollo Económico Social, 1987.

Reclus, Élisée. *L'Homme et la Terre.* Paris: Librairie Universelle, 1905–1908.

Redding, Arthur F. *Raids on Human Consciousness: Writing, Anarchism, and Violence.* Columbia: University of South Carolina Press, 1998.

Renshaw, Patrick. *The Wobblies: The Story of Syndicalism in the United States.* Garden City, N.Y.: Anchor Books, 1967.

Rey, A. "Pedagogía estética y militancia política a través de la revista *Ideas y Figuras* (1909–1916)." In *IV Jornadas de Historia de las izquierdas, prensa política, revistas culturales y emprendimientos editoriales de las izquierdas.* CeDInCI, 2007.

Ribera Carbó, Ana. *La Casa del Obrero Mundial: anarcosindicalismo y revolución en México.* México: Instituto Nacional de Antropología e Historia, 2010.

———. "Ferrer Guardia en la Revolución Mexicana." *Educació I Història: Revista d'Història de l'Educació* 16 (juliol–desembre 2010): 139–59.

Ringrose, David. *Spain, Europe and the Spanish Miracle, 1700–1900.* Cambridge: Cambridge University Press, 1996.

Rivera, Librado. "Prologo," in *Ricardo Flores Magón, el apóstol de la revolución social mexicana.* By Diego Abad de Santillán. México: Centro de Estudios Históricos Sobre el Movimiento Obrero, Cuadernos Obreros 18, 1978.

Rivero Muñiz, José. "Los Cubanos en Tampa." *Revista Bimestre Cubana* 74 (January–June 1958): 5–140.

———. "La lectura en las tabaquerías." *Revista de la Biblioteca Nacional* (October–December 1951): 190–272.

Rocca Torres, Luis. *De la multitude a la soledad: La vida de José Mercedes Cachay Líder Popular Lambayecano.* Chiclayo, Perú: Centro de Estudios Sociales Solidaridad, 1993.

Rocker, Rudolf. *Nationalism and Culture.* Los Angeles: Rocker Publications Committee, 1937.

Rodrigues, Edgar. *Alvorada operária.* Rio de Janeiro: Mundo Livre, 1979.

———. *Os libertários: Ideias e experiências anárquicas.* Petrópolis: Vozes, 1988.

———. *Nacionalismo e cultura social.* Rio de Janeiro: Laemmert, 1972.

Rodríguez, Carla. "El feminismo anarquista en Argentina: *La Voz de la Mujer." Jornadas: "Los Terciarios Hacen Historia"* ISP Dr. J. V.González, 2006. http://en.calameo.com/read/000068238eb7c31534800.

Rodríguez Díaz, Universindo. *Los sectores populares en el Uruguay del novecientos: Segunda Parte.* Montevideo: TAE Editorial, 1994.

Rodríguez Terrazas, Ignacio. "Protesta y soberanía popular: Las marchas del hambre en

Santiago de Chile, 1918–1919." Unpublished thesis, Pontífica Universidad Católica de Chile, 2001.

Romani, Carlo. *Oreste Ristori: Uma aventura anarquista*. Annablume, 2002.

Romero Pérez, Jorge Enrique. *La socialdemocracia en Costa Rica*. San José: Editorial Universidad Estatal a Distancia, 1982.

Ronning, C. Neale. *José Martí and the Émigré Colony in Key West: Leadership and State Formation*. New York: Praeger, 1990.

Rosemont, Franklin. *Joe Hill: The IWW and the Making of a Revolutionary Workingclass Counterculture*. Chicago: Charles H. Kerr, 2003.

Rosenthal, Anton. "The Arrival of the Electric Streetcar and the Conflict over Progress in Early Twentieth-Century Montevideo." *Journal of Latin American Studies* 27 (1995): 319–41.

———. "Radical Border Crossers: The Industrial Workers of the World and their Press in Latin America." *Estudios Interdisciplinarios de América Latina y el Caribe* 22, no. 2 (July–December 2011): 39–70.

———. "Streetcar Workers and the Transformation of Montevideo: The General Strike of May 1911." *Americas* 51, no. 4 (April 1995): 471–94.

Rosenzweig, Fernando. "El desarrollo económico de México de 1877–1911." *El Trimestre Económico* 32 (July–September 1965): 404–54.

Rotóndaro, Rubén. *Realidad y cambio en el sindicalismo*. Buenos Aires: Pleamar, 1971.

Rouco Buela, J. *Historia de un ideal vivido por una mujer*. Buenos Aires: self-published, 1964.

Russell, Bertrand. *Proposed Roads to Freedom: Socialism, Anarchism and Syndicalism*. New York: Henry Holt, 1919.

Sábato, Hilda. "Ciudadanía, participación política y formación de una esfera pública en Buenos Aires, 1850–1880." *Past and Present*, no. 136 (August 1992):139–63.

———. *La política en las calles: Entre el voto y la movilización. Buenos Aires, 1862–1880*. Buenos Aires: Sudamericana, 1998.

Salazar, Orlando. *El Apogeo de la República Liberal en Costa Rica 1870–1914*. San José, Costa Rica: Editorial de la Universidad de Costa Rica, segunda reimpresión, 1998.

Salazar, Rosendo. *Historia de las luchas proletarias de México, 1923 a 1936*. Mexico City: Editorial Avante, 1938.

Salerno, Salvatore. *Red November, Black November: Culture and Community in the Industrial Workers of the World*. Albany: State University of New York Press, 1989.

Samis, Alexandre. "Desvio e Ordem: anarquismo e pólicia na República Velha." In *História do Anarquismo no Brasil*, v. 1, edited by Rafael Borges Deminicis and Daniel Aarão Reis Filho, 57–74. Rio de Janeiro: Eduff, 2006.

———. *Minha patria é o mundo inteiro: Neno Vasco, o anarquismo e o sindicalismo revolucionario em dois mundos*. Lisbon: Livraria Letra Livre, 2009.

———. *Moral pública & martírio privado: colônia penal de Clevelândia do Norte e o processo de exclusão social e exílio interno no Brasil dos anos 20*. Rio de Janeiro: Robson Achiamé, 1999.

Sánchez Cobos, Amparo. *Sembrando ideales: Anarquistas españoles en Cuba (1902–1925)*. Sevilla: Consejo Superior de Investigaciones Científicas, 2008.

Sandos, James. *Rebellion in the Borderlands: Anarchism and the Plan de San Diego*. Norman: University of Oklahoma Press, 1992.

Sapriza, G. *Memorias de rebeldía: siete historias de vida*. Montevideo: Puntosur, 1988.

Saulquin, Isabelle. *L'anarchisme littéraire de Octave Mirbeau*. Villeneuve d'Ascq: Presses universitaires du Septentrion, 1998.

Schmidt, Michael. *Cartography of Revolutionary Anarchism*. Oakland: AK Press, 2013.

Schmidt, Michael, and Lucien van der Walt. *Black Flame: The Revolutionary Class Politics of Anarchism and Syndicalism*. Oakland, Calif.: AK Press, 2009.

Schwarz, Roberto. *Misplaced Ideas: Essays on Brazilian Culture*. London: Verso, 1992.

Scobie, James. *Buenos Aires: Plaza to Suburb, 1870–1910*. Oxford: Oxford University Press, 1992.

Servier, Jean. *La utopia*. Mexico City: Fondo de Cultura Económica, 1982.

Sevilla Exebio, Julio César. "La Montonera del Cura Chumán, Ferreñafe 1910." *Utopía Norteña* (1995): 147–71.

Shaffer, Kirk. "Tropical Libertarians: Anarchist Movements and Networks in the Caribbean, Southern US and Mexico." In *Anarchism and Syndicalism in the Colonial and Post-Colonial World, 1870–1940: The Praxis of National Liberation, Internationalism, and Social Revolution*, edited by Steven Hirsch and Lucien van der Walt, 273–320. Leiden: Brill, 2010.

Shaffer, Kirwin. *Anarchism and Countercultural Politics in Early Twentieth-Century Cuba*. Gainesville: University Press of Florida, 2005.

———. *Black Flag Boricuas: Anarchism, Anti-Authoritarianism, And the Left in Puerto Rico, 1897–1921*. Urbana: University of Illinois Press, 2013.

———. "By Dynamite, Sabotage, Revolution and the Pen: Violence in Caribbean Anarchist Fiction, 1890s–1920s." *New West Indian Guide* 83, nos. 1 and 2 (2009): 3–35.

———. "Contesting Internationalists: Transnational Anarchism, Anti-Imperialism, and U.S. Expansion in the Caribbean, 1890s–1920s." *Estudios Interdisciplinarios de América Latina y El Caribe* 22, no. 2 (July–December 2011): 11–38.

———. "Cuba para todos: Anarchist Internationalism and the Cultural Politics of Cuban Independence." *Cuban Studies* 31 (2000): 45–75.

———. "Freedom Teaching: Anarchism and Education in Early Republican Cuba, 1898–1925." *Americas* 60, no. 2 (October 2003): 151–83.

———. "Havana Hub: Cuban Anarchism, Radical Media, and the Trans-Caribbean Anarchist Network, 1902–1915." *Caribbean Studies* 37, no. 2 (July–December 2009): 45–81.

———. "Latin Lines and Dots: Transnational Anarchism, Regional Networks, and Italian Libertarians in Latin America." *Zapruder World: An International Journal for the Study of Social Conflict* 1 (June 2014). http://www.zapruderworld.org/content/kirwin-r-shaffer-latin-lines-and-dots-transnational-anarchism-regional-networks-and-italian.

———. "Prostitutes, Bad Seeds, and Revolutionary Mothers in Cuban Anarchism: Imagining Women in the Fiction of Adrián del Valle and Antonio Penichet, 1898–1930." *Studies in Latin American Popular Culture* 18 (1999): 1–17.

———. "The Radical Muse: Women and Anarchism in Early Twentieth-Century Cuba." *Cuban Studies* 34 (2003): 130–53.

Silva, Adhemar, Jr. "A bipolaridade *política* rio-grandense e o movimento operário." *Estudios Ibero-Americanos* 22, no. 2 (1996): 5–26.

——. "A Confederação Operária Brasileira e o Rio Grande do Sul (1913–1915)." *Logos* (Canoas) 7, no. 1 (1995): 45–54.

Silvestri, Susana. *El color del río: Historia cultural del paisaje del Riachuelo.* Bernal: Universidad Nacional de Quilmes, 2003.

Sitrin, Marina. *Everyday Revolutions: Horizontalism and Autonomy in Argentina.* London: Zed Books, 2012.

——. *Horizontalism: Voices of Popular Power in Argentina.* Oakland, Calif.: AK Press, 2006.

Skirda, Alexandre. *Facing the Enemy.* Oakland, Calif.: AK Press, 2002.

Skuban, William E. *Lines in the Sand: Nationalism and Identity on the Peruvian-Chilean Frontier.* Albuquerque: University of New Mexico Press, 2007.

Slater, David. "El capitalismo subdesarrollado y la organización del espacio: Peru: 1920–1940." *Allpanchis* 12, no. 13 (1979): 87–106.

Smith, Donald B. *Honoré Jaxon: Prairie Visionary.* Regina, Saskatchewan: Coteau Books, 2007.

Smith, Robert Freeman. "The Díaz Era: Background to the Revolution of 1910." In *Mexico: From Independence to Revolution, 1810–1910,* edited by W. Dirk Raat, 192–205. Lincoln: University of Nebraska Press, 1982.

Socarrás, Fernando Figueredo. *La Revolución de Yara, 1868–1878: Conferencias.* Havana: M. Pulido y campaña, 1902.

Solomonoff, Jorge N. *Ideologías del movimiento obrero y conflicto social.* Buenos Aires: Editorial Proyección, 1971.

Somers, Margaret. "Deconstructing and Reconstructing Class Formation Theory." In *Reworking Class,* edited by John R. Hall, 73–105. Ithaca, N.Y.: Cornell University Press, 1997.

Sonn, Richard. *Anarchism.* New York: Twayne Publishers, 1992.

Soria, Carmen, ed. *Letras anarquistas: José Santos González Vera y Manuel Rojas.* Santiago: Planeta, 2005.

Soto Rivera, Roy. *Victor Raúl: El hombre del siglo XX,* vol. 1. Lima: Instituto Víctor Raúl Haya de la Torre, 2002.

Soto Valverde, Gustavo. *La Iglesia costarricense y la cuestión social: Antecedentes, análisis y proyecciones de la reforma social costarricense de 1940–43.* San José: Editorial de la Universidad Estatal a Distancia, 1985.

Souza, Newton Stadler. *O anarquismo da Colônia Cecília.* Rio de Janeiro: Civilização Brasileira, 1970.

Souza, Robério Santos. *Tudo pelo trabalho livre! Trabaljadores e conflictos no pós-abolição (Bahia, 1892–1909).* EDUFBA/FAPESP, 2011.

Spalding, Hobart A., Jr., *Organized Labor in Latin America: Historical Case Studies of Urban Workers in Dependent Societies,* New York: Harper Torchbooks, 1977.

Spalding, H., and M. Hall. "The Urban Working Class and Early Latin American Labour Movements, 1880–1930." In *The Cambridge History of Latin America,* vol. 4, edited by Leslie Bethell, 325–66. Cambridge: Cambridge University Press, 1986.

Stanfield, Michael Edward. *Red Rubber, Bleeding Trees: Violence, Slavery, and Empire in Northwest Amazonia, 1850–1933.* Albuquerque: University of New Mexico Press, 1998.

Starr, Frederick. *In Indian Mexico: A Narrative of Travel and Labor*. Chicago: Forbes & Co., 1908.

Steffy, Joan Marie. "The Cuban Immigrants of Tampa, Florida: 1886–1898." MA thesis, University of South Florida, 1975.

Stephen, Lynn. *Zapata Lives! Histories and Cultural Politics in Southern Mexico*. Berkeley: University of California Press, 2002.

Struthers, David. "The World in a City: Transnational and Inter-Racial Organizing in Los Angeles, 1900–1930." PhD diss., Carnegie Mellon University, 2010.

Suiffet, Norma. *Rafael Barrett: La vida y la obra*. Montevideo: Edición de la autora, 1958.

Suriano, Juan. *Anarquistas: Cultura y política libertaria en Buenos Aires 1890–1910*. Buenos Aires: Ediciones Manantial, 2001.

———. *Paradoxes of Utopia: Anarchist Culture and Politics in Buenos Aires, 1890–1910*. Oakland: AK Press, 2010.

Swain, James O. "Costa Rican Mystics." *Hispania* 25, no.1 (February 1942): 79–84.

———. "Some Costa Rican Writers as Topics to Research." *Hispania* 22, no. 2 (May 1939): 183–88.

Tarcus, H. *Diccionario biográfico de la izquierda argentina: De los anarquistas a la "nueva izquierda" (1870–1976)*. Buenos Aires: Emecé, 2007.

Taussig, Michael T. *The Devil and Commodity Fetishism in South America*. Chapel Hill: University of North Carolina Press, 1980.

Tauzin-Castellanos, Isabelle, ed. *Manuel González Prada: Escritor de dos mundos*. Lima, 1977.

Taylor, Lawrence Douglas. *La campaña magonista de 1911 en Baja California: El apogeo de la lucha revolucionaria del Partido Liberal Mexicano*. Tijuana: El Colegio de la Frontera Norte, 1992.

Taylor, William B. *Drinking, Homicide and Rebellion in Colonial Mexican Villages*. Stanford, Calif.: Stanford University Press, 1976.

Tejada R., Luis. *La cuestión de pan: El anarcosindicalismo en el Perú, 1880–1919*. Lima: Instituto Nacional de Cultura, 1988.

Thomas, Hugh. *Cuba: The Pursuit of Freedom*. New York: Harper and Row, 1971.

———. *The Spanish Civil War*. Harmondsworth, U.K.: Penguin Books, 1965.

Thompson, Guy. Introduction to *The European Revolutions of 1848 and the Americas*, edited by Guy Thompson. London: Institute of Latin American Studies, 2002.

Tilly, Charles. "Contention and the Urban Poor in Eighteenth and Nineteenth-Century Latin America." In *Riots in the Cities: Popular Politics and the Urban Poor in Latin America, 1765–1910*, edited by Silvia M. Arrom and Sevando Ortoli, 225–42. Washington, D.C.: Scholarly Resources, 1996.

———. *Trust and Rule*. London: Cambridge University Press, 2005.

Tinajero, Araceli. *El Lector de tabaquería: Historia de una tradición cubana*. Austin: University of Texas Press, 2007.

Toledo, Edilene. *Anarquismo e sindicalismo revolucionario: Trabalhadores e militantes em São Paulo na Primeira República*. São Paulo: Perseu Abramo, 2004.

Toledo, Edilene, and Luigi Biondi. "Constructing Syndicalism and Anarchism Globally: The Transnational Making of the Syndicalist Movement in São Paulo, Brazil, 1895–1935." In *Anarchism and Syndicalism in the Colonial and Postcolonial World, 1870–1940*:

The Praxis of National Liberation, Internationalism, and Social Revolution, edited by Steven Hirsch and Lucien van der Walt, 363–93. Leiden: Brill, 2010.

Torre, Juan Carlos. *La vieja guardia sindical y Perón: Sobre los orígenes el peronismo*. Buenos Aires: Editorial Sudamericana/Instituto Torcuato Di Tella, 1990.

Torrealba Z., Agustín. *Los Subversivos*. Santiago de Chile: Imprenta Yara, 1921.

Trachtenberg, Alexander, and Benjamin Glassberg, eds. *American Labor Yearbook, 1921–1922*, vol. 4. New York: 1922.

Tragtenberg, Mauricio. "Editorial." *Educação e sociedade* 19, no. 65 (1998).

True, Marshall McDonald. "Revolutionaries in Exile: The Cuban Revolutionary Party, 1891–1898." PhD diss., University of Virginia, 1965.

Turcato, Davide. "Italian Anarchism as a Transnational Movement, 1885–1915." *International Review of Social History* 52 (2007): 407–44.

Turner, Ethel Duffy. *Revolution in Baja California: Ricardo Flores Magón's High Noon*. Detroit: Blaine Ethridge Books, 1981.

Turner Morales, Jorge. *Raíz, historia y perspectivas del movimiento obrero panameño*. Mexico, D.F.: Editorial Signos, 1982.

Valle Ferrer, Norma. *Luisa Capetillo: Historia de una mujer proscrita*. Río Piedras, PR: Editorial Cultural, 1990.

———. *Luisa Capetillo, Obra Completa: "Mi patria es la libertad."* Cayey, Puerto Rico: Departamento del Trabajo y Recursos Humanos, Universidad de Puerto Rico en Cayey, 2008.

Van der Esch, Patricia. *La Deuxième Internationale, 1889–1923*. Paris: Marcel Rivière, 1957.

Vanger, Milton I. *José Batlle y Ordóñez of Uruguay: The Creator of His Times, 1902–1907*. Cambridge, Mass.: Harvard University Press, 1963.

———. *The Model Country: José Batlle y Ordóñez of Uruguay, 1907–1915* (Hanover: University Press of New England for Brandeis University Press, 1980).

Vargas Arias, Claudio. *El Liberalismo, la Iglesia y el Estado en Costa Rica*. San José: Editorial Guayacán, 1990.

Vargas Martínez, Gustavo. *Colombia, 1854: Melo, los artesanos y el socialismo*. Bogotá: La Oveja Negra, 1972.

Vásquez Presedo, Vicente. "Navegación y puertos en el desarrollo de la economía argentina en el período 1875–1910." In *Temas de historia marítima argentina*. Buenos Aires: Fundación Argentina de Estudios Marítimos, 1970.

Vassallo, A. "'Sin Dios y sin jefe': Políticas de género en la revolución social a fines del siglo XIX." In *Historia de luchas, resistencias y representaciones, Mujeres en la Argentina, siglos XIX y XX*, edited by María Celia Bravo, Fernanda Gil Lozano, and Valeria Pita. Tucumán: Editorial de la Universidad Nacional de Tucumán, 2007.

Vega Jiménez, Patricia. "Consumo y diversiones públicas en Costa Rica (1850–1859)." In *Industriosa y sobria: Costa Rica en los días de la Campaña Nacional (1856–1857)*, edited by Iván Molina Jiménez, 81–109. South Woodstock, Ver.: Plumsock Mesoamerican Studies, 2007.

Vicuña Fuentes, Carlos. *La tiranía en Chile: Libro escrito en el destierro*. 1938–39. Reprint, Santiago: LOM, 2002.

Viñas, David. *Anarquistas en América Latina*. México: Editorial Katún, 1983.

Viotti da Costa, Emilia. "Liberalism: Theory and Practice." In *The Brazilian Empire: Myths and Histories*, edited by Emilia Viotti da Costa, 53–77. Chicago: University of Chicago Press, 1985.

Vuotto, Pascual. *Vida de un proletario: El proceso de Bragado*, 5th ed., Buenos Aires: R. Alonso Editor, 1975.

Ward, Colin. *Anarchism: A Very Short Introduction*. Oxford: Oxford University Press, 2004.

Ward, Thomas. *La anarquía inmanentista de Manuel González Prada*. New York: Peter Lang, 1998.

Waterbury, Ronald. "Non-Revolutionary Peasants: Oaxaca Compared to Morelos in the Mexican Revolution." *Comparative Studies in Society and History* 17 (1975): 410–42.

Watson, Bruce. *Sacco & Vanzetti*. New York: Viking, 2007.

Weber, Devra. "Historical Perspectives on Mexican Transnationalism: With Notes from Angumacutiro." *Social Justice* 26, no. 3 (Fall 1999): 39–58.

———. "Keeping Community, Challenging Boundaries: Indigenous Migrants, Internationalist Workers, and Mexican Revolutionaries, 1900–1920." In *Mexico and Mexicans in the Making of the United States*, edited by John Tutino, 208–35. Austin: University of Texas Press, 2012.

Westfall, Loy Glenn. *Key West: Cigar City U.S.A.* Key West, Fla.: Key West Types, 1984.

Whitecotton, Joseph W. *The Zapotecs: Princes, Priests and Peasants*. Norman: University of Oklahoma Press, 1977.

Williams, Michael G. "Politics without Love: Anarchism in Turgenev, Dostoevsky, and James." PhD diss., University of Michigan, 1974.

Williams, Raymond. *Marxism and Literature*. Oxford: Oxford University Press, 1977.

Wilson, Elizabeth. "Against Utopia: The Romance of Indeterminate Spaces." In *Embodied Utopias: Gender, Social Change, and the Modern Metropolis*, edited by Amy Bingaman, Lise Sanders, and Rebecca Zorach, 256–62. London: Routledge, 2002.

Wilson, Peter Lamborn. "Caliban's Masque: Spiritual Anarchy & The Wild Man in Colonial America." In *Gone to Croatan: Origins of North American Dropout Culture*, edited by Ron Sakolsky and James Koehnline. London: Automedia/AK Press, 1993.

Woodcock, George. *Anarchism: A History of Libertarian Ideas and Movements*. London: Penguin Books, 1986.

———, ed. *The Anarchist Reader*. Atlantic Highlands, N.Y.: Harvester Press, 1977.

Worley, Matthew, ed. *In Search of Revolution: International Communist Parties in the Third Period*. London: Tauris, 2004.

Yankelevich, Pablo. "Los magonistas en *La Protesta*: Lecturas rioplatenses del anarquismo en México, 1906–1929." *Estudios de Historia Moderna y Contemporánea de México* 19 (1999): 53–83.

Yoast, Richard. "The Development of Argentine Anarchism: A Socio-Ideological Analysis." PhD diss., University of Wisconsin-Madison, 1975.

Zaragoza, Gonzalo. *Anarquismo argentino (1876–1902)*. Madrid, Ediciones de la Torre, 1996.

———. "Anarquistas españoles en Argentina a fines del siglo xix." *Revista de la facultad de filosofia y letras de la Universidad de Valencia* 26 (1976).

Zeledón, José María. *Alma infantil*. San José: Imprenta Lehmann, 1928.

———. *Jardín para niños*. San José: Imprenta Falcó y Borracé, 1916.

———. *Musa Nueva: Cantos de vida*. San José: Ariel, 1907.

Zeledón Venegas, Jorge. "José María Zeledón Brenes." In *Cincuentenario de la letra del Himno Nacional de Costa Rica, 15 de setiembre 1903–1953*, edited by Carlos Meléndez Chaverri, 13–18. San José: Imprenta Nacional, 1954.

Zogbaum, Heidi. *B. Traven: A Vision of Mexico*. Wilmington, Del.: SR Books, 1992.

Zubillaga, Carlos. "El batllismo: Una experiencia populista." In *El primer batllismo: Cinco enfoques polémicos*, edited by Jorge Balbis, Gerardo Caetano, and Ycette Trochon, 11–45. Montevideo: Centro Latinoamerican de Economía Humana y Ediciones de la Banda Oriental, 1985.

———. *Pan y trabajo: Organización sindical, estrategias de lucha y arbitraje estatal en Uruguay (1870–1905)*. Montevideo: Librería de la Facultad de Humanidades y Ciencias de la Educación, 1996.

———. *Perfiles en sombra: Aportes a un diccionario biográfico de los orígenes del movimiento sindical en Uruguay (1870–1910)*. Montevideo: Librería de la Facultad de Humanidades y Ciencias de la Educación, 2008.

Contributors

James Baer is professor of history at Northern Virginia Community College in Alexandria, Virginia. He is coeditor with Ronn Pineo of *Cities of Hope: People, Protests and Progress in Urbanizing Latin America 1870–1930* and the author of *Anarchist Immigrants in Spain and Argentina*.

Raymond Craib is associate professor of history at Cornell University. He is the author of *Cartographic Mexico: A History of State Fixations and Fugitive Landscapes* and coeditor of the volume *No Gods, No Masters, No Peripheries: Global Anarchisms*.

Evan Matthew Daniel is instructor of history at Queens College, City University of New York and is affiliated with the Percy E. Sutton SEEK Program for working-class and low-income students. His research interests include nineteenth-century American and Cuban labor and intellectual history with an emphasis on radical ideologies and political movements as well as Cuban immigration to the United States. His work is published in the *Journal of Southern History* and the *Journal for the Study of Radicalism*.

David Díaz-Arias is associate professor and director of graduate studies for the Department of History of the University of Costa Rica. He has published several essays and books, including *La Fiesta de la Independencia en Costa Rica, 1821–1921*; *Historia del 11 de abril: Juan Santamaría entre el pasado y el presente*; and *Historia de la Infancia en la Costa Rica del siglo XX*.

Shawn England is assistant professor of history at Mount Royal University in Calgary, Alberta, Canada. He researches issues surrounding indigenous peoples in Latin America with a particular focus on Mexico. He is coeditor of *Globalization and Human Rights in the Developing World*.

Laura Fernández Cordero is a researcher at CONICET (National Scientific and Technical Research Council, Argentina) based in CeDInCI/UNSAM (Center of Documentation and Research of Left Culture).

Steven J. Hirsch is professor of practice in the Department of International and Area Studies at Washington University in St. Louis. He is coeditor with Lucien van der Walt of *Anarchism and Syndicalism in the Colonial and Post-colonial World, 1870–1940.*

Geoffroy de Laforcade is associate professor of Latin American and Caribbean history and director of International Studies at Norfolk State University. In addition to several articles and book chapters on the history of anarchism and syndicalism in Argentina, his publications and research address migration, popular culture, diaspora, and transnational networks in the Atlantic world. He is the coauthor of *The How and Why of World History* and coeditor of *Transculturality and Perceptions of the Immigrant Other.*

Beatriz Ana Loner has been associate professor of history at the Federal University of Pelotas (Brazil) and visiting professor of history at the Federal University of Santa Marta (Brazil). She has published numerous works on anarchism, labor, and race in Brazil, including *Construção de classe: Operários de Pelotas e Rio Grande (1888–1930).*

José C. Moya is professor of history and director of the Forum on Migration at Barnard College and director of the Institute of Latin American Studies at Columbia University. He has authored more than fifty publications, including *World Migration in the Long Twentieth Century* and *The Oxford Handbook of Latin American History*, an edited volume on Latin American historiography.

Lars Peterson completed his doctoral degree in history at the University of Pittsburgh in 2014. His research examines Uruguayan social, political, and cultural history at the beginning of the twentieth century, especially the progressive Batlle government.

Anton Rosenthal is associate professor of history and associate director of the Center for Latin American and Caribbean Studies at the University of Kansas where he teaches courses on global, comparative, and urban history. He is also a member of the board of directors of the Urban History Association.

Kirwin Shaffer is professor of Latin American Studies at Penn State University–Berks College. He is author of numerous articles and book chapters on the history of anarchism in the Caribbean Basin. In addition he is the author of two books: *Anarchism and Countercultural Politics in Early Twentieth-Century Cuba* and *Black Flag Boricuas: Anarchism, Antiauthoritarianism, and the Left in Puerto Rico, 1897–1921.*

Index

www.ingramcontent.com/pod-product-compliance
Lightning Source LLC
Chambersburg PA
CBHW020817270326
41928CB00006B/383